# READINGS IN

# MISSIONARY ANTHROPOLOGY

# READINGS IN MISSIONARY ANTHROPOLOGY

**William A. Smalley, Editor**

PRACTICAL ANTHROPOLOGY
Box 307
Tarrytown, New York 10592, U.S.A.

Library of Congress Catalogue Card Number: 67-17463

*$3.50 paper*

*$4.50 cloth*

PHOTOLITHOPRINTED BY CUSHING - MALLOY, INC.
ANN ARBOR, MICHIGAN, UNITED STATES OF AMERICA
1967

# CONTENTS

## CHRISTIANITY IN HUMAN CULTURES

## THE MISSIONARY IN AN ALIEN CULTURE

## ANTHROPOLOGY: ROLE AND METHOD

# PREFACE

THE insights of the social sciences, and particularly of cultural anthropology, are making an ever-stronger impact on Christian missionary method, clarifying problems in the development of churches in different cultures, and contributing to the effective communication of the gospel. Since 1953, when it was started as a very modest mimeographed publication, the bimonthly periodical PRACTICAL ANTHROPOLOGY has grown to be an outlet for the publication of ideas, questions, discussion, and reports of successes and failures in this field.

The demand for some of the articles in back issues of PRACTICAL ANTHROPOLOGY remains high. Many articles have been reprinted elsewhere, a few of them several times. New subscribers, once they begin reading the current issues, often order those back issues which are available in order to get a wider outlook on the questions being discussed or greater understanding of the area of the world in which they are working as missionaries. Courses in missionary strategy and in anthropology for missionaries often require the reading of articles from PA.

In order to help supply this need and to make available in one volume the earlier contributions of PA to missionary anthropology, we now publish these *Readings in Missionary Anthropology*. Included here are all the articles of missionary significance in the first six years of PA publication (1953-1959), except those reprinted from other publications. Book reviews, notes, and other miscellanea are not included.[1] Two articles from 1960 are also included to round out the volume.

The reprinted articles have been rearranged under broad topics, as can be seen from the table of contents. They cluster around four different problems. How do human cultures differ,

1 Articles in the *Supplement*, published in 1960 to make available the material of missionary significance from the first four years of publication, are included here *in toto*.

and what effect do these differences have on the effective communication of the gospel? What is the church like in different cultures? What are the problems of a missionary in a culture different from his own? What is the place of anthropology, and its method, as applied to the problems of the church of Jesus Christ? There is, of course, considerable overlap from one category to another. The decision as to where to put an article was sometimes somewhat arbitrary. These categories do, however, reflect to a considerable degree the areas of PA contribution to the missionary effort, where the social sciences have a great deal to say to the church.

In producing this volume a few of the articles have been reset in type and sometimes slightly edited, but most are reproduced photographically from earlier printings. This has resulted in some minor inconsistencies of format. Some of the articles, for example, contain brief accounts of the author and his background, while others do not. Some of the data included are out of date. All contributors, however, are introduced with fuller, up-to-date information separately in this volume, superseding those descriptions which appear scattered through the book. Not all footnotes could be adjusted to include a cross-reference to articles which had been reprinted in this volume, although this was done where possible. There are two type styles and two slightly different page formats.

The publication of PRACTICAL ANTHROPOLOGY is a service to the church, to Jesus Christ, and to his ministers. It makes its contribution to missionary scholarship, and to the stimulation and inspiration of individual missionaries and others concerned with Christ and culture. It is a tool for the training of missionaries. It is also used by some anthropologists interested in studying simply as cultural problems the questions with which it deals. We hope that *Readings in Missionary Anthropology* will make the magazine's usefulness all the greater.

WILLIAM A. SMALLEY

# CONTRIBUTORS

**Paul R. Abrecht** is Executive Secretary, Department of Church and Society (Division of Studies) of the World Council of Churches, 150 route de Ferney, Geneva, Switzerland. After earning the B.D. from Union Theological Seminary in 1946, he did graduate studies in economics and ethics at Columbia University from 1946 to 1949. From 1955 to 1961 he was director of a special World Council study program on Christian responsibility toward areas of rapid social change, culminating in the publication of *The Churches and Rapid Social Change* (New York: Doubleday, 1961).

**G. Linwood Barney** is Associate Professor of Anthropology at the Jaffray School of Missions, Nyack, New York 10960, U.S.A., and Associate Director of the Toronto Institute of Linguistics. His M.A. in anthropology from the University of Minnesota was followed by further study and the completion of all requirements for the Ph.D. except the thesis. He also studied in the Summer Institute of Linguistics program at the University of Oklahoma in 1947 and 1949. Mr. Barney spent 1950-1954 as a missionary linguist, working on the Meo language in Laos under the Christian and Missionary Alliance. His M.A. thesis, *The Meo of Xieng Khouang Province,* was reproduced as Laos Project Data Paper No. 13, Department of Anthropology, University of California, Los Angeles, 1961.

**Ann N. Beardslee,** c/o Nesmith, 1726 Ryan Road, Jacksonville, Florida 23316, U.S.A., was a missionary of the Christian and Missionary Alliance in Mali and Upper Volta, West Africa, from 1955 to 1963. Her husband is now directing a program for training Bible Society colporteurs in Africa. Mrs. Beardslee took the course offered by the Summer Institute of Linguistics at the University of North Dakota in 1959.

**John Beekman** is Chief Translation Consultant in Mexico and General Translation Coordinator for the Wycliffe Bible Translators (Apartado Postal 13, Ixmiquilpan, Hidalgo, México). He took the courses of the Summer Institute of Linguistics at the University of Oklahoma, and served from 1947 to 1959 as a missionary translator among the Chol Indians of Chiapas, Mexico, where he contributed to the translation of the New Testament.

**Robert C. Blaschke** is a missionary working in Segbana par Kandi, Dahomey, West Africa, where he has been pioneering new work among the Boko (Bussa) people since 1954. Mr. Blaschke studied anthropology at Wheaton College, took a B.D. at Gordon Divinity School in 1952, and is a candidate for the M.A. at Hartford Seminary, where he is studying anthropology and linguistics. He took the Summer Institute course in London, England, in 1953.

**Albert Buckwalter,** Casilla 53, Pcia. R. Sáenz Peña, Provincia del Chaco, Argentina, has been a missionary to the Toba Indians under the Mennonite Board of Missions and Charities since 1951. He took the course of the Summer Institute of Linguistics in Norman, Oklahoma, U.S.A., in 1955, completed his B.D. at Goshen College Biblical Seminary in 1956, and is working toward the M.A. in linguistics at Hartford Seminary.

**Florence Hansen Cowan,** 2218 W. Edinger, Apt. 3, Santa Ana, California 92704, U.S.A., spent 1936-1960 in Mexico among the Mazateco Indians translating the New Testament, teaching people to read, and teaching the Bible, under the auspices of the Wycliffe Bible Translators. Since 1960 her husband has been in administrative work with the same organization, but she has made yearly field trips to Mexico for Bible distribution and short-term Bible institute work. Mrs. Cowan has written several articles on Mazateco language, culture, and Bible translation. Among them, "A Mazateco President Speaks", is an article in applied anthropology which appeared in *América Indígena* (October 1952).

**Barbara F. Grimes** has been a missionary translator among the Huichol Indians since 1952, working with the Wycliffe Bible Translators, Instituto Lingüístico de Verano, Apartado 22067, México 22, D.F., México. She is also an instructor in phonetics and phonemics at the Summer Institute of Linguistics, Norman, Oklahoma, U.S.A. In addition to taking the courses of the Summer Institute of Linguistics, she attended the Linguistic Institute of the Linguistic Society of America in 1953. Mrs. Grimes has collaborated with her husband in writing articles on Huichol kinship. One of them, "Semantic Distinctions in Huichol (Uto-Aztecan) Kinship", was published in the *American Anthropologist* in 1962.

**Joseph E. Grimes** has been a missionary translator among the Huichol Indians since 1952, working with the Wycliffe Bible Translators, Instituto Lingüístico de Verano, Apartado 22067, México 22, D.F., México. He is also Lecturer in Descriptive Linguistics at the Summer Institute of Linguistics, University of Oklahoma. He took the M.A. and Ph.D. in linguistics at Cornell University in 1958 and 1960 respectively, minoring in anthropology. Dr. Grimes has published several articles on American Indian linguistics, has contributed to *The Bible Translator,* and recently prepared an article on the Cora and Huichol Indians to be published in the *Handbook of Middle American Indians.* He has also led in efforts of the Summer Institute of Linguistics to apply the use of electronic computers to problems of language analysis, and has contributed articles to computer journals.

**David L. Hamm** is studying toward an advanced degree in the Department of Missions of the Divinity School of the University of Chicago. He has the B.D. from Union Theological Seminary, 1943. He is also the pastor of the United Church of Christ of Fox Lake, 36 Glen Ave., Fox Lake, Illinois 60020, U.S.A. Mr. Hamm was a missionary in the Philippines from 1946 to 1959.

**Mahlon M. Hess** is Assistant Secretary of the Eastern Mennonite Board of Missions and Charities, Salunga, Pennsylvania 17538, U.S.A. He took the courses of the Summer Institute of Linguistics in 1945 and 1951 and studies in sociology at Union Theological Seminary and Columbia University. Mr. Hess was a missionary in Tanzanía from 1945 to 1965.

**Dale W. Kietzman** is director of the work of the Summer Institute of Linguistics in Brazil (Caixa Postal 4216-ZC-OS, Rio de Janeiro, GB, Brazil). He took an M.A. in anthropology at Northwestern University in 1952 and followed the Brazilian Studies program at Stanford University in 1961-1962. Previous to his time in Brazil, Mr. Kietzman spent some years in Peru and Mexico. Publications on anthropology and linguistics from his pen have appeared in Latin America journals.

**John C. Messenger, Jr.,** is Associate Professor of Folklore, Anthropology, and African Studies at Indiana University (Folklore Institute, Indiana University, 714 East Eighth St., Bloomington, Indiana, U.S.A.). He received the Ph.D. in anthropology from Northwestern University in 1957. Professor Messenger spent fifteen months among the Anang of southeastern Nigeria during 1951-1952, eighteen months among the Aran Islanders in western Eire between 1958 and 1964, and two months among the Montserrat Islanders in the West Indies during 1965. He is author of numerous articles based on his field work and other research. His book entitled *Folk Culture of Aran* is to be published by Holt, Rinehart, and Winston.

**Eugene A. Nida** is Secretary for Traslations, American Bible Society, 1865 Broadway, New York, New York 10023, U.S.A. His Ph.D. is in linguistics from the University of Michigan. In addition to several books in the fields of linguistics and Bible translation, including a new and important *Toward a Science of Translation* (Leiden: E. J. Brill, 1964), Dr. Nida has written extensively in the field of the missionary implications and application of anthropology. In the first ten years of the publication of PRACTICAL ANTHROPOLOGY he produced thirty-three articles and reviews for it. Two of his books *Customs and Cultures: Anthropology for Christian Missions* and *Message and Mission: The Communication of the Christian Faith* (both published by Harper and Brothers, 1954 and 1960 respectively) are in this field also. He is associate editor of PRACTICAL ANTHROPOLOGY.

**Eunice V. Pike** is a Linguistic Consultant and a translator among the Mazatec Indians of Oaxaca, Mexico, working with the Wycliffe Bible Translators (Instituto Lingüístico de Verano, Apartado 22067, México 22, D.F., México). She started working among the Mazatecs in 1936. More recently a considerable amount of her time has been given to work as a linguistic consultant in Peru, Ecuador, New Guinea, and Mexico. Miss Pike is the author of several articles in the fields of linguistics, language learning, and anthropology. In addition to her work reprinted in this volume, she has written "Mazatec Sexual Impurity and Bible Reading" (1960) and "Mazatec Focus" (1962) for PRACTICAL ANTHROPOLOGY.

**Marie Fetzer Reyburn,** Box 495, Jos, Nigeria, received the M.A. in anthropology from Columbia University in 1948. She undertook field work in anthropology applied to missionary problems in South America from 1952 to 1955, and since then has been living in Africa, first in the Cameroun and now in Nigeria. She is a member of the editorial committee of PRACTICAL ANTHROPOLOGY.

**William D. Reyburn** is a Translations Consultant for the American Bible Society, based in Nigeria (Box 495, Jos, Nigeria). He took an M.A. in anthropology from the University of New Mexico in 1947 and a Ph.D. in linguistics from the University of Pennsylvania in 1952. From 1952 to 1955 he did research in anthropology and linguistics as applied to missionary problems in Ecuador, Argentina, and Central America. Since 1955 he has followed a similar course in Africa, being based first in Cameroun and then in Nigeria. Dr. Reyburn has written extensively for PRACTICAL ANTHROPOLOGY, as this volume shows in part, and is a member of its editorial committee. He is also author of *The Toba Indians of the Argentine Chaco: An Interpretive Report* (Elkhart, Indiana: Mennonite Board of Missions and Charities, 1954).

**William J. Samarin** is Associate Professor of Linguistics, Hartford Seminary Foundation, 55 Elizabeth St., Hartford, Connecticut 06105, U.S.A. He was granted the Ph.D. in linguistics at the University of California, Berkeley, in 1962. He spent 1951 to 1960 under the Foreign Missionary Society of the Brethren Church, in the Central African Republic. He has written grammatical descriptions of two different African languages, which are in press.

**William A. Smalley** is a Linguistic and Translations Consultant under the American Bible Society in Southeast Asia (Box 103, Chiengmai, Thailand). He took the courses of the Summer Institute of Linguistics at the University of Oklahoma in 1947 and 1948 and received the Ph.D. in anthropological linguistics from Columbia University in 1956. He spent 1950 to 1954 as a missionary linguist in Laos and Vietnam. Dr. Smalley is author of books and articles in the fields of linguistics and the application of linguistics and anthropology to missionary problems. One of these, *Introducing Animism* (New York: Friendship Press, 1959), was coauthored with Eugene A. Nida. He is editor of PRACTICAL ANTHROPOLOGY and of the present volume.

**Lois Sorensen** (now Lois Sorensen Avoian, Box 1237, Juneau, Alaska) took a B.A. in anthropology from Wheaton College in 1960. She has lived in southeastern Alaska for six years.

**William L. Wonderly** is a Field Associate in the Translations Department of the American Bible Society, responsible for Mexico and Central America (Sociedades Bíblicas en América Latina, Apdo. 6-820, México 6, D.F., México). He received the Ph.D. in linguistics from the University of Michigan in 1948. Dr. Wonderly has been in Mexico since 1939, first as a missionary translator under the Wycliffe Bible Translators and then with the American Bible Society. He is the author of various articles in linguistics and of several contributions to PRACTICAL ANTHROPOLOGY, of which he is also on the editorial committee.

# Introduction

*William A. Smalley*

**Reprinted from Vol. 7, No. 3 (1960), pp. 113-123.**

# Anthropological Study and Missionary Scholarship

*The growing interest in the study of anthropology among missionary scholars and prospective missionaries in the United States prompted the Missionary Research Library to ask for a bibliography of anthropology for missionaries[1] together with an interpretive introduction. The article which follows reproduces that introduction, with minor changes. Many of the readers of* PRACTICAL ANTHROPOLOGY *have had little or no formal training in this field, and perhaps this article will help to place the contents of this journal in greater focus.*

OVER the last two decades there has been spreading through missionary scholarship, and into the ranks of active missionaries, a rapidly increasing awareness of the relevance of the study of cultural anthropology. Anthropology is becoming a unit in the curriculum of prospective missionaries of some sending agencies. A nod in its direction is often made at missionary orientation conferences. Some missionaries go out of their way to study it on furlough, or before they go to the field for the first time. And whether they are aware of it as a separate academic discipline or not, almost any missionary reads with absorbed interest, and appreciation, a good anthropological study of the people among whom he is working, or of some nearby and related group.

## The Science of Cultural Anthropology

In the United States cultural anthropology is the largest and most flourishing branch of the general field of anthropology, which also includes linguistics, archae-

1 William A. Smalley, *Selected and Annotated Bibliography of Anthropology for Missionaries.* New York: Missionary Research Library, January 1960. The bibliography is mimeographed as part of the Occasional Bulletin series of the library. It differs from the bibliography by James O. Buswell, III, "Anthropology in Paper-Backs" appearing serially in PRACTICAL ANTHROPOLOGY, in that it attempts a rounded coverage, and includes a high proportion of missionary material, rather than restricting itself to inexpensive paperback volumes. In addition to the introduction reproduced here, the bibliography consists of some three hundred annotated entries under the following topics (with subheadings): I. General; II. Nature of culture: theory, history, and methods of anthropology; III. Culture change; IV. Aspects of culture (with separate headings for A. Economy, technology, ecology; B. Social organization, kinship, family, marriage; C. Political organization, law, government; D. Religion, magic, taboo, witchcraft; E. Language, gesture, communication; F. The arts; G. The individual in culture); V. Anthropology and the missionary; VI. Non-missionary applications of anthropology; VII. Periodicals. Included also are specific recommendations for a graded reading course in cultural anthropology. Individual copies of the bibliography are available for 25 cents from the Missionary Research Library, 3041 Broadway, New York 27, N. Y. Annual subscription to the Occasional Bulletin (which publishes articles and bibliographies of interest to missionaries and missionary scholars) is one dollar.

ology, and physical anthropology. The unifying concern of these four very different specializations is *man* (in his origins and physical variations through time and space) and *culture* (in its origins and variations through time and space). In their contemporary phase these branches of anthropology are especially concentrating upon the dynamics of man and culture. What are the processes by which differences arise? How are they transmitted within the society? In this world of "rapid social change" how does change take place in deep-seated human habits? What is the effect of such change upon the society as a whole? upon individual reactions?

Because cultural anthropology is the largest and best known of the branches of anthropology in the United States, it tends to be called by the generic term "anthropology." In general, we will follow that usage here. Because it is the area of anthropology most relevant to the Christian mission, our attention will be restricted to it, except for a brief discussion of linguistics. Although the specialized techniques of linguistics make it a separate branch of anthropology, in academic practice a man's language is in reality a most significant part of his culture.

Cultural anthropology is most fully developed in the United States. For this reason, non-English-speaking parts of the world use the word "anthropology" in a different sense from what it is used here. In Europe it refers usually to physical anthropology, rather than cultural. "Ethnology" is often the closest European equivalent to our "cultural anthropology," although for us ethnology is a much more restricted word, referring to the description of individual cultures rather than the science of culture. In Britain the term "social anthropology" refers to the cross-cultural study of societies. It, again, is a more restricted label than "cultural anthropology."

One evidence that anthropology is gaining a wide influence in its sister sciences (such as sociology and psychology) and among the general public (including the missionary public) is the fact that in this introduction it no longer seems imperative to make a lengthy explanation of the anthropologist's use of the word *culture.* Not many years ago it would have been necessary to make much of the fact that anthropology uses the word to cover all of man's learned behavior, not just the arts and other symbols of refinement. In the anthropological sense all men have culture. It is not restricted to "cultured" people. This use of the term has become commonplace in American vocabulary in the last few years.

## Missionary Anthropologists

Some of the subject matter of cultural anthropology has been uppermost in missionary consciousness whether or not the missionary was aware of any academic discipline by that name, or even before there was such a discipline. The conflicts of the Hebrew and Greek Christians in the New Testament were over culture change, and over differences of cultural standard in relation to the new faith which was so important to them. The journals of early missionaries, Protestant and Roman Catholic, are often crammed with observations and comments about the life of people around them. Anthropologists have combed some of them, to glean information about the earlier stages of a people's life, or about a people now extinct as a separate cultural entity.

The early missionary, impelled by his calling, lived and observed, even though he did not always understand what he observed as fully as he would have the opportunity to understand it now because of anthropological analysis available to him. Sometimes he felt impelled to destroy what he saw; sometimes it frightened him, or disgusted him, or irritated him. Sometimes he was captivated by phases of life around him.

Until recently, in fact, the missionary was the most frequent Western observer of non-Western cultures. This observation, when recorded, has provided much data for anthropology, but it is not in itself anthropology, for like any science, anthropology classifies and interprets its data. There have been missionaries, however, who have not only contributed data, but who have also been keen interpreters of their data. In a few cases they rank with some importance in the history of anthropology.

One such missionary, for example, was the English Bishop Robert H. Codrington, who studied the Melanesians of the Pacific first-hand as a missionary among them. He wrote several books on their languages and cultures, including his classical *The Melanesians.*[2] Codrington is particularly famous for his discussion of *mana,* the belief in supernatural power which is both non-physical and non-personal, being unrelated to spirits or gods. The phenomenon is found in many areas of the world, but Codrington's examination of it greatly clarified it, and his work marks an important base line in the anthropological study of religion for that reason.

Edwin W. Smith, missionary to South Africa and later Versions Secretary of the British and Foreign Bible Society, was also an influential anthropologist in England. He was at one time president of the Royal Anthropological Institute and is author of several books including *African Ideas of God*[3] and *The Golden Stool.*[4]

We could mention Maurice Leenhardt[5] of France for his excellent work on New Caledonia and his place of leadership in French anthropological circles until his death in 1954. The bibliography, in its annotations, names more such men who, as missionaries, or having started as missionaries, have made a substantial contribution to this field.[6]

These men are representative of Protestant missions. The Roman Catholic group is much larger. Catholic anthropologists in the United States have a professional journal, *The Anthropological Quarterly.* The most famous school of Roman Catholic anthropologists is the "Vienna School" of which Father Wilhelm Schmidt was the founder and guiding light for decades. Schmidt and his school produced the weighty journal *Anthropos,* one of the great journals in the field. Unfortunately a great deal of the energy of Schmidt and many of his colleagues has gone into trying to prove a hypothesis which most other anthropologists feel is untenable. It is that primitive peoples the world over are characterized by a concept of a "high

2 A reprint of Codrington's classical work has been published in New Haven by the Human Relations Area Files, 1957.

3 London: Edinburgh House Press, 1950.

4 London: Holborn Publishing House, 1926.

5 See William D. Reyburn, "Notes on Maurice Leenhardt, French Missionary Anthropologist, 1878-1954," PRACTICAL ANTHROPOLOGY, Vol. 3, No. 4 (July-August, 1956), pp. 63-68.

6 For a more extended discussion of the contribution of missionaries to anthropology see Annette Rosenstiel, "Anthropology and the Missionary," *Journal of the Royal Anthropological Institute,* Vol. 89, Part 1 (1959), pp. 107-115

god," and that this points back to an original monotheism.[7] Attractive as such a theory may sound to some Christians (including Samuel Zwemer, who picked it up and advocated it in the United States),[8] there are far too many variables in the various "high god" concepts of different peoples to make the data mean very much even if the concept could be shown to be universal. Many anthropologists, furthermore, feel that Schmidt has had to stretch his data badly to find a "high god" concept everywhere. Be that as it may, Father Schmidt and many Catholic missionaries have contributed enormously to anthropological discussion and anthropological ideas as well as anthropological data.

### American Missionaries and Anthropology

Among American missionaries there have not arisen any such anthropological figures as these and others which could be mentioned in Europe. With the exception of the field of linguistics, no American missionary has done work as widely recognized by anthropologists as have these Europeans. However, as the results of anthropological investigation began to filter more and more into general American education, as works of anthropologists such as Margaret Mead, Ruth Benedict, Bronislaw Malinowski, and scores of others became current in paperback editions in thousands of drugstores and news stands, as more information about anthropology became current before and after World War II, American missionaries were increasingly attracted to its study. We seem to be in the interesting position where at present American missionaries do more formal academic study of anthropology than do their European colleagues, but the Europeans seem to do more field study of the peoples around them, and are more prone to publish the results.

Two institutions in the United States pioneered courses in anthropology with the missionary group specifically in mind. At the Kennedy School of Missions (Hartford Seminary Foundation, Hartford, Conn.) Morris Steggerda taught anthropology for many years, and Edwin W. Smith, to whom reference was made above, was on the faculty for a brief period. This tradition continues at Kennedy and has had its influence on many missionaries. At Wheaton College (Wheaton, Illinois) Alexander Grigolia and his successors have taught anthropology for a similar period of time. Many anthropology majors at Wheaton plan to be missionaries.

In more recent years the teaching of anthropology has spread, in one degree or another, to scores of other schools which emphasize the training of missionaries. Many of these schools are of the Bible institute or Bible college type. Some of them are small, but the cumulative effect is that ever larger numbers of outgoing missionaries have had at least one course in anthropology. It is debatable as to how valuable one isolated course may be, but the trend toward increased study of anthropology is clear, and some missionaries have studied rather extensively in it. It is also clear that some groups not related to the Division of Foreign Missions of

---

[7] An English summary of Schmidt's major work is *The Origin and Growth of Religion*. London: Methuen and Co., 1931.

[8] Samuel Zwemer, *The Origin of Religion: Evolution or Revelation*. New York: Loizeaux, 1945. (Currently out of print.)

the National Council of Churches are placing more stress on anthropological training for their missionaries than are most DFM-related groups.

One reason for the growing interest in the study of anthropology on the part of missionaries is the work of Eugene A. Nida and of some his colleagues in the Translations Department of the American Bible Society. Nida's *Customs and Cultures: Anthropology for Christian Missions*[9] has provided a much-needed popular introduction to the subject since it appeared in 1954. *Introducing Animism,*[10] by Nida and Smalley, is a brief popular introduction to this topic. PRACTICAL ANTHROPOLOGY is privately published by the editors, but several of the Bible Society's Translations Department staff are on the editorial committee. These same individuals have repeated opportunities to advise missionaries whom they meet on the field in the course of consulting with them on Bible translation problems. Occasionally the consultation leads these missionaries into some kind of formal or informal study of anthropology.

## Missionary Linguistics

It has been stated earlier that language is a part of culture, and that linguistics as often practiced in the United States is a part of cultural anthropology, but that in its techniques it is so specialized as to be a clearly marked sub-discipline. It is in this area where American missionaries, and men devoting their life to the training of American missionaries, have made a notable professional impact. Kenneth L. Pike of the Summer Institute of Linguistics (and the Wycliffe Bible Translators), Eugene A. Nida of the American Bible Society, and H. A. Gleason of the Kennedy School of Missions have all written important pioneering textbooks in the field. These men, and others, have made contributions in theory, method, or pedagogy. A list of those missionaries who have made and published field studies which are up to professional standard would include many more again.

The major part of the present missionary productivity in the field of linguistics comes from impetus and leadership provided by the Summer Institute of Linguistics, which is the academic organization of the Wycliffe Bible Translators. This organization now has translators working on Indian languages in Mexico, Guatemala, Peru, Ecuador, Brazil, and the United States. It has workers also in the Philippines, Vietnam, and New Guinea. It has summer academic sessions which offer highly intensive courses in beginning (and in some cases advanced) descriptive linguistics at the Universities of Oklahoma, North Dakota, and Washington, as well as in London and Melbourne (Australia). Several thousand missionaries have taken their courses, missionaries of many groups besides their own. For the most part these missionaries have been of the "conservative" wing.

Admittedly, not all of the thousands of missionary candidates who have studied linguistics have made any significant use of their study in the field. A large number have, however, and current linguistic information is rapidly spreading among missionaries. In this connection, the Toronto Institute of Linguistics (conducted by the mission boards of the Toronto area) and the Missionary Training Conference (conducted by the DFM at Meadville, Pa.), each summer help to dissemi-

[9] New York: Harper and Bros., 1954.
[10] New York: Friendship Press, 1959.

nate such information in a practical way, although they do not attempt formal linguistic training.

It is, furthermore, difficult to study much linguistics without being exposed to some of the rest of cultural anthropology. Thus the spread of linguistics has contributed to the rising interest in the whole field of anthropology.

### Changing Trends in Anthropology

The relevance of the study of anthropology has not always been clear to some missionary scholars. At earlier points in its history cultural anthropology was dominated by physical anthropology, the study of human fossils, the evolution of man, race, genetics, etc. On the other hand, if the anthropologist was not completely absorbed in fossils, he seemed to be preoccupied with primitive cultures, and the relevance of the study of remote New Guinea tribesmen sometimes seemed rather small to the missionary in urban Japan.

Many of the contemporary emphases of anthropology, however, are highly relevant to any missionary, and that relevance is emerging ever more clearly. It must be admitted that after more than a hundred years of activity largely restricted to the more primitive parts of the world's population, the data of anthropology still seem heavily weighted in that direction. Our bibliography is evidence enough of that fact. However, from the study of small, relatively uncomplex societies, there have emerged concepts and tools which are being applied with ever-increasing fruitfulness to folk and peasant societies (such as are the rural areas of most of the world today) and to subsegments, at least, of urban life. Although we have somewhat arbitrarily excluded such studies from the bibliography, American communities have not been immune to anthropological investigation in the last two decades.

Some of the most fruitful modern trends in anthropology, so far as the missionary is concerned, are represented in the areas of the bibliography labeled "Culture Change" and "The Individual in Culture." These studies emphasize the dynamics of culture, the way in which it grows, changes, decays, in which it is passed from one society to another, or the ways in which culture molds the individual through his training and participation in it. Another increasing concern of anthropology is the problem of cultural values. Anthropologists are seeking to probe more fully into the different sets of assumptions, unformulated codes of ethics, "world views" of different peoples.

In much of this current interest which anthropologists share with missionaries, the study is at least partially interdisciplinary with sociology, psychology, psychoanalysis, etc. Contemporary anthropology is borrowing concepts from such fields as freely as it is loaning its own to them. The *sine qua non* contribution which anthropology makes in such study, and also in missionary scholarship, is the habit of viewing human phenomena cross-culturally, or studying human institutions comparatively.

There was a period in anthropological history (not fully over yet) when it was devoting an enormous percentage of its scholarship to refuting assumptions made on the basis of Western culture or some branch of it. A classic example of this is Margaret Mead's *Coming of Age in Samoa,*[11] a superb study of Samoan ado-

[11] New York: New American Library, 1949.

lescence, in which she found no "stormy adolescence" as was supposed to be a universal characteristic of growing up. A multitude of small, unrelated, primitive societies was the nearest that science could come to a controlled experiment in human life. The missionary badly needs this lesson from anthropology. The cross-cultural viewpoint which it fosters is perhaps its greatest single contribution to him.

At the same time, new kinds of generalizations about human behavior are emerging from anthropological study. As the knowledge of human culture worldwide increases, it becomes increasingly possible to find the small core of real universals in human life, and to determine the dynamics of culture and of the individual in culture. In doing this the anthropologist is turning more and more to the less primitive peoples of the world. Current anthropological field research is substantially the investigation of folk and peasant groups, the rural areas, in many cases, of the great countries of the world. Not that anthropologists have lost their delight in the opportunity to investigate one of the dwindling groups of "untouched" primitives, but the focus of attention no longer lies there. The time has come when no serious missionary anywhere can afford to ignore the contributions of anthropology.

In a very real sense anthropology today is the science of peoples, languages, and cultures. Sociology and psychology and economics have specialized in certain phases of the culture of the West. But it is precisely beyond the limitations of Western horizons which the missionary must see if he is to minister in other parts of the world. We could go much farther than this. Current trends in anthropology are throwing more and more light on cultural differences within the West. This kind of study is more difficult because some of the differences are not as great, but differences there are, between South American and North American, between Frenchman and citizen of the U.S.A., between Londoner and Bostonian, between the inhabitants of Main Street, Little Rock, and Main Street, Buffalo. In a time of cooperative missionary activity, when missionary diplomacy is often preoccupied with problems of coordination between members of different cultures in a common Christian task, may we not hope that anthropology may sharpen those cross-cultural insights which will give us more understanding of our brother's motives, the reasons for the behavior which seems so inexplicable to us? And may we not hope that it can help us to reach that stage of sophistication which will make us realize that we are as inexplicable to him, and proceed from there to find a common ground of action for Christ?

## Specific Values to the Missionary Scholar

A word about the relevance of anthropology to the trends and movements in the missionary cause would perhaps be in order. That complex of attitude and behavior known as "paternalism" is badly out of fashion now, but what is replacing it? The answer often comes in terms of "equality," "fraternal relationship," "independence," "identification," etc. Much of this important current emphasis risks being a travesty if it is not based on profound mutual understanding between those who are in "fraternal relationship." One of the important roads to mutual understanding and respect is the insight which anthropology can offer.

Anthropology has a great deal to offer to the younger churches and to outsiders who try to work with the younger churches. It has much to offer to the contemporary emphasis on the church *in* society and the church *as* society. As churches seek, under God, to find solutions to the social problems of the culture in which they are growing, anthropology can help them to see these institutions or patterns of behavior more objectively. This, we might add, is equally true of the church in the United States.

Anthropology offers specific techniques for learning about people and their culture. As with all sciences, these techniques are occasionally beyond the reach of the missionary with limited training and funds, but for the most part they are readily applicable. These techniques are best learned in formal anthropological study, but they can also be gained through extensive reading. The best guide to anthropological field research is *Notes and Queries on Anthropology*.[12] Before undertaking systematic field study of any group the missionary should also read several good monographs by different authors in different areas of the world, to give him some "feel" for the approach to problems.

Anthropology offers source materials and analyses of specific societies in many parts of the world. For some groups of people the missionary can find numerous volumes of anthropological study. For others there is sketchy work, or none at all. Most important culture *areas* of the world, however, do have representative works which are most helpful because of resemblances between peoples within the area. Our bibliography cannot begin to cover this enormous volume of material.

When specific studies are available they differ, of course, in scope and value. Some are general studies, giving an outline of the major features of the culture. Others are more detailed specific studies, as may be seen in some of the categories of the bibliography. Many are dated in that they were made a generation or more ago. If the missionary will, however, consider such studies as starting points for his own exploration in attempting to understand the culture around him, almost any such earlier study is of some value at least. In some cases the work is superb.

Insight into the meaning of behavior is another important contribution of anthropology. People in different societies sometimes mean entirely different things by the same action. The thoughtful study of anthropology inevitably breeds a healthy degree of cultural relativism as an institution such as the "bride price" or subordinate status of women, or marriage arranged by parents, or a definition of incest which includes the father's brother's children, but not the father's sister's children, are seen in terms of their functional relevance within a society; and, on the other hand, some of our most cherished customs are seen to be the product of our own particular history. This kind of cultural relativism, a degree of freedom from ethnocentrism, is essential if we are not to insist on the automatic importation of our cultural behavior as we witness to a supercultural God and the supercultural faith and love which he engenders in men on the basis of his revelation of himself to them in cultural form in the Scriptures and in the lives and words of his missionaries.

Anthropology offers the value of seeing cultures as "wholes." Anthropology studies social structure in relation to eco-

---

[12] London: Routledge and Kegan Paul, 1954.

nomics, to religion, to technology, etc. Agricultural techniques are not enough in themselves, but they have a relation to the family structure of the people who perform them, to religious rites, to the yearly cycle of labor, etc. Above all, religion cannot be isolated from the remainder of life. The tendency to compartmentalize its religion, which is a characteristic of American culture, is not shared by most other societies in the world. Conversion, and resulting changes in behavior, will have far-reaching effects if they are at all profound. These secondary effects can sometimes be most undesirable both from the standpoint of the missionary and from the standpoint of the members of the changing culture.[13] They may, however, be beneficial. Most often they are mixed. Anthropology has a great deal to offer the church and its leaders in a time of culture change. Missionary technicians, doctors, agriculturalists, and other specialists should all take seriously the wide ramifications of some of the changes which they introduce. Ultimately all of these contributions, or potential contributions, boil down in one way or another to the communication of the gospel. It is for this purpose that the church spreads out through the world in the person of its missionaries. In one way or another, a message which has been understood in the framework of one cultural system is being transmitted into that of another. The message is entirely outside of the province of anthropology, but the process of transmission, the men who stand talking to each other, and the cultures which frame their thoughts and guide their reactions, these are all in the field of anthropology.[14]

## Opportunities for Missionary Anthropologists

Aside from the opportunities involved in the teaching of anthropology to missionaries, there are at least two major kinds of situations in which missionary anthropologists are needed. The first of these is in the professional application of anthropology to missionary problems of the kinds hinted above and many others. This would involve full professional anthropological training, and would involve field research with a view to the solving of specific or general problems in the communication of the gospel, relations between Christian groups (such as missionaries and church), etc. A brief example of such a study can be seen in William D. Reyburn's *Toba Indians of the Argentine Chaco*[15] and his articles in PRACTICAL ANTHROPOLOGY.[16] To do creative work on this scale requires unusual gifts. The number of qualified people is small, as is the number of situations where the need for such study is seen by the mission or church involved. The sense of need, however, is growing.

Much more typical, and much more common, however, is the opportunity for the individual missionary, no matter what

---

13 The anthropological literature is full of examples, but see particularly John C. Messenger, Jr., "The Christian Concept of Forgiveness and Anang Morality," PRACTICAL ANTHROPOLOGY, Vol. 6, No. 3 (May-June 1959), pp. 97-103, and in this volume.

14 Eugene A. Nida is writing a book, *Communication and Christian Faith* (to be published by Harpers in 1960), which will highlight, among other things, the cultural factors involved in the Christian witness.

15 Elkhart, Indiana: Mennonite Board of Missions and Charities, 1954.

16 Particularly Vol. 5, and the early numbers of Vol. 6.

his location or his specialty, to make, as his avocation, an anthropological study of the people with whom he is living and working. In a sense the word avocation is misleading. His study may start as a hobby or sideline, but if it reaches any depth at all, it becomes a foundation for his whole approach to the culture around him.

Many missionaries have undertaken such study, more or less unsystematically, and would be most amazed to hear it called "anthropology." Others have sought what professional or published anthropological help they could find, and have proceeded as systematically as they knew how. Most of these have remained on the amateur level, their materials (often very valuable) unpublished, many generalizations unformulated, some areas of knowledge patchy, but nevertheless with a respectable understanding of the life around them.

Some missionaries, on the other hand, have felt that they did understand the people with whom they were dealing, but through some influence or other have begun more systematic anthropological study, and have been amazed at the richness of the culture which opened up to them. Some journals, like *Africa* or PRACTICAL ANTHROPOLOGY, are anxious for articles containing the anthropological findings of missionaries. Other professional journals, though not seeking the work of missionaries, are glad to publish anything which meets professional standards.

An intelligent, sensitive missionary, after following a course of reading such as suggested in the following section, and with the help of a manual such as *Notes and Queries on Anthropology,*[17] a filing system modified from Murdock's *Outline of Cultural Materials,*[18] and correspondence with other missionary anthropologists, should be able to do some substantial field research and record it in systematic fashion.

## A Reading Course in Anthropology

The coverage of the bibliography is too broad to be of much help to the individual who wants a basic reading course to give him a well-rounded knowledge of the field. The following books, in approximately the following order, are therefore suggested as a beginning. From there the individual can read whatever interests him the most.

1. Eugene A. Nida, *Customs and Cultures: Anthropology for Christian Missions.* New York: Harper and Bros., 1954.
2. Clyde Kluckhohn, *Mirror for Man.* New York, McGraw-Hill Book Co., 1949.
3. An up-to-date introductory general text or two such as Ralph L. Beals and Harry Hoijer, *An Introduction to Anthropology.* New York: Henry Holt and Co., 1942; Raymond Firth, *Human Types: An Introduction to Social Anthropology.* New York: New American Library, 1958; Walter Goldschmidt, *Man's Way: A Preface to the Understanding of Human Society.* New York: Henry Holt and Co., 1959. Melville J. Herskovitz, *Cultural Anthropology.* New York: Alfred A. Knopf, 1955; E. Adamson Hoebel, *Man in the Primitive World.* New York: McGraw-Hill Book Co., 1958; Felix M. Keesing, *Cultural Anthropology: The Science of Custom.* New York: Rinehart and Co., 1958. If the reader wants a more specific suggestion he might try Keesing.
4. One or two collections of brief

[17] Op. cit.

[18] New Haven: Human Relations Area Files, 1950.

ethnographic surveys such as George Peter Murdock, *Our Primitive Contemporaries.* New York: Macmillan, 1934; Elman Rogers Service, *Profile of Primitive Cultures.* New York: Harper, 1958; Ralph Linton, ed., *Most of the World: The Peoples of Africa, Latin America, and the East Today.* New York: Columbia University Press, 1949; Margaret Mead, ed., *Cooperation and Competition among Primitive Peoples.* New York: McGraw-Hill, 1937; Irwin T. Sanders and others, eds., *Societies around the World* (two volumes). New York: Dryden Press, 1953.

5. Edward T. Hall, *The Silent Language.* Garden City, N.Y.: Doubleday, 1959.

6. One or two readers in general anthropology such as those of Carleton S. Coon, ed., *A Reader in General Anthropology.* New York: Henry Holt, 1948; Morton H. Fried, ed., *Readings in Anthropology* (two volumes). New York: Thomas Y. Crowell, 1959; Edward Adamson Hoebel, Jesse D. Jennings, and Elmer R. Smith, comps., *Readings in Anthropology.* New York: McGraw-Hill, 1955; Margaret Mead and Nicolas Calas, eds., *Primitive Heritage: An Anthropological Anthology.* New York: Random House, 1953.

7. From this point on, all reading of general or theoretical material should be interspersed with the reading of book-length studies of specific cultures, whether listed under "Ethnography" or under one of the more specialized headings of the bibliography. This reading should be taken from outside the area in which the missionary is specifically interested almost as much as from within it, in order to gain the cross-cultural perspective which is so important to anthropological study.

8. Alfred Louis Kroeber, *Anthropology.* Rev. ed. New York: Harcourt, Brace, 1948.

9. Representative readings from the remainder of the bibliography. By this time the missionary will have some background on which to make his own choices.

10. One or more professional journals.

## ADDENDUM

Since the above article was written many books have appeared, a few of which might be substituted for some of those mentioned. One book, however, must be mentioned as essential in any reading course for the missionary. It is Louis J. Luzbetak, *The Church and Cultures, An Applied Anthropology for the Religious Worker.* Techny, Illinois: Divine Word Publications, 1963. It should be fitted in early after Nida's *Customs and Cultures.*

Luzbetak is a Roman Catholic priest and anthropologist who has written an introductory textbook and has included in each chapter a section on the missionary implications of the anthropological principles discussed. It is highly recommended to Protestants as well as Roman Catholics.

# Cultures of Man
# and the Communication of the Gospel

*Eugene A. Nida*

# Mariology in Latin America

WITHIN the last few years, there has been a marked increase of interest in Mariology within the Roman Catholic Church. This increased focus of attention upon Mary has found expression in the establishment of many shrines, wide publicity of alleged miracles, numerous books and articles on the significance of Mary for the modern world, and intense promotion of the Virgin of Fatima as the protectress of Christendom against Communism. The recent promulgation of the doctrine of the assumption of the Virgin has augmented Mary's theological status, and the much-discussed doctrine of Mary as coredemptrix with Jesus Christ seems to be gaining in influence within the Roman Church.

For the most part, this development in Mariology has been discussed by Protestants primarily in terms of the theological implications of the ever-increasing centrality of Mary within the Roman system. In large measure, however, Protestants have failed to see this development in terms of the broader cultural implications. In order to understand and more fully appreciate what is happening within the Roman Church, we need to view this extraordinary emphasis upon Mary in the light of the anthropological background involved.

## Dying Christ and Living Mary

In trying to understand the reasons for the focusing of attention upon Mary, some persons have readily seen that this is an almost inevitable result of making Christ less and less attractive to the people. Rather than portraying Christ as a victorious "culture hero" (if we may be permitted to speak in purely anthropological terms), Christ is the defeated, dying victim. Such a Christ produces feelings of pity and compassion, but he does not inspire with confidence and hope. Christ on the cross reminds the sinner of his sins, but this symbol does not suffice to make the average person want to identify himself with the suffering Savior.[1] Contemplation of the dying Christ does elicit strong emotional feelings, but they tend to drain one of nervous energy. Accordingly, they do not result in a feeling of well-being or confidence.

On the other hand, in contrast with the dying Christ there is the symbol of the radiantly beautiful Mary, the benevolent person who is always accessible and always giving. It is Mary who has compassion for the multitude, and it is the contemplation of this symbol which brings reassurance and a sense of hope and well-being. As the mediatrix between the worshiper and Christ, or God, she becomes the

[1]Masochistic individuals are of course the exceptions to this general scheme, and it is not without significance that a number of the more rigorous orders of the Roman Church have been characterized by masochistic rites centering in identification with the crucified Christ.

**Reprinted from Vol. 4, No. 3 (1957), pp. 69-82.**

giver of life, the source of health, and the means of power. It is not strange, therefore, that the center of worship in the Roman church should shift from Christ to Mary, for people prefer to identify themselves with a living Mary rather than with a dying Christ.

### The Mass and Fertility Rites

This contrast between death and life has been further accentuated in the Roman development of the mass, which in its early New Testament form reflected the covenant meal of the Old Testament. However, during the first few centuries it became in many aspects almost totally assimilated to the fertility cult rites of the mystic religions. Whether as reflecting the rites of Eleusis, Isis, or Osiris, or those which centered in the cult of Astarte, the same dominant principle prevailed — the dying god-son raised to life through the principle of female productivity. As the mass developed, it became no longer a commemorative feast, but a miraculous re-enactment of the shedding of blood. The worshiper was not just reminded of the fact that Christ died and rose again, but that he was constantly dying for the people, and they partook of his very body and blood, whether directly or in the person of the priest. This symbol served only to reinforce their equation of Christ with death, and not with life. The emotional unattractiveness of this procedure left a spiritual and psychological void which was filled by the symbol of the Virgin — readily borrowed from the pagan mystery religions and taken over with very little adaptation into the practices of the Church, though with a certain measure of theological polishing.

### The Latin Culture Context

The fact that the symbol of the suffering, dying Christ was gradually replaced by the loving, living Mary is, however, by no means all of the story, particularly in the case of Latin America. There the developments have an even deeper significance as far as their relationship to the cultural themes are concerned. In the Ibero-American culture (excluding the Indian elements) the Church and the society seem to fit like a glove on a hand, and quite understandably so, for in a sense the glove and the hand "grew up together." The Latin culture has, of course, been in a large measure the product of the teaching of the Church, and in turn the Church has adapted itself to the special Latin characteristics. Any attempt to discover the order of priority (the old problem of the chicken and the egg) is a relatively fruitless undertaking, for such adjustments always come as successive waves of give and take. However, within the contemporary life of Latin America there are certain important observations which can be made concerning the reciprocal re-enforcement of the related institutions, and it is this phase of the cultural pattern which we need to note briefly.

### Female Orientation

There are three underlying factors which must be understood if we are to appreciate the close relationship between the Roman church and Latin American society. In the first place, Latin American culture is female-oriented. By this we do not mean to imply that this orientation is the only or even the dominant one, but in contrast with other cultures which in this area of life may be described as sex-oriented, certainly Latin American culture shows a dominant tendency toward female orientation. In our own U.S.A. society, as well as in the culture of ancient Greece, the dominant element seems to be more a matter of sex itself than of interest in the female. These differences may be noted in such characteristics as (1) less homosexuality than in our own culture, (2) more overt attention paid to sex characteristics of females, and (3) greater concentration of interest in eliciting female response than in simply gratifying sexual drives. Furthermore, the greater distinctiveness in male and female roles tends to re-enforce the female-oriented nature of Latin society.

### The Mother Role

In the second place, in Latin American society the mother is the emotional center of the family. The father is more or less expected to have extramarital relations, whether with prostitutes or mistresses. In fact, in some regions of Latin America the number and quality of one's mistresses is a more decisive factor in gaining prestige than the number of cars one owns. Since the father is expected to have divided loyalties and to possess other emotional attachments, it is not difficult to understand why children should feel greater emotional attachment to the mother, even though they may continue to have a deep respect for their father. In saying that the father is expected to engage in extramarital affairs, we do not imply that all men do, for some are very faithful to their families, especially some in the middle and lower income groups. However, though some fathers may not be unfaithful, there is nevertheless the general attitude that if such men should become unfaithful, it is not to be too severely condemned. Furthermore, the wives in such circunstances are supposed to be more or less tolerant toward such affairs and to accept the fact of competition with equanimity.

A more or less natural consequence of the mother's role as bestower of benefits from the time the children are quite small is that she continues to function in this same way, though in a somewhat different form. Rather than being the direct source of help, she becomes the intercessor of the children with the less approachable father. In fact, fathers are supposed to be somewhat standoffish and mothers are supposed to be more indulgent. Of course, there are numerous exceptions to these roles, but this is the general pattern. Even though in a particular community this pattern may not be the statistically dominant one, it is, nevertheless, regarded by most Latins as being the way Latin life is organized. Hence, the "myth" (or the reality) of the more distant father and the interceding mother becomes a cultural framework in which the concept of an exacting God and a benevolent Mary can have meaning.

### Women in the Church

In the third place, there is a very well-defined relationship of re-enforcement between the status of women and the position of the Church. The status of the wife in an outwardly monogamist society is maintained by the Church by denying the validity of divorce. In fact, in some countries of Latin America the Roman Church has had such influence upon the governments that there is no possible way for a person to obtain a legal divorce. The Church, accordingly, confirms and maintains the wife's status by legally preventing or by placing severe obstacles in the way of any other female's threatening the position of the wife. At the same time, the mores of the society permit almost wholesale competition for the romantic affection of the husband, but by threat of excommunication against divorcees (though not against mistresses or adulterers) status is maintained, even though in the actual role of women there is often a wide discrepancy between real and ideal roles and behavior.

It is, accordingly, quite understandable that the wife and mother should be concerned with the re-enforcing of the authority of an institution, such as the Church, which does so much to protect her status. As the faithful, interceding mother, she identifies herself with the Virgin and finds her confidence in the strength of the one institution which maintains her status and which seems to defend her role.

Since there is also a rather well-defined pattern of indulgence of mothers towards sons, it is not difficult to see how in this aspect as well the people assume that the most effective way of reaching the somewhat formidable Christ is through the indulgent, benevolent mother. Accordingly, not only do women find in Mary a cultural type with which they may identify themselves, but many men, whether consciously or unconsciously, tend to transfer their feelings of dependence upon their mother to worship of the Virgin Mother.

All this means that loyalty to the Virgin is not the result primarily of instruction by the Church itself, but of a kind of unconscious reflex of the underlying emotional patterns in Latin life. This is perhaps the principal reason why the Roman Church continues to be so strong, despite the strong liberal and intellectual movements in Latin America. Time and again, the Jesuits have been forced out of various countries, and in many areas there are strong anticlerical movements, but despite such anti-Church attitudes there seems to be a continued devotion to the Virgin as an unconscious symbol of the life of the people. It is not without significance that for each of the countries or principal regions in Latin America there is some patron Virgin. Individual areas may also have their patron saints, but the overruling focus of emotional attachment is to the Virgin. This promotion of the Virgin as the patron of the nation is a natural outgrowth of the role of the benevolent mother on the lower level of the family unit.

## Male-oriented Cultures

In contrast with the centrality of Mary in Latin America, it is interesting to note the differences in the Greek Orthodox Church, as well as such other Eastern Churches as the Coptic, Armenian, and Ethiopic. Though the Eastern as well as the Roman Churches had a very similar early history as regards certain aspects of the mass and the recognition of Mary as "Mother of God" (a significant feature of the Athanasian and Arian controversy), nevertheless the Eastern Church has not made Mary the center of adoration to the extent that the Roman Church has done, especially in Ibero-American culture. Part of this disparity may be attributed to the fact that the Eastern Church rejected the use of images and sensuous art forms. The icons, relics, and mosaics were not particularly well adapted to emphasizing a female sex element. On the other hand, the Eastern Churches are studded with frescoes and murals, but these are predominantly of masculine persons: Biblical heroes, early saints, and Jesus Christ. However, despite the difference in the art forms and objects, one basic reason for this diversity between the Eastern Churches and the Roman ones is to be found — the fact that in the area of the Eastern Churches society is much less female-centered. In this feature there has no doubt been some influence from Islamic culture during the last thousand years or so. But one must also recognize the fact that the culture of the Eastern Mediterranean, even before the rise of Islam, was essentially male-oriented. Important broad patterns of life have had a significant influence in molding the Churches of both the East and the West.

## Theology and Emotions

The most frequent criticism leveled against the Protestants is that they do not "believe in" the Virgin. The arguments used by Roman Catholics do not betray any special theological concern for the Virgin. It is only that they cannot understand what seems to be gross lack of respect, gratitude, and filial loyalty. For the average Latin Roman Catholic the Virgin is not primarily the historical personage who lived in Nazareth, gave birth to Jesus Christ, and nurtured him to manhood; the Virgin is the symbolic projection of a series of emotional attitudes formed within the very first years of a child's life. Emotional attachment to the Virgin is thus acquired as one of the deepest and earliest psychological experiences. For the most part, this attitude toward the Virgin is without overt reasoning, though it may be formulated in memorized doctrines and expressed in overt acts of prayer. The fact that Virgin adoration is largely implicit within the cultural framework greatly increases its hold upon the person, for any rejection of the Virgin is tied up with rejection of mother, home, and family love.

To a great extent, Protestant missionaries in Latin America have failed to understand fully the place of the "Virgin-symbol" in the lives of Roman Catholics. They have tried to employ theological arguments against what they have denounced as "Mariolatry." However, for the most part, Roman Catholics have been entirely unmoved by such theological arguments. The reason for this is that they learned to believe in the Virgin not from theological arguments but because of family relationships. Even though admitting the validity of arguments based upon historical revelations in the Scriptures, Roman Catholics find themselves emotionally unable to consider rejecting the Virgin. In fact, they often insist that they know God (even as revealed in the Scriptures) would not want them to do so, for they have never distinguished between filial loyalty and the religious symbol of the Virgin.

## The Living Christ

If, however, the break from the Virgin-symbol is so difficult for Roman Catholics, how are we to explain what has happened for so many tens of thousands (about five million in all) who are Protestants in Latin America? There are, of course, a number of more or less overt "anthropological" reasons for people turning from Catholicism to Protestantism: (1) reaction to the authoritarianism of the Church, (2) special educational advantages offered by Protestant missions, (3) personal resentment against the behavior of persons who were identified with the Roman Church, and (4) a sense of frustration which ends up in a nonconformist defiance of the status quo and all it stands for. To this list may be added a number of other minor overt reasons for people becoming Protestants. However, there is another reason which is far more important than any of these "trigger" causes. This is the substitution of the symbol of the victorious, living Christ for the defeated, dying one.

One of the effective ways in which this new symbol has been communicated is through the Scriptures. Time after time, Roman Catholics have commented when they read the Scriptures that they "did not realize that Christ lived." They had thought of him only as dying. The fact that his life was filled so full of service and identification of himself with people and that, though he suffered, he rose from the dead and ascended to glory, seems to be an almost incomprehensible revelation.

Furthermore, in the message of the Scriptures Roman Catholics discover that it was God who identified himself with man in Christ (God is no longer screened off by the ever-present Virgin) and that it was Christ who identified himself wholly with man. It is this identification of Christ with man (he was one like us) which finally reaches through to men and women. Furthermore, Roman Catholics learn that this Christ who lived also lives today and by his Spirit walks with men. Here is the fullness of fellowship and the certainty of penetrating through the veil of uncertainty which always shrouds the well-meaning but sometimes thwarted efforts of the kindhearted Virgin-symbol.

It is not without significance that, for the most part, individual Roman Catholics do not become Protestants over night. In fact, during the process of learning about the living Christ, they often go back time and again to praying to the Virgin, and in times of severe family crisis they feel an almost irresistible urge to seek refuge in prayers and candles to the Virgin. When they do make a final break (sometimes after a number of years), they do so only when the symbol (and the reality) of the Christ as living intercessor has been completely substituted for the earlier symbol of the interceding Mother.

It is just as well that Protestant missionaries recognize the fact that the symbol of the Lord Christ cannot hope to be as popular as that of the benevolent Mother, if by "popular" we mean that which has the greatest appeal to man's sinful nature. In the first place, the Virgin-symbol involves aphysical attractiveness with sex appeal (whether admitted overtly or not — but whoever saw an image of a homely Virgin?) and an emotional identification with mother-love. On the other hand, the symbol of the Lord Christ, though it may have some of the popular appeal of the culture hero, can never become simply a Davy Crockett. As God himself, Christ always possesses for man that "otherness" which mystified even his closest disciples. He was one with them, and yet they recognized that he was utterly different. This mystery of the incarnation never escaped them and continues both to mystify and to inspire the believer's deepest thoughts and his highest aspirations.

### Celibacy of the Priesthood

In the conversion of a person from Catholicism to Protestantism there is an important shift or orientation from female to male symbolism, with a much-decreased concentration upon the sex element, for it is much easier to identify oneself with the sex element in the more earthly Mother than to symbolize the sex relationship with the more distant Christ.

On the other hand, the celibacy of Roman Catholic priests would seem to deny this sex element, but in reality it only confirms the sex factor. In his function as the earthly representative of Jesus Christ, the Pope and the priesthood which receive their sanction through him must be symbolically identified with Christ. However, in order to be intimately associated with the Virgin-Mother symbol, they must be *symbolically* incapable of sex relations. Otherwise, there would be danger of "spiritual incest." On the other hand, the Protestant minister has no such attitudes toward the Virgin-symbol, and in his status of prophet, rather than primarily as priest, he identifies himself with the people, in order to bring them to God. The Roman priest, however, is primarily a priest, identified with the bestower of benefits (i.e. the Virgin-Mother) and transmitter of blessings to the people.

The close relationship between celibacy of the priesthood and the Virgin-symbol may be seen by comparing further the practices of the Eastern and Roman Churches. Asceticism began in the East as the result, it would appear, of predominantly Syrian influences, in which celibacy of priests in numerous pagan cults was regarded as an essential requisite for attendance upon the goddesses of fertility. (In a number of these religious cults castration was the symbol of identification with the goddess.) However, though celibacy began in the Eastern churches and was widespread during early centuries, it is not now regarded as a requisite for the priesthood, even though it may be encouraged in some of the orders and for certain higher posts in the ecclesiastical hierarchy. On the other hand, though celibacy was relatively slow in coming to the Western churches, it is now obligatory in the Roman Church, for the very reason that only in this way can the priest (whether consciously or unconsciously) attain full identification with both Christ and the Virgin-Mother without the guilt of incest.[2] In the male-oriented culture of the East, where the Virgin is not the dominant symbol, celibacy is not so essential, and hence not obligatory.

## Symbols

Perhaps one of the most difficult tasks for the Protestant missionary in Latin America is to realize the nature and importance of symbols, whether verbal or visual. This does not mean that the Protestant does not possess a number of symbols; he does. But for the most part his symbols are primarily words and verbal descriptions of people and events. When the Protestant thinks of Saint Peter, a whole series of images immediately come to the surface of his thinking. They include the denial at the trial, the three questions posed by Jesus after the resurrection, Peter cutting off Malchus' ear, etc. For the average Roman Catholic in Latin America, Saint Peter means a statue in a particular church, a patron saint of a nearby town, a statue before which he prays in times of sickness in the family, a personage in heaven who intercedes with Mary, who in turn goes to Christ. If a Roman Catholic happens to have read the Bible, he may have some mental images similar to those of the

---

[2] It is quite true that these explanations involve several important features of Freudian psychology, but they are by no means dependent solely upon an acceptance or rejection of Freudian theories. These fundamental psychological relationships are recognized in one form or another by practically all psychoanalysts.

Protestant, but for the most part, even if the Protestant and the Catholic use the same words "Saint Peter," they are very likely to be talking about entirely different things.

A number of Protestant symbols are words which stand for important beliefs (many of which the average Protestant cannot explain). These words symbolize important experiences in his life and doctrine which he believes are indispensable to faith: repentance, conversion, redemption, blessing, Holy Spirit, justification, sanctification, the dying Savior, the blood, the cross, the open tomb, saints, confession, prayer, faith, hope, assurance, etc. For the Roman Catholic a number of these words are associated with specific objects (or images) which he can see or rites in which he overtly participates: the blood (the wine at communion or red paint on the crucifix), the dying Savior (the crucifix), the cross, saints (heavenly intercessors and images within the home and at church), prayers (it is not without interest that the Catholic "says prayers" or "recites," but the Protestant "prays"), faith (as a list of doctrines), confession (to the priest), etc. However, for a number of word symbols which the average Protestant possesses there is often no corresponding object or mental image for the Catholic. For the most part, Roman Catholicism has objectified its symbols in attractive or awesome objects or in impressive rites. On the other hand, the Protestant emphasizes much more the abstract or historical value of the word symbols.

## Protestant Symbolization for Catholics

If, however, a missionary is going to communicate effectively with people of Roman Catholic background, he must try to bridge the psychological gap which exists between the two systems by choosing word symbols which will help the Roman Catholic to understand the Protestant beliefs. Accordingly, rather than use words which may carry little or no meaning (or which may only define more or less abstract doctrines prior to their being explained at length), he needs to employ figures which will approximate in some measure the degree of objective symbolization which is so common to Roman Catholics. One of these symbols, and a very important one in communicating with Roman Catholics, is that of the rent veil. By means of this symbol one can indicate the significance of the Mediator of the new relationship with God. The symbol of the covenant meal, consecrated by the death of the One who offered himself, can help explain the Biblical meaning of the communion. The symbol of the Risen Lord can help to transform the crucifix and give assurance that death is swallowed up in victory.

One of the reasons for the spectacular success of the Pentecostal churches of Chile is in their rich use of verbal symbols which help to create for their people the vivid impressions of Biblical events and characters, with whom the people in their dramatic times of united prayer and demonstrations identify themselves psychologically. In the relatively unattractive, stern atmosphere of Protestant churches of Latin America some attempt should be made to find compensatory verbal substitutes by which the symbolism becomes as meaningful as possible and the group fellowship as emotionally rewarding as the corresponding sense of beauty and pageantry in the Roman Catholic edifices and rites.

For the missionary one of the most essential elements is adequate understanding of the underlying factors influencing behavior. Without this knowledge we are sometimes immobilized, not knowing what to say nor where to turn. Our understanding of the fundamental concepts of Latin American life is still very rudimentary, but we must make every effort to understand and to appreciate the basic nature of any society, if we are to have any appreciable success in communicating to such people the full meaning of Christ as Savior and Lord.

*William D. Reyburn*

# The Transformation of God and the Conversion of Man

THE major obstacle to the effective communication of the Christian message of God's redeeming love looms up in the receiver's notion of God. The universal question which should be posited by Christian missions is, *Can a man be converted to Christianity without the transformation of his idea of God to conform to a Christian concept of God?*

In order to throw some light on this question a discussion of these matters will be given within the framework of two disparate folk cultures, the peasant Quechua Indians of the Ecuadorean Andes and the hunting Kaka tribe of the southeastern French Cameroun. These two societies provide a widely divergent cultural base from which to view this problem.

The notion of God as held by any group of people is one of the most vital keys they can offer the missionary as an insight into the depths of their human feelings about a score of subjects other than the purely religious. In fact, the missionary who will know his people will have to first know their God. How a people symbolize the supernatural, and the way they think and feel toward their God or gods is not only a clue to the stuff of which the society is made, but also an indication of what in Christianity will be immediately relevant. It shows also what will undergo radical reinterpretation to fit the existing scheme of things, and what will have to be rejected as unintelligible (although it is possible to embody paradoxes and contradictions and to make little or no attempt to have things logically consistent). What a society or any individual will think about man is not determined so much by his method of studying man (as historian, anthropologist, or biologist) but by what he assumes man to be. Likewise, what a society thinks about man's relation to God and vice versa is not set by the manner of approaching God, but by what it assumes man and God to be.

The two societies dealt with here assume similar yet quite different things about God. These in turn are reflected in basically different human orientations which give life's purpose (or lack of it) different ends. Knowledge of a man's view of God is not immediately given by simply asking for it but is gotten at rather through his practices, attitudes, values, institution, systems of beliefs, and relations to other human beings.

It is no exaggeration to say that man creates God in his own image. This creation of God in the image of the people likewise affects and determines much of the way in which man creates his culture. The two things are interdependent. Christianity's claim to withstand this charge is contained in the view of God which originates from a self-disclosing God who reveals himself to man.

**Reprinted from Vol. 4, No. 5 (1957), pp. 185-194.**

In order to catch a comparative view of God, we will first give Christian conceptions of God with their counterparts seen from Kaka and Quechua concepts. This may be done best by separating the Christian set into (1) God as God, and (2) God as Redeemer. The confusion of these two aspects of God in the minds of the Kaka and Quechua creates a barrier to understanding Christianity.

**God as God**

*Christian*: God is perfect.

*Kaka*: God is a spider, Ndjambie. His character is impersonal, thus perfection or lack of it cannot be one of his attributes.

*Quechua*: God is Father, Taita Dios, who is as personal as Taita may decide to be. He is not granted a state of perfection. He is only reckoned as good or bad according to his acts.

*Christian*: God is one and infinite.

*Kaka and Quechua*: Ndjambie and Taita Dios are not infinite but submerged in an infinite cosmos. Therefore they are not the creator even though called that. Not being truly creator, Ndjambie and Taita Dios are not infinite.

*Christian*: God is lawgiver and judge.

*Kaka*: Ndjambie is not connected with enforcing supernatural sanctions, such as punishment for incest. The "law" is given through the ancestors whose spirits enforce its sanctions.

*Quechua*: Taita Dios is judge without being lawgiver; therefore his judgment is capricious.

*Christian*: Since God is perfect and the lawgiver, humans are dependent morally.

*Kaka*: No such dependence follows.

*Quechua*: Dependence is entirely on a material level since Taita Dios is unrelated to perfection.

*Christian*: God is the creator and author of cosmological order.

*Kaka and Quechua*: Such order as exists is unquestioned and indifferently ascribed to Ndjambie and Taita Dios.

*Christian*: Individual feeling of responsibility on part of man to God; man therefore acknowledges himself as sinful.

*Kaka and Quechua*: Ndjambie and Taita Dios are responsible to man; no feeling for the converse. Therefore, man is not a sinner before Ndjambie and Taita Dios, nor responsible to them.

*Christian*: Anthropomorphizes in God the essence of the highest moral and spiritual values.

*Kaka*: The highest moral and spiritual values are held to be in the spirits of the dead who attained to socially approved status in this life.

*Quechua*: The highest moral value is one which is sanctioned by the group and the Quechua seeks in no way to universalize it.

*Christian*: God is personal, the Father of man.

*Kaka*: Ndjambie is totally impersonal, a spider.

*Quechua*: Taita Dios ("Father God") may be cajoled into being personal, but his impersonality shares in the impersonality of volcano peaks which are co-divinities with Taita Dios. These are also called Taita. The fatherhood of volcanoes comes about through the marriage union of these mountains which gave origin to man (Quechua man).

*Christian*: God is eternal and man's relation to God is an eternal one.

*Kaka*: Ndjambie is eternal but remains so independent of man.

*Quechua*: Life and Taita Dios are viewed as static without reference to eternity.

*Christian*: God is omniscient but loving and caring for man.

*Kaka*: Ndjambie neither knows nor cares about human beings. His job is to help keep the cosmos regulated.

*Quechua*: Taita Dios knows only what the saints or the Virgin may care to pass on to him. These may be cajoled through fiesta rites.

*Christian*: God is unchangeable.

*Kaka and Quechua*: Ndjambie and Taita Dios are egocentric and can and do look after their own interests first. They are not attributed any persistent unchanging personality qualities. While Taita Dios is quite durable and static he is characterized by whimsical moods.

*Christian*: God is the embodiment of all truth.

*Kaka and Quechua*: The existence of universal truth is not posited.

*Christian*: God is just, holy and good independently of man.

*Kaka*: None of these qualities are attributed to Ndjambie.

*Quechua*: Taita Dios is good if he accords the request of his petitioners. Otherwise he is bad or angry, getting revenge on man.

## God as Redeemer

This second view of God, *the Christian revelation*, does not come ordinarily to such people as the Kaka and Quechua after they have cleared the ground for a redemptive God, but at the very outset. The confusions which result are directly or indirectly responsible for the general syncretistic conceptualizations of God one finds on the mission fields.

*Christian*: Man stands guilty before God as a sinful creature.

*Kaka and Quechua*: Man is simply an unfortunate die tossed by fate.

*Christian*: God is moved through loving compassion to deliver man from his sinful state.

*Kaka*: Ndjambie has no care and man is not sinful. Men simply do bad deeds.

*Quechua*: Taita Dios can be placated for his wrath and provoked to help man in his unfortunate conditions. Man is not a sinner but does wrongs such as stealing.

*Christian*: God initiates a plan to bring man unto himself motivated through love. Such a plan becomes a part of human history. God the lawgiver and judge receives in himself his own penalty because of his love for man.

*Kaka*: Ndjambie has had no plan because he has had no concern for man as man. History to which Christianity refers its revelation does not exist. The personalized dealing of the Christian God can in no way fit impersonal Ndjambie.

*Quechua*: Taita Dios in the Roman Catholic notion is admitted to have made a plan of salvation. However, the purpose for this plan remains an anomaly for the Quechua since after four hundred years of indoctrination he still does not make the assumptions about man's conditions which would prompt Taita Dios to reveal himself.

*Christian*: God is the self-disclosing God of revelation unfolding in history and witnessed to in Scripture.

*Kaka and Quechua*: The non-present world is not historical but mythological. The witness of a written record for Ndjambie would presuppose that the Bible Ndjambie begins with the contact with the literate white population. For the Quechua the written record of Taita Dios is denied by the local parish priest, which strengthens and confirms the Quechua hold on a syncretized Taita and Dios.

## Religious Views Revealed in Culture

If we keep these religious assumptions in mind and trace through some of the aspects of these cultures we will see readily how these unvoiced statements of faith provide a key note for behavior. Some examples follow.

1. "God" is not infinite to the Kaka and Quechua and is not in control of the universe. He is enmeshed in the cosmos in such a way that he is totally lacking in concern for man as such. This lack of concern for man flows on through to man's lack of concern for man.

2. Ndjambie and Taita Dios are totally removed from ethical considerations because they have no attributes of perfection. Among the Kaka the idea of God the Judge is also lacking. Consequently behavior is curbed by the fear of being caught by another man. What is expedient is right. Ends justify means.

3. Men do not assume that they are guilty sinners before Ndjambie and Taita Dios. Hence they are not responsible before these gods. This freedom from responsibility before Ndjambie and Taita Dios allows a freedom from responsibility on the human level also. The Kaka and Quechua do not make assumptions about their gods which would allow them to be morally dependent upon these gods. It is much safer to be independent of these capricious divinities than to trust one's lot to their whims.

4. The core of ethical behavior for the Quechua and Kaka does not arise from feelings about the perfection and moral attributes of Ndjambie and Taita Dios. Ethical considerations are based upon the idealized behavior of the ingroup. However, the ethical relations of one's kin or social group are of such deep value that they are held to be sacred. Among the Kaka the violation of such proper behavior can result in supernatural punishment. Since these punishments are not forthcoming for "unethical" behavior outside of one's own group, there is a double standard of ethics fully consistent with the dichotomy of the sacred society and the indifferent and impersonal Ndjambie. Man does not compare his ethical or moral self with a holy, righteous Ndjambie but with the accepted standards of behavior for his ingroup, a heritage from the ancestors.

5. Ndjambie and Taita Dios are unrelated to "truth." Therefore, there is no search for truth with respect for the truth. One is more interested in establishing a point of view favorable to the support of the ego.

6. A major orientation in both societies is that of being controlled by fate. Ndjambie and Taita Dios are not the creative Will, they are not infinite. They do not have personal concern and love for man in his plight. They are whimsical, changeable, impersonal and show no concern nor love for man. A major difference between the Kaka and the Quechua is that the latter assume one can solicit through Catholic fiestas the aid of Taita Dios through his mother (the Virgin). The Kaka, because Ndjambie is too far removed to be concerned, rely upon magic, mainly in the form of medicines. If the medicines fail, the Kaka appeals through the sorcerer to spirits in nature or the spirits of the dead. The Quechua may pray for help from the spirits of the volcanoes. In both cases, if failure results one has completed the circle of fate and is ready to start again. The Quechua's subservience makes him a ready pawn of fate but basically the two meet at the same point.

## Translator's Dilemma

When the translator writes Ndjambie or Taita Dios in the context of the Christian Scriptures, is he really translating? There is no better native term in these two cultures and a foreign word would be lacking entirely in the few equivalences which do exist. On the other hand, Ndjambie and Taita Dios, in spite of the fact that converts use them, are not on their face value equivalent to the Christian God. However, it is precisely the convert who is attempting to fit to his god concepts for which he has derived little or no feeling from his culture. The Biblical Ndjambie who cared for man, worked out a plan, carried it out at a certain point in history and plans ahead for the future is hardly recognizable to the average Kaka tribesman. His Ndjambie shares with the tribe the lack of concern for men outside of the clan. The thinking forward to carry out a plan and then actually doing it is contrary to the ideal of Kaka effort which makes no plan ahead of today because no one knows what might happen tomorrow. Because of this he does not recognize his relation to any such farsighted Biblical Ndjambie.

The comparative assumptions about God as God are quite different between a Christian concept and the Kaka and Quechua notions. There are some similarities, however. When we move to a comparison of notions of God as Redeemer, the disparities between the Christian on one hand and the Kaka and Quechua on the other become immense.

## Conclusion

Christian missions compound confusions with their ubiquitous catechisms which begin by parading past a multitude of unknown Bible characters from Genesis through Revelation in order to show the learner who God is. These names, usually adaptations from a colonial language, fully convince the would-be convert that the white man's God is not only a trinity but a pantheon of immense proportions. These catechisms assume the convert's religious mind is an empty basin to be filled for the first time in his life. This procedure not only defeats the purpose of catechising but leaves the learner with a fragmented confusion of his own god and little or no idea of the Christian God. The result of this can hardly be called Christianizing. It could be more properly called "detheizing." Such a process leads naturally among many complacent nonliterate people to a general apathetic "Christian" life. Essentially this is what has happened to millions of the inhabitants of Andean South America and is one of the great moral blights in history.

A conceptual transformation of God as God is necessary before man can understand and grasp the idea of God as Redeemer. People are known to have thrown over their gods. The Hawaiians are an example. People everywhere in history have been putting away old gods for new. However, such a total renunciation comes from a motivation to do so completely. It does not follow that such a transition means an automatic preparation to accept a radically different notion of God. The task for Christian missions is to so deal with man's religious ideas that the Christian notion of God prepares a man to accept the Redeemer notion of God. Merely renouncing a pagan god or belief system does not in any way in itself mean that the renouncing individual is thereby prepared to grasp in faith the idea and spiritual reality of the Christian God of loving redemption.

*Eugene A. Nida*

# The Roman Catholic, Communist, and Protestant Approach to Social Structure

EVEN the most casual observer of what is going on in the world today recognizes that there is something essentially different in the approach which Roman Catholicism, Communism, and Protestantism make to social structure. In country after country, one finds the Roman Catholic hierarchy concentrating on the elite, drawing its principal leadership from this class, and seeing that important members of the class feel no lack of education or spiritual assistance. At the same time, Roman Catholicism has a wide appeal to the impoverished masses, while among the middle classes there is often a strong anticlerical sentiment.

On the other hand, Communism talks of a classless society and yet has succeeded in creating the most class-conscious structure known in the Western world (almost equivalent to the caste system of India). The Communist leadership itself constitutes a special elite, which is drawn principally from the proletariat — a dictatorship by representatives of the proletariat.

Protestants, however, have their strength not in the elite classes nor in the lower classes, but primarily in the middle classes, and especially in those segments which are on the upward move in the socio-economic scale.

Reprinted from Vol. 4, No. 6 (1957), pp. 209-219.

Do these differences in Roman Catholic, Communist, and Protestant "societies" reflect simply an accidental development? Or are they the result of well-thought-out plans of social organization? Or are such developments an inevitable reflection of other fundamental features of these rather diverse ideologies? The answers to these questions can only be found in an analysis of the structure of society and certain significant features of social control and movement.

## Diagrammatic Representation of Social Structure

As a means of visualizing something of the nature of social structure (though with obvious oversimplification and hence skewing of the data), we may diagram a typical social structure as follows:

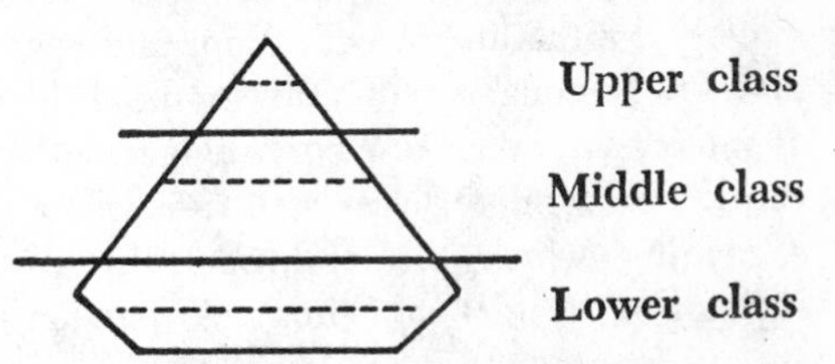


In this diagram the various classes are schematically arranged as higher, middle, and lower, with a subdivisional distinction within each class, thus giving us a traditional six-class structure (which may or may not be true of particular societies, but which is typical of a number of societies). Rather than being a strict pyramid (as is usually taught by Communist propaganda), most structures tend to be a kind of inverted diamond, since the indigent population is actually less numerous in most societies than other segments of the lower class, such as factory laborers, unskilled day laborers, and tenant farmers. The middle class is generally divided between the independent tradesmen and small merchants in the lower middle class and the semiprofessional persons, clerks and lower-bracket white collar workers in the upper middle class. The upper class is divided usually between the "older families," constituting the first-class elite, and many of the leaders in business and the professional world. However, in many instances some members of the "old families aristocracy" are not as wealthy or as politically influential as many members of the second-class elite (or the lower upper class).

Class structure is not to be considered simply a classification of earning power or occupation. It involves such additional factors as family lineage, education, personal attractiveness, basic attitudes (such as attitudes toward the chances of success, value of hard work, saving of money, desirability of education, and sex mores), personal talents (as in the field of music, art, entertainment), and friendships. Furthermore, class structure is not something which the anthropologist or sociologist decides to "impose" on the society in order to describe it. The social structure is there and recognized in covert or overt forms by the people. Although in some societies many persons tend to deny its existence (something which is true of a number of communities in the United States), the behavior of people within such societies reveals a set of human relationships which are based upon such class structuring.

Because of the wide differences in types of social structures, it would scarcely be fair not to emphasize such diversities by comparing certain widely varying structures. For this we may take the following diagrams, based on an impressionistic view of the structures of the U.S.A. and of India:

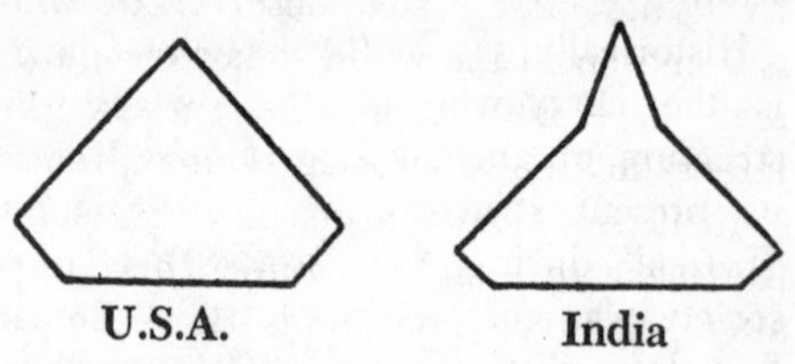


## The Roman Catholic Approach to Social Structure

Without exception, the Roman Catholic approach to the social structure is through the elite, who are provided with good schools, considerable personal attention, and from which group the leadership of the Church comes. There are, of course, many priests drawn from the lower classes, but with very rare exceptions any member of the priesthood having a rank of bishop or higher is drawn from the elite, and, if possible, from the first-class elite — the aristocracy. Moreover, the Church exerts its control on the society by means of the elite, who generally dominate the political and economic life of the people. This means that the Roman Catholic clergy are almost without exception on the side of the conservative political party.

It is quite understandable that the Roman Catholic Church should approach the social structure in this way, for the Church itself is a strictly pyramidal structure with very overt ranking of authority. In a sense the Church is a kind of institution apart from the society and regarded as being above the society, for the laity are not really members of the Church, only adherents. Accordingly, the Roman Church, which has never relinquished its claim to complete temporal as well as spiritual authority, proceeds to exercise whatever control it can by means of the same type of hierarchical attitude toward the social structure as is contained within its own organization.

Historically, the Roman Catholic Church is the carry-over of the authoritarian structure of ancient Roman society, and its present structure was more or less "frozen" during the Renaissance, when society was completely controlled by the first-class elite. There have been some notable attempts to introduce certain changes in such structuring, and in a sense the equalitarian character of certain of the Catholic orders (not, of course, the Jesuits) fulfills this function, but these orders have not gained control of the papacy. Most recently there was a very significant attempt to bring the Church closer to the people by instituting the role of "worker-priests" in France. However, the authorities of the Church abandoned this scheme entirely when they discovered that the priests were themselves becoming "too sympathetic" with the workers. Had such a movement continued, it would have undermined the authoritarian structure, based upon a definite class consciousness, which identified itself with the elite, not with the workers.

In the almost exclusive identification of the Roman Church with the position and interests of the elite there lie the seeds of greatly diminished power and influence, for the future is with the masses. The general repudiation of the Roman Church by the masses in Europe, the rise of strong anticlerical movements, especially among the middle classes, and the indifference of the average man to the doctrines of the Church, in favor of the new cult of "scientism," poses a real threat to the Roman Church.

On the other hand, in countries in which the Roman Church is the exclusive dictator of the school system or where the elite have almost complete control of the masses, the lower classes continue to have a strong allegiance to the Church. In the elaborate and attractive ritual the people participate vicariously in a pageantry provided by the elite and characteristic of their opulence. The Church provides the only evident hope of any changed status in the next life. Furthermore, the dependency relation to the Church in spiritual matters is only a symbolic continuation of economic and social dependency upon the elite. In these circumstances, however, the middle classes are often anticlerical, for they recognize in the Roman Church their principal obstacle to breaking into the elite position. Accordingly, politicians, who arise primarily from the upward-moving segments of the middle class, cultivate the masses by means of liberal political doctrines and thus lay the groundwork for taking over governments from the conservatives. When, however, as has happened several times in Latin America, the amoral attitudes of certain liberal leaders (as reflected in their evident concern for purely personal gain) leave the masses disillusioned, they are then amenable to overtures from the conservatives, who promise law and order, even at the expense of freedom.

### The Communist Approach to Social Structure

The Communists are authoritarian and totalitarian, even as the Roman Catholics are, but their approach to social structure is very different, even though in the end they create a strictly pyramidal structure with highly centralized controls. In the first place, the first- and second-class elite (the upper class) must be liquidated by killing (in which case the property may be expropriated) or brainwashing. The first process is employed primarily with the rich, and the second is used on intellectual groups. Once these two classes of elite have been eliminated, the party can superimpose upon the society a new ruling clique, a new elite. This new elite, however, is not drawn from members of the former elite, except in rare instances. It is drawn, rather, from members of the lower class or from certain disillusioned persons of the middle class (especially members of rejected minority groups) who have tried to break through into the upper class but have been prevented from doing so, despite their evident personal capacities. This is a reason why in a number of countries of western Europe and the United States there is such a high percentage of Jews in the Communist movement, and why in the United States Communism has had such a wide appeal to certain intellectuals in the Negro population.

The purposeful and planned discrimination against representatives of the upper middle classes or former upper classes is evident in eastern Germany, where the sons of professors are often rejected for advanced studies, despite their high qualifications, in favor of the sons of tradesmen or day laborers who may actually be somewhat inferior in intellectual ability. By plucking a person out of a lower class and thrusting him into the elite in such a way that the person is completely dependent upon party loyalty for every advance in status or advantage in living, the Communist leadership knows full well that it can produce a much more loyal servant of the state. Such a person is not so likely to want to push into the first-class elite, but will be more content with second-class elite status. His viewpoints are likely to be more amoral with regard to party loyalty than if he felt that he had a right to certain prerogatives. As a "representative" of the lower classes he can more satisfactorily live the fiction of the "dictatorship of the proletariat."

The Communist emphasis upon creating a big social gap between the elite leadership and the rest of the populace helps to provide a distance which can better justify the doctrine of "infallibility," which the Communists have been entirely too clever to formulate as a creed (in contrast with the Roman Catholics), but which constitutes an implicit doctrine. This is evidenced in the fact that the people are never provided with more than one slate of officials to approve. In other words, the State knows best, in the finest paternalistic and Tsarist fashion. By providing a large gap between the governing elite and the masses the party is able to place a higher "price tag" on membership (the price of unquestioned loyalty), and not only will men do anything to get in, but they will perform any type of function in order to stay in.

On the other hand, the social structure of Communism contains the seeds of crisis, for what is to happen with the second and third generation of Communists? Human nature being what it is, is there not a possibility that the elite class will want to perpetuate itself as an aristocracy, in which case the Soviet social structure will then be frozen into a kind of caste system? Even at present the Soviet system is not a dictatorship of the proletariat, but a dictatorship of men of whom the majority arose out of the proletariat. But there is every likelihood that within two or three generations there will be a dictatorship of an aristocracy which in times past arose out of the proletariat, and there will be only a propagandistic touch with the masses. There is no doubt but what such a fiction may be maintained for some time, especially in an age where controls of power and communication can be so centralized. However, the dictatorship of the proletariat will only be a fiction, even as "the classless society" is also a fiction.

## The Protestant Approach to Social Structure

On the whole, Protestants have not purposely avoided any class, but have infiltrated all classes, as reflected in churches which range from Episcopal to Pentecostal. It is quite true that during the Reformation the decisions of princes were of great importance in the political struggle, but the real strength of the Protestant movement existed in the rapidly growing merchant classes, not primarily among the ruling classes. It can still be said that the major strength of Protestantism exists in the lower middle and upper lower classes.

By concentration on doctrines involving personal salvation, moral integrity, thrift, financial responsibility, hard work, and the elimination of personal vices, Protestantism has not only attracted people who are interested in personal improvement, but has started many people on the upward "climb" in the social structure, since precisely these virtues are important in the individualistic, profit-motive society of the West. The Methodist movement in England, for example, began primarily among the lower classes, but within a short time the descendants of these people were predominantly middle-class people, and now there is a sizable group of British Methodists who are members of the lower upper class.

In this upward movement of Protestant groups there has always been the tendency of the group to lose effective contact with the class out of which it has come. Accordingly, Methodism, which "outgrew" its appeal to the lower classes, indirectly fostered a Nazarene revival, and the Nazarenes and similar groups, who tended to move away from the lower classes, made room for Pentecostals, whose principal appeal is directed primarily to such classes.

Protestantism does not have a particularly strong appeal to the very wealthy, for in general it demands too high a standard of stewardship of money and too great a sense of responsibility for social ills. Furthermore, since salvation cannot be purchased by money, there is no guarantee of special favors for the rich. (There are, of course, some unfortunate exceptions in which Protestantism falls far short of its historical and Biblical basis.)

Protestantism is far more racially prejudiced and class conscious than Roman Catholicism. The principal reason for this is the fact that in Protestantism the laity are "members" of the church (not just "adherents," in contrast with the ordained who alone constitute the Church, as far as Roman Catholicism is concerned), and hence they have a greater sense of congregational participation and oneness. This type of in-group consciousness leads to greater class awareness and the tendency to segregation, following the patterns of the social structure.

On the whole, the Roman Catholic Church has a greater appeal than does the Protestant to the very poor. It is less bothered by problems of class consciousness and prejudice, which arise from the congregational character of the Protestant movement. It also provides elaborate, beautiful ritual in which the poor may participate and thus identify themselves with something immeasurably higher than their own humble status. The poor remain attached to the Church in the same dependent relationship which they have toward the elite on whom they are socially and economically dependent, and the Church may provide a sense of status and well-being, even in the worst of circumstances, for it is the one claim which such persons have for "pie in the sky by and by." Furthermore, in order to attain these ultimate goals the Roman Church does not make the same demands upon the lower classes for personal initiative, responsibility, and ambition — factors which are noticeably lacking in members of this class.

The ideal Protestant approach to society is the incarnational one, in which those of any one class are willing to reach down and, in identification with those who have not found the way, introduce them to "the Way, the Truth, and the Life" in Christ Jesus. This is the way of the *kenosis* (the "emptying") of prerogatives in order that men beneath may be reached and raised up. However, except for the foreign mission enterprise, it is not usually the case that members of a church have such a ministry of reaching down as Christ did, but they reach out to those of the same social class. In fact, those who reach down (who dare to preach in the streets and without official sanction, as Wesley did) are often ostracized from the original constituency and excluded. They accordingly form a new denomination, with a distinctive message for and appeal to a particular social segment. Since Protestantism not only directly and indirectly fosters such movements, but refuses to censure such departures as heresies (as is the case with parallel departures from Roman Catholicism), it is inevitable that Protestantism will continue to produce a series of different denominations. Actually, however, this capacity to reach new and different segments within the social structure and to bring into leadership (often quite unintentionally) persons of ability within the diverse social groupings is the genius of Protestantism. If, on the other hand, in pursuance of the ideal of a united Protestantism this belief in the priesthood of the believer is denied to the point of crushing such new and creative movements (a kind of totalitarian ecumenicity), Protestantism will have sown the seeds of its own destruction. It could only be successful in such a pursuit of conformity by becoming a completely totalitarian organization. However, those whose ecumenical thinking is most realistic within the Protestant movement recognize that the high-priestly prayer of our Lord (John 17) does not mean organizational identity as much as spiritual unity. In the age of the mass man one must not be deceived into thinking that only in organizational identity is there strength, for masked beneath an outward unity may be smoldering antagonisms, while within a group of freely cooperating entities there may be the greatest capacity for the fullest expression of latent human creativity.

*Eugene A. Nida*

# The Relationship of Social Structure to the Problems of Evangelism in Latin America

FOR many years those concerned with the problems of evangelism in Latin America have been keenly aware of some of the significant correlations between differences of social structure and the response of the people to the gospel. For one thing, relatively few people from the upper classes and not too many from the middle class ever become associated with evangelical churches. This has meant that the membership of most of the Protestant churches has come from the upper brackets of the lower class. The leadership within the churches has seemed to come primarily from the families of independent tradesmen and merchants, e.g. carpenters, shoemakers, blacksmiths, and shopkeepers. It would appear as though the gospel had an attraction for just those groups which had much to gain, e.g. education for their children, a sense of importance (as co-laborers with God in the Kingdom of Heaven), and recompense for having been so largely excluded from the upper brackets of Latin American society. Conversely, these same people had very little to lose by becoming Protestants, for they were not so likely to lose their jobs, were not dependent upon some one person for their social and economic security (as in the case of the day laborer or peon), and had never been cultivated to any great extent by the Roman church, which has concentrated most of its attention upon the elite classes.

The phenomenal growth of the Pentecostal movement among the people of Latin America has also served to highlight the relationship of social classes to the communication of the gospel, for not only is the Pentecostal movement as large as all the other denominations put together, but it has had success not only among the lower classes, from which its membership is largely drawn, but also among some of the upper classes.

Furthermore, missionaries have been quick to note that it is ever so much easier to begin work in new towns or recently built communities than in areas where people have lived for a long time. All of these facts have served to focus our attention upon the possibilities of understanding more adequately some of the fundamental problems of social structure in Latin America and their bearing upon the task of evangelism.

## Acute Problems in Evangelism

On almost every hand the average missionary faces certain acute problems in evangelism, and a number of these seem to be directly related to factors in social structure. For example, not infrequently

**Reprinted from Vol. 5, No. 3 (1958), pp. 101-123.**

there are churches which have flourished and grown for a period of five to ten years, only to be followed by twenty years of almost complete stagnation. Such churches seem to have reached a particular group within a community, and then to have stopped growing. In some instances, a few persons are won to the gospel in the initial attempts to start a new church, but their very presence within the church seems to prevent the entrance of others. In other churches the social standing of the members rises rapidly through improved education, greater ambition, and the indirect results of a higher sense of responsibility — characteristics which lead to greater financial rewards. However, the tendency is for such churches to lose touch with the very classes from which most of the members originally came.

A particularly difficult problem exists in Protestant churches in which there is a class cleavage within the church. In one church in Cuba there is a morning congregation composed primarily of upper middle class young people, many of whom have a university education. The evening congregation consists of older people from the lower middle class and upper lower class. The rivalry between such groups in all phases of the church life is pathetic, for it hampers the potential ministry of such a group and serves to rob the people of a true sense of fellowship.

The differences of response between people in small rural communities and those in the cities has always called for certain adaptations in missionary approach but the basic problems become increasingly more acute as churches in the urban centers assume responsibility for work in rural areas. So often they fail completely to establish a really vital work in which the rural people feel anything more than a kind of "poor country cousin" relationship to the city congregation. This distinction of class levels becomes even more difficult in a divided society, that is to say, one made up of a Spanish and Indian constituency. The Indians are usually left out, not because of any desire on the part of the Spanish-speaking people to thrust them aside, but simply because they do not understand the means by which they may effectively develop and promote a vigorous Indian constituency.

### The Role of Schools

In the early years of Protestant missionary work in Latin America the establishment of schools, both primary and secondary, was supposed to be a major factor in overcoming certain of the major difficulties inherent in the social structure of Latin America as it was related to the development of the Evangelical church. These schools were not only supposed to educate the children of Evangelicals, but were calculated to create among the non-Evangelicals a favorable attitude toward the Evangelical cause. Some schools have largely fulfilled this purpose, but a number have singularly failed. By an essentially secular viewpoint these schools have educated certain people away from the Evangelical community, and have often failed to bring into the Evangelical group those from the outside who might have special talents or abilities. The so-called neutralist view of many so-called Evangelical schools is well illustrated by the recent boast of a principal of one of the largest mission schools of Latin America, who insisted that during the last eleven years of the school's existence not one student had been converted.

In view of the numerous problems posed by various factors in the social structure of Latin society, we cannot help but ask ourselves such questions as, What is the basic class structure of these societies? What explains the acceptance of the gospel by one group and not by others? What are the forces and techniques of social change? How do people change their class status within Latin American society? What bearing has the proclamation of the gospel on such changes? What should be our basic strategy in approaching Latin society?

## The Structure of Latin American Society

The structure of society in Latin America is highly complex and differs considerably from area to area. However, despite the possibility of a certain amount of error resulting from oversimplification, we can describe certain essential characteristics of Latin American society by means of a type of inverted diamond diagram:[1]

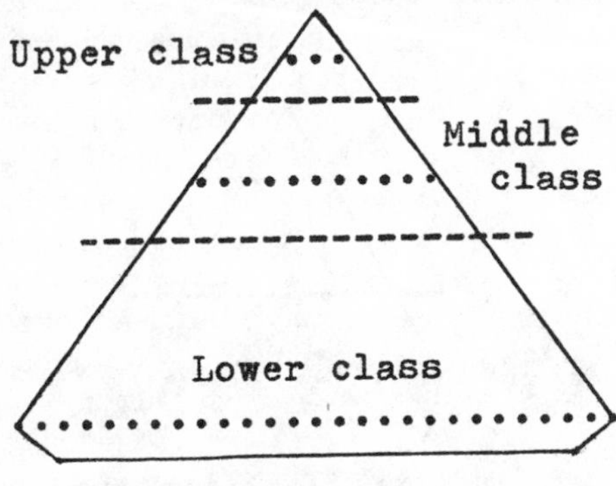


Figure A

Figure A symbolizes what are probably the major characteristics of most societies in Latin America, in which the narrow point represents the elite, the central portion the middle class, and the base portion the lower class. The upper class is divisible generally into two classes of elite: (1) the old families, representing the traditional aristocracy, and (2) the *nouveaux riches,* who have only recently acquired wealth and prestige. Some very rich people in the lower upper class may be accepted into the upper upper class, if they have some special influence or political power, but in general the two layers of elite are rather well defined.

The middle class is similarly divided between (1) the upper middle class, consisting of successful but not so wealthy professionals such as doctors, lawyers, professors, politicians, engineers, and businessmen, and (2) the lower middle class, consisting of the white-collared workers, e.g. clerks, bookkeepers, small businessmen, schoolteachers, and preachers.

The lower class is divided between (1) the upper lower class, made up of less prosperous tradesmen, factory workers, independent small farmers, domestic workers, and day laborers, and (2) the lower lower class, consisting of the extremely poor seasonal workers, indigent sharecroppers, and the habitually unemployed.

We must not assume that diagram A reflects accurately the actual proportion of the respective population, for the relative size of the various classes differs greatly in the various countries. We do not have the necessary statistics in order to produce a thoroughly accurate picture of the various societies, but we can approximate something of the diversity in types in the diagrams in Figure B, designed to portray Haitian, Cuban, and Peruvian societies.

There are several significant features of the diagram in figure B. Diagram 1 has a definite constriction between the

[1] See Eugene A. Nida, "The Roman Catholic, Communist, and Protestant Approach to Social Structure," in this volume.

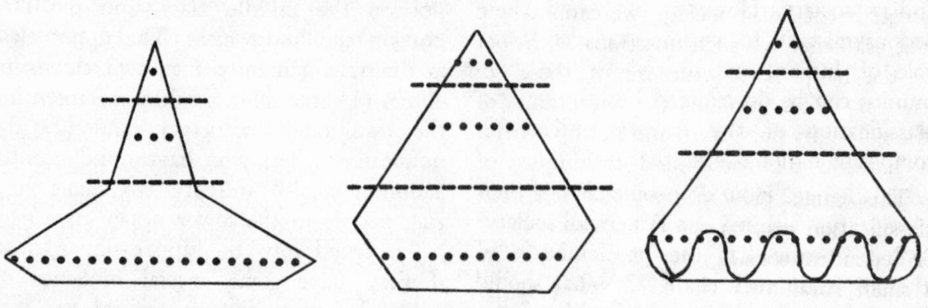


Figure B

class one elite and the class two elite, a distinction which is fully recognized by the Haitians themselves and a boundary which is as difficult to pass over as any in the social structure. The Haitian middle class is also quite restricted, and the lower class is largest at the lowest level.

In Cuban society the middle class is not only relatively large, but the transition from the lower class and into the upper class is not so pronounced as in the case of Haiti. Moreover, the number of people who are indigent is not as great as in Haiti, hence the narrower base.

In the case of Peruvian society the middle class is proportionately less than in Cuban society, with a gradual transition from the upper lower class, but the society bulges in the lower portions of the upper lower class. In diagram III, however, there is an additional feature, namely, the wavy solid line which marks the division between the predominantly Indian population (classified roughly on the basis of habitual use of an Indian language and the wearing of Indian type clothing) and the Spanish-speaking people. It should be noted that the Indian population is the lowest in the social structure, as far as general prestige is concerned, but some members of this class reach up into the upper lower class. However, if they are to go up very far, they must adopt the classificatory symbols of the dominant group, namely, the Spanish language and the "Western" dress.

In the case of Peruvian society it would be more accurate to diagram the relationships between the two co-existing subcultures as follows:

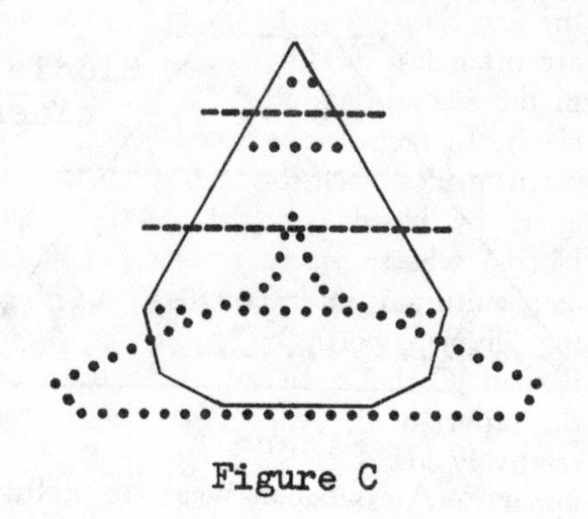

Figure C

In this structure an individual may possess a double status. For example, he may be in the elite within the Indian society, but only in the upper lower class or lower middle class of the non-

Indian society. However, it would be a serious mistake to assume that the social role of Indians within the Indian community can be determined by any general classification of the Indian within the composite national structure.

This same principle of the multiple classification may apply to any subculture or dependent social group. For example, in a small rural area the local "elite" may only rate as upper middle class in the society of the nearby town and as lower middle class in the still more inclusive structure of the nation.

**Bases of Class Structure**

From our description of the constituencies of the respective classes one could presume that wealth would be the primary criterion of class membership. There is no denying the importance of money, but it is certainly not the only factor, nor even the principal one, at least not for certain divisions. For example, some members of the first-class elite (the upper upper class) are often less wealthy than many persons in the second-class elite (the lower upper class). In fact, the so-called "aristocracy" often prides itself on being a class set apart by blood (i.e. the so-called bluebloods) who spurn the criterion of money as a culturally inferior basis of ascertaining "human worth." The position of the Roman Catholic clergy also contradicts the criterion of wealth, for priests from relatively low classes are accepted in the upper brackets despite their lack of personal wealth, but they are usually never admitted into the highest class, unless a papal appointment to the hierarchy overrides local class lines (something which rarely happens). Persons with exceptional talents, e.g. artists, singers, and dancers, or those with gifted intellects, e.g. writers, professors, and orators, may be admitted to a class which for the most part consists of considerably more wealthy members.

Class membership is thus not simply a matter of wealthy or family lineage or special talents. It includes all of these plus political influence, leadership ability, and the favor of influential friends.

In speaking about such classes we tend to give the impression that they are perfectly obvious to everyone, including the members of the society in question. However, these class distinctions are not fully evident, for people do not wear labels. Nevertheless, people are quite conscious of the class to which they belong (something which is much less true in the life of the United States, where the classes are less well defined and where people are supposed to deny the existence of classes and most people insist that they belong to the middle class). The classes in Latin America can, however, be delineated without too much trouble by determining those groups which (1) participate together in social functions, (2) tend to intermarry, and (3) recognize their essential identity of outlook and mutual interests. Furthermore, each class is aware that those "above" have greater prestige and those "below" have less. Accordingly, all classes, except the top, want to climb up in the scale of prestige.

What we have described as the different social classes are essentially prestige classes. There is no inherent reason why certain groups should be granted more prestige than others (other societies in the world have quite different prestige systems), but the Latin American societies do possess their typical structure, and with this we must reckon.

In describing classes as lower and higher, we only have reference to the built-in prestige factor. Certainly such terms as "higher" and "lower" must not be interpreted as representing any moral evaluation (though that is what many members of the upper classes would like to have others think). If we were to judge the social classes on the basis of such criteria as honesty, reliability, sense of responsibility to family, hospitality, and willingness to sacrifice for the sake of the community, it is quite likely that the upper lower class and the lower middle class would come out on top, with some notable examples of these virtues in the other classes, but not as predominant features. Accordingly, our isolation of classes and their scaling from high to low is based essentially on one principle, namely, the degree of prestige which the members of a society associate with the respective classes.

In speaking of prestige as a determinant of classes we recognize that the pattern is not one of absolute grades and fixed boundaries. That is to say, the classes of Latin American society are not castes, as in India. Rather, they are somewhat fluid groupings of people who associate together in various ways and who recognize in some measure the equality of their status. Prestige, therefore, is a polar element easily recognizable in the extremes, but less obvious in the central zones. Moreover, within the six classes, which constitute the major divisions recognizable in Latin life, there are numerous minor scales of prestige.

## Orientation of Classes

The orientation of most members of all but the highest class is upward. That is to say, most people want to have more prestige. A number of people in the lowest classes have seemed to be largely resigned to their prestige status, but within the last few years the development of leftist labor movements in Latin America has resulted in a widespread concern for upward drive among the lowest class.

Most members of the highest class are relatively content with their lot. Their only concern seems to be the preservation of the *status quo*. Hence, they are skeptical of any radical changes and unwilling to make room for many competitors in the highest class. In fact, any major assault on their class of top elite by the "newly rich" is usually resisted vigorously with all the snobbishness of which this snobbish class is capable.

The pressures for change of class status are strongest in the rising elements of the middle class, but liberal political ideas have also induced major segments of the lower class to believe that what they would like, namely, more prestige and a greater share in the material rewards, are not only desirable but attainable, and if not by their own efforts then by means of political revolution. The creative minority within the proletariate is thoroughly convinced of this fact and hence is ready to rally the masses behind almost any leader who will promise them a higher status and more things.

On the other hand, while this upward-reaching group in the lower classes is intent on changing the *status quo* for them and their supporters by any and all means, the top classes are intent on preserving the social structure and the rewards which it provides. In most countries the intensity of the conflict is directly proportionate to the degree of separation and the strength of the intervening barriers.

## Techniques of Mobility

Though we often speak as though political events were the dominant factors in the change of class membership, this is essentially a false assumption. A change of political parties may slightly modify the rules by which persons may change social status — e.g. giving preference to those of liberal or conservative orientation, as the case may be — but for the most part it takes a thoroughgoing revolution to break open the social structure. Even the Mexican revolution, the most drastic in Latin American history, did not completely overturn the social structure. What it did accomplish was to remove some of the first-class elite and to remove the caste restrictions on the lowest classes. It ultimately had a profound effect upon Mexican society in that it released social pressures bent on upward mobility, but it was far from being a Communist-style revolution in which the higher classes are liquidated or reduced to lower-class status and the revolutionary leadership takes over the place of the elite and erects a high wall of isolation between the party leadership and all the rest of the classes. What is more, the Communist social structure functions so as to draw its leadership, not from the immediately inferior middle class of professionals, but from exceptional persons in the lower class, who are not likely to favor competition from the potentially "dangerous" professionals.

For a woman, the surest means of raising one's status is to marry into a family with higher social rank, for the husband's social position is largely the determining factor in a wife's status. If a man marries "above himself," he may or may not make the grade. This will depend upon personal charm, money, and, in the case of the first-class elite, primarily the determination of his father-in-law to give him social status.

In many segments of Latin society the parents' obtaining for their children a *compadre* 'godfather' or *comadre* 'godmother' of a higher status than themselves is a means of going up in social rank. This is only a kind of indirect benefit, but it does serve to enhance the prestige and tie the social unit together.

Obtaining a *padrino* is an even more important method of advancing in social standing. A *padrino* is a person who agrees to help someone in business, often guarantees loans, protects him against abuse by other elite, seeks opportunities for the advancement of his "client," and introduces him to a higher social group than the person enjoys at the time. In return the "client" always supports the *padrino's* political ambitions, will carry out any favors he is asked to do, and if the *padrino* should ever have need, the "client" is supposed to help to the limits of his resources. This is, of course, a carryover from feudal times, but it is a very important contemporary feature of Latin American life, and though it exists on a strictly informal basis (that is to say, there are no legal contracts binding the two parties), the social institution lies at the very heart of Latin life.

A number of other techniques in upward mobility have already been mentioned in other connections, namely, the acquisition of wealth, distinction in artistic performance, brilliance of intellectual endowments, and unusual leadership ability.

## Orientation of the Roman Catholic Church Toward Latin American Society

In view of the fact that the Roman

Catholic Church is a strictly authoritarian institution with a completely pyramidal structure (after all, the Roman church and Latin society both arose from the hierarchical structure of Roman society), it is not surprising that the Roman Catholic Church has concentrated its attention on the cultivation of the elite. Not only are all the benefits of the church open to such people, but the church obtains practically all its leadership (from bishops on up) from the elite and in turn provides the elite with the best possible education in the Roman Catholic tradition. Whether the masses remain illiterate or not is not the primary concern of the church. What does count is the identification of interests and viewpoints with the ruling minority.

On the other hand, the Protestants have directed their appeal to the masses, not only because they were the most numerous, but because they were the most concerned with change and responded to the hope of a better chance.

The Protestant appeal to the masses has seemed to many Roman Catholics as being nothing but a veiled form of Communism, for Communist agents likewise appeal to the lower classes and hold out promises of a better life. Any further comparison between Protestantism and Communism immediately shows the profound differences, but there is enough superficial similarity to convince the less-informed or the already prejudiced that they must "repudiate the Communist and Protestant propaganda," as Roman Catholic publicists have repeatedly declared.

## Justification of the Protestant Approach

Some persons have questioned whether Protestant missionaries did right in appealing primarily to the lower classes. Certain individuals have contended that a concentrated "attack" on the leadership of Latin America would have ultimately resulted in greater gains. However, it is extremely doubtful that this would have been the case, even if the personnel capable of such an appeal to the upper classes had been available. All that we can judge from the results of Protestant work in the light of the structure of Latin society seems to confirm the view that early missionaries acted in accordance with sound sociological principles, even though at the time they did not analyze the problems nor define the goals in these terms.

The sociological principles which seem to amply justify the course of Protestant missions in Latin America are three:

1. *The future always rests with the masses.* This is particularly true in contemporary society in which the vestiges of feudalism are rapidly crumbling in the assault of the so-called "mass man."

2. *The creative minority* (to use Toynbee's phrase) *which is reshaping Latin life has its origin primarily in the upper lower class and the lower middle class,* the very groups to which Protestantism has directed its approach.

3. *The only way to raise the masses is to become identified with them.* The Biblical principle of the leaven in the lump is the only means of altering in any substantial way the condition of the masses. Even if the elite were won to Protestantism, there would be no guarantee that these persons, whose social position depends upon preserving the *status quo,* would feel any constraint to change the condition of the lower classes, except in some superficial manner of urging a change of ecclesiastical loyalty on the part of the lower class "subjects."

### Theological Justification

Despite what seems to be an evident sociological justification for our Protestant strategy, we also need to ask ourselves as to whether there has been a corresponding theological basis, or has our historic approach been essentially opportunistic? The answer to this question seems to be quite clear. We do have a theological justification, for in fundamental essence this approach to the masses reflects the divine principle underlying the incarnation, namely, (1) humbling of oneself in order to identify, and (2) giving leadership to others by participation and the challenge to "follow me."

### The Face-to-Face and the Urban Societies

Though the general principle of appeal to the masses is fully justified, it is quite evident that in working out the implications of this principle there are wide differences of practice and response between small face-to-face communities and large urban agglomerations. What works in an urban situation often fails miserably in a small town, and conversely what appeals to rural people falls on deaf ears when directed to an urban audience. What, then, are the basic differences in the social structures and the effective means of communicating to these diverse constituencies?

A face-to-face society is just what it implies, namely, one in which all the members are known to each other, and everybody knows all about everyone else. What is more, in such a group most people are related, either through blood or marriage, and if not in this way, then through the godparents and *padrino* systems. Such a face-to-face society functions in many ways like an extended family and as such tends to (1) make collective decisions, (2) have considerable inner cohesion, (3) present a unified front against intrusion, (4) be conservative in orientation, and (5) be centralized in its control, in the pattern of the family.

If, in approaching one of these face-to-face communities, it is possible to win over the leadership, one can soon gain access to the entire group. That is to say, the community follows the lead of the "ruling" family or group of elders, even as members of a family tend to follow the direction of the father or other strong personality. On the other hand, if one succeeds only in isolating some of the disgruntled members of such a community and in making them the "leaders" of the newly formed Protestant church, it is very likely that one will never be able to penetrate very deeply into the community structure. Such a "church" will always be a kind of appendage to the social structure, isolated from its essential life and a haven only for the community outcasts.

Many missionaries have felt that the best approach to a face-to-face society is to preach the good news to the entire group and to challenge the community to accept the gospel as a group. This procedure does not overlook the necessity of individuals making personal commitments, but it proceeds on the basis that a group which is accustomed to making group decisions should be confronted as a social unit. Some German missionaries have been singularly successful in this approach in some of the face-to-face communities in Indonesia. Dr. Alcibiades Iglesias, who has carried on a remarkable work among his own San Blas people in Panama, has adopted a somewhat similar approach. He has not isolated the Christians nor himself from the community, but has related the message of the gospel to the entire life of the community. A very similar approach has been employed by the Baptists of the eastern part of Cuba, who have sought to minister to all the needs of an entire community and to make the gospel relevant to all without attempting to isolate or estrange individuals within the community life.

On the other hand, it must be recognized that in Latin America the likelihood of an entire community accepting the gospel as a unit is not very great. This means that any Evangelical church will be made up of people who are more likely than not to be a minority in a community. As a minority they will be subjected to all kinds of severe social pressures depending largely upon (1) the extent to which the church group is composed of those who are already regarded as community outcasts (hence the importance of not formally organizing a church until it contains at least some of the responsible members of the community, who are not subject to the same patterns of rejection), and (2) the degree of pressure which the Roman Catholic clergy can arouse concerning this "intrusion" into the community life.

## Compensation for Social Pressures

When social pressures are brought against a newly established Evangelical church, there must be some types of compensation or the entire church structure is likely to collapse. These people need to experience a kind of fellowship which is even more satisfying than what they have known in the community as a whole. If people can be taught the meaning of their new fellowship in Christ Jesus and what the "new community of the saints" can and should mean, they can be brought into a type of fellowship which will be not only satisfying but creative. The difficulty is, however, that too often this out-group feeling within the Protestant communion is largely defensive rather than creative; and though it does protect the members, it is largely ineffective in reaching out for others.

One of the very important ways of compensating for the loss of a feeling of social security within the immediate face-to-face community is to relate the small Protestant community to a larger fellowship of other believers in the country. This is done by attendance at rallies, conventions, and official meetings of various church associations, so that they may realize that they are a part of a large, growing body of believers. In Peru one missionary discovered that it was of immense importance to have such meetings in towns which had newly established churches. If the small, struggling church could be the host to a relatively large group of people, who by their dress and behavior exhibited obviously higher social status than was regularly attributed to such Protestant groups, the impact upon the community would be of great importance in the evangelistic efforts of the church in question.

The approach to the urban community is by no means as restricted as that involving the face-to-face society. The urban community is made up largely of people who are dislocated from their former face-to-face communities. They are more independent, more easily attracted into new movements, and more anxious to find means of personal profit and advancement. In the largely impersonal atmosphere of the city, where one fights with one's neighbors but does not know them, the Protestant church has a very special ministry, for it can help to create an effective, mutually beneficial social group in the midst of the impersonal environment and thus meet peoples' basic need for fellowship.

This aspect of personal fellowship in the midst of an impersonal society is one of the keys to the unusual success of the Pentecostal churches in Latin America, which, in addition to a number of other extremely significant appeals to the Latin temperament (factors which are beyond the scope of this article), have succeeded in large measure in making people of all classes, and especially the very lowest, to feel that they belong, are needed, and must make their own distinctive contribution within the community of believers which recognizes them as an integral part. This sense of belonging, of social security, and of being "indispensable" has resulted in the Pentecostal group's far outdistancing so many of the denominations which have depended more upon trained leadership, foreign funds, and an emphasis upon what the church could do for the people, rather than what the people must do for the church. In other words, the Pentecostal churches have succeeded in large measure in creating a face-to-face, living fellowship in the midst of a competing, impersonal agglomeration of people.

## Problems of a Divided Society

Within a face-to-face society there may be an almost insuperable barrier which excludes one group from any vital social contacts with the other. In Latin America this situation exists in those communities which contain both Indians and Latins. Except for some of the strictly primitive groups (as in Amazonia and a few other marginal areas), the Indians of Latin America are a part of the larger social unit. The culture is basically a folk culture, and the Indians stand in a dependency relationship. The whites are dependent upon the Indians for some simple artifacts and for work and raw products from their small farms. The Indians are dependent upon the whites for legal rights, guarantee and possession of their farms, rudimentary education, and all sorts of manufactured articles. There is an almost complete symbiosis, but with the white community being largely parasitic upon the labors of the Indians.

This type of arrangement, involving dependency and exploitation, almost inevitably produces severe strains of feeling, deep suspicion, and outright antagonism. One would think that in view of this situation the Protestant missionary could make a strong appeal to the Indian to "throw off the shackles" and to separate himself from the religious system which is identified with the upper class. However, this is not so easy, for the Indian knows full well that this economic and social security depends very largely upon his keeping in good with his *patroncitos* 'landlords' or 'sponsors,' or *palancas* as they are called in Ecuador.

Some missions have attempted to minister exclusively to Indians and peons and have discovered that unless they actually controlled the land, as in the case of the Canadian Baptist mission in Guatajata, Bolivia, they had little or no success. In fact, some of the people whom they helped the most seemed most intent upon proving their continued identity with the upper class by spending large sums of money on liquor with which to entertain the *patroncitos*. Wherever missions have experienced any appreciable success in working in such divided societies it has been found that in some measure they either acted as the *patrón* (as in the case of the Canadian Baptist mission in Guatajata, Bolivia), or there were some Evangelicals in the Latin society who would act as *padrinos* for the Evangelical population. This means that the presentation of the gospel must be directed at the entire society, so that within the newly formed Protestant group there may be some who may fulfill the vital function of the "upper class."

## Means of Communication

Without doubt, one of the most difficult aspects of evangelism in Latin America is to discover those means by which the communication of the gospel may be made in a relevant and socially acceptable manner. This does not mean that the Good News must be distorted in order to accommodate it to men's ideas. Rather, it must be presented in such a context as to make it really "Good News," not just foreign propaganda.

One Protestant missionary working in an Indian community of Ecuador discovered that the people were not at all interested in the beliefs of the Protestants, but they were very anxious to know about the Catholic doctrines. Accordingly, he offered to tell them about the various Roman Catholic beliefs and in a series of evening meetings in his own home he explained to them, without attempting to criticize or argue, the various doctrines of the Roman church. He used a Roman Catholic catechism and employed a Roman Catholic copy of the Scriptures. After several evenings of teaching and discussion, some of the group insisted that he tell them what the Protestants believed. At their invitation, he then explained, in the same objective and meaningful way, what he as a Protestant believed. In the very community where other missionaries had been singularly unsuccessful in presenting the gospel this missionary was able to communicate effectively, because he spoke to their need and in a context which was relevant to their understanding at the time.

A missionary in West Africa made it a regular practice in his earlier days of itinerant evangelism to stop in villages for several days and in the evenings to inquire of the elders as to their belief in God. He never tried to explain his own faith until asked to do so by the leaders, who invariably inquired of him after he had spent long hours in learning from them. The missionary's purpose was not, however, just to elicit curiosity. He was convinced that in order to tell the people about God he had first to learn what they knew about God, or otherwise he might fail utterly to make his message relevant.

One outstanding missionary in Peru has made it a practice never to enter a village to evangelize the people except at the express invitation of some person within the village. His Quechua helpers often enter new villages in order to establish important first contacts, but the missionary has become convinced that if he is not to thwart the ultimate effectiveness of his ministry, he must enter a village as a guest of a member of the community, who will not only guarantee his safety during his stay but will be an important means of inviting others to hear the Good News, brought by the "foreigner."

There is a considerable tendency for missionaries to "barge ahead" irrespective of the local situation. One way in which this is done is through the free distribution of Scriptures and other Christian literature. Such materials seem to be so cheap and people appear to be so ready to accept whatever is offered free that missionaries are deceived as to the ultimate effectiveness of their endeavors. In the first place, a high percentage of such literature is never read, and not infrequently the people react to the gospel as being nothing more than cheap propaganda. What is even worse, the distributor loses the priceless opportunity to communicate to the people in a context which they can fully understand, namely, the necessity for the bookseller to convince people of the desirability of his product. In the process of selling, whether or not the person buys, the bookseller has the chance of witnessing to the truth and effectiveness of the Good News. He also has a chance to challenge the prospective customer to study this for himself and to accept it. However, the man who is distributing free literature is immediately classed as a propagandist, a job for which he must be well paid, and his own testimony is relatively valueless.

The necessity of communicating within a meaningful context may sometimes lead to amazing methods. One agriculturalist working with the YMCA in Mexico discovered that in the area in which he had set out to help the people, everyone was suspicious of his efforts and refused to listen to his advice. Accordingly, the agriculturalist proceeded to introduce improved varieties of vegetables, grains, and fruits, and employed new methods of putting humus back into the soil by the generous use of compost made from abundant organic material in the area. So the villagers would not "misinterpret" his efforts, he put up a high fence around his gardens and ostensibly attempted to protect his choice products. The inevitable result was that the people stole his products in order to sell in the nearby markets. This method of teaching might seem unnecessarily "indirect," but it was effective for it was fully meaningful within the context of these people's lives.

The importance of communicating by identification has been so emphasized that some missionaries have wrongly exaggerated its significance to the point of thinking that identification consisted primarily in imitation, largely of an external type. This has led some missionaries purposely to dress poorly and to live in ostensibly humble quarters. The people, however, have detected the false ring in this type of superficial imitation and have reckoned it as a kind of cheap paternalism, which in fact it is. The identification which is required is not imitation, but full participation as a member of the society. In order to participate effectively one must not deny his own cultural heritage — something which cannot be done even if one wished to do so — but to employ this background for the benefit of the total constituency.

Some missionaries have assumed that "natives can best reach natives" (as they have so often framed the principle). In a sense this is quite true, but at the same time it is a general experience of missionaries that Latin American converts often refuse to work among people of the very class from which they themselves have come or among those who are in the immediate class below them, especially if these classes are both rather low on the social scale. This should not be too hard to understand, for any convert who has advanced in the social structure as the result of hard work and diligent application often feels quite insecure in his new social position. To return immediately to work among people representing the very class from which he has raised himself would seem to endanger his status. Furthermore, a great deal of the education which he probably has received in mission schools has prepared him for a middle class social position and in a sense he has been "de-classified" as far as his original status was concerned. He no longer really feels at home.

But even those who have not been educated up and out of a class are often reluctant to minister to people immediately beneath them, for it would seem to imply that they are lowering their own status and hence endangering their prestige position within the society. On the other hand, such persons are often quite willing to work among those considerably below their own status, for then they do not feel that there is any danger of being mistaken for a member of such an inferior class. In a sense this explains why it is somewhat easier to get missionaries from the United States to work in areas in which nationals of the respective countries are reluctant to serve. The missionary runs no risk of losing status. In fact, among the in-group of which he is a part in the United States his very going to such "benighted heathen" enhances his prestige, but this is not the case with so-called "national workers."

The sensitivity of national workers to these problems of class within their own society must be fully recognized if one is to understand their special problems and some of the reasons which dictate what appears to be such strange behavior. In one instance, for example, an Indian from southern Mexico went off to study in a Bible school in Guatemala. Upon his return he began preaching in Spanish, which he did with considerable skill, but of course his audience understood little if anything of what he was saying. This continued for about three weeks, after which time this young Indian pastor shifted to the Indian language and has continued to use it ever since. The ability to use Spanish was an essential symbol of his new status, and once this was adequately confirmed, he could then safely afford to identify himself with the Indian constituency.

This principle of security in social position helps to explain why it is sometimes easier to get university students to undertake work in some slum area than to get people who have just emerged from the slums to return to them in order to minister. This also explains why one Negro pastor in Cuba found it difficult to work among his own people, for they preferred to have a white minister, for this gave their church more prestige. On the other hand, a well-educated constituency of whites was quite willing to accept this brilliant Negro, for the prestige of this group would not be endangered.

## Backsliding and Class Identification

One of the apparently puzzling phenomena in the experience of some evident converts is the almost pathetic concern for reinstatement which characterizes those who turn from Protestantism and go back into their former socio-religious grouping. Time and again missionaries have mentioned how incredible it was that certain outstanding people who seemed to show every promise of developing into outstanding leaders within the Protestant movement would go "so far back into sin," once they dissociated themselves from the Evangelical constituency. In fact, such persons often become far more addicted to their favorite vices than they ever were before coming in contact with the gospel. It would seem that the more conspicuous has been their testimony the more severe is their backsliding.

The sociological explanation for this is the fact that such persons feel constrained to do all they can to be accepted again in the constituency of which they were formerly a part. To do this they must completely violate the mores associated with the Protestant element in order to prove to their non-Protestant friends that they no longer belong to the Protestant group. A somewhat similar reaction occurs, of course, with the new convert to Protestantism. In order to be accepted within the Evangelical community, he often symbolizes his break with the past by strong denunciation of his former friends, publicized breaking or burning of images, unnecessarily harsh denunciation of the Roman Catholic Church, and even unwarranted disrespect for the religious sentiments of conscientious people.

## The Work of the Holy Spirit

From what has been said up to this point some readers might conclude that we have little or no regard for the role of the Holy Spirit in the program of evangelism. Quite to the contrary, the more one studies the methods and procedures of foreign missions the more one becomes convinced of the function of the Spirit of God in transforming the lives of people. However, it does seem quite evident that God's Spirit works with and not contrary to the basic need of human beings, as exemplified in certain aspects of social structure. A study of the human elements in the divine-human drama of God's role in human history does not deny God's part; it only helps one to appreciate better the way God has chosen to work within the context of human life by the principle of incarnation, rather than from outside by a continued series of supernatural interventions.

Those who fully appreciate the living reality of the incarnational element in our Christian faith take seriously the meaning of revelation by word and by life ("the Word became flesh"). On the basis of this the fundamental procedure of missions may be developed in terms of identification ("He humbled himself") and participation ("He was tempted in all points"). Herein lies the key to effective witness, sacrificial ministry, and vital growth for the churches in Latin America.

*Eunice Pike and Florence Cowan*

**Reprinted from Vol. 6, No. 4 (1959), pp. 145-150.**

# Mushroom Ritual versus Christianity

*How can one effectively present the message of divine revelation to a people who already have, according to their belief, a means whereby anyone who so desires may get messages directly from the supernatural world via a more spectacular and immediately satisfying way than Christianity has to offer? The Mazateco Indians equate the hallucinogenic mushroom with Jesus Christ himself, believing that when Jesus lived on earth he spat on the ground and his saliva sprang up as the mushroom. Through it as his mouthpiece, he speaks to them in the hallucinations which its chemical content induces. Christian hymns taught by the missionary are sometimes believed to be inspired by the mushroom and are probably sung to it by its devotees. Taboos applicable to mushroom eating are transferred to the Bible and result in fear of reading it. The partaking of the divine mushroom poses potential problems in relation to the Christian concept of the Lord's Supper. The use of the mushroom in southern Mexico in the quest of visions and supernatural revelations would appear to have many points in common with the use of peyote by the Indians of northern Mexico and the U.S.A., where there has been extensive syncretism of peyote ritual and Christian forms.* PRACTICAL ANTHROPOLOGY *would welcome further contributions on the problems of communicating the Christian message in this type of context. It is a subject that still needs much careful and prayerful study.*

SOME of the Indian groups of southern Mexico make ritual use of certain species of mushroom which have hallucinatory powers. The ceremonies are performed by a *curandera* or shaman but with the participation of other persons. Pagan and Catholic traits blend in the ritual, which is carried out in the presence of Catholic images. This use of the mushroom is centuries old, having been described by the early Spanish writers. The present article is based on the ritual as it is observed today among the Mazateco Indians of the State of Oaxaca. Our information for the most part comes from four sources: from the people who participate in the ceremonies, from shaman women who have become our friends, from overhearing the ceremony as it took place in a house next door to us, and from tape recordings of two all-night

**Miss Eunice V. Pike and Mrs. Florence Cowan are members of the Wycliffe Bible Translators, working among the Mazateco Indian group of Oaxaca, Mexico. During their years of service in this field they have participated in the translation of the New Testament in Mazateco, which is currently in the process of publication.**

sessions which were made by R. G. Wasson and which he permitted us to hear.[1]

### Deceptive Mixtures

From all four of these sources we learn that the old tribal beliefs and Christian ideas and terminology have become mixed. One minute the shaman (a woman in both ceremonies which were recorded) would chant that she had the heart of Christ or the heart of the Virgin Mary; the next minute she was chanting that she was a snake woman, a moon woman, a bird woman. At both sessions she sang the Lord's prayer as it is sung in the Catholic church in the town of Huautla; but the next moment she was chanting about being a southern cross woman, or talking about a tiger eating someone's soul.

Many kinds of mushrooms grow in the Mazateco area, but only certain ones are used in the ceremony and only these will be discussed in this paper. Some informants say that the mushroom grows wherever a drop of Christ's saliva fell, and that for that reason when the mushroom speaks it is Christ himself speaking. Other informants say that the mushroom grows wherever a drop of Christ's blood fell, and that for that reason the Huautla region has living land — land where the mushroom does not grow is dead.

[1] For specific details see V. P. and R. G. Wasson, *Mushrooms, Russia and History*. New York: Pantheon Books, 1957. A popular but valuable presentation of the mushroom ritual appears as a feature article by R. G. Wasson, "Seeking the Magic Mushroom," in *Life*, May 13, 1957, and *Life International*, June 10, 1957. See also Valentina P. Wasson, "I Ate the Sacred Mushroom," in *This Week Magazine*, May 19, 1957. For a later news report on the medicinal qualities of the hallucinogenic mushroom, see "Mushroom Madness," in *Time*, June 16, 1958.

The most common reason for eating the mushroom is in behalf of someone who is ill. One informant said, "Jesus Christ himself gave us the mushroom because we are poor people and have no doctors or medicine to help us" At other times the mushroom is used for divining such things as who stole a certain horse, who killed a certain man, whether or not a sick person will die, or the welfare of a person who is away from home. At the ceremony anyone present may eat the mushroom, but the shaman eats several times as many as the others. All see visions (beautiful colored moving pictures, they say), but the shaman chants and sings while the others lie quietly on straw mats. They may speak encouraging words to the shaman or make comments to one another. Somehow when the session is over, they have the impression that 'Jesus' has given them the answers. They know that the sick person will get better or die, that they must get the help of the doctor, call in the witch doctor, or look for certain herbs. They know that their relative in the faraway city is well or in trouble.

However, we have conflicting reports on how 'Jesus' goes about telling them these things. Our information differs sharply depending on its source. The patients, or people who hire the shaman, say, "Jesus said that my son would get better," or "Jesus told me to stop drinking liquor," or "The little mushroom said so." The patients never say, "The shaman said that Jesus said. . . ." But one of our shaman friends insists that 'Jesus' doesn't 'tell' her anything. She insists that he never actually speaks to her. She 'sees' the sick boy well, or she 'sees' a tiger eating his soul. Her visions are like movies or television and she just talks about what she sees going on.

In the tape recording of the two ceremonies we were not able to pick any place where a supernatural being talked in first person giving a message. It was just the shaman singing about what a wonderful person she herself was. However, a mother told one of us that the mushroom had told her that her daughter would die and then added, "But don't be afraid, I'll take her soul to be with me." We have had hints that 'Jesus' talks directly to the sick person, or to the relatives by means of the mushrooms that they themselves have eaten. All our sources, however, agree that somehow those asking for guidance receive it, and that 'Jesus' is the one who gives it to them.

### Attempts at Separation

We find that the deep-seated belief in the mushroom frequently causes the Mazatecos to misunderstand our witness for Christ. We must ever be alert to their way of thinking so that we may choose unambiguous words. Examples of some of the problems follow.

1. At least twice when describing heaven as a beautiful place, a place where there are no tears, etc., Eunice Pike has been asked, "Have you seen it?" She answered, "No," and at that time thought the question very queer — didn't the person know that only the dead have seen heaven? Later she realized that a high percentage of Mazatecos claim to have seen heaven — the mushroom gives them moving pictures of it. Now she tells people, "The Book which tells us about God says that heaven. . . ."

2. A shaman is respected and called a 'wise man' by the Mazatecos. One time a shaman stood listening to one of the authors witness about Christ. The expression on his face was one of sympathy and understanding. After a bit he spoke up, "I, too, am a wise man." The missionary didn't recover fast enough to tell him that she differed from him in that the things she taught were only those things which are in accord with God's written Word.

3. One time when one of the writers was objecting to the use of the mushroom she was told, "But what else could I do? I needed to know God's will and I don't know how to read."

4. One cloudy day the missionary was sitting at the local airstrip hoping that the plane would arrive. A number of Mazatecos were also waiting. To redeem the time she sang a hymn, planning to use it as a starting point for witnessing. The hymn she happened to choose was a new one that no Mazateco knew yet; in fact, she had translated it just the day before. As she sang she heard two of the women talking. "Isn't that beautiful! How lovely! It's just like the mushroom." They had not been talking to her, but she couldn't keep out of that conversation. "No, it's not like the mushroom. This is different." The women would not listen. Emphatically they broke in to say, "We mean, wasn't it gracious of the mushroom to teach you that song!"

Many people have learned a number of the hymns in Mazateco, since at least five hundred phonograph records with hymns and a gospel message have been sold in the area. We now suspect that some of the hymns have been sung to the mushroom by the shaman. In fact, one Christian Mazateco warned one of the authors against teaching any hymns to her shaman friend. "She may sing them to the mushroom if you do!" All this poses many problems. Should we limit the sale of records to Christians only? But the wonderful thing about a record is that it can go where there are no Christians and no missionary. Should we teach hymns only to Christians? But singing a hymn is one of the easiest ways to start a conversation about Christ. We have gone on teaching the hymns, but now we are alert, ready to point out that a hymn is in accord with the Scriptures, whereas many of the shaman's chants are contrary to them.

5. There is one taboo that most people consider very necessary to observe when eating the mushroom. That is, they have to be ceremonially 'good' or 'clean'. Specifically, they must refrain from sexual intercourse for four or five days both before and after eating the mushroom. One of our shaman friends said that she had started eating the mushroom in behalf of others when she was twenty years old, but that she had stopped completely when she married. After her husband died she took up that work again. Then she married a second time, and again she stopped. Widowed the second time, she took up the work of shaman again.

This taboo which is imposed in connection with eating the mushroom has, it seems, been a direct source of difficulty in the distribution of the Scriptures. We tend to call the Scriptures 'God's Word'. The Mazatecos have considered the mushroom a means of getting a message from God, and hence the two things tend to get grouped in the same category. If such a taboo applies to the one, in the minds of at least some Mazatecos it applies to the other.

One young man of marrying age had been reading the Scriptures and enjoying them. Then one day he told us that he was thinking of getting married, and he wondered whether he could go on reading the Scriptures, or if he must stop once he was married. A leader in one village, a married man, seemed hungry for the gospel, listened eagerly when taught, asked pertinent questions, and seemed to accept the Lord and prayed for forgiveness of sin and for the Lord to bless his wife and children. But although well off financially he refused to buy the Scriptures and never read them for himself. When urged, he objected with, "People say that we will go crazy if we read God's Word." It was at least a year later that it dawned on us that the same reason is given for observing the taboos when eating the mushroom. One of our neighbors went crazy and we were told in a whisper that is was because he ate the mushroom when not 'clean'.

These and other incidents make us suspect that the taboo is so interpreted as to make people in general afraid to read the Scripture. Parents are afraid that their children will die. We are struggling with the problem and perhaps we are making progress. When selling Scripture in the market, we no longer use the term 'God's Word'; rather we say, "This book teaches us about God."

Also we have made up a wedding song which gives advice to the Mazateco couple. (Old folks are supposed to give advice to a Mazateco couple.) The first verse tells of a couple getting married, and urges that they take the Jesus road. The husband is urged to love his wife. The wife is urged to respect her husband. Then in the second stanza they are urged to read the Scriptures. In the third stanza they are told to teach their children the Jesus way. That song is a good jumping off point to urge that the couple read and pray together.

6. It would appear that the eating of the mushroom has features in common with the Christian Eucharist, which are a potential source of confusion. During the mushroom ceremony the people all nibble on the mushroom at the same time. They make a kind of unit listening to the shaman sing and seeing visions together. In his description Wasson applied the word "agape" to the ceremony, and we have been asked (by outsiders) if the Mazatecos confuse it with the Lord's Supper. Does the eating of the divine mushroom have for the Mazateco a psychological value comparable to that which the Eucharist has for the Christian? What teaching must accompany the introduction of the Lord's Supper to the Mazatecos to prevent the Christians among them from seeking the same experience from the bread and wine that they have formerly gotten from the mushroom — and being disappointed? All this needs careful study and development in the local church context. We can see possibilities of confusion. One Mazateco said that the mushroom must not be cooked because it is considered as a living person. However, since there is still no organized Mazateco church there has as yet been no celebration of the Lord's Supper, and therefore as of this date we know of no confusion. We have hopes that there will be none, for at least a handful of individuals have not stumbled when they received private instruction.

## Supplying the Need now Filled by the Mushroom

Medicine has given at least some Christians the courage to reject the mushroom. When a non-Christian sister-in-law says, "You are killing your husband! Why don't you call the wise man?" (meaning that, if the wife does not call a shaman when her husband is sick, then she is the same as a murderer), the Christian can save face by answering, "I'm using medicine instead." That not only keeps the relatives from pressing so hard, but the medicine sometimes cures the patient.

The Mazatecos have occasions when they desire some special knowledge for which they usually turn to the mushroom. Sometimes this desire has been met by citing the admonition in James 1:5. We point out that God has promised to give us wisdom if we ask him. Once, when a Mazateco Christian asked, "How does a Jesus-follower go about finding a horse?", we prayed with him, asking for wisdom and guidance, and then suggested that he go out and hunt. He found the horse!

Perhaps part of the reason for using the mushroom is to have a party-like thing, or some special attention for the sick relative. If that be the case, then the need might be filled by public prayer for the sick one during the Christian service.

## Surpassing the Mushroom

The shaman sings that the mushroom says she is clean, good, victorious. It calls her a humming bird, the moon, the morning star, the southern cross. She is an interpreter, a woman by whom others live, the law, medicine, justice. The mushroom says that she is the child god, a spirit, a saint, a creator, the heart of Christ, the heart of the Virgin Mary. She is light, speech, thought. But in spite of the pretty words the shaman is afraid. Even as she sings she fears her earthly enemies. She is afraid of the harm that may be done to her or her family by witchcraft (i.e. by a type of witchcraft that is completely apart from the mushroom). We had noticed in listening to the tapes that at times the shaman was weeping as she chanted. Upon being questioned, she explained to us that she was weeping because she was remembering that one of her sons had been murdered and she was concerned for the one that was left.

The mushroom often breeds fear. The visions may show the shaman that the patient is dying of 'fear sickness' with no suggestion of how to cure him. The relatives accept the diagnosis and prepare for the funeral while they wonder what it was that frightened him. In contrast, our Lord said (John 14: 27), "Peace I leave with you, my peace I give unto you; not as the world giveth, give I unto you." In practice we have found this passage of Scripture to be true; many of the Mazateco Christians, with turmoil around them, have come to have hope and an inner peace — a peace that comes from knowing that they have a Savior, and Someone who loves them.

By contrast, in neither of the two mushroom tapes could we discover help for someone who knows that he is a sinner and needs salvation. The shaman sings of the greatness that she is said to have, but that greatness is of no real help to her; she is as bad off as any of the other 90,000 Mazatecos. Our Lord, however, can take a down-and-out repentant sinner and clean him up until he can bear the fruits of the Spirit.

The ethical values mentioned in the mushroom ceremony are in keeping with the values generally recognized in Indian cultures, but they fall far short of the ethics of Christianity. In the long list of virtues that the shaman claims for herself during the ceremony, there is no love, joy, peace, kindness, grace, or gentleness — none of the qualities that we recognize as fruits of the Spirit. These, however, are things that mark one who has become a Christian in the Mazateco society: love for family and for fellow Christians, joy in spite of hardships, peace in the midst of village wars. "By this shall all men know that ye are my disciples, if ye have love one to another" (John 13: 35).

## Conclusion

Some Mazateco believers, chiefly new Christians, have continued to use the mushroom for a while. Arguments against it have accomplished very little. The thing that has helped is study of the Scriptures — any and all parts of them — until the person concerned comes to understand God's idea of sin, his love and plan for the sinner, and something of God's greatness. That seldom happens after the study of a few brief passages; it seems to take a considerable amount before a person's eyes are opened.

*William J. Samarin*

**Reprinted from Vol. 6, No. 4 (1959), pp. 179-182.**

# Gbeya Prescientific Attitudes and Christianity

MOST of us in Oubangui-Chari have witnessed at one time or another the celebration of the killing of a leopard. But I dare say that most of us did not draw too near the merrymakers, for we did not know what to think of it. We did not know whether it would be "right" for a missionary to seem interested — or even inquisitive — about such "pagan practices" for fear of seeming to give our approval of them.

A missionary is struck at this time by the marked change in behavior of people who he thought were "good Christians." Most of the people are stripped of most of their clothing. (If the men happen to be wearing trousers, they roll up the legs.) The women put on makeshift leafy bustles over their cloth skirts. The men brandish spears. There is drumming and singing — songs which are never heard in regular church activities. There is dancing — the swaying of the body and the shuffling of the feet, as people keep in time with the music. Every now and then one of the crowd approaches the leopard, which is slung on a pole carried by the men, and cries out and jabs at the animal. The leopard's face is wrapped so that its eyes and muzzle are covered, for, we hear, "the leopard might see the person who killed it and get revenge," and "the leopard's whiskers are a very powerful medicine."

We stand at the edge of the crowd, unable to understand what people are saying and singing about, for we know only the lingua franca. So we remain embarrassed, not knowing whether to smile or frown, whether to stay and see more (so that we could have more to say on deputation!) or whether to leave in a hurry.

Need we be embarrassed at witnessing such a celebration? Are we justified in going so far as to condemn any part or the whole of the activities, or is it advisable to participate with the people? Questions of this sort about this particular event in an African's life, or any others about which we have some misgivings, cannot be properly answered without an analysis of the forms involved and their meaning or function in the culture complex. We shall shortly see that several very important features of African culture converge and intermesh in this event.

## An Act of Celebration

Basically, we are concerned here with a *celebration*. The people rejoice because they have killed a destroyer of stock, namely, goats. This is no insignificant fact, for goats constitute one of the marks of wealth, and even in this day of money exchange goats persist as a stable and conclusive payment in many transactions.

Another reason for rejoicing is that a

man-killer has been liquidated. It is not that leopards are a real threat to human life, but that when they are accosted, they present themselves as a formidable foe, one that can kill or maim. When we realize that one of the foci of Gbeya culture, for we are talking only of the people with whom we are well acquainted, is survival — the daily fight against sickness and death — we can begin to understand what the defeat of such a foe means to them.

The leopard is not the only man-killer. The others are (in addition to man, of course) the elephant, the lion, the crocodile, the eland, and the anteater. It is significant that the buffalo, which certainly kill many more people than the eland do, are omitted. In fact, it is doubtful that many people can remember anyone's being recently killed by an eland. What characteristics these animals seem to share is their size, potential threat, or their rarity in the area occupied by the Gbeya. The anteater, however, seems to kill only with its sickness (about which more is said below).

But such celebrations, i.e. those characterized by the singing of certain songs and the brandishing of spears, do not follow the killing of all the animals listed above, but only the lion, leopard, and, before the arrival of the European administration, man. There are also scattered and less intense celebrations when the new moon introducing the dry season first arises. The dry season, the people explain, is the time when animals are killed.

### Danger of Contamination

The second basic feature of the leopard celebration is that it is a *time of danger*. The corpse of any of the predatory animals listed above contaminates all who come in contact with it. It is said that these people, unless they are ritually cleansed, will be affected by a sickness described as a cough without any expectoration of mucus but of ultimate expectoration of blood (tuberculosis?). Therefore, he who first found the leopard (if it was in a trap), he who killed it, and they who carry and butcher it — all these are automatically contaminated. Special care is taken of the whiskers. They are removed and burned, for it is believed that one's enemies will use them to put them into one's food and cause one's death. Likewise, the claws of the anteater are used in such sorcery.

The cleansing takes place in the following way: Those who are contaminated give all that they had on the day of the killing, as well as the spear, to an initiate, someone who has already gone through the cleansing ceremony. They sleep outdoors, and at daybreak they are washed with a certain potion prepared by the initiate. He it is who gets all their contaminated articles of clothing or hunt that they had on them the day before. He then instructs them to observe certain taboos until the first rains. At that time he kills a chicken and prepares the sauce. Three times he dips a bit of the meal into the sauce and puts it into the palm of the one being cleansed, and three times the latter throws it over his shoulder. The fourth time, the initiate takes the other's hand and helps him to dip up the sauce and put it to his mouth. That being done, he is pronounced clean.

### Relation to Pagan Religion

There appears to be no fetishistic worship connected with this rite. It is simply a matter of washing away the carrier of the disease. The main features of this rite (those mentioned above) characterize many other cleansing rites, some of which, of course, *are* connected with fetishistic practices.

Once the animal is butchered it is no longer "contagious." If one's clan is permitted to eat leopard meat, one can eat it. This leopard taboo is different from the taboo having to do with one's clan's totem. There are, however, rules which govern the eating of leopard meat, as with any "man's animal," namely, lion, lynx, hyena, civet, red monkey, and gray monkey. Only male elders may eat. Once one has become the father of two or three children, he qualifies as such an elder, but if one's father is still living, it is considered rude and disrespectful to partake. For these clans, anyone who violates the taboo is subject to the contaminating disease. In the clans which are not restricted by this taboo, the elders refrain from eating, deferring to the young men who are supposed to beget stronger, healthier children for having eaten leopard meat.

## The Fabric of Gbeya Life

This discussion, brief though it may be, has revealed the fact that we have to do here not with an isolated incident in the life of the Gbeya, but the realization of an intermingling of cultural themes. Were we to analyze this event in such a way as to make a list of subjects for further study, information that would certainly help us to better understand the Gbeya, we would have at least the following: recreation (the lack of it, the need for it, the forms it takes), sickness and death (causes and remedies, including fetishistic and nonfetishistic practices), taboos (their ritualistic and "real" function), the concept of the relation of the material to the nonmaterial world and God's relation to them.

This event is not a burr which has attached itself to the fabric of Gbeya culture and which can be plucked off with impunity. Rather, it is a design in this fabric, not printed on, but woven into it. We can tear out this practice only at the cost of leaving a hole with loose ends to all the threads. Were we to legislate against it without applying our teaching and guidance to its roots, such as correcting the Gbeya's unscientific (not necessarily "un-Christian") views of the world, which we have wisely never done, we should not be making any contribution to a healthier African church. Rather, we should reveal to our fellow Christians that we had no confidence in their judgment, no ability to see evil when it exists. And if they should yield to the pressure of our exhortations without being convinced that there is an evil involved, we would be encouraging, nay, forcing them to shallowness and hypocrisy.

For, after all, what is there pagan or heathen in this celebration? Is it wrong to sing? Is it wrong to move one's body rythmically? And what about American football games and all of their hypnotic fanfare — the yells and songs and all?

We concede that the Gbeya have erroneous ideas of the world. We admit that they are wrong in believing that leopards can kill simply by contamination. But is this heathen? Is it even superstitious? — a term having more connotative than denotative value, a pejorative really. Is it not simply prescientific thinking?

Prescientific views are not banished by evangelical preaching alone. Before the scientific era there was a great deal of nonsensical thinking even among good Christians. And even today, among folk cultures one finds many views which the more sophisticated city-dweller smiles at. On the other hand, these members of folk cultures shed many of their views along with the old ways of living very quickly after being urbanized.

The Gbeya, then, are a prescientific people whose world view is still intact in spite of various cultural innovations, material and nonmaterial. Christianity has been well accepted by them, but they do not see any inconsistency in having faith in Christ and believing that animals contaminate people. Some day they, too, will be wiser, but in the meantime they are not really poorer, weaker Christians for it.

---

*William A. Smalley*

**Reprinted from Vol. 6, No. 4 (1959), pp. 182-185.**

# Vocabulary and the Preaching of the Gospel

*Readers who are familiar with Eugene A. Nida's books[1] have read his discussions of the fascinating differences between religious terms in different languages, and of the widely different areas of meaning which words in different languages may have because of the difference in cultural background of the people using the languages. We present here a most practical problem in the vocabulary for 'sin' and 'taboo' in one of the Senoufo languages of West Africa, as presented by Mrs. Howard Beardslee. When, as in this case, there is very little of either linguistic or cultural correspondence, the task of communicating the gospel is challenging indeed.*

## The Problem

As missionaries we have come to communicate the message that God sent His Son into the world reconciling the world unto Himself. A part of this message is the fact that sin separates man from God and obstructs the fellowship between God and man. We are puzzled as to how adequately to explain sin, for the word we have been using means both 'sin' and 'taboo.' The gospel was first preached to the Senoufos in the Bambara trade language which has different words for sin and taboo. When it was interpreted into Se-

1 Especially *God's Word in Man's Language* (New York: Harper and Bros., 1952) and *Bible Translating* (New York: The American Bible Society, 1947).

noufo the word *kapini* incorporates the two ideas in one word.

Taboos among the Senoufos are innumerable. It is taboo for a man to see his wife sewing, or to hear her sing the "marriage song." It is taboo for a man to whistle in a field except when he is resting, or for a woman to whistle except to make a little wind when trying to blow the chaff off the grain on a still day. It is taboo for the women to see a certain fetish, or for anyone to watch the old women when they go out to perform a certain ceremony to bring rain in a drought. One night a woman said to me, "We have so many deaths in our country because our taboos are so many." They believe that they will be harmed in some way or that God will kill them for breaking a taboo.

A Senoufo who had often heard the gospel preached said that adultery and lying were 'sins' or 'taboos.' However, some who had had no contact with the gospel said that adultery was not a *kapini,* but that if the husband found out about it he beat up the wife and the guilty man. An adulterer is sometimes called a 'person without shame,' but adultery is still commonly practiced. When we inquired of the Senoufos about things commonly considered sinful by us, we found that before they ever saw the white man those who habitually practiced adultery, lying, and stealing were called *silegebafeebi,* or 'without-shame-people.'

It presents a problem when preaching to those who have had no contact with the gospel, since when we preach against sin they think of taboos. Would it be possible or practical to give an adequate explanation every time one preaches, showing the difference between their taboos and sin as we know it to be revealed in the law of God? How much do the Christians understand when we preach against sin? We are sure they continue to practice their taboos, with very few exceptions. This word *kapini* seems to be the most natural one for the Christians to use when they are testifying or preaching and it was they who first used this word when interpreting from the trade language into the tribal language.

*Ann Beardslee*

It seems apparent that *kapini* is not in itself an adequate way to translate 'sin' into Senoufo. No matter what explanations were given in sermons, hearers would tend to identify *kapini* with the kinds of behavior it covers, and not the extended meaning of the missionary. But how will we find better vocabulary?

## The Catalog Approach

One way is to assume that we know in most cases whether a man's behavior is sin or not, and what the difference between sin and taboo always is. By such a point of view we could make two lists, one of "sins" and one of "taboos" and be guided thereby in our dealing with the Senoufos, in our preaching to them, and in our judgment of their behavior. The one list might contain items of behavior such as adultery, lying, and stealing; the other might include seeing one's wife sewing, hearing one's wife sing the marriage song, etc.

Now we want to talk to unevangelized Senoufos about these things. The behavior in the second list they consider dangerous, likely to bring death, possibly wicked or fearful. Many of the items in the first list they consider reprehensible, but not fearfully dangerous or subject to the punishment of God or nature. Our temptation is to consider the second group petty and irrelevant, the first extremely serious.

Our word 'sin' was probably translated *kapini* (the Senoufo word for the second group) because it was presented as fearful and bad, subject to divine sanction. A word to cover the first group is hard to come by. We understand that people who do these things are "without-shame-people," and at least this is a starting point, though there is no indication of divine displeasure in the term.

In other words we can have two terms for the two lists, but the "feeling" behind them, the really significant meaning seems reversed to us. We run into other problems also, because the longer our lists, the more certain it is that somewhere on them there are going to be items for which these Senoufo terms do not apply. Perhaps many of the items on the "sin" list will not be thought of as "without-shame" behavior.

However, at least we have a starting point, and we decide to teach people the rest of the list of "without-shame" behavior, as we have compiled it. We construct our catechisms, prepare our sermons, and organize our ministerial training program so that people understand completely that God will not tolerate "without-shame" behavior, and just what that behavior consists of.

In this way we have a terminological distinction between taboo and sin, and we have overcome what seems to us to be a serious mistake in informing people that God does not want them to whistle. Thus we feel that we are more adequately communicating the gospel.

## The Communication Approach

Or are we?

On the other hand, we could start from another direction and ask, ourselves what sin is, basically, theologically, and culturally. How is it defined cross-culturally?[2] If we decide that sin is that which disrupts man's fellowship with God, disobedience and rebellion against God, or indifference toward Him, rejection of His Lordship and of His Son, it casts the whole problem in another light. Specific acts then become symptoms of our allegiance, or of our rebellion, or even of our vacillation between. As our preaching and teaching starts with God, moves through the level of redemption through Jesus Christ into the behavior of Christian people in a given culture, we are faced with the profound question of the transformation of a world view of a group of people, and of their knowledge of God. As men learn to know God, His Son, and discipleship, a profound transformation can then take place in their lives.

But sin and sins are Biblical concepts, and the need to discuss them does not go away by changing the viewpoint. However, we have stopped shifting individual acts of behavior around from one category to another, and we have changed instead to inquire about motives, about the nature of sin, and about the character of God. This is a very Biblical thing to do, and it is basic to the communication of the gospel. Our search for vocabulary becomes less one of a search for a label

[2] I am not here dealing with the question of who should make and enforce value judgments and decisions of right and wrong in a church. This complex problem has been discussed in a variety of articles in PRACTICAL ANTHROPOLOGY.

to cover a catalog of actions, and more one to describe a range of attitudes.

In order for any Biblical sense of sin to become real to the Senoufos, their understanding of God must first become in some measure Biblical.[3] It is only as they recognize the antithesis between God's nature and their own that talking about sin takes on any relevance at all.

I would certainly want to avoid using the term *kapini* as a general term for sin or sins. "Without-shame-people" or some other expression like "without-shame-deeds" (if this is possible) may be applicable to some situations and some behavior. It could perhaps take on the meaning of divine sanction in time. I would seek, however, as much as possible, to preach about God and His revelation of Himself in His Son Jesus, our love and obedience to Him, and showing that love in behavior which does not come in to disrupt it. I would emphasize God's abhorrence of the human selfishness and disobedience which disrupt fellowship, in order to make sense, linguistically and theologically. It is God's relation to man which is the most significant from the Christian point of view, not whether an individual act is good or bad in itself alone.

The solution to intercultural communication is not so much to translate as to re-express in another language and cultural system. If words for sin are hard to come by, then other, longer, more paraphrastic ways may have to be found, which of course implies fundamental decisions about basic meaning rather than glib identifications of the vocabulary of one language with that of another. What do we want to say to the Senoufo? Do we want to tell them that they should not steal? Well, then, let's say it. Do we want to help them live in a way consistent with the Lordship of Christ? This is more subtle, and harder. It subordinates the question of finding the right vocabulary to the question of finding the effective way to express a whole range of message.

[3] See William D. Reyburn, "The Transformation of God and the Conversion of Man," PRACTICAL ANTHROPOLOGY, Vol. 4, No. 5 (Sept.-Oct., 1957), pp. 185-193.

*William D. Reyburn*

**Reprinted from Vol. 6, No. 1 (1959), pp. 1-19.**

# Polygamy, Economy, and Christianity in the Eastern Cameroun

*Polygamy as a desired form of marriage among the tribes represented in this study appears to be inseparably linked with economic aspects of life as these are developing in the eastern Cameroun today. Motivations for polygamy are a complex set of cultural factors which have not and will not be readily changed. Christianity in its total condemnation of polygamy has failed to discriminate between things which are totally different. The emphasis upon monogamy has often led Africans into a false picture of the monogamous union and a resultant reaction to it. While there are certain immediate and practical steps Christian churches can take concerning polygamy, the church is neither equipped nor is it operating in the real sphere of its message by following these superficial approaches to the problem. The Christian church, particularly Protestant, makes its fatal mistake in attempting to operate with neither a formulated missionary science nor an articulate missionary theology. From the side of missionary science we must learn that the case involved in this area is primarily economic and not primarily isolated polygamy. From the side of missionary theology we need to take the findings of such information and in true Christian identification with the human being involved move with our theology to his inner longings and* WITH HIM *communicate a gospel that speaks to the roots of his real need and show him that Christ is the ultimate answer to the* POWER *problem of his heart. When this has been done the transformed individual displays a transformation of symbols in his new relation to the power of the gospel and his regenerate life.*

A KAKA tribeswoman, the mother of three children, sat on a low stool with a mortar between her bare legs. Rhythmically she raised her right arm high above her head, then brought a heavy wooden pestle down with a sharp blow, beating the manioc into flour for the evening meal of *kamo*. Her left hand shot into the mortar to stir around the manioc meal and then was quickly pulled aside as the pestle hammered down again and again. A child sat silently in the dirt beside her tugging gently at a fetish hanging about its neck. Soon the child arose and tried to move in toward a lank breast that was bobbing back and forth on the mother's chest. The woman stopped, took the child and

---

**Dr. William D. Reyburn's article on polygamy is based on a talk given in September 1958 in Douala, French Cameroun, at a conference on the social responsibility of the church before the social changes in the Cameroun. The report provoked a vigorous discussion among the delegates and some of their conclusions are incorporated in the article.**

put it to her breast, wiped the sweat from her forehead, and turning to her husband said, "If you had two wives I could go to my mother's tomorrow." Her husband lay stretched out on a mat, appearing to pay no attention to his wife. The woman continued in a louder voice: "Look across the courtyard at Abele. She sits and plays with her children while Kana cooks tonight." Turning toward her husband she picked up a stick and pointed it at him, and with an angry scowl on her face she called out, "Poor man, poor man, who respects a poor man?" The husband arose from his mat, walked to the fire, picked up a live coal between his leathery fingers and dropped it into his pipe. Turning toward his wife he spat, cursed softly, then slowly walked away. The woman sat the child on the ground, picked up her pestle and continued to prepare the evening meal which her husband would eat by himself by the embers of his fire while her half would be for herself and his children to be eaten in the flickering light of her mud floor kitchen.

## Motivations for Polygamy

The Kaka woman described above reveals something of the feminine motivation for the polygamous[1] family. She wants more freedom for herself and blames her husband's poverty for not securing this liberty. She often provokes her husband into a polygamous union by employing the ridicule of "poor man." Polygamy is an institution which appears to many modern Africans as something natural to Africa. As some say, "Polygamy is beautiful; it is a symbol of that which is truly African." Since a very large number of modern Africans were born into polygamous families and have experienced both the rewards and frustrations of westernization, it is not surprising that many Africans feel a strong pull toward the polygamous family as a satisfying security in a world that is changing perhaps too quickly. The gregarious nature of the large polygamous family fits the Kaka[2] personality, which is constantly endeavoring to express itself in interpersonal relationships.

## The Desire for Children

Perhaps the most commonly voiced reason given by people of the Cameroun for the continuation of polygamy is the desire to have numerous children. The African looks upon offspring in a way which is often different from European ideas. In the first place the traditional African conceptualizes a marriage union as centered primarily around fertility. This view that all things should produce their kind causes him to conceive of humans as producers of their own kind. He views his life as a gift which he has received from his father, who received it in turn from his father, and so on. The gift of life has been handed down from generation to generation and each one is morally responsible to participate in that continuity. When a man has been given the gift of life from his father he will be most unfaithful to his father, if he fails to pass it on himself. Not only is there a sense of responsibility for reproduction among men, but the woman is likewise prepared to conceive of herself as the property of a man who has paid

1 Because of the popular usage of *polygamy* to denote plural wives, it is used here in that sense. More exactly, it should be called *polygyny*. *Polygamy* actually refers to plural marriage, whether of husband or wife. *Polyandry* is the technical term for plural husbands.

2 The Kaka are the group in the Cameroun with which the author is primarily working.

for her productive rights and she is responsible to produce children as well as gardens. It is little wonder then that many Africans read the accounts of Jacob, his wives and concubines, in the book of Genesis with a greater avidity than they read the Gospels or the Epistles.

Children are a great asset in the African household particularly in the traditional village life. There is a separation of boys and girls which takes place even before puberty in which boys are associated with the male segment of the patriclan (the father's family and line of descent) and girls with the female side. This separation is often a further motivation for children. If a woman has only sons she has no one to associate with her and to identify themselves with her in her work and life. She is therefore anxious to have boys for her husband but also to have girls for herself. Girls are particularly valued in the monogamous marriage where they will for a certain number of years be available to assist the mother in her work. Girls are the source of dowry payment which will increase the father's wealth and give him the opportunity to form a marriage union between his daughter and a friend who may often be of his own age group. It is this friendship pact between men which gives rise so often to the marriage of young productive girls to old senile men. The girl's father is more concerned to prove his long standing friendship to a man of his own age class than to arrange a compatible marriage for his daughter. To the traditional Kaka father his friendships come before the assumed conjugal compatibility of his daughter. He conceptualizes his daughter in terms of *service* and not in terms of happy marriage union. It is because of this attitude, which many young African girls no longer share, that such marriages become extremely pathetic.

Boys are desired particularly because they are the visible continuation of the father's lineage. They will continue to inhabit the paternal village and to continue the family names which have been handed down through the generations. The father of an African household expects his offspring to help him and to provide him with a retinue of servants. The African father who is visibly well serviced by his many offspring is considered as a man of standing and is envied by others who for lack of children are forced to perform many menial tasks for themselves. In African societies such as in the southern French Cameroun, where land is plentiful and every man is an independent cash crop producer, it is impossible to hire workers. Consequently a man who has a large number of children can increase his cash crop production through the labor of his children. The economic aspect of polygamy will be taken up in more detail below.

A modern development of child motivation for polygamy in some African areas, particularly French, is the financial compensation for children. Many men in government service as well as private service are extremely anxious to increase the size of their families in order to receive this financial aid. Since children belong to their fathers and will not be lost due to separation of father and mother, there is often not much restraint in divorce and a turnover of wives is often common.

The high infant mortality rate of children is another factor which increases the pressure of polygamy. Africans are vividly aware that only a portion of the children born to them will live to serve them and to grow up and reproduce themselves. As one man said to me once, "I have eighteen children. Some are bound to die, some will be of no account, and I hope that the few that are left will grow up to be worth something."

Not only is the African man aware of the fact that he will lose children through death but also that he may lose his wife through death or for some other cause, such as interclan disputes. Since a marriage union is not often viewed as being a lifelong association, a man is prone to view the taking of a woman as a temporary arrangement in life. Many Kaka men have said that they would not have much security if married to only one wife. "What would I do if I had only one wife and she died?" It is especially true that a man who has had plural wives and has a large number of children feels it necessary to keep a retinue of mothers for his children.

### Sexual Contact

While sexual considerations per se are probably secondary as a motivation for polygamy, Kaka men often express their concern that the death of a wife would leave them deprived of sexual contact. Also a man finds it convenient to have more than one wife for sex contacts when one wife is sick, called to her paternal village, or is having her monthly period.

The literature on the subject of polygamy often cites the long period of abstinence between birth and the weaning of the child as a reason for polygamy. This may have been true at an earlier time, but at least among the Kaka it is presently insufficient reason. Sex relations with a nursing mother are tabooed, but this is primarily to protect the child. If a Kaka man has a sex contact with a nursing woman, he must carefully bathe himself and put medicine on the eyes of the child. Otherwise his impurity will pass on to the infant and cause it to die. Kaka men do not observe a strenuous abstinence code during the period of lactation and are unable to defend this as a reason for wanting plural wives. Christian Kaka men who do not practice fetish medicine and who do not plan to enter a plural marriage are beginning to have children more frequently than before. They are not entirely free from a sense of shame in doing this.

Failure to have children is perhaps one of the strongest motivations to enter a plural marriage today among the Kaka. If a woman is sterile a man is often compelled to take on a second wife so that he may have offspring. Among some Kaka families it is felt to be an obligation of the father-in-law to provide another daughter when the first has proven sterile. Among many Kaka this involves the husband in no additional dowry payment, but for others the husband is instructed to return the daughter and his money is refunded and it is entirely up to him to find another wife. In many cases in the Kaka tribe men have been able to keep the first wife, who continues to serve her husband, but always with remorse over the fact that she gave him no children. Some monogamous men who have large families in the villages of this study are not as a rule anxious to enter a polygamous union.

On the basis of demographic counts of male and female births as well as marriageable youths, there is in this area no disproportionate female excess in population. Men disappear earlier in the upper age grades leaving a larger group of old women than old men. However there is no population imbalance at the marriageable age level to motivate polygamy. If one counts the number of young males and females living with their fathers, there is always a great excess of sons over daughters. This is due to the fact that daughters are placed in marriage shortly after sexual maturity while sons must wait considerably beyond maturity to amass the money necessary for dowry payment. It is very rare to find a Kaka girl over fourteen in her father's family village, while his unmarried sons may be there at twenty to twenty-five years of age without having been able to take a wife. *Hence it should be underscored here that the two most common reasons for polygamy given by French administrators and missionaries in particular (viz., long sexual abstinence and female population excess) are in this area of no motivational validity whatsoever.*

### The Role of the First Wife

The role of women and their attitude toward the family and marriage is a major aspect of monogamy and polygamy. A woman who has more work than she can handle is often anxious that her husband take on another wife. This frees the first wife from much of her burden and gives her free time to take produce to a market, sell it and perhaps spend her money. She will be free to go to her village and visit, to spend more time with her small children and to undertake other tasks in which she finds pleasure. In addition to the freedom that polygamy gives the woman, it creates a special position of authority for the first wife, called *nya toū* in Kaka, which means "woman of the house." It is *nya toū* who directs the other wives and makes the final decisions when problems and arguments arise among the co-wives. Only *nya toū* has direct access to her husband and may call him by his name, and it is she who receives the orders from the husband. In many Kaka marriages in which the husband is advanced in years, *nya toū* may be an elderly woman managing the polygamous compound made up of co-wives and junior wives who are expected to obey her commands. *Nya toū* plays a very important role in the husband's decision to espouse another woman. *Nya toū* usually talks over with her co-wives the advisability of another wife, and if they are agreed that the presence of the potential wife would disrupt the harmony of the compound, *nya toū* presents these facts to her husband and often makes alternative suggestions to him. If the husband disregards *nya toū*'s advice, he soon finds out that the price of peace means returning the new woman to her family. In the case where a man marries a young girl, it is the responsibility of *nya toū* to take care of the girl like a mother and the husband does not sleep with the girl until *nya toū* advises him. Hence, the attitude of the first wife toward the possibility of co-wives is a very important factor in the creation of the polygamous family. In the villages of this study it was often found that the first wife was not anxious to have co-wives provided that the husband's demands were not too great. Also, if he bought her European goods which represented an equitable share in the cash income and if she had children, she did not feel extremely anxious for the presence of co-wives.

### Frequency of Polygamy

In order to investigate the relation of polygamy in the changing economy of the eastern French Cameroun, a survey was made of five villages. The area covered by this survey represents a zone which is sparsely inhabited and consists of some seven relatively small tribes (Kaka, Yengele, Mponpong, Bizom, Ngounabem, Mpomam, Bangando). The distance by road between the two most extreme villages (Gounté and Mbateka Ndjong) is approximately 650 kilometers. The results obtained showed that the detailed study of this problem at Lolo was quite typical of the greater area. A full account of the Lolo study will be prepared at a later time. In order not to burden this paper with statistics I will give only the summary figures for the various villages.

1. *Ngola.* An Mponpong speaking village in the Subdivision of Yokadouma and located twenty kilometers south of Yokadouma on the Yokadouma-Molondou road. Ngola has 58 husbands and 95 wives, making a ratio of 1.6 wives per husband. Thirty-nine percent of the husbands are polygamous, 56 percent of the wives are in polygamous unions.

2. *Mbateka Ndjong.* A Bangando (Gbaya dialect) speaking tribe in the Subdivision of Molondou, located 20 kilometers north of Molondou on the Molondou-Yokadouma road. Mbateka Ndjong has 16 husbands and 22 wives, making a ratio of 1.37 or 1.4 wives per husband. Thirty-one percent of the husbands are polygamous, and 50 percent of the wives.

3. *Mindourou.* A Kaka speaking village in the Subdivision of Batouri, located 40 kilometers south of Batouri. Mindourou is divided into two halves; one is Protestant and the other Catholic. The statistics on this village include only the Protestant half of Mindourou. Mindourou has 35 husbands and 50 wives, making a ratio of 1.4 wives per husband. Thirty-seven percent of the husbands and 56 percent of the wives are in polygamous marriages.

4. *Gounté.* A Kaka speaking village in the Subdivision of Batouri, located 25 kilometers east of Doumé Station. There are 25 husbands and 38 wives, making a ratio of 1.5 wives per husband, with 44 percent of the men and 63 percent of the wives in polygamous unions.

5. *Lolo.* A Kaka village in the Subdivision of Batouri, located 80 kilometers east of Batouri on the Batouri-Gamboula road. Lolo has 56 husbands and 78 wives, making a ratio of 1.4 wives per husband. Forty-three percent of the men and 50 percent of the women are in polygamous unions.

From the foregoing data, the following conclusions may be drawn.

1. The percentage of wives in polygamous marriages is greater than that in monogamous marriages. In Lolo and Mbateka Ndjong they are equally distributed.

2. The percentage of husbands in polygamous marriages is always less than the number of husbands in monogamous unions.

3. The ratio of wives per husband is in all areas less than 2.

4. The overall frequency of polygamy and the ratio of wives to husbands is essentially equivalent throughout the entire area of this study.

## Sexual Reproduction at Lolo

It was stated above that one of the major motivations for polygamous unions is to increase the number of children. In the following paragraphs we will examine briefly the sexual productivity in Lolo and then proceed to review these factors in the light of the changing economy.

In order to study the productivity of polygamous and monogamous marriages, it is impossible to arrive at just conclusions without comparing women of similar age groups whose productive activity has been over a similar span of years. In the data given below such a grouping has been done and only the final figures are given. Children here refer only to surviving offspring.

In Lolo 10 percent of the polygamous women have produced no children while nearly half of the monogamous women have produced no children. This statement must be understood in terms of the general age grouping of these women because there are just as many polygamous women in Lolo as monogamous. A detailed explanation will be given under the section on polygamy and the new economy. The polygamous women of Lolo have produced on an average 2.5 children per polygamous mother, while the monogamous women have produced an average of 2 children. On the surface it appears that the comparable age group of polygamous women has many more children than the equivalent group of monogamous women. However in Lolo nearly half of this group of monogamous women have had no children at all. If we remove them from the group, the monogamous women have produced an average of 3 children as compared with 2.5 for the productive polygamous women.

This quantitative view of productivity looked at from the male's position is somewhat different. The average number of children per polygamous male household is 5.3 while the average number per monogamous household is only 2.

It is extremely difficult to provide a quantitative account of this kind of data. In the first place no marriage is conceived in Lolo as being permanently monogamous. Likewise what are today polygamous unions may be tomorrow monogamous and next month will revert again to polygamy. However a qualitative account of child productivity in polygamous and monogamous unions in Lolo helps to show that certain kinds of monogamous unions are tending to produce more children than polygamous unions taken as an average. This is extremely valuable in the light of the fact that selected monogamous unions in Lolo are achieving what 90 percent of the men of Lolo claim can only come through polygamous unions.

It was said above that only 10 percent of the polygamous women have failed to produce children while 50 percent of the monogamous women have had no children. Does this then prove that the polygamous union is more productive? If so, why? The answer to these questions is entirely one of *selection*. The matter may be stated very simply. If a woman has given birth (before marriage or after), she is marked as productive and this in turn increases the price of her dowry. A polygamous man with wealth can afford to pay for a proven producer whereas a poor man with little source of income is doing well to get a low-priced wife who may often be a woman sent away from another marriage for her failure to give birth. If a man has money he can afford to buy the producing wife; if not, he cannot. Consequently we may say that financial position (usually gained through polygamy) makes possible the *choice* of productive wives. When this form of village capitalism was pointed out to a group of anti-capitalist college students, it came to them as quite a shock.

Monogamous marriages that can be compared in terms of time of monogamous union and period of productivity potential fall into two groups: those that bear children and those that do not. A further comparison shows that the 18 child-bearing monogamous unions tend to be stable and with less desire to seek extramarital sex contacts than the other 18 unstable nonproductive monogamous unions.

### Venereal Disease

It has long been noticed by Africans and missionaries alike that pastors and catechists have often tended to produce large families. At least one of the reasons for this is the fact that sex relations in these cases are restricted to the husband and wife, thus reducing the possibility for contracting venereal disease. Among the Kaka the wide-spread occurrence of venereal disease may be attributed largely to the wide-spread practice of premarital and extramarital sex relations. It is estimated by one doctor working among the Kaka that nearly half of his women patients are cases involving a venereal infection and resultant sterility.

The spread of venereal disease, which in many cases eventually prohibits conception, is due to two main sets of factors. In the first place is the commonly accepted practice among the Kaka of sharing wives between close friends[3] and the premarital promiscuity practiced by the young. The second set of factors stems more from the economic development. Many young men are unable to secure the money required for dowry payment. Consequently they seek relations with prostitutes and transmit venereal disease. Many wives find that their husbands do not share with them enough of the income from the cash gardens, and so these women seek sexual relations with other men in exchange for money, cloth, or other gifts. These women feel that European goods are necessary to life now and find this as a means of obtaining some of them.

In view of these factors it is exceedingly difficult for a Kaka man to maintain a selfish economic control of his wife and expect her to be faithful to him. It has been found in Lolo that the productive monogamous and polygamous marriages cannot indulge in outside sexual contacts if they expect to have large families.

### Polygamy and Economy

So far we have only alluded to some of the effects of the desire for money and European goods. It will now be necessary to describe briefly the type of economic development taking place in the eastern Cameroun and to show how this economic activity and polygamy are interrelated.

The economic life of the eastern Cameroun has been retarded, due mainly to its distance from the coast. Before the arrival of European colonizers in the Cameroun in the last quarter of the 19th century, coastal tribes were trafficking in ivory, rubber and slaves, which they secured from interior tribes. These coastal tribes maintained an exclusive contact with Spanish, Portuguese, German and French merchantmen sailing the west coast of Africa. Following the German occupation of the Cameroun it was discovered that the Kaka area contained considerable quantities of native rubber. Before establishing contact with the Kaka, it was necessary for the Germans to cross the hostile Meka tribal area as well as several other smaller tribes who had killed and eaten the few German merchants and officers venturing into this part of the

[3] See the description of Kaka sexual practices referred to here in William D. Reyburn, "Kaka Kinship, Sex, and Adultery," PRACTICAL ANTHROPOLOGY, Vol. 5, No. 1 (Jan.-Feb. 1958), pp. 1-21, and in this volume.

Cameroun. Punitive expeditions were carried out against various tribes and a communications route established, opening up the southeast Cameroun for rubber exploitation. Rubber and ivory were exchanged for European trade goods from approximately 1906 until the Germans were driven out in 1914. Following this initial period of influx was a period of some fifteen years in which the French attempted to organize its administrative units and did practically nothing to encourage economic development in this area. It was not until about 1935, when the road connecting Batouri in Cameroun and Gamboula in French Equatorial Africa was built, that the economic aspect of this country came again under outside stimulation.

In 1907, at the time of the first rubber exportation from the Kaka country, an average dowry payment was twenty *boukas,* which is a flat hoe-like piece of iron. By 1914 the price was still twenty *boukas,* but also included some European trade goods, especially cloth. In the 1920's the number of *boukas* was about five, but the amount of trade goods was greatly increased and in addition money was included. By 1939 the *boukas* had disappeared entirely and the dowry payment was entirely cash and trade goods.

This change in the dowry payment reflects the way in which the economy of the country was changing. *Soumba* is the term used in Kaka for iron, dowry, wealth and money. From time immemorial the dowry and iron have been synonymous. All wealth was in iron, and iron was used primarily in agriculture, hunting, war and marriage. The iron ceases to be the token of wealth today, but money, also called *soumba,* is used in payment of dowry.

The introduction of cash into the eastern Cameroun has been based upon two principal sources, labor and crops. Labor has always meant working for the administration, merchants or missions, in each case European institutions. Job opportunities have been relatively few. However, the introduction of money crops of cacao, coffee and tobacco have recently become available to all. The opening up of the roads in the eastern Cameroun (and in all other areas) made it possible to market crops in local central markets as well as to transport them off for exportation. Cacao was introduced into the western Cameroun before 1900. However, in the area of this study it was greatly delayed due to the lack of roads and communication and did not get started in the grasslands until in the last fifteen years.

### Effect of Changing Economy

Cacao and coffee began to be exported from the forest areas of the eastern Cameroun as early as 1920. However it was not until 1946-50 that the tobacco development began in the forest and grasslands. The result of tobacco production has had a vast effect on nearly every aspect of the life in the area. Throughout the area of this study, social organization, village settlement patterns, daily routines, economic values and a host of other aspects of these cultures have been vastly affected. Some of those factors relevant to polygamy are presented here.

1. Most outstanding is the increased work burden for the woman. The men of this area (if not of Africa in general) do not believe that a man is obliged to work to the same extent as a woman. A man is responsible for numerous details of village and family life which require hours, days and weeks of deliberation which cause him to be absent from his

gardens. However, he expects his wife or wives to spend full time on the job. The result of greatly increasing the woman's work with all of the detailed jobs in the production of coffee, cacao and tobacco has the effect of causing the woman to object to her disproportionate burden. She is therefore, in many cases, obliged to seek help in her tasks through the assistance of a co-wife or wives.

2. The general increase in wealth tends to make those who have money appear richer than those who do not. Consequently the feeling of being "poor," which is opprobrium to the African, is increased. He feels impelled to avoid being left behind while others gain more wealth. Polygamy is a way to keep up and avoid the ridicule of poverty.

3. It is impossible in the area concerned to hire workers. Land is free and available. Every man is in competition and attempts to make gardens as large as his work force will allow. In some cases, extended families or subclans work cooperatively and in this way assist one another in their gardens. However, this form of cooperative labor is not extensive and it is not aimed at increasing everyone's garden but rather to reduce the total amount of heavy labor for the men. A man must depend upon himself, his wives and children to produce his income from his gardens.

4. The increase in cash has meant the increase in dowry price. In the area of this study, the majority of the money that is earned goes into dowries. Trade goods such as clothing, bicycles and sewing machines come next, and education lags far behind. Many young men find that their fathers do not pay them anything when the crop is sold. Hence they are not motivated to remain and continue the work. It is also the case that marriage has become exceedingly unstable due to the increase in available cash and the competition for wives as laborers. Many a father will encourage his daughter to leave her husband so she can go into another marriage where the father will receive a larger dowry. Consequently the father-in-law may blackmail his son-in-law for additional payments. If the son-in-law is unable to pay, the girl is forced by her father to leave her husband and enter another marriage. The original dowry is then repaid and the girl's father has made a handsome profit. With this profit he may be able to buy another wife for himself.

### Sex and the Changing Economy

It is a thesis of this paper that the desire for the possession of wealth among the peoples of the eastern Cameroun has caused them to make certain adjustments which are tending toward their own ruin. In early times extramarital sex relations were formally forbidden and to break this law meant death, war or separation of subclans. With the coming of the European administration, particularly the French, all of this has been changed. Former controls have been lifted. It was formerly part of the responsibility of village elders or parents to guard their daughters from too frequent sex contacts. Any infraction of the laws of extramarital sex relations (except in *wandja,* the exchange of wives between close friends) was dealt with by the most serious punishment, usually death. The French administration, unlike the German, put the political responsibility into the hands of *chefs de canton* who were backed by French authority. Courts were set up to put into practice French laws. Punishment for sex offenses were adjusted to the levying of a fine. This was new to the Kaka and was entirely removed in his thinking from any moral dimension. The French authorities encouraged people to be married civilly, and when a man committed adultery with a woman having had a civil marriage it was in the eyes of the French an infraction upon a person who was in the process of becoming *evoluée*. Consequently the fine for such a case of adultery is fixed at 3,000 francs while the fine for adultery with a woman married only by traditional arrangement is only 1,500 francs. Since the responsibility for acting against adultery was removed from the hands of the village notables and placed in the courts, there was no longer any fear connected with adultery. In fact, often a man has found that if he can successfully accuse another man of committing adultery with his wife, he can collect the money from the offender and the matter is settled entirely on the basis of a financial agreement outside of court.

The codification of adultery as an offense against the colonial law had the effect of removing the traditional control of adultery. Since the payment of a fine was such a meager punishment and a new means of securing money for the offended party, it actually served to vastly encourage extramarital sexual relations with the result that in recent years the spread of venereal disease has become a front rank social problem among the Kaka, reaching the point of social pathology.

The result of the widespread occurrence of venereal disease has been, as was cited above, a sharp decline in the number of births in Lolo.

It is only fair to point out that it has not been the administration's policy alone which has created this situation. The cultural preparation which had been laid for many millennia before the arrival of the European colonizers has also contributed its part. This orientation among the Kaka as among many other African ethnic groups has been one which viewed the woman primarily in terms of sexual fertility and social inferiority. As long as the Kaka lived within a closed kinship world, his sexual behavior toward all the women with whom he associated was extremely well defined. However the extension of that small world through roads, the cessation of interclan and tribal wars, the opening of schools, and migrations sent him abroad into a new world where his rigid village *structural morality* was insufficient to guard him. Mission schools have often been more of an open temptation to sexual promiscuity for young people than a place where new moral attitudes were instilled. The traditional attitude of the young male has been that of sexual aggression, and the cultural and psychological preparation of young girls has been that of submission as part of the preparation for fertility expected of females.

The Kaka practice of *wandja,* in which two men in close friendship trade wives for sexual purposes, has had certain economic aspects which have come into play in the extension and reinterpretation of this practice. When two men establish the relation of *so* ("friend"), they trade gifts. Each takes turn giving the other a gift, which must be increased with each exchange. The *so* relation has not been primarily concerned with wife exchange but with material gain. The giving of a wife creates a new relation between the two men and their wives, in which the men are now expected to pass gifts to the wives. However, these gifts do not remain the property of the wives but are given to the husbands. Consequently the institutionalized practice of *so* has been extended in recent years in order to gain gifts through the lending of one's wife. This in turn has increased the spread of venereal disease, and when gone unattended for long periods, sterility has been the frustrating result. This in turn has caused the husbands to seek other wives for the production of children. Other practices of this type could be cited; however, the *so* relation is typical of the ways in which certain Kaka practices have undergone extension in practice motivated primarily out of economic considerations.

## The Problem Is Economic

It is evident now that polygamy as well as freedom of sexual relation, the spread of venereal disease, the sterility of many women, and associated problems share a common nucleus which is of an economic nature. That is, there is a conceptualization of wealth which is the heart of this problem. Women and children are viewed largely as laborers and producers. Wives produce children and gardens, girl children produce dowry and provide personal service and are valuable for increasing garden income. The cash income from all a man's gardens belongs to him exclusively and he shares as little as possible with his wife or wives. Wives have a great desire to own, and if they do not find that they receive an equitable proportion of the cash income from their labor, they are anxious to seek other means of securing money. This they may do by encouraging and helping the husband to secure other wives. This gives each wife an opportunity to free herself from the close control of her husband, to sell her garden produce in a market town, to find employment, and to have financially rewarding extramarital sex relations.

It is then in conformity with the facts that the matter of polygamy in the eastern Cameroun today is motivated more out of economic consideration than from anything else. Consequently it is both futile and dangerous for the Christian church to set up ecclesiastical laws against polygamy. What is needed rather is a reorientation of both men and women concerning money and wealth, and in particular a new conceptualization of the African family, in which economic considerations are secondary to other values. Such an attitude should have to begin with the male.

## What Is Polygamy and What Is a Marriage

The mission and church in the Cameroun have at various times attempted to legislate the admittance of polygamous women into the church. In essence the approach has been that the polygamous man is viewed as guilty of polygamy while the wives are innocent. This judgment has been based upon the fact that the man in these societies, because of the dowry, is the instigator of marriage. This is true in principle since the woman has had very limited choice in matters of marriage.

This position is not entirely just, however, since in many cases it is the first wife who provokes the husband into marrying a second wife, a third, and so on. Where only one wife in a polygamous marriage is admitted on the assumption that the man has only one real wife, the first one, there is the problem which often occurs due to the dictatorial power of the first wife over the co-wives. A second or third wife may be one who merits church membership but the first wife becomes a member in spite of the fact she may be unfit. If a man returns his wives in order to be a church member, he normally keeps the one which pleases him and who is fertile. He and his *selected* wife are then eligible for admittance.

It appears that by condemning polygamy per se, Christianity in Africa has done needless harm by a lack of discrimination. The question of a type of marriage union has appeared to be more important than the nature of the family involved in any kind of parental union. In the first place, the Christian church in its absolutist position of monogamy has impressed Africans that monogamy automatically produces a wholesome Christian family. While this has not been the purpose of Christian missions, it has nevertheless been implied.

The various kinds of polygamous unions found throughout Africa do not display the same basis for the foundation of the family. Neither are all polygamous marriages to be simply lumped together without discrimination.

In the French Cameroun today there are polygamous marriages involving chiefs who have upward of thirty wives. These wives are given out for child production and are exchanged quite as freely as merchandise. This is the exception. It is the remnant of the chief-polygamous marriage of the past generation, in which a chief might have a "wife" in nearly every village in his tribe. These wives played a definite political role as well as serving as wives and child producers and economic exchange. In the Cameroun today there are also polygamous marriages in which the family is the center and the relations in the polygamous family are most pleasant. Co-wives treat each other like sisters and all appear to be interested primarily in the welfare of all the members of the polygamous family group. The husband has a genuine concern for his wives and children and provides for them in a truly benevolent fashion. After one has lived in close contact with such a family, there can be no doubt why some Africans say: "I am proud of the fact that I was raised in a peaceful, compatible polygamous household." It would be extremely false to classify a peaceful, happy polygamous marriage and family with the type of chief-polygamy cited above. Likewise it would be unjust to lump a wrangling, arguing polygamous group of co-wives with either of the two cited above. It is a true and unfortunate fact that the majority of polygamous unions in the area of our study classify themselves as "incompatible marriages," due often to reasons related to the economy. In all five villages there is at least one generally recognized "ideal" polygamous family. It is possible to set up four types of family groups in these villages based upon the general peacefulness and compatibility that exists in the parental union and family group. There are two types of monogamous family and two types of polygamous family: (1) incompatible monogamous, (2) compatible monogamous, (3) incompatible polygamous, and (4) compatible polygamous.

### Objections to Polygamy

If we admit that all polygamous unions and families are not made of the same stuff, just as all monogamous-based families are not of the same moral quality, we are brought back to the question: Should some cases of polygamy be admited to the church and others not? This is the question that the ecclesiastical authorities of churches ask themselves and they will continue to legislate the matter. Our purpose here is not to plead for one decision or another but to examine some of the implications of polygamous unions in the light of Christian thought.

The Christian church bases its objection to polygamy upon the Scriptures. However, on the level where these anti-polygamous decisions are made, it is commonly assumed that the New Testament is explicitly clear on the subject. This is not the case. The New Testament is conspicuously unconcerned with the subject. There is ample historical evidence to show that monogamy was the accepted and honored form of marriage among both Jews and Gentiles in the time of Jesus. Geoffrey Parrinder states in his study of polygamy:[4]

> Much of the teaching of Jesus on moral questions seems to have been given in answer to queries brought to him, on matters that were keenly debated at that time: for example, the penalty of stoning for adultery, divorce, the payment of taxes, the greatest law.
>
> Now it is very significant, and a point often overlooked, that there is no record of a question about whether a man might, in any circumstances, take a second wife. If there had been any doubt at all about whether a serious-minded Jew could have several wives, we should very probably have some reference to it in the Gospels or the Epistles. This would certainly have been preserved by the early Christian communities, if the problem had ever arisen in their own moral life. The absence of a negative command against polygamy, in the New Testament, is therefore very significant, in exactly the opposite direction to that which is commonly and rashly assumed. It shows that the question no longer arose among the Jewish or Gentile communities to whom the gospel was addressed.

If it can be accepted that the teachings of Jesus and the apostles took place among monogamous people where polygamy was not common enough to be in the minds of the people, we may ask if the New Testament has nothing to say on this subject. The answer, of course, is that the New Testament teaching regarding marriage and the family are fundamental attitudes which are often incompatible with polygamous unions as we know them. Jesus exalted sexual morality, and the permanence of the marriage union (Mark 10: 2-12). Paul exhorted wives to obey their husbands, but also placed a responsibility on the husband to love his wife. The emphasis in the Gospels upon a marriage between two people is a

> . . . quotation from Genesis given in the Gospels, as also in the Epistles, (which) is from the Greek Septuagint translation of the Old Testament. It is even stronger than the original in Genesis, where the words "the twain" did not occur. The Gospel still further reinforces this by adding, "So that they are no more twain, but one flesh."
>
> If, then, a man cannot leave his wife, it is obvious that Jesus would not countenance a man's taking a second wife. This would be sheer adultery. The "one flesh" makes this quite clear. It is not permissible to have two marriage contracts at once, "two flesh." Nor can the unity of man and wife be broken up by the admission of a concubine.

[4] Parrinder, Geoffrey: *The Bible and Polygamy*, S.P.C.K.: London, 1950, p. 43.

"They are no more two, but one flesh," excludes a third party.[5]

Another serious objection to polygamy which should be presented is suggested in the Golden Rule. Now polygamy is the *ideal* form of marriage in the villages investigated in this study; over 90 percent of the men in Lolo replied that they preferred a polygamous marriage. This means that the majority of men in these areas are monogamous by circumstance and not by choice. In these villages we have shown that only slightly more than one-third of the men presently have plural wives. Between one-half and two-thirds of the men are not being able to realize their ideal. Polygamy as an ideal form of marriage union if conceived as permanent is an *impossibility*. Only under the most rare circumstances would it be possible for every man to have at least two wives. Since ideal polygamy is not practicable and the available women go to the men with the money to pay for them, many young men are therefore driven to seek relations with prostitutes and to be late in marriage, and to spend long frustrating years attempting to amass the necessary wealth to afford a wife. During this process a man is tempted to steal, usually contracts venereal disease, and often becomes quite cynical desiring to have wealth more than anything else. It is only natural that such a person would believe that adequate wealth would purchase all kinds of happiness.

The objection may be raised here that in most societies there are things which cannot be shared equally. The American executive position may be cited as a parallel in our own society. Other things such as driving Cadillacs, owning a suburban home, having a swimming pool, may be indicated as desired aspects of American life which are wanted by the majority but of nearly impossible realization. We may certainly admit to the truth of this and show the frustrating effects upon our society due to the fact that the *personal failure* is a resultant institution which fills psychopathic wards, amusement escapes, crime and even evangelistic halls. However, the parallel is not complete due to the fact that the marriage union is a universal form basically necessary for the continuation of mankind.

Polygamy as it is today in the eastern Cameroun is an open attempt at female monopoly and is incompatible with the Golden Rule. Any people who idealize and live in expectation of that which is unrealizable and impossible are thereby imposing serious strain on the structure of their society. This is particularly true when it concerns something as expectable as is the marriage union and the family.

We may sum up the past two sections now by saying that polygamy varies and in some cases it is concerned for the family welfare and in others, just as in many cases of monogamy, it has no such concern. We are also safe in saying that there are basic attitudes in the New Testament which are contrary to the principle of polygamous unions when this is an ideal form of marriage for the majority of men. We may go further and question whether or not a Christian conception of marriage partnership would allow the continuation of polygamy. Polygamy dies out where the status of the woman is raised and where the woman becomes highly conscious of her own personality and aware of marriage as a sharing reciprocal relation rather than a servient relationship. It is safe to say that modern Africa cannot make the

[5] *Ibid.*, p. 48.

adaptation to the modern world without allowing and favoring the changed status of its women. Consequently, by moving toward an identification with the other countries of the industrialized world, African societies are of necessity moving toward monogamy. Independence for African nations will bring women into positions and responsibilities which they never knew under colonial administrations. These adjustments will unquestionably create conditions unfavorable to "buying wives."

## Approach to the Solution

Having described the nature of polygamy in one large area of the Cameroun and having stated that polygamy is an institutionalized form of wealth today, we are now ready to outline how this problem may be faced by the Christian church. In the first place, for the church to preach against polygamy is simply going at the matter backwards. Legislating against it by church councils, while at the same time encouraging the economic build-up of the churches, creates a contradiction which the Africans in the area do not comprehend. The orientation of Christian missions is definitely cast in a financial mold which it brings from its home churches and ecclesiastical heritage, in which self-propagation means often that the local church needs to pay the catechist or pastor and keep books. This is to the missionary a mere step which the indigenes must learn if they are to be a self-supporting church. Actually many native churches would be self-supporting if missionaries had not made such an issue of it and caused it to become a front line aspect of the missionizing movement. European backgrounds with money-conscious values and organizations have in effect often impressed native groups that upon the financial handling of the church depends everything else. Consequently the conceptualization of the church has often been in the natives' mind a kind of primitive bank in which everyone is a member of the board. There is probably nothing in the native churches of the Cameroun today which merits one tenth of the time taken up in budgets and money matters. As one well educated Cameroun pastor put it, "All the work of the church depends upon money, and if we don't make our budget we are weak and unable to work."

The native church in the Cameroun feels a dilemma in that money is felt to be so terribly necessary for the ongoing of the church, but those who can often contribute most (the polygamous men) are excluded from its membership. It is as though General Motors Company were told to increase its total output of automobiles, but also to send its employees on vacation. The African is not entirely responsible for the situation in which he finds himself. Neither is he entirely free from responsibility for it. Christian mission churches are over-concerned with the idea of membership which no doubt helps to assess increase and decrease and provides figures for the home board. A first step in a Christian solution to the problem in the eastern Cameroun would be to reconsider the idea of church membership and to embrace a fellowship of families without consideration for the status of the marriage union. As it is presently, the father of the family is forced to be an outsider. The source of authority is excluded. The family takes on a feeling of separation from the one they really honor, the father. Anywhere in the Cameroun where a person is asked if X is a Christian, the reply is Yes, or No; and if No the qualification is frequently added that X is a polygamist. The church in the Cameroun is by and large a female church where the man who needs the teaching of the church is felt unwanted. However, there are certain basic attitudes shared by the men which will not be affected by the church as long as the church communicates itself along the artificial lines of "membership." Consequently the church has no choice but to work in reverse and tell women (who have little choice or voice in the matter) that polygamy is wrong.

If the church does not want to re-adjust its lines of communication and prefers to be based upon membership, then the church will have to get out of its narrow confinements and address itself to the males in other ways. It may hold men's institutes, sponsor gatherings for men outside of the church atmosphere, and through the personal contact of its present male constituency attempt to bring about a changed attitude toward money and wealth. Where polygamy is a sign of status, it is sometimes possible to take on a new sign which serves the old purpose. Cement houses in the villages of the Bulu tribe are beginning to receive the recognition formerly granted to polygamists only. Careful financial arrangement may enable male Christians among the Kaka to build such houses and the prestige accorded to the polygamist only may be shifted to the owners of cement houses. The church could help by advising Christian men on how to economize and to plan their expenditures.

The status of women must be visibly changed. This is being started through education, but here again we cannot assist present adults by thinking always of people of a generation or two in the future. Christian men and women who have proven that marital fidelity produces more children today than unfaithful polygamy or monogamy, will continue to be a strong influence for the cause of Christianity.

**Reorientation of Values**

Most fundamental of all perhaps is the necessity for Christian village men to conceptualize their wives as partners in a permanent marriage concerned for the welfare of their families. In order to do this, it is absolutely necessary that these men change their attitude toward work. In spite of the fact that they are ridiculed, they must not demand of their wives more than they are willing to do themselves. Here is precisely one of the greatest problems. Christian missions have created the specialized class of African pastors who see themselves as professional men who do not work in gardens if at all possible to avoid it. Seminaries have failed to take into sufficient account the social reality of African life. It may be necessary that the Cameroun seminary student be taught to appreciate a new meaning of physical labor and actually be taught to work with his hands as an integral part of his training. This would mean that his teachers, Europeans and Africans, would also have to participate. Pastoral theology is not enough. If the African pastor conceives of himself as above work, he will be at a loss to bring about any fundamental change in the male attitude toward work.

A great danger for the Christian church which concerns the matter of polygamy is that the church gives the impression that a monogamous marriage is automatically good. The African knows that this is not necessarily so. In fact he knows that monogamous marriages are sometimes completely impracticable.

For instance, a village or clan chief with heavy responsibilities and a constant flow of visitors to feed would not be able to perform his expected duties with one wife. If he tried, his wife would soon die of overwork. Polygamy cannot be viewed from European labor class and economic points of view.

There can be no doubt that two factors would automatically lead toward monogamy: male and female equality of rights with mutual respect, and the existence of a complex class system where hired laborers were available. As for the first of these, the Christian church may have a great deal to say. The second matter is a problem of cultural change which fortunately or unfortunately may come eventually. Probably the thing which will have the greatest practical influence in the Cameroun for some years to come will be the fact that many Christian men have taken on a new idea of womanhood and marital fidelity and this has in turn often been rewarded by numerous offspring. These outward signs will change with the time. The Christian message must continue to seek in the African's heart and in identification *with him* the answers to the deeper longings that find their outlets in polygamy. I suggest one of these here because of the fact that Christianity can effectively work in this sphere. I refer to it as "transformed symbolism." The argument is essentially that the African feels a compulsion to represent in tangible form his innermost feelings. That which is purely symbolic to Europeans the African fills with a meaning and action. The Christian sacrament of the communion cannot be equated for the European and African. To the latter the Roman Catholic doctrine of transubstantiation is real and meaningful. The Protestant view is given lip service but is not satisfying to the heart. It would take us too far afield to follow up this discussion in detail. However, it has its outworkings in the matter of marriage and the family, wealth, and polygamy. Children, crops, gardens, and wives are all aspects of the traditional African's compulsion for a visible sign to mark what he believes. They are the tangible living representations which guarantee for him the meaning of life. Life is an aspect of power. All that polygamy ideally produces are vivid signs of the presence of this power. Now we have come to the core of this longing. This deepseated emotion, which silently lies hidden in the heart beckoning and calling, is a desire for power. The possession of force is the possession of being and vice versa. Everything in the African's life partakes in this power and life is conceived as a gamble for the gain or loss of power. One need only listen to the prayers of the African Christian to witness the extent to which this concept of power is the truly motivating aspect of his life. Life needs to be continually reinforced through the addition of power, by the increase of life. All life is lived in a dynamic drive for power, for human vitality. It affirms this life and finds it totally inconsistent with some aspects of the Christian message aimed at renouncing life. All in this life exists to serve man and to affirm his living presence. Is there little wonder, then, that a living compulsion moves the African toward all those outward symbols of such a world outlook? The Christian songs that are choices among the people of this study are ones which affirm this life or look forward to the eternal life which is a blessed continuation of this life. Christ has come "that they might have life, and that they might have it more abundantly."

It is absolutely necessary that Christianity not confuse this existence in power of the African with European ideas of power. This is not power as an idea. It is not just power as a lust for submitting others to one's will. The *ddeti* of the Kaka is a dynamic force in all existence which one must partake of and be a part of in order that life may be guaranteed. This power naturally plays its role now as it mingles with political ideas and nationalism. It was all-important at earlier times in war. It is the nucleus of medicine, of fetishism, of magic. It is the essence of the African's concept of God. It makes even the most stubborn western forms of Christianity take on an African feeling. It is the generating principle behind ancestor worship and kinship bonds, social structure and village life. African Christianity, as it matures, comes back to it and makes it serve its task of revealing the meaning of life.

The insipid nature of much of the African's Christianity stems from the fact that he joins a church and relies upon this association (church contagion) to place him nearer to the source of power. The step which is badly needed in the communication of the gospel to the African is that the presence of this power is realized in submission to the role of the humble servant to be filled with a power for service to others. This means the acceptance of a new and vital aspect of this dynamism which the African hopes for. It means that the tangible symbols of its presence must be seen. It is for this reason that the African believes when he sees and one act speaks more than a thousand words.

*William D. Reyburn*

# Kaka Kinship, Sex, and Adultery

A DETAILED description of Kaka kinship system and the socially regulated behavior that is built into it would require more space than would be justified here. Hence I will attempt to develop only those points in Kaka kinship and social behavior which have a bearing upon sexual mores. It is hoped that a review of these factors will structure for us the context from which the Kaka Christians and non-Christians derive their sexual codes which are so divergent from our own.

In stating these matters I wish to remark that in attempting to understand Kaka sexual values from the kin and social system I am not hereby pleading for the justification of such behavior nor for the defense of the Kaka traditional ways of thinking about such things. Evangelization of an African tribe is very much tied up with sexual behavior. This is as true to state as the remark that frontier evangelization in the western U.S. in the last century was involved in horses, six-guns, agriculture, and law enforcement. The fact that church sessions are swamped with adultery palavers in African communities is sufficient reason to warrant an attempt to understand the foundations of sexual values in African societies.

---

**Reprinted from Vol. 5, No. 1 (1958), pp. 1-21. This paper was originally prepared for a mission meeting and was not written with PRACTICAL ANTHROPOLOGY directly in mind. This accounts for its question-and-answer form.**

While the data here are drawn from personal investigations among the Kaka of the Eastern Cameroun, it should not be thought that the Bulu and Basa are radically different. In a general way the systems, attitudes, and values are essentially similar. The details will vary. Any missionary can and should investigate these subjects for his own comprehension of his work. In order to assist missionaries who care to follow up these leads among the tribal peoples among whom they work, I have set this paper out in the form of a series of questions and answers.

One should be cautioned on two points, however. First, the questions that I have written are too generally stated to be of value to ask an African. However, within the replies following each question there will be found material which will be suitable for more specific questioning. Also, questions should be addressed to people who are sure where you stand. If the informant feels that you are out to trap him, his replies will be nothing more than a defense for himself. There is no substitute for confidence and close rapport. Christians and non-Christians, young and old, male and female should be questioned. If a missionary has lived with a people for a number of years and suddenly appears to become inquisitive about many aspects of the African's private life, it may be resented and the African will politely sidestep each question. The best informant is one who is convinced that the missionary is respectfully attempting to *learn* the African way of doing things.

## 1. What is the largest socially cohesive group to which every Kaka individual belongs?

The clan. Every Kaka person belongs to a patriclan which is made up of all the people who issue from a common legendary male ancestor. Descent is reckoned through the male line only. Hence each person, male or female, belongs to the clan (*mbo*) of his father. The clan is an exogamous group, meaning that no man or woman of the same clan may intermarry. Furthermore, premarital and extramarital sex relations between members of the same clan are considered incestuous and the offenders subject to supernatural punishment. The clan often coincides with the village, but in many cases a clan is large and is spread over a number of villages. It is not infrequent that struggles for clan leadership cause one portion of a clan to split into several subclans. These continue to practice clan exogamy and other clan taboos and rituals. The strength of a clan depends upon its population and wealth. It is the desire of each clan to be the largest dominating force among many clans.

In the clan, be it Bulu, Basa, or Kaka, one regards all the other people in the clan as being related to himself, and he calls them by classificatory kin terms. His real father and father's brothers and other men of his father's generation are all "fathers." His grandfather and grandfather's brothers are all "grandfathers." His cousins are all "brothers" and "sisters," and his nieces and nephews, along with his own offspring, are all "sons and daughters." His mother belongs to a different clan (that of her father) and in that clan he has many "mothers," since he extends this terms to cover all the female members of his mother's clan. Likewise among the Kaka, he calls all the women of his father's mother's clan "mother," and the same for the women of his mother's mother's clan.

## 2. What is a "family"?

In addition to being a member of a clan, a Kaka individual is born into a specific family group. However, "family" does not mean to an African what Europeans and Americans take it to mean to them. The lack of an equivalent term in the language of the South Cameroun for the European elementary family reflects the fact that the Africans do not conceive of the elementary family as being a valid concept. A Kaka belongs to a residence group (*ddité*, 'a common fireplace'). A lineage group within the clan forms a cluster of residences. There are brothers and their wives and offspring.

Looking at this lineage group from the viewpoint of a child, I see a cluster of houses in which are living my fathers and my brothers and my mothers. Since I am treated the same in any one of them and will be fed and helped or scolded alike at any one of these, there is little point in singling out "my family" as against "your family." Consequently, the residence group of the Kaka is a cooperative, sharing-common-authority residential group where the European idea of "family" is spread over and completely mixed into several elementary families. The residence group is a more personal one than the clan taken as a whole. While a person calls many men "father," he knows which is his real father and the behavior toward him differs from that of more removed "fathers." Likewise, the boys in one residence group have a stronger feeling as "brothers" than they do for all the other "brothers" in the other residence groups of the clan.

To summarize, then, the patriclan is a male descent group. It is like a club in which every child born belongs to his or her father's club. The rules of the club say that girls must go and live where their husbands' fathers' club men are. Also there are strict prohibitions against marriage between members of the same club, or even into the club of your mother or your two grandmothers. One classifies people in his clan roughly into four groups: grandfathers, fathers, brothers and sisters, and offspring.

### 3. What is the basis for authority in the clan and residence group and how is it structured?

The Kaka conceive of authority as an aspect of the male lineage. The greatest authority is the one who originated the clan. Consequently, each male ancestor receives his authority from his predecessor and passes it down through the lineage. It is because of this that the dead are literally more powerful and respected than the living. The oldest living male, unless he has become too senile to function, is the respected authority of the clan. The outstanding elderly leader of the largest clan in a village is normally the village chief. Wealth and numbers are the criteria for strength in the clan. Among the Kaka it is common for a village to include a half dozen clans. Bulu villages are commonly one clan only. The married women are, of course, outsiders and belong to clans other than their husbands'.

Authority may be transferred at the will of a chief who does not wish to pass it on to his incapable son. In this case the new chief accepts the members of the expiring chief's clan as his "orphans" and he thereby puts himself under great obligation to those people.

In a village consisting of several clans each has its own clan head man. These individuals form the group of notables who are present for discussion of village affairs with the village chief. A village chief may be much younger than his notables, but his authority rests not in his personality but in his relationship as heir of his father's lineage group. The power and authority in the ruling lineage does not cease unless another lineage becomes stronger and takes over by sheer weight of wealth and numbers.

The lines of respect within the residence group flow from the oldest males (grandfathers) down to fathers and on down to sons and finally to grandsons. A female has authority in the residence group as a paternal aunt. She functions as a "female father" in authority over her brother's children. Women and girls are on the bottom rung of the hierarchy and do not count in the general scheme of things as people with authority. However, a mother who comes from a large clan and residence group may call on the help of her fathers and brothers to assist her in exerting influence in her family.

It should be remarked that the real authority in the Kaka areas is the village chief. The "Chef de Canton" is an administration-linked position created by the whites. The success of the Chef de Canton depends upon his ability to secure the cooperation of the *real* village authorities, the village chiefs. It is still common for a village to put up a straw chief who will receive the abuse and probings of the administration. They value their native authority too much to expose him to the often crude and unwelcomed contacts with administrators engaged in such tasks as recruiting laborers, taking census, and collecting taxes.

### 4. What are the primary kin relations within the clan and residence group, and what are some of their socially established relations?

In the following discussion we will speak from the point of view of a male "I". Remember that I am of my father's clan. My mother belongs to a different clan.

*Grandparents.* As a child my relationship to grandparents is the most pleasant and most indulgent experience imaginable. I can get away with anything. If I break their dishes, they think I am the cutest little thing. If I cry, they bounce me on their knees and coo at me, and if I scream to the top of my voice, they merely laugh and howl with me. They will stop anything they are doing to get food for me, and if I have a long, heartbreaking experience to relate, the most tender, sympathizing hearts in all the world are my grandparents'. My paternal grandfather, I later come to learn, is the most feared and respected of all the men in my residence group, but since we have all learned to love him for his indulgence we continue as men to love him for his ability and old age. He will someday be joining the big grandfather in another world, and they will be strong to help our residence group. Someday I shall grow up to have the power of my grandfather.

*Fathers.* I have lots of fathers: my real father who says he bore me, and his brothers. They are the ones who teach me to hunt and fish and to make my way in the world. They instruct me about women, and they tell me the secrets of our clan. I never question their authority because they are the sons of my grandfather. Someday they will have his power. I have many other fathers. All the men in my clan who are of my father's generation I call "father," and "grandfather" those in the next older generation. These men are like real fathers, but they have their own residence groups and they are not quite so close as my real father and his brothers. Other men I call "father" are the husbands of my father's sisters and of my mother's sisters. You may wonder how I know to call all of these men "father." It is real easy; as a child I heard them all call me "my son." So I know which ones to call "my father."

*Mother.* Just as I have many "fathers," I also have many "mothers." First, there is my real mother who gave birth to me. Then there are all of her sisters. For all of the men whom I call "father" I likewise call their wives "mother." This includes the many wives of my father. While I call all of them "mother," I know that my heart is always on the side of just one when I hear them argue and fight; that's the one who bore me. My real mother gives me lots of "mothers" because I call all of the women of mother's clan by the term "mother." When I say "mother" to all of these women of many different ages, I don't really mean "mother of my residence group." It is just a way I have of showing respect for all the women of my mother's clan.

Sometime I may see a girl who is very pretty and want to have relations with her, but if I call that girl "mother" I would get sick in my stomach if I should think of her genitals. If I know one of these "mothers" is bathing in the river, there is something in my heart that causes me to turn my head and not see her, or I cross the river at some place where I won't see her. This is true also for all the girls and women in my maternal and paternal grandmother's clans. They all call me "son" and I call them "mother." My fathers have always told us that, if we had sex relations with a "mother," both the mother and the man would die an awful death and no medicine, not even the Christian's God, could prevent it.

Once one of my "fathers" dreamed of sleeping with one of his "mothers." In the morning he awoke with a fever and after he confessed what his spirit had done in the night he became terribly ill and in a few days was dead. My fathers use this story to remind us never to allow our spirits to stray toward "mothers." We hear that white people can marry nearly anyone except sisters and that they don't die. The fathers that come back from the cities tell how our tribe brothers in the cities are beginning to do like the whites. Maybe someday we will start trying the white man's ways in the villages, too. The Christian God may protect us like he does the whites.

*Brothers and sisters.* Just as I call every woman "mother" who calls me "son," so I call every boy "brother" and every girl "sister" who calls me by those terms. Speaking of people of my own generation, I make a distinction between all those born before and after me. So I am careful to recognize the difference between older and younger brothers and sisters. This is very important for us Kaka people because the wives of all my older brothers are "my wives" also. At least that is how I'm taught to call them. And since I call them "my wives" they call me "their husband." I can marry them if my older brother dies. However, for my younger brothers I call their wives "sisters-in-law" and can never look forward to marrying or being given one of these "sisters-in-law." All of the children of my generation in my clan are brothers and sisters to me. If I am ever in doubt about whether a certain boy or girl is a brother or sister, I merely stop to ask whether his father is a "father" to me, too. In mother's clan there are no brothers or sisters, however, just "mothers" and "fathers" (except for mother's brothers).

The closest relations I have are with my brothers. I look up with respect to older brothers because they stand closer to my father's authority than I do. I am likewise respected by my younger brothers.

As for my sisters, it is not a question of authority. We have that same feeling for "sisters" that we do for "mothers." For instance, if some boys from another clan are joking with me about a sexual affair and my sister is present, I feel compelled to go and hide in the grass. My sister, too, will get up and leave. If we go to bathe after eight or ten years of age and there is a "sister" bathing, we will pass on and come back after she is gone. If I should be with girls who are not "mothers" or "sisters" and we would see two dogs copulating, the boys will point to it and laugh and try to get the girls in a similar mood. But if I should see such a thing while in the presence of a "mother" or "sister," I would feel embarrassed and would act as though I had never noticed the copulating dogs.

We know that the young white people kiss their sisters, but if such a thought makes you sick at your stomach, it must be best to avoid such close contact with a sister. There are many words in our language which signal a sexual connotation. When I speak around "mothers" and "sisters," I talk with guarded lips so that these words do not offend them and embarrass me.

*Uncles.* In a patrilineal society the main spot open for an uncle is mother's brother. In Kaka I call mother's brother *koko* and he calls me *taa.* Our relationship is a difficult thing for the mind of a white man to grasp. Here are some of the things maternal uncle and I do. I can go into his house and help myself to about anything he has and he doesn't say a word. If he buys a new bicycle, I will probably be the first to break it for him, but I won't have to pay for it. If I am hungry, I will go catch a chicken or goat belonging to maternal uncle and carry it off without saying "Please," "Thank you," "Hello," or "Goodbye." We feel that is just the way maternal uncles are. We children often say that God made two good people in the world, grandpa, who is so indulgent, and maternal uncle, who is so naive.

Another aspect of the maternal uncle complex is that I call his wife "my wife" and she, of course, calls me "my husband," just like she calls her husband, my uncle. This is about like the wives of my older brothers, but in the case of this "wife" I can have free sexual access to her while maternal uncle is alive. If I am at maternal uncle's house and "my wife" (maternal uncle's wife) is not too busy, we get together on uncle's bed. If uncle comes home while we are engaged, I merely call out, "It's sister's son," (*taa*), and he acts as though he doesn't know what is going on inside. When I have finished with uncle's good wife, I may pick up a chicken in the yard and amble back home. When maternal uncle sells his tobacco, all of his sister's sons really become pests, for we go sit down at his house and joke with him about his wealth. Finally he goes to my father and gives him some money. Then we leave him alone until we hear he has gotten hold of some more cash. Soon we do it all over again.

However, custom declares that I pay my uncle in certain cases, too. If I kill an animal, the whole front quarter belongs to maternal uncle, and if he doesn't get it there will be trouble afoot. If maternal uncle kills an animal, sister's son gets the head. Since there are many maternal uncles with still more *táa,* who is the one to get the meat? Every *koko* has his favorite sisters' sons, and certain nephews have favorite uncles. However, the first nephew or uncle to appear may often be the recipient of the meat. It is for this reason that we nephews always make it a point to know what maternal uncle is up to. If I suffer a wound which disables me in the slightest, I am obligated to make a payment to my maternal uncle. If he is wounded, he must pay the father of one of his sister's sons, or the nephew himself if the latter is an adult. If my child dies, I must pay that child's maternal uncle for the death. (That is, my wife's brothers.) I pay also to my maternal uncle if I am ill, and he pays his sister's son if he is ill. If I go to prison, I pay him, or if he goes, he pays me. A sister's son may inherit the wives of his maternal uncle upon his death. However, the maternal uncle's younger brothers have first choice. If there are no younger brothers, the sisters' sons are the next in line. (The woman has considerable freedom to choose for herself.)

You may ask why all this reciprocity between sister's child and maternal uncle. We Kaka see it like this. First, the marriage relationship surrenders the girl's productivity to another clan. This girl's brothers do not wish it to be entirely a onesided affair. Hence her brother retains an economic relation with her sister's offspring. While a male from another clan has paid for the productive rights (the dowry), the woman's brothers keep a secondary utilitarian interest in the offspring. Under the Kaka life of the hunt, the meat which a sister's son provides for uncle is considerably more than the older maternal uncle provides for the nephew. Consequently, the death, illness, imprisonment, or other indisposition of a nephew means less meat supply for his maternal uncle. Therefore a financial settlement is felt to be in order.

To make the distinction between maternal uncle's wife (who is not of my mother's clan) and her offspring who are in my mother's clan, it follows that "my wife's" daughter turns out to be "my mother." Likewise, maternal uncle's son is also called *koko,* and his wife is "my wife," while his daughter is again "my mother." In English this first "mother" would be my first cousin and the second "mother" a second cousin (or first cousin once removed).

*Wife.* The people whom I call "my wife" (they call me "my husband") are: (1) maternal uncle's wife of wives, (2) the wives of my older brother, and (3) my wife's younger sisters. Maternal uncle's wife is sort of a self-service kind of a neighbor. However, I am not free to have promiscuous relations with my older brothers' wives. I may have relations with my wife's younger sisters, but after these are married this is less frequent. They are potentially "wives" for me, since I may marry one or more of them after I marry the first. For this reason it is advisable to marry an older sister always so that you can get the younger ones, too, later on. One cannot marry the older sisters of one's wife. If my first wife does not bear children, her family is obligated to provide another "sister" without the additional payment of dowry.

The relation of husband and wives is complex, and we won't discuss it here except as this relation bears upon the sexual code.

*Fathers- and mothers-in-law.* My father- and mother-in-law represent two highly respected symbols for me. Not only do I pay them for the productivity rights of their daughter, but I will continue throughout their lifetime to pay in cash and kind if I am satisfied with my wife as producer of children and garden stuff. I shall never enter the sleeping quarters of my parents-in-law. This spot I hold to be holy. If I should ever trespass here, I might behold the sex act which brought forth my wife, and this would be against all proper thought and conduct. Because I respect my in-laws, I will not use their names in conversation nor address them as anything other than the respected term *ki.* If I have a relative with the same name as my in-laws, I will pay at the wedding for the right to speak this name. In this way my in-laws will know that I am not being disrespectful if he or she should overhear me pronouncing his or her name.

Just as I avoid all sexual symbolism with my "mother" and "sister" kin, so I do the same with in-laws. Furthermore, I am not free to joke with them like I do with mother's brother. When I meet an in-law my face is long and sad, reflecting my deepest humility and highest respect. My mother- and father-in-law are not my only such relative. My wife's older sisters are also called *ki* and merit the same kind of preferential respect.

**5. How is the sexual orientation of a Kaka tribesman determined by his kinship system?**

Within the kinship system there are two sets of females: those who are considered *sisters* and *mothers* (the incest block), and the *wife* group who are potential spouses (the sex contact block). Consequently, the Kaka makes a fundamental separation between this incest group and the available or potentially available set on the basis of linguistic symbols. The word *nyari* 'wife', which includes maternal uncle's wife or wives, my wife's younger sisters, and my older brothers' wives, signals to me a potential sex contact, and the behavior that follows is according to the expected signal. "Sister" and "mother" are terms which signal "incest, stop, on guard, death to the offender, etc."

The symbolism associated with both these categories builds itself into a full-blown world of symbolic reality that is transformed into real behavior. The result of having linguistic symbols to mark off sexual behavior is very neat and precise as long as the old kin groups remain in contact and as long as outside influences do not intervene. This means merely that a Kaka depends upon language signals to provide for his primary clues as to how he should or should not behave as regards the opposite sex.

**6. What does this imply as to non-kinship sexual attitudes?**

It implies that one knows how to behave sexually within the kin system. This system reveals that the outer limits (maternal uncle's wife, wives of older brothers, etc.) of the kin group are the starting point for increased sexual interest which begins by the signal "my wife." Every other female who is not a mother or sister (or grandmother or female father, i.e. father's sister) is a potential spouse, although all of these outside women do not carry the kin term of "my wife." The African has a polar concept of sex (not frigid as an iceberg). At one pole he lumps together the incest block and closes his thought to it. At the other pole is an open accessible female world, all of whom are potential wives. It is into this world he moves with sexual aggression which is as positive at this pole as it is negative at the other.

**7. Does the kinship orientation of sexual behavior explain the Kaka sexual attitudes?**

It does to a large extent. At least it sets the position from which he views sex, i.e. the incest block vs. the rest of the female world. The one is associated with supernatural punishment, while the other attains to life's greatest good — productivity and continuation of the male lineage, which is his greatest moral obligation to the fathers of the clan.

**8. How do premarital sex relations affect extramarital ones?**

When a girl reaches puberty or near puberty, the women begin to remind her that her nubile state is given her to produce children. At her first sex contact at puberty the father will be wounded in the hunt or at his garden work. This is a signal for him to inquire as to his daughter's sex relations. If the girl admits having had a contact (there is no punishment or disgrace connected with it, and hence no reason to conceal it), the father will collect a "defloweration" charge from the boy. This means that the girl is now available for dowry payment. If a dowry is paid, the father of the future groom requests that the girl be protected from further sex contacts. If the girl's marriage is not begun at this time, she is free to indulge in sexual promiscuity as often and with as many males as she chooses.

The reason for requesting that a future bride not be allowed promiscuity is that a partial dowry payment has been made, and if the girl becomes pregnant, there will be a struggle over the ownership of the child. During this period of open or hidden promiscuity (hidden somewhat if a partial dowry has been paid) a girl picks up dozens of suitors. These males never relinguish their claims on the girl even after marriage. Consequently, her premarital suitors often continue to seek relations after marriage.

**9. What does a Kaka understand in the term adultery?**

Sex contacts are defined according to the persons involved. Relations between an individual and maternal uncle's wife are simply "sex relations." This is considered about on the level of paying a social call. Premarital relations, called *bindi,* is an act which young people are expected to indulge in. It is the way in which girls prepare themselves for the ends to which a woman has been born, to produce children. Extramarital relations called *wandja* is a complex of its own with no exact equivalent in Euro-American societies.

*Wandja* is like a game in which I win a *ko-mbe* 'comrade', much to my delight and to his disgust. If I have sex relations with Mvondo's wife Mata, then I get to call Mata my *wandja* 'mistress', and Mvondo has to call me his *ko-mbe* 'comrade'. It is the desire of most men to be able to call as many women as possible "mistress" and thus to be called "comrade" by as many men as possible. However, to become a comrade I must pay a "fine" for getting a man's wife as my mistress. Once she is my mistress, she is under obligation to feed me if I am hungry and to take care of me when I pass through her village. I, in turn, am expected to present gifts to my mistress. A woman wants to become a mistress, as she will receive gifts from many men in this way. None of these acts are understood in the same way missionaries take the term adultery. The Kaka concept of incest is much more serious than the Christian idea of adulterous unions. In other words, there simply is no exact equivalent.

**10. Can the idea of wandja serve as an equivalent for adultery in the Euro-American sense of the word?**

It is true that *wandja* is an offense to the husband of the adulterous female. However, it is not so because the wife has broken the "sacred vows of marriage," nor is it because a man would suspect the paternity of his wife's offspring. The offense is in the thought of having been forced into the comrade relation which gives the adulterous male a position of superior social prestige. Also important is the fact that an adulterous woman implies that her husband is less potent than some other male. This is a bitter bit of ridicule which no Kaka man can easily take. Consequently, his reputation as a sire of offspring is belittled in the eyes of the other village women and his chances of gaining mistresses for himself are crippled. It often results in the man taking his wife and family and moving from the village. A further factor is that of the food relation between a man and his mistress. If a husband's meat from the hunt is going to feed his adulterous comrade, he himself will suffer and such meat will injure his chances in the hunt as well as his medicine for the traps.

### 11. Who is actually wronged in a wandja relation?

The answer again is the economic one. The rights of ownership for the purpose of production paid via the dowry is the thing which is wronged. No person as such is wronged. If the adulterous wife bears a child, the paternity of the child is never a question. It is ownership that counts. The owner of the child is the one who has paid the dowry. If no dowry has been paid, the offspring belongs to the mother's father's brothers or some other male relative.

### 12. How important is the woman's attitude in adulterous unions?

Younger and middle-aged women encourage adulterous unions by ridiculing men as impotent if they do not make sexual advances. It is common for a group of women to mock a man and jest with him ridiculing the size of his genitalia. The natural defense of the male is to subdue one of the women and convince her or them that he is equally as potent as the other men of the village.

### 13. What is the symbolism of sex dreams?

The incestuous dream is often a foreboding of death. There are dozens of other dreams among the Kaka which are interpreted as omens of evil luck and death. However, there is one dream which can issue only in the greatest of all good fortune: *extramarital sex relations.*

### 14. How do Kaka Christians rate adultery in their moral concept of right and wrong?

First of all, the greatest wrong is incest, the stinginess within the residence group, and then theft. *Wandja* or adultery is a wrong against the dowry, but since it is an act into which two agreeing parties enter, it is not looked upon as harmful to any party on the order in which incest, stinginess, and theft are.

### 15. Why is there such a moral gulf between incest and wandja?

Simply because incest violates religious values, the sanctity of the clan and residence group, and is punishable by the spirits of the dead, while *wandja* is a misuse of ownership rights which can always be righted by payment in cash or kind. The spirits cannot be satisfied with money payment because they are the supernatural defenders of the holiness of the tribe or clan.

### 16. How does polygyny figure in the sexual foundations of the Kaka?

First, a man who stands to inherit wives from his older brothers or his maternal uncle is likely to become a polygynist. Polygyny is dominated by economic interests. We discuss three kinds here. (1) Chief polygyny is the possession of plural wives in order to feed and care for the large number of notables who are necessary for handling village affairs. (2) Fonctionnaire polygyny is an institution developed by the French administration by adding to the salary of government employees for each of their children. This is the reflection of the economic bent of polygyny. (3) Ordinary polygyny or village polygyny is the possession of plural wives in order to provide the work force necessary to keep up large gardens, tobacco, coffee, and cocoa farms. Polygyny is the "desired" form of marriage among the Kaka. At Mindourou, the oldest center of Protestant influence in the subdivision of Batouri, one third of the husbands have two or more wives. Fonctionnaire polygyny is doing the greatest moral harm to the Christian efforts of the South Cameroun.

Polygyny should be considered primarily from its economic position. In this way a woman may be thought of as a bond or stock. (1) There is always full return on the cash investment. (2) The woman produces steady dividends in the form of children and labor. (3) If the woman is in default (no children), another will be given in her place. Polygyny is not primarily related to sexual matters. However, some women prefer to be co-wives as they will have less sex contact from the same man in this way.

**17. Is the dowry related to sexual values among the Kaka?**

The dowry is a financial or economic arrangement between two clans or families in which the one group recompenses the other for the right to claim the offspring born into the marriage. The dowry (or lack of it) secures for the child his right to claim his legal position as a member of his father's or mother's clan. In a patrilineal society he naturally belongs to his father's clan, provided, of course, his father has him through dowry rights of clan possession. Otherwise he is the property (member) of his mother's clan. Hence the dowry establishes clan rights and is not concerned with sex behavior as such.

**18. Is there no end in sight for the dowry?**

The dowry will last probably as long as the clan does because they are integrally related. The dowry is a woman's pride. If women had independent careers and educational opportunities, they would not feel the need of the dowry. However, the desire of some pastors to do away with the dowry for their children's marriage must assume two basic considerations. (1) That the establishment of clan identity is no longer important and functional. (2) That the girl involved is sufficiently independent and satisfied with her status in the world that other females cannot bring ridicule pressure upon her. The pastors who make these assumptions often fail in the second requirement. The women of the Cameroun do not have economic and social status of sufficient ranking to free themselves from the stigma of "dowrylessness."

**19. Christians often have huge families which are the envy of non-Christians. Does this mean they have been given God's special blessing for becoming Christians?**

I do not believe that God blesses fourteen or fifteen children on a poor pastor or catechist just because he has become a Christian, especially in view of the fact that the mother may be neurotic with frequent childbirth and the father, living on a small salary, is unable to feed, clothe, and educate the offspring. This problem occurs everywhere throughout the Christian world where people have been accustomed to having free extramarital relations and then become conjugally faithful after becoming Christians. Rather than blaming or crediting God for rewarding a Christian for what he is normally expected to do anyway, one can expect that the faithfulness of man to wife and vice versa prevents the malfunction of organs through venereal infections and allows the wife to become pregnant more readily. Also important is the fact that the husband is more likely to be seeking relations from his own wife during her fertile period, whereas before he may have been indulging in extramarital relations at the time when his wife could have conceived.

**20. The transitional life among the Kaka has produced many changes. What is the nature of some of these?**

(1) The loss of former moral supporting beliefs. The Kaka, like many other African tribes, have, through European contacts, questioned some of their strongest moral linking beliefs. The idea that incest would result in immediate death is a very rigid belief which snaps when too much pressure is brought to bear on it. The witness of Christianity is often only a one-sided communication in which the new symbols and the new life are readily accepted. Those who are accepting the new life are readily accepted. Those who are accepting the new *cannot* continue to hold on to the old. Consequently, unless there is a filling of the old moral support, the tendency to be a Christian with a crumpled moral life is the result. Many African Christians are capable of the transition to Christianity while others merely find the transition a happy escape from an older order which wore heavy on their conscience. A truly converted African may find no inner weakening; on the contrary, the Christian life is apt to provide him with a renewed spiritual energy which has deep moral ramifications. However, the loss of old moral supports creates new problems for Christian as well as non-Christian. Often the Christian, while having made a successful adaptation to Christian standards, simply has no precedent or tradition for coping with newly developed situations.

(2) The economic base that is replacing the kin group orientation. Formerly when one's entire universe was the village or clan there were, as indicated here, strong orientations toward the economic and ownership aspects of life. As people have come out of the village and gone into education and work they have carried these orientations with them. The kin group direction is not possible where one is disassociated from that group. The Kaka have learned that the only way to have recognition from the whites has been to simulate as nearly as possible the white man's standard of living. Money is required to do this, a great deal of money. Consequently, many Kaka impress the whites as having an abnormal lust for money and material goods. The payments which are exchanged between *taa* and *koko* continue in force today even where *taa* and *koko* are living separately and engaged in professions. In the village the payments are greater in cash due to the decrease in meat supply and the increased desire for European goods.

**21. Can the mission help the African church in such problems as sex and adultery?**

In the first place, Christianity among the Kaka (peoples of the Southern Cameroun) must not be envisioned in the Euro-American family setting. The problem for Christianity among the Kaka people is the establishment of a Christian patrilineal society and the Christianization of the residence group and clan. If the only way in which Christianity can be implanted is to supplant the patrilineal clan with some form of European society, then Christianity is nothing more than an elaboration of our Western ideas and forms of life.

The Kaka view of sex, kinship, and adultery is undergoing change. Part of this transition is stimulated by Christian and part by non-Christian sources. These elements are working directly against each other. Sexual perversions, prostitution, and other institutions are making themselves felt right along with endeavors to maintain standards of conduct which have constituted the central stream of Christian tradition. In this conflicting picture of multiple stresses, the Kaka are sure only within the familiar direction of the residence group and clan. Consequently, a Christianity which does not make itself intelligible on familiar grounds runs the chance of becoming irrelevant.

An example of how such relevancy can be established is the case of the African concept of productivity. The African is oriented toward productivity on the basis of what constitutes the *good life*. As long as productivity leads to the good, then all things associated with productivity are good. This is in essence how a Kaka philosopher might state the case. Consequently, premarital relations, extramarital relations, extreme sexual indulgence, plurality of wives, and many children are all aspects of the good life. The Christian does not and need not give up entirely this African view of the good. However, as a Christian he is expected to transform the value and associations of productivity. This transformation does not come simply by becoming a church member.

There needs to be a joint effort of African Christian leaders and missionaries to examine these questions together so that the younger churches may be informed as to the biological bases of human productivity. However, in so doing it will be necessary for medical missionaries and other whites to remember that the high value which the African places on fertility and productivity arises from a moral obligation to his patrilineal society in which man is expected to maintain the continuation of his lineage. This obligation is to him close to the deepest moral springs of his being. The mechanization of biological facts must be woven into a moral fabric in order that the African will benefit from these facts as he should. Such an exchange should go a long way to assist foreign missionaries to appreciate and sympathetically understand the African transitional viewpoint as well as to assist the young churches to face this changing life with a satisfactory set of values.

### 22. Looking at Kaka life from the side of Christianity, what is the major problem?

The conversion of the Kaka concept of God.[1] The Kaka concept of God is that of a spider, *Ndjambie,* who before the coming of Christianity quietly spun the heavens and kept the stars and clouds in their place. Since Christianity, *Ndjambie* has been asked to give up his patient impersonal toiling and to come down and intervene in the lives of men. *Ndjambie* is, according to Christian teaching, the God of history who thought ahead, conceived of an idea for many years in advance, worked out a plan and carried it out, and now, having made a huge personal sacrifice, remains intensely interested in man as an individual. This planning ahead for the coming of Christ,

---

[1] See William D. Reyburn, "The Transformation of God and the Conversion of Man," in this volume.

doing it, and being interested in man in a personal dimension does not in any way fit the personality of the unpredictable *Ndjambie,* who never had any plan, never could have brought forth a son, and who, of all things, was never interested in the ethical doings of anybody. *Ndjambie* (the spider) was not and is not predictable. He is part of the whole world, which has no history but which is punished along by accident and the cosmos. If *Ndjambie* had been interested in doing anything for anyone, the people might have felt like asking him for something. No one ever did.

As in the case of most nonliterate peoples, the idea of *Ndjambie* is tied up with the undifferentiated Cosmos. The Cosmos-God is the least personal any concept can become. Consequently, it is not surprising to see that *Ndjambie* is *Fate* and that man is utterly controlled by a cruel, unpredictable, and impersonal fate which is symbolized by *Ndjambie.*

The greatest transformation which can come in the life of any society is the conversion of their God to the personal Christian idea of God. The societal changes which will follow in the wake of such a conversion may be witnessed in the history of the Hebrews, who separated God from nature, or better, whose God through his self-revelation separated himself from the primitive nature idea imbedded in man's thinking.

This task is not accomplished by missionaries speaking and assuming that *Ndjambie* and God are equivalent substitutable symbols. They are not. For most, *Ndjambie* in 1957 is not the Christian God, even though the translated Scriptures call him by that name. The missionary who will make a contribution to the Christian transformation of Kaka ideas will first recognize the nonequivalence in our terms and then will make his teaching relevant and instructive to the Kaka world of reality.

*Robert C. Blaschke*

**Reprinted from Vol. 6, No. 5 (1959), pp. 193-197.**

# A Franco-African Cross-Cultural Clash

*French colonial policy and Administrators' lack of knowledge of the prerequisites for leadership in the Sabu tribe of Central Africa led to a clash between clans. Mr. Blaschke, who knew of the bitterness which had been built up between the groups, found out what had led up to it and here tells the story. Most interesting of all is the way in which the puppet chief appointed by the administration sought to defy the traditions of his fathers and acquire the real chiefly power which was in the control of the land.*

THE sun stole quickly into the eastern sky on the 8th day of March 1958. Omar Gisa, chief of the canton of Sena, head of the *kaasu* clan of the Sabu tribe, sat astride his white Arabian stallion. He moved cautiously with warriors (armed with bows and poisoned arrows) out of the forest into the clearing surrounding the small village of Sogote.

Simultaneously, almost as if it had been planned, the French administrative officer and a captain of the French police drove into the same clearing from the motor road.

The strained look fell from the warriors' faces. The fingers which had been clutching their bows now relaxed. The tension-charged air was dispelled as the white and black leaders approached each other. The Africans, though momentarily unhappy with the white man's intrusion, somehow sensed that this was a providential meeting which had prevented much bloodshed. This feeling was confirmed some months later when it was learned that Giba, the head of the *nesa* clan and chief of Sogote, had laid a trap which Omar Gisa, unknowingly, was about to spring. He had been about to call down upon himself and his men a barrage of poisoned arrows from the ring of Giba's warriors who were concealed in the forest which surrounded the village.

## Sabu History

In order to understand more fully the foregoing action, we must turn back the pages of Sabu history a bit. In Sena, during the days of preparation for this encounter, the most frequent answer to my question, "Why is the chief going to war?" was, "Giba and his people refuse to pay their taxes. Furthermore, they threatened that if Gisa and his son came to collect taxes, they would kill them!" It seemed strange to me that such a small group of people should rebel

---

Rev. Robert Blaschke has spent one term as a missionary with the Sudan Interior Mission in the Republic of Dahomey, West Africa. His formal study of anthropology includes the B.A. in anthropology from Wheaton College, and graduate study at the Kennedy School of Missions. He also has the B.D. from Gordon Divinity School.

against this French-empowered chief. In a sense, to refuse to pay taxes was a revolt against the French as well. I credited these people with more intelligence than to revolt against a modern-arms-supported power.

Further investigation, however, gave me new insight into why Giba had revolted. It was revealed that (1) the Sena chief had added 100 francs to the tax money already stipulated by the French official, (2) Gisa was demanding from Giba in addition his due tribute in food, etc., (3) Giba was desirous of splitting the already small canton in two, himself becoming a chief of canton along with Gisa, and (4) Gisa had tried to appropriate the land belonging to Giba. As I suspected, the fourth reason proved to be the most important.

A couple of months later a visit to Giba and his elders not only confirmed the truth of these four factors, but showed them to be quite secondary in light of the Sabu history that was to be unfolded to me.

Giba and his elders declared that their clan, called *nesa,* belongs to the royal family of the former Kingdom of Nikki. This clan had migrated from Nikki to Sogote, becoming the first inhabitants in this area. Many years later (no one knew how long) some strangers, possibly of the Kyensa tribe, came to salute Giba (the name for the *nesa* clan chieftaincy) and asked him for a grant of land. The property surrounding what is now Sena was given to them.

When troubles and difficulties arose at Sena, those involved were taken to Giba for a judgment. Even after a successful elephant hunt all the meat was brought directly to Giba for distribution. All important events, traditions, and ceremonies either originated or were performed at the seat of authority, the Sabu capital of Sogote.

Giba, realizing the inconvenience of the trek to Sogote for every little judgment, decided that he would inaugurate a chief in Sena. This chief would judge the minor cases. So, with much pomp, ceremony, and feasting, Giba named the first Sena chief. He was called Sena Gi of the *gaasu* clan. To impress me as to whose authority had priority, one of the elders inserted, "Until this day there have been seven Sena chiefs, but the number of Gibas there have been no one knows."

### Arrival of the French

Life among the Sabu continued in this manner until the French conquered them. The army installed an outpost consisting of several huts for an officer and several noncommissioned officers. The ruins may still be seen just north of Sogote. All liaison between the French and the Sabu tribe was directed through this center until the time when the grandfather of the present Sogote chief died.

None of the eligible candidates for this vacant chieftaincy understood French at that time. Since the chief of Sena had attended French public school in his youth and was known to the French, they told him whom they had chosen and gave him the authority to name the chief so designated by the government. This was outrageous so far as the people and their customs were concerned.

Orders to be carried out in Sabu country henceforth were issued by Gisa, a descendant of strangers in this land and a member of a socially inferior clan. From this time on the French used Gisa as a liaison. No longer was Giba the recognized authority as far as the French were concerned. Gisa was not slow in recognizing the potential in this French-given power. He did not hesitate to exploit its possibilities. Though this action of the colonial power caused no immediate overt reaction, it had nevertheless sown seeds of discontent and rebellion in the hearts of Giba and the *nesa* clan.

After nearly twenty-five ignominious years of the "head" paying tribute to the "tail," the "man" serving the "woman," and the superior groveling on the ground before the impetuous inferior (as the *nesa* clan regarded their relationship to the *kaasu* clan), this ripened ulcer of resentment burst forth into open rebellion. It just had been too much. This to which they had been subjected was criminal.[1]

In retrospect, we wonder how the French could have blundered so badly. Yet this was the result of their regular colonial policy with regard to the status of chiefs.

## French Colonial Policy and the Chief

The concept of *Liberté, Egalité, Fraternité,* which came out of the French Revolution, was applied not only to France but to her colonies as well. All the territories of the French Empire were considered one with the great "mother" soil, *la France*. The inhabitants in these far-off places were deemed full-fledged French citizens with all the inherent rights and privileges of the Frenchman born on French soil.

It was the desire of the French to develop an élite class, called *les évolués,* who would become the black Frenchmen through the acquisition of the French language and the assimilation of French culture. On the shoulders of *les évolués* would rest the privilege of carrying on and transmitting the great traditions of France to others in overseas territories.

In fact, the French conceived the eventual annihilation of the indigenous culture. Mair points out: "The tendency of the French administration to think in terms of grand general schemes applicable to a whole federation of colonies simultaneously militates equally against any recognition of local differences of culture."[2] In fact, any power or custom that could not lose its identity through assimilation into the French culture was either destroyed or irreparably weakened.

## Implementation of French Policy

In order to establish protectorates organized and operated by direct administration, certain drastic steps were necessary. Thompson and Adloff noted that the first step was to dissolve the ethnic basis of political formations, and to set up a territorial type grouping. Deliberate or not, this had been done by both the French and English colonial powers as well as within the French territories themselves. For instance, the boundary line between Nigeria and Dahomey divides the Yoruba, the Fon, the Bariba, and the Busa. By the same token, these same tribes have been divided up within the French territorial system by the administrative organizational district called *le cercle*.

The second step was to remove the paramount chiefs. In spite of the fact

[1] The foregoing information was supplied by the present chief and the elders of Sogote. It was checked and confirmed, though sometimes reluctantly, by several informants, young and old men in Sena. The facts are true, but the names of people have been changed.

[2] L. P. Mair, *Native Policies in Africa,* London: Oxford University Press, 1937, p. 209.

that a chief may have exploited his own people and lived like a medieval feudal lord, the chief was the symbol, the depository, the trustee, and in some places the semideity with whom resided the sacred traditions of the tribe, with the promise of their perpetuation.[3] Regardless of the high honor inherent in the office of the paramount chief, Mair adds, "The idea of a native chief exercising any kind of independent initiative seems to be alien to the conception of most French colonial authorities."[4]

The removal of a paramount chief did not mean the replacement of that office with a European administrative post. Since it was still necessary to have direct contact with the people, the French installed the "desirable" kind of chief. Mair enumerates the following qualifications for such a chief: "Literacy, ability in accounting, loyalty, assiduity in carrying out official orders."[5] These traits are strictly Western. Whether or not the puppet chief belonged to the indigenous royal family was immaterial. Quoting Mair again, we see that the French "... even set [a chief] in authority over alien people."[6] Whether he was capable of leadership within his own society was inconsequential.

For all practical purposes, then, traditionally speaking, the chiefs have lost all of their power, "... so that their function is reduced to that of a mouthpiece for orders emanating from outside, ..."[7] according to Mair. While it is perhaps true that they do not have their former power, nevertheless they do have a job to do. A list of these functions, as gleaned from Thompson and Adloff's volume, is as follows: (1) religious prestige, (2) traditional revenues, such as tribute, etc., (3) collecting taxes, (4) recruiting laborers and soldiers, and (5) conciliating minor chiefs.[8] In return for carrying out these responsibilities, the paramount chief is paid a small salary.

In the light of what happened in Sogote, one would be inclined to agree with Thompson and Adloff's evaluation of French policy when they say that by means of the "principle of the separation of powers, the French have unwittingly undermined what was traditionally an undivided religious, economic, and political authority."[9]

### The African Custom of Land Tenure

Lest we denounce the French too vehemently for following such antitraditionalist policy, we should consider the fourth reason previously stated for Giba's revolt: "Gisa had tried to appropriate the land belonging to Giba." For here we see that Gisa in full knowledge of native customs, "riding the horse" of white man's power, chose to violate the traditions of his own people. The more one understands of the African custom of land tenure, the more audacious becomes this act of his.

Let us first of all recognize that, as E. W. Smith says, "... African society does not comprise the living only; the living and the dead compose a close interdependent community, and anything which disturbs the harmony between

[3] Virginia Thompson and Richard Adloff, *French West Africa,* Stanford, California: Stanford University Press, 1957, pp. 204-213.

[4] Mair, *op. cit.*, pp. 210-211.

[5] *Ibid.*, p. 209.

[6] *Ibid.*

[7] *Ibid.*

[8] Thompson and Adloff, *loc cit.*

[9] *Ibid.*, p. 24.

them is regarded as crime."[10] The African is repeatedly drawn back to this association.

Since he realizes that his ancestral spirits "are regarded as the guardians of tribal morality," he is very careful about "the land where their bodies lie buried and the forest which harbors their spirits," for "African religion is rooted in the soil and bound to the parcel of ground hallowed by the presence of the dead."[11]

It is here that the question of land ownership arises. T. O. Elias, quoting an African chief, says, "I conceive that land belongs to a vast family of which many are dead, few are living, and countless members yet unborn."[12] Under this system, then, not even the living can claim land ownership. Elias continues that it was just this desire to preserve land for the requirements of this owning group, past, present, and future community and family, that land has been held inalienable.[13] Obviously, then, no individual can hold land either. The individual, by reason of his being a member of either a community, a kinship group of families, or a family, has certain rights on that land, but never the right of ownership.

The chief is considered the trustee, the custodian, the representative of the tribe with respect to the land. Though he has the power to parcel out the land with the consent of all the elders of the village, he is not the owner, and he cannot alienate the land, for reasons already stated.

By reason of the fact that a chief holds sacred land in trusteeship, he becomes in this capacity a mediator responsible, both to the ancestor spirits and people alike, for the proper disposal of the land. One can understand then why, as Meek puts it, "the authority of chiefs, subchiefs, and heads of clans and families is bound up with the land."[14] An Akan proverb of the Gold Coast states it even more tersely: "All power lies in the land."[15]

Perhaps it was this power that Gisa was after when he strove to bring Giba's land, the *nesa* land, under his control. Traditionally, he knew that "... those who committed offenses against their kinsmen could be punished with moral, ritual, or ... legal sanctions";[16] he also knew that being French-sponsored, as he was, Giba would not be able to take any retaliatory action against him. However, Giba did display his contempt for Gisa by refusing to pay his taxes and threatening to kill anyone coming to collect them. This open defiance to Gisa's authority and prestige brought him and his warriors into the clearing surrounding the small village of Sogote. But here he found himself frustrated by the power which had given him the initiative from the start — the white man.

[10] E. W. Smith, *The Golden Stool,* New York: Doubleday, Doran and Company, Inc., 1928, p. 191.

[11] *Ibid.,* pp. 191, 202.

[12] T. O. Elias, *Nigerian Land Law and Custom,* second edition, London: Routledge and Kegan Paul Ltd., 1953, p. 173.

[13] *Ibid.,* p. 172.

[14] C. K. Meek, *Land Law and Custom in the Colonies,* second edition, London: Oxford University Press, 1949, p. 10.

[15] *Ibid.*

[16] P. Brown, "Patterns of Authority in West Africa," *Africa,* Vol. 21, No. 4 (October 1951), p. 267.

*Eugene A. Nida*

**Reprinted from Vol. 6, No. 1 (1959), pp. 20-23.**

# Drunkenness in Indigenous Religious Rites

*Drunkenness, like other human activity, has to be viewed cross-culturally to be seen in the light of its meaning in any particular culture. In this article Dr. Eugene A. Nida suggests briefly that the motivations behind drunkenness in the United States do not necessarily apply in other societies, and particularly that drunkenness has a ritual, ecstatic function in many religious rites.*

THERE is a tendency for some missionaries to regard drunkenness in indigenous religious rites as nothing other than a sign of total moral degeneracy. It is quite understandable why missionaries should do this, for especially in Protestant circles drunkenness is strictly prohibited and has strong moral implications. If, on the other hand, a missionary has read about Alcoholics Anonymous or has become acquainted with some of the psychological and sociological studies on alcoholism in American society, he is likely to decide that the use of liquor in indigenous religious celebrations indicates a basic inferiority complex on the part of the worshipers, who as a group are suffering from some form of cultural morbidity and are hence seeking a sort of escape from real or imagined threats. We must not deny the fact that alcoholism can be a characteristic of a group which is suffering from extreme cultural pressures, and under the influence of liquor such a group may be able to create a kind of make-believe world in which the people can experience a "release" once they are free from the inhibitions imposed by the threatening social, economic, and political woes.

However, there are certain situations in which drunkenness in religious celebrations does not fit such an easily constructed picture of moral or cultural disintegration or escape. For example, many Mexican Indian religious festivals mark a period of excessive drunkenness, but the people are not particularly addicted to drunkenness at other periods of the year. Moreover, many of those who imbibe the most at such religious festivals are often those who are quite restricted in their alcoholic intake during other times. In other words, there is no close correlation between persons who are habitual alcoholics and those who become thoroughly drunken in these religious rites. Such fiestas, however, are not merely occasions sanctioned by religion in which drinking is quantitatively increased for all members of the group. There is something selective involved, and it is this selectivity which is important if we are to understand ritual drunkenness.

Another area of the world in which alcoholic consumption is closely tied with certain religious practices is in West Africa, where some religious festivals involve the consumption of enormous quantities of palm wine, with resultant drunkenness. Moreover, there is no reason to think that these festivals are particularly diagnostic of cultural morbidity or degeneracy. There does not appear to be any special reason prompting any "escape." From every observation the people are simply "reveling" in what many missionaries have denounced as wanton debauchery.

There are many such places in the world in which drunkenness has been closely associated with religious rites, but perhaps in no area was it so elaborated as among the ancient Greeks, who worshiped the composite figure of fertility and drunkenness in the person of the god Dionysus, also known as Bacchus. The rites of Dionysus involved some of the most extreme orgies of frenzy and group hysteria ever recorded. In the enactment of these rites the drinking of wine was an indispensable part, not as an expression of bravado or intemperance, but as something far more profound, namely, as a means of attaining religious ecstasy, in the form of a "divine madness." It would seem that here is a fundamental factor in alcoholic consumption in religious rites which has often been overlooked by those who have viewed such events from an "alien" standpoint.

## Drunkenness and Religious Ecstasy

One of the most powerful emotions which can be associated with religion is ecstasy, whether discovered by the mystic, as the result of long periods of meditation, or by the hysterical voodoo dancer, who finally collapses when he is at last "touched by his god." Alcohol has been discovered by many peoples as being one of the "drugs" by means of which such an ecstatic state may be attained. Here is a method, not merely for escape from the world of mundane reality, but of access to the supernatural world where one can enjoy the ecstatic thrill of identification with the supernatural. Other means employed to accomplish much the same purpose are peyote, mescal beans, mushrooms (among the Mazatecs of Mexico), and hashish (or marihuana) in the Middle East. Alcohol, however, seems to have certain special advantages for worshipers, for it removes normal inhibitions (thus permitting greater freedom of expression), provides a sense of well-being, increases suggestibility, and stimulates sexual desires, where in many religious rites drunkenness is associated with fertility cult practices.

One must not presume, however, that alcoholic consumption in religious ritual must necessarily be directed toward the goal of complete ecstasy or utter physical collapse. The Tarahumaras of Northern Mexico, for example, consume vast quantities of beer (called *tesgüino*) during socio-religious dances which may last all night. Though some of the participants collapse either during the night or on the paths back to their homes, the beer is not drunk in order to provide an escape, but to promote a sense of uninhibited participation by all those present — a kind of social ecstasy, with religious overtones.

## Drunkenness in Latin America

Of course, it is not easy to determine just where the factor of ecstasy may leave off and mere escape begins, nor is it always possible to know whether part of what may be observed in "religious drinking" may have a carry-over into non-religious alcoholism. However, it has been my observation that among many of the lower classes in Latin America drunkenness is not just what it is so often in the United States. The alcoholics of

Skid Row in America seem so often intent on merely "blacking out," with the avowed purpose of drinking themselves to death. Our bars are frequently filled with relatively quiet men seeking to forget, with the entertainment consisting mostly of television or radio, punctuated by a fight or by some slap-happy customer who wants to yell or sing. But bars in the small towns of Latin America seem to provide in many instances a quite different kind of picture. There is a good deal more singing, whether by individuals or groups, more drinking for the extreme "delight" of it, more boisterous, convivial "hoopla," and more real "charge" out of the experience. People drink because they enjoy drunkenness. In general, they do not appear to be trying to "show off" or to exhibit "cockiness" (as in American patterns of drinking where our individualism is at its worst); they get drunk for the sheer exhuberant joy of drunkenness — an emotional reaction evidently not too distantly related to the dionysian reveling of ancient times.

The apparent differences in certain motivations for a good deal of drinking deserve much careful study if we are going to fully understand some of the acute sociological problems of Latin America. But apart from some of the more far-reaching implications of such contrasts, there is one factor which may be significant in interpreting certain developments in the response of people to particular types of missionary work. For instance, a Pentecostal type of approach has been highly successful in reaching the lower classes in Latin America. There are undoubtedly a number of reasons, such as the very dramatic forms of ritual (which substitute for the spectacles of the Roman church), emphasis upon healing (also an integral part of Roman Catholic appeal and a pressing need for people who lack means for medical assistance), a highly developed sense of group participation, and a well-motivated sense of responsibility (since so many Pentecostal movements have not been hampered by being dependent upon foreign missionaries). However, there is still an additional factor which may be very important in the case of a number of conversions involving notorious drunkards, namely, the fact thay they find in Pentecostalism something of the same type of intense ecstasy which they formerly endeavored to attain through alcohol. (It is not without significance that on the day of Pentecost the people interpreted the ecstasy of the disciples as being drunkenness. Moreover, Peter did not deny the similarity, but insisted that it could not be drunkenness since it was so early in the day.)

It would be wrong to imply that Roman Catholicism does not emphasize the ecstatic element in worship. The truth is that there is much more importance attached to such experiences by Roman Catholics than by Protestants. The Roman church provides the people with unusually thrilling spectacles, encouraging ecstatic visions of the saints and the Virgin, and propagandizes miracles of healing. Protestantism, except for the more emotional groups, is largely devoid of such elements, and the focus of attention is upon true religion as a pattern of conduct rather than an emotional outburst.

### Cross-cultural Study of Drunkenness

In making certain of these suggestions as to the possible link between the ecstatic nature of a good deal of drunkenness in Latin America and certain aspects of the appeal of Pentecostalism, I am not suggesting for a moment that the ecstatic phases of Pentecostalism are essentially unworthy, unreal, or anything more than mere psychological substitutes. Moreover, an analysis of motivations prompting certain types of drinking in Latin America is entirely inadequate to explain the Latin's propensity for intense emotional responses. The forms of drinking are only symptomatic of a whole complex of related characteristics which combine to explain the so-called Latin temperament. What we are trying to suggest in this presentation, however, is that drunkenness in other societies cannot be judged merely from observation of our own culture, and that drunkenness cannot always be analyzed merely as an attempt to escape from one's own sense of inferiority. Rather it is a technique, widely practiced now and throughout the centuries, whereby people have sought for ecstatic religious experiences.

**Reprinted from Vol. 5, No. 5 (1958), pp. 222-233.**

*Lois Sorensen and William A. Smalley*

# Planting the Church in a Disintegrating Society

## I

I HAVE spent two years in southeastern Alaska doing secretarial work. The first year I worked for the territorial government and the second in a mission school. I had the opportunity of knowing and working with many of the Thlinget[1] Indian people. At the school I also had contact with students who were of Haida, Tsimpshean, and Athabaskan Indian background, as well as a few Eskimos. This paper will concern the Thlingets of southeastern Alaska only. While there I had no knowledge of anthropology, and at the same time made no attempt to study these people. Much of this paper, therefore, is written in retrospect.

During these two years, many times I asked the question, "Why aren't there more native Christians?" I worked with a native pastor who is one of the most outstanding Christians I have ever met, and there were a few other native Christians, but in relation to the number of churches (at least 10 in Sitka, which has a population of 3,500), their extensive work, and the length of time the church has been there (about 80 years), the number of Christians seemed very small to me. The answer I was constantly given was, "Well, the church has been here less than 100 years, and this is not very long when you consider the effect the Gospel has had in other areas." Another answer that I actually heard a couple of times from evangelical ministers was that "the Holy Spirit must have departed from Southeast Alaska!"

### Conflicting Influences

The Russians occupied Alaska in the late 1700's and most of the 1800's, and organized many Russian Orthodox churches. American missionaries entered Alaska about 1870. Dr. Sheldon Jackson was among the first. He started a school for some of the boys in Sitka. The purpose of the school was to give them a Christian education which included such things as cleanliness, sanitation, and higher moral standards. To accomplish this it was necessary to separate the boys from their community life, and an American-type school was built. Dr. Jackson was the leading spirit in revolutionizing that part of Alaska in terms of the acceptance of education and in opening up the territory to Christian missionary

[1] In this paper I am using the most common spelling seen in Alaska, rather than "Tlingit" which is seen in most anthropological literature.

---

**Miss Lois Sorensen, after a term of missionary service in Alaska, took a course in anthropology at Wheaton College. There she found the theoretical and factual basis for some of the "feelings" which she had had about the Alaskan work. Some of the problems about which she has been thinking were drawn together and described in this paper and in correspondence with friends in Alaska.**

activity. However, the consequences of his program, as it has been carried on through the years, have had their unfavorable aspects. Although it was not expressly spoken, the actions seem to imply that it would be best to destroy everything in local culture and make white men out of these students as quickly as possible. The students were forbidden to speak their native language while at the school; they therefore had to learn English.

This attitude of the necessity of turning the Indians into cultural white people as soon as possible has continued, and after 80 years of existence the school is hard at work with this problem. Dr. Jackson was also the first Education Commissioner for Alaska; the government schools were therefore all started with this same pattern. Not only has such an attitude been held by the missionaries and educators, but it has carried over also into the government departments as well. There has been little real attempt at identification with the natives, but simply a one-way communication in most cases. I realize what has been said, and will be said throughout the rest of this discussion, may seem highly critical. However, I think it will be found to be a realistic picture of the situation in this area.

White people in Alaska have not gone there to establish homes and remain for the rest of their lives, but are transient. There is a large number of service men with their families who are there, usually for two years, and then leave. The government term of service for nurses, teachers, and clerical workers is also two years. Many people who go are looking for excitement, and two years is enough for them. Life is slow in the towns because of isolation, and the excitement soon wears off. Other people go to Alaska to "help humanity," and often after two years feel they have done enough. Others go to escape or solve a personal problem. Alaska is often thought of as a wild place, but also as a good place to be a hermit. Many individuals live by themselves and have very little contact with others. This assortment of kinds of people is represented among staff members of the hospitals, schools, and offices. Sometimes they have not been able to get along well in the States and as a last resort have come to Alaska. Almost anyone can get a job in Alaska as the demand is so great, and the pay high, attracting many people whose feeling of security in other communities has worn thin. As a consequence, there are ill-advised adventure-seekers — often with a very minimum of training — leading the native people and setting examples by which they should live.

Not all of the people are like the former. There are *many* educated, well-adjusted, and well-trained people, but often they are in administrative positions. Even though they are the ones making decisions on policies affecting the natives, they often sit behind a desk all day and never mingle with the native people.

With the great turnover in personnel, each new group of workers that comes in is inclined to think they know how everything should be run, and immediately set about to change everything and get rid of the "old fogies" who have tested and tried many of these methods and adopted the ones that worked best. The native sees instability again and again.

### Some Consequences

Even though the Thlinget language is used very little today, in the villages many still speak their native tongue. There are still a number of the older people who do not understand English. Last June a friend and I took our violin and flute and went to see a bed-ridden Thlinget friend who lives with her mother. The mother cannot speak English. After we had played a few hymns, her mother started singing in Thlinget for us. We were thrilled, as she had never done this before, and we tried to learn some of the words and sing with her. The mother, who is about 80 years of age, was literally jumping up and down with excitement, and her daughter exclaimed over and over again, "They're singing in Thlinget; they're actually singing in our language!" Yet I have been told by missionaries that it is absolutely useless to attempt to translate the Bible into this language as they know English well enough. Another friend told me of how his family made very little use of their radio until a news broadcast was started in the Thlinget language once a week. His mother, who usually retired at 9 every evening, would stay up until 10:30 just to hear that broadcast. Just listening to this once a week encouraged her to use the radio more frequently. A parallel effect might be had upon translating the Bible — the people will desire to read the Bible, and also have a greater desire for education.

## The Native Social Structure

The family structure, although quite strong, is rapidly breaking down. Feelings many times continue to be strong where clan membership in matters of courtship and marriage are involved. It is no longer absolutely necessary that marriage be outside the clan, but this is still desired. One daughter remarked to her mother, "Every time I date a fellow I like, you tell me he's related to me." They have adopted the American dating system, but still do not feel entirely free to marry anyone they please. Many of the natives feel it will advance their status if they marry white people, and there is a great deal of interracial marriage. The missionaries have told them that their matrilineal clan structure is not in accordance with the patrilineal structure of the Old Testament and they should therefore give up their matrilineal structure. The natives have probably held on to their matrilineal system more firmly, however, than many other of their cultural features. The children are confused. They are told by the white people that their parents' ideas are wrong and old-fashioned. On one hand they are drawn towards accepting the white man's way, and yet their family ties are so strong that they cannot entirely reject them.

## Alcoholism

Among elders and young people, alcoholism is one of the main results of the transition process. Many of the Thlinget are confused and frustrated. They cannot live in their old way, and they cannot live in the white way either; so they turn to drink and soon become alcoholics. The police are often bribed and they pay little attention to it. It seems that almost every other door in the downtown area is a liquor store or a bar. The example of most of the white people has encouraged drinking because most of them drink. One former minister drove a cab and delivered liquor to help out in his support. The liquor business is a major business in Alaska, and since there is no law against the sale of it, the natives are often led by white example to think that there is nothing wrong with it.

### Extramarital Relations

Alcohol and the presence of members of the armed services have both contributed to the presence of many illegitimate children. The parents feel badly when this happens, but do not turn their daughters away. Most of the girls refuse to marry the father of the baby because it would usually necessitate leaving home and Alaska. Of course, it is sometimes true that the father refuses to marry the girl. The Welfare Department, therefore, must support the child and its mother. When a young girl sees that she can get money for having an illegitimate child, she will often have others in order to get more money. This fact is commonly known, yet the schools and churches do very little teaching of moral principles. Most churches do not teach Christian concepts of marriage, or that one's body is a temple of the Holy Spirit.

### Remnants of Old Culture

Superstition still exists, but most of it is under cover. No native would admit to a white person that he still believes in the supernatural powers remaining from the old religion, yet occasionally there will be a flare-up, or someone in close contact with the native will relate things he has observed. Such information in all probability is transmitted among people who are in church on Sunday mornings.

In earlier days the potlatch was a feast at which the host gave gifts to his guests and destroyed enormous amounts of valuable property like blankets, skins, oil, and valuable "coppers" which were symbols of wealth. This was done in order to shame the guest, and to assert the superiority of the host, or to honor someone who had recently died. A form of the potlatch still exists today; however, this too is under cover. A present-day potlatch corresponds more to our big parties where there is much eating and drinking. A very important part, also, is story-telling. The different clans represented may tell their various legends. There may be even deeper significances to the potlatch that remains in its present form which have not been obliterated nor superseded by the teaching that they have received.

### Personal Suggestions

1. I believe that the native language should be used, not primarily in order to preserve the language, but as a means of teaching the older people who are the ones who rule the homes and families. It may also be used to reach the younger and middle-aged people who have been brought up in homes where the native language was spoken and native expressions and ways of thinking were learned. Many feel that this will encourage the people to go backwards. I feel that it will not do that, but will recognize the fact that the language is being used and show the people the value of their culture. The adjustment to white cultural patterns will be easier and less painful for them; and this will also give the white people a greater appreciation of the natives. Together they can then share a new if changed world. If this, and the probable strengthening of whatever cultural integrity is left, is going "backwards," it is only if becoming a "white man" is considered "progress." The entire population of North American Indians is facing white sentiment, as well as legislation, born of this notion, that assimilation equals progress.

Recently I was talking to a young Thlinget who is studying in Chicago to be a doctor. I asked him his opinion of translating into the native language. At first he saw little value in it, but later he said, "Well, if you do that, perhaps the people will quit being the spectators and become the players, and they will see that the Gospel is really for them too, and will understand it better."

2. Potluck suppers, which have already been established, can serve as a partial substitute for the potlatch. It would be valuable to have a planned program after the supper which might be recreational, spiritual, or both. Perhaps one of the native people could tell a Thlinget legend or some of their history. (I was greatly impressed at a Sunday School picnic when the native minister told a story in Thlinget of the Raven and the Wolf, and another man translated into English.) At other times a short devotional message could be brought, preferably by a Thlinget. A greater and stronger fellowship of the Christians is possible through these potluck suppers.

3. Native leadership should be encouraged in the churches. Attempts have often been made to get native Sunday School teachers, but these have not been very successful. I think that one basic reason for the failure is that the native people do not like to be responsible to a white person. If a native were in the position of leadership, however, they would probably be more willing to help in the church. Perhaps a native could teach a small Sunday School class of adults or children in the Thlinget language. Native deacons, ushers, and choir directors have proved very effective and should be encouraged to continue.

4. The godly Thlinget pastor mentioned above is preaching to his congregation mainly in English because of the nature of the missionary methods which have prevailed. Although it has been the tradition and all of his "education" has been against using the Thlinget language, and about half of his congregation are white and English-speaking, I believe that he should be encouraged to expand a ministry in his native language. If people will stay up an hour and a half later at night to hear the news in their language, the Gospel in their language, both in the churches and on the radio, should have far-reaching results. During the summer most of the people are out fishing and have very little opportunity for worship. Some other form of worship should be substituted, and the radio might well be a means of doing this. During the winter, when many of them are not working, they sleep late in the mornings, which means that Sunday School and morning worship are poorly attended. Many of the villages have found that it is better to have Sunday School in the afternoon and the main worship service in the evening. Many ministers, however, have felt that the morning service should be emphasized. I think that the worship service should be fitted to their schedule, as there is nothing supernatural or supercultural about holding a worship service at a certain hour in the morning or evening as it is done in the United States and Canada.

5. As much as is possible, the newcomers to Alaska should be screened and should have a good orientation and know what to expect *before* going. Although this is desirable, it is impossible for all personnel. But it should be imperative for missionaries. I also feel that it is impossible for a person to do a lasting job on a short-term basis (such as a 2- or 4-year term). The need is so extensive that the emphasis has often been on quantity, and not on quality, both in the church field and government work. This needs to be changed, or the results

that have already appeared will become worse, and greater problems will develop. An anthropological orientation program, I think, is vital, especially to those who expect to work with the native people.

Even if one is not working with the native people, his influence in the community will spread to the natives. This orientation needed cannot be accomplished in a 3-day training session or even a week. At least a month, plus reading of many background books would be more desirable. If someone is willing to go through all this, then chances of being accepted by the natives will be much greater because he has already shown his desire to learn and not to teach, or force (as has been the result in many cases) his knowledge on the people. Someone who is willing to go through this is probably a better adjusted person.

I found that even though I was not particularly interested in learning about the customs of the people, many times the native people would tell me about them. I think the reason for this was that I did not have a critical attitude toward them or their culture as so many white people did. I think they sensed that I was honest in wanting to help them and they did not feel that whatever they told me would be used against them. It is necessary to stay there a long time to win their confidence. The Thlinget people *will not* open up to strangers, and when someone such as a writer asks prying questions they may give him a partial answer, or say they do not know, that there is nothing unusual, or even give a wrong answer. We would react the same way if someone came prying into our personal affairs. Writers, for instance, will go to Alaska for two weeks to two months and then go back to the States and write a book of stories on Alaska. These stories cannot possibly be altogether factual, although they have some truth in them. Above all, "the love of Christ constraineth us" is the important qualification and attitude.

6. The importance of lay workers in this area cannot be overemphasized. There are already so many churches, with just a handful of people (usually untrained) in each church. The minister is faced with being head of the Sunday school, church janitor, doing all the secretarial and bookkeeping work, making repairs, etc., plus preaching and visiting his parish. The lay worker, someone living in the community and working so that he has his own support, has an unlimited opportunity. Also, the natives can see in someone besides their minister — who gets paid for doing it — how the Christian life should be lived. There is a tremendous ministry among the white people also, both Christian and non-Christian, for the lay worker.

**Unanswered Questions**

So far I have said very little about how to go about developing the native church, mostly because I do not know the answer. How does one go about establishing an indigenous church in such a place where people stand between two cultures and where there is so much ambiguity in the cultural framework? Does the matrilineal system have to be replaced by the patrilineal system? Will the potlatch have to be destroyed, and if so, how? Should Alcoholics Anonymous or a similar group be sought to aid in the alcoholic problem?

Lois Sorensen

# II

THE picture which you draw of Thlinget and other people of Indian background in Alaska is not as unusual as you may think. Many of the details of your description can be paralleled in one society after another around the world, places where the impact of the West upon an aboriginal culture has left a people in transition, as you say: disoriented, insecure, afraid. It has often happened that a society has been shaken to its very roots by contact with another. Its major presuppositions have been challenged. Its way of life has been changed either through force or influence. It sees a way of life which has many of the earmarks of power and the glitter of wealth — a way of life which seems materially desirable; and yet the Western alternative presented to it is too complex for it to understand. It holds tenaciously, and a little bit hysterically sometimes, to certain aspects of its past. Its insecurity, its fear, breaks out sometimes in a violent movement such as the Mau Mau and sometimes in emotional apathy and resignation. As different as the atrocities of the Mau Mau and the lethargy of many American Indian groups seem, they are but two symptoms of the same conflict of cultures, the same breakdown of values. In your case the cultural apathy carries along with it a religious apathy, and even among those Thlinget who have become Christians the spirit of the present Thlinget world is that spirit of lethargy and deadness.

## History Cannot Be Reversed

Much as you may regret it, you can never turn back the Thlinget clock. The unfortunate train of events, the unfortunate influences of the past, can never be removed. Like every other realistic missionary in the world, you have to accept people where they are and move on from there. We have outstanding precedent in this; this is the way in which God has dealt with mankind all down through Biblical history.

You might as well face the fact that by and large the Thlinget language is probably on its way out. And the truth of how long it will last probably lies somewhere between the extremes of those missionaries who feel that by teaching a few more people English they have ensured its death, and those missionaries who feel that it must be maintained at all costs. Nobody can predict without a careful ethno-linguistic survey how long the language will last as a functional part of Thlinget life. But we can be reasonably sure that eventually — in a matter of generations — it will pass on, whether we like it or not.

In the meantime, we must realize that for some of the Indians there is security and prestige in the use of English, that to some of them no doubt the use of their native language seems a mark of backwardness and inferiority. To others, as you point out, the native language is still that emotional vehicle through which they feel and to which their hearts respond.

The relationship of the church to all of this is a very serious matter. The ministry of the Gospel is to all people, including both the ones who look forward to English and those who look backward to Thlinget. It seems to me that an adequate ministry will have to provide for both. However, a missionary should not be misled by ideas about the effectiveness of Biblical translation in isolation. It is not going to be enough to translate the Scriptures and to present them to a handful of individuals who would be interested in reading them. If work is undertaken in Thlinget literature, it should be undertaken enthusiastically and fully to the point where there is some functional use for written Thlinget. This would involve reading materials both of a religious and non-religious nature. It would involve, in short, the provision of enough materials for the Thlinget reader such that he would feel that reading was worth while for him and, more than that, would provide him with these materials cast in such a way that he would not feel that it would be better to have them in English.[1]

History cannot be reversed, but a new future can sometimes be fashioned out of some of the relics of the past, and, like some other groups in the world, the Thlinget language perhaps can be an important vehicle again (along with English) if it is made functional and relevant in a way that seems worth while for the modern world (as the Thlinget looks upon it) and not simply a fossilized vestige of an unhappy past.

### The Planting of the Church

Your question, "How does one go about establishing an indigenous church in such a place where people stand between two cultures and where there is so much ambiguity in the cultural framework?" is an agonizing one for many a missionary; but I think first of all we can arrive at a better understanding of its implications by foregoing the concept of "establishing" a church and speak instead of "planting" the church.[2] "Planting" essentially involves communicating. It involves the transfer of a message from one individual to another, not the concerns of organization and procedure which so occupy the thinking of many missionaries.

The task of communicating the Gospel among the Thlinget is fundamentally, of course, the same task that it is anywhere else. It is that of finding out how the message which came in the cultural garb of the Middle East hundreds of years ago, and which the missionary understands principally in the cultural garb of Western 20th century, can in turn be made to strike with impact and sharp force in the cultural garb of an Indian of Alaska. The difficulties involved are especially severe, however, because of the tensions and disintegration within the society there. There is no single unambiguous language and culture pattern for them. Instead, there is flux and insecurity, change and instability. This complicates the task but does not change its essential nature.

[1] See William D. Reyburn, "Literacy in Primitive Society," *The Bible Translator,* Vol. 9, No. 2, (Apr. 1958), pp. 76-81.

[2] See William A. Smalley, "Cultural Implications of an Indigenous Church," PRACTICAL ANTHROPOLOGY, Vol. 5, No. 2, (Mar.-Apr. 1958), pp. 51-65, and in this volume.

The problem remains one of speaking to the issues which the Indians see and stimulating them to put their reliance upon Jesus as Savior and Lord. It is in the determining of the issues as the Indians see them that anthropology first fits into the picture.

This is not just a matter of orienting newcomers to Alaska. Neither three days, nor three months, nor three years will do it for some people; and yet a few rare souls have such sensitivity and perceptiveness that they learn whether they are "oriented" or not. I thoroughly agree with you that all newcomers should be oriented as you suggest. But the point is that this orientation will not lead people to an effective communication of the Gospel, although it may help them to avoid many mistakes which could be a serious hindrance to the preaching of Christ.

We are going to have to be careful not to project our sense of needs completely into the Thlinget situation. When we think of religion we think of the need for morality, honesty, hard work, social consciousness, love of one's neighbor. These and a thousand other things are specific needs in our life, which the Gospel fills. Some of these needs the Thlinget will sense, and others they will not, at least not at first. I suspect that their needs would be phrased in much more highly emotional terms if they were to be phrased at all. I suspect that the need for security and protection and stability in life would rank high if the Gospel could be so presented to them. I suspect that an emotional outlet such as the Indians of the Southwest achieve through the Peyote or the Sun Dancers or which some groups of Christians achieve through highly emotional evangelistic services would rank high among Thlinget needs. It is hard to predict, but I suspect that some of the things which you have particularly mentioned like alcoholism and illegitimacy of children might not be listed at all and some things that we would never think of would be extremely important.

By this I am not saying that the needs which we see in Thlinget life are not also very real, but my point is that for the communication of the Gospel to them, the needs which they sense are those which motivate them toward Christ if they feel that He has an answer for them. After their initial contact with Him, after their conversion and that subtle transformation that occurs in culture as the result of the Holy Spirit operating through it, other needs of which they were not conscious before may well come to the surface. A new dimension of definition of needs becomes relevant to them because of the Scriptures and because of a wider outlook and understanding of God in their relationship to man.

A church springing up from such soil as this could have many forms. It might show an identification with the past, a strong sense of Thlinget solidarity, a re-expression of Thlinget moral values in a Christian setting. As such it would probably be repudiated by "progressive" elements in the Indian population. Or then it might show an identification with the West, with Western cultural forms and Western ideas. In such a case it would emphasize the use of English, the Western English Scriptures, and education in English. As such it would leave the older folks and the less Westernized people cold. Then again the new church might be a new synthesis of cultural elements such that in it and around it Thlinget of all kinds, those whose eyes are essentially on the past and those whose eyes are essentially on the West, would find a new expression, a new synthesis, a new way of life. I should hope that a church of this kind would grow out of the soil that you have described.

But for such a church to grow, what will be needed? We have already mentioned the nature of the communication that will have to take place. But I doubt if a church of this kind will really grow as a direct result of missionary activity. Usually such churches are one step removed from the missionary; they result from the work of some outstanding leader himself perhaps brought under the influence of the Gospel by a missionary, but recasting his message in terms of the aspirations and needs of his people and presenting the Gospel to them in a way that strikes home to their very souls. This is the role of the prophet, of the man who has that extra margin of vision to see beyond the horizon of his traditions, to stretch the borders of his own background, to interpret what God has for His people to them.

Should such a prophet arise and should a church be established through his work, we could almost predict that the major mission forces in Alaska will look askance at the results. The movement will most certainly be an emotional movement, and with a highly intellectual Western Christianity most of us find it hard to appreciate the Holy Spirit working through the emotions of less emotionally strait-jacketed people than ourselves. A movement of this kind, even though it may not be the immediate direct product of a missionary's activity and even though it may seem strange to him in its overt expression, can still provide a tremendously significant area of work for him in his relationship to the developing group of Christian people. If he has tact and consideration and is willing to work with the Holy Spirit and the forces of culture which are bringing the church to fruition, his ministry of translation, of teaching, of stimulation, of bringing new ideas, can be a very profund one. I know of no greater place of trust than that of a sensitive missionary in such a position as this.

I take it that a movement of this kind has not yet sprung up among the Indians of Alaska and we cannot wait for it to do so but must push ahead, seeking to understand the Indians in such a way that our feeble message as foreigners will come to them, that the Holy Spirit will supply that measure of power which will overcome our deficiency, and that God will be pleased to move in His own way and in His own time.

### Some Matters of Detail

There were several specific questions of a cultural nature which were raised in your article. For example, there was that of the matrilineal system versus a patrilineal one. In the past the Thlinget people have reckoned their family systems through the mother instead of through the father and American missionaries and American administrators steeped in the traditions of the Hebrew Old Testament and the good old American way of life have felt that this is wrong. To be realistic again, we must realize that in time probably the matrilineal social structure of the Indians in Alaska will break down through the influence of the West, and its courts, and its schools. But, as I think you sense, this issue is really an irrelevant one for the church. God worked through a patrilineal society in the Hebrew people and He has worked through matrilineal societies elsewhere. There is nothing intrinsically moral or right and wrong about social structure as such. The many different social structures as found today in the world are simply many different ways of organizing group behavior into useful channels and of making life more valuable to the participants in the society. The missionary's role in relation to this as in relation to other cultural matters is to let history take its course and to concern himself with more important issues. Not that he should not understand the social structure as it exists and the tensions within it. That is very important, but it is not his place to make changes. Should the society, on the other hand, be in the process of changing, it is not his place, either, to hold tightly to the past and try to thwart the changes. It is perfectly legitimate for him to participate by pointing out difficulties or problems which he may see and possible avenues of change. He is not in a cultural vacuum and should not pretend to be so, but that is a far different matter from the deliberate and energetic attempts to promote change or resist it which have so characterized Americans, including missionaries, in their dealings with other people.

The potlatch is, of course, famous in anthropological literature. It has long fascinated me as being the symptom of a type of attitude toward one's fellow human being that also characterizes so much of American life. The potlatch was an instrument of aggression. As you well know, the Indians of the Northwest Coast destroyed or gave away property in order to shame their neighbors, in order to get the best of them. This is fantastically similar to the society of many of our big cities where people spend money so lavishly in order to best their neighbors in the continual competition of keeping on top of the social heap. And just as the spirit which prompts these American displays of wealth can be identified as part of the American brand of worldliness, so I am sure the spirit which prompts the potlatch exhibit is likewise the Thlinget brand of that same unhealthy hold that our culture sometimes has upon us. Here again it is not the potlatch in itself as an institution, but the meaning that motivates it, that is unchristian. That same spirit that motivates it is very parallel to the spirit behind much of American life, including the life of many of the missionaries who would condemn the potlatch institution. Simply because the forms which it takes in American life seem more civilized to us, the potlatch seems a more barbaric custom, but in terms of Christian values it reflects the same agressive selfishness we show.

Again I feel that the potlatch as an institution is not really any of the missionary's business. As men are confronted with Christ in a way that makes Him seem relevant to them, a transformation takes place in their lives and it is quite possible that the spirit behind the old potlatch will be part of what is transformed into the image of God's Son.

Alcoholism likewise is a symptom. It is a symptom of the cultural tensions, the breakdown of values, the lack of moral pressures that exist. As serious as its social consequences are, no treatment of this symptom is going to have much lasting value. It is not until men have seen in Christ the fulfillment of the needs which they sense, that such problems as alcoholism will find a solution. I doubt that any such group as Alcoholics Anonymous would have much effect in Thlinget society. That particular group works on the basis of a strong desire to overcome alcoholism and upon the pressure created by the group to help each member to keep in line. An entirely new set of pressures and of values would have to be met and would have to be created in order to be based upon the needs which the Thlinget feel.

Illegitimate birth and extramarital sex behavior are again part of the frequent symptoms of this type of a cultural situation. They too will not be remedied by any direct action upon them as such, but only through a restructuring of the whole value system of the people involved. Here again the answer can ultimately only be that of the effective communication of the Gospel, to the answering of the questions which the Thlinget people unconsciously ask themselves.

I would be very cautious about functional substitutes as well. I do not think it is the missionary's place to institute functional substitutes, although it is certainly his place to suggest them at times. I think that functional substitutes are inevitable, that they must inevitably come when in the process of culture change an empty place, a vacuum, is left unmet in the needs which the society feels. Unless functional substitutes are genuinely incorporated by the people themselves, however, they are too divorced and do not really meet the need but instead simply satisfy the qualms of the missionary's conscience.

### Warmth and Security of the Gospel

These brief rambling notes in reply to your article will, of course, never really come to grips with the problems that you see around you in Alaska. No one can do so from the outside. If they have any value in stimulating fruitful ideas for you or others, we will be most grateful. Let me come back once more to the basic feeling, the basic impression that I get from so many groups such as the Thlinget. It is that the church which meets their needs will be a church of warmth, of emotional activity — a church where the inhibited, the insecure, the fearful, will be able to give release to their emotions and worship their God spontaneously and freely and openly among their fellows. If I am not mistaken, Christ can be to these people a protector, an older brother, a guard, in a sense that we in our self-sufficient way will never know. There is much that we can teach the Thlinget, but I suspect that if a people's movement breaks out among them there will be aspects of their understanding of God which we have never really appreciated. If we would listen, perhaps there is much they could teach us, too.

W. A. S.

**Reprinted from Vol. 6, No. 3 (1959), pp. 140-144.**

*Paul Abrecht and William A. Smalley*

# The Moral Implications of Social Structure

*It has not been often that the editor of* PRACTICAL ANTHROPOLOGY *has received a letter raising serious objection to any of the many viewpoints which have been expressed in the pages of the magazine. We welcome such letters, of course, as they draw attention to weaknesses of presentation, faulty logic, wrong data, unwarranted conclusions, and many other possible problems with material published in PA. We did receive one such letter from the Rev. Paul Abrecht of the Department on Church and Society, Division of Studies of the World Council of Churches in Geneva. Since it was in reference to something I had written, I am taking this opportunity of printing the letter along with an explanation of my earlier statement.*

**The Letter From Mr. Abrecht**

With much of Mr. Smalley's interesting statement on "Planting the Church in a Disintegrating Society" (PRACTICAL ANTHROPOLOGY, September-December 1958) I can agree. However, I would like to take issue with some of his remarks on page 232. He writes:

> There is nothing intrinsically moral or right and wrong about social structure as such. The many different social structures as found today in the world are simply many different ways of organizing group behavior into useful channels and of making life more valuable to the participants in the society. The missionary's role in relation to this as in relation to other cultural matters is to let history take its course and to concern himself with more important issues.

There is, I agree, no "Christian" structure of society; all social structures stand under the judgment of God. But from the Christian point of view, might it not be argued that some social structures are definitely *bad*? How to go about changing them is another question. Would not Mr. Smalley agree that the Christian has a responsibility today to work for change in the structure of racially segregated communities in the U.S.A.? And suppose a Christian convert in a colonial society complains of the injustice of the political setup. Is it not within the missionary's responsibility to help him understand his responsibility — as a Christian — in working for change in the political structure? Or suppose that a woman living in a polygamous society has become a Christian and begins to understand the meaning of the monogamous family ethic developed in the New Testament. Is she not to be encouraged to think out the meaning of responsible change in the structure of family life?

Mr. Smalley reacts very rightly against missionaries who have attempted to promote change or resist it in a tactless way in the past. But in reacting to this he goes to the other extreme adopting a positivistic attitude of ethical neutrality to structures. It is true that later in this message Mr. Smalley qualifies his statement by declaring that the missionary may point to "possible avenues of change." But the suspicion remains that Mr. Smalley believes social structures are really outside our Christian concern.

Toward the end of his statement Mr. Smalley says in regard to the problems of illegitimate birth and extramarital sex behavior, "They too will not be remedied by any direct action upon them as such, but only through a restructuring of the whole value system of the people involved." Who is to do this restructuring of the value system? The government administrator? The lawyer? The anthropologist? May not the Christian community itself have a role in such "restructuring"?

The Christian, I believe, is concerned with the whole of life including the moral basis for the structures of society. In the change or reform of such structures the Christian has the duty to work for responsible human relations. Mr. Smalley's view would seem to deny the obligation of the church to express its concern for man in all his social relationships. At least his way of stating his position might give rise to that suspicion.

### Form and Meaning

In replying to Mr. Abrecht's well-taken comments, I would first like to point out a distinction in my own thinking which I obviously did not make clear in my earlier article under discussion. It is the difference between a structure, and the meaning of that structure. To take a clear-cut case from language, many different structures can convey roughly equivalent meaning, and the same structure can carry different meanings. To illustrate with two languages which are rather alike in structure, as languages in the world go, "He read it to me" and "Il me l'a lu" (literally "He me it has read") are pretty much the same, meaning-wise, but very different structurally. They belong to entirely different language systems, involve different kinds of grammatical agreement, consist of different sounds, etc. On the other hand, "He is in the dog house" (to use a hackneyed example) has two entirely unrelated meanings for the same English sentence.

To say that language structure and meaning are different is not to say that they can ever be divorced from each other. But they are different, and the ability to keep this difference in mind is of great importance to the linguist who works with a variety of languages in an analytical way. It can make his understanding of both form and meaning clearer as it separates out the variables which are found from language to language. An extreme case of the confusion of form and meaning in language is the situation where the actual phonetic form of the name of God becomes sacred, as it did among the ancient Jews, where to utter the name of Yahweh was sacrilege. Less extreme examples of this kind of confusion of linguistic form and meaning may be found in many churches today.

It seems to me that it is important to keep this kind of distinction in mind for other kinds of cultural behavior as well as for language. Let's take one of Mr. Abrecht's questions as an example: "Racially segregated communities in the U.S.A." carries a charged meaning to almost any American. But is it the structural fact of segregation of race which is bad, or is it the tremendous variety of meaning overtones which such segregation happens in this cases to imply: "second-class citizens," unequal opportunity, contempt, suppression, congenital inferiority, etc.? The simple formal, structural fact of segregation in itself is not evil. French- and English-speaking Canadians live relatively segregated lives. So do the various ethnic groups of Switzerland and Belgium. Why is the segregation of Negroes and Whites in U.S.A. communities evil but the segregation between millions of African Negroes and American Whites (or Negroes) not bad? It surely is not the Atlantic Ocean which makes the one immoral and the other amoral. The meaning underlying the two forms of segregation is entirely different.

To us, slavery is "bad." It was a burning issue at one time in American history until we eliminated it to replace it with other evils. The Biblically oriented Christian, however, would have a hard time justifying the idea that the structure, the institution of slavery, is universally bad. St. Paul was certainly not bothered about it. It was not one of the issues that Jesus made anything of. The "badness" of slavery is related to new meanings which have been read into it since New Testament times, meanings of the degradation of the individual, deprivation of spirit, destruction of human dignity and independence, to name only some.

## Restructuring Comes from Within

If it is granted that there is a distinction between structure and its meaning, what is the practical relationship between them when it comes to culture change? Structures which acquire unfavorable meaning often have to be changed. In language we see clear examples of this. A word like "damn" (and many much more vulgar words) in English has nothing wrong with it so far as its structure is concerned. The sequence of sounds is no better or worse than any other sequence of sounds. "Nice" people are careful about the use of it, however, and some children will in fun use the homophonous word "dam" because of the association of the sound of the two words. The meaning makes it relatively taboo. The illustration could be made stronger if it were not that some other words are so more decidedly taboo that I do not even feel comfortable in using them as an illustration.

In similar manner, as the meaning of slavery in the Western world gradually changed because of new ideas about human dignity and justice, the form of slavery became intolerable. An internal restructuring of values resulted in the elimination of those social structures which seemed to reflect outgrown attitudes. But here lies a very interesting fact about human culture. Such a change in values results in change in social structure only in those social relationships which at the time symbolize the repudiated meaning. Slavery was abolished, but it was to be another generation before issues of colonialism would be called into question. The same changes in values concerning human beings eventually found a new symbol to fight against in the structure of colonialism. I doubt that the men who worked so energetically for the freedom of the American slaves would have seen colonialism as being a related issue at all. At that time colonialism meant Christianizing the heathen, medical facilities for the sick, philanthropy for the underprivileged, education and enlightenment for darkened minds.

In other words, a change in values, new ideas, a sharpened sensitivity will produce structural change, but it will produce it only in those structures which *seem to the participants* to be symbolic of the "badness." The new values, the new sense of right and wrong, the new feeling against injustice, may well be due to stimulation from outside the culture. I suppose that it usually is. Any significant change, however, comes only from within the culture. It is only as people in a particular society begin to attach new meanings to old forms (or old meanings of badness become intensified to the point where the form becomes intolerable) that change in structure which has any significance takes place.

The new meanings which bring about changes in habits of behavior are not necessarily what the outsider would expect. There is, for example, an ancient custom among some of the mountain tribes of Vietnam, in which the upper incisors of adolescent children are sawed or hacked out as a beauty measure, and as a symbol of growing up. Missionaries have long opposed the custom as being unhygienic (because of resulting infections), cruel, and evidence of heathen superstition and degradation. The custom has been disappearing, until now it is rather rare except in remote areas, but I am sure it is not disappearing primarily for the missionaries' reasons. There are certainly some cases of Christians who have been taught and believe that this is an unchristian type of behavior, but they believe this ritually, without emotional conviction. The real reasons for the change are probably simply that the mutilation symbolizes cultural "backwardness," and that there are more and more people who want their children to look more like the neighboring Vietnamese and even the Westerners living there. What was once a beauty mark has become a symbol or mark of lack of cultural progress and development. There is certainly not the same horrified meaning of savagery and badness which the outsider feels about the custom. This change, then, has little or no significance in terms of Christian ethics, humanity, mercy, or anything of the kind. It is much more a matter of keeping up with a new set of Joneses.

Mr. Abrecht's question about the Christian convert in a colonial society who complains of the injustice of the political setup is a case in point. Is it, or is it not the missionary's responsibility to help him understand his responsibility, as a Christian, in working for change in the political structure? Put in those terms, terms of helping a man understand his responsibilities, there can be only an affirmative answer. But it is precisely here that the rub comes. The missionary in this situation may assume that the man's responsibility is to work for culture change. But is that necessarily so? Biblically, the themes of resignation to one's social lot are as strong as the denunciations of social injustice. What is the man's responsibility in working for change in political structure? This is something the alien missionary can never really know. The missionary's role here as always must be primarily that of leading the convert to an ever-deepening understanding of God, of His revelation in Jesus Christ, and of the relationship of responsible obedience and fellowship which God seeks in His people. He must encourage and stimulate the Christians to seek that cultural expression which will best reflect within the meanings of their cultural habits these new values which they are gradually coming to understand. He must help them see in the Scriptures some of God's history of dealing with men in an enormous variety of cultural circumstances, and to seek from the Holy Spirit that intimate personal guidance which God seeks to give His church in all times and cultures. If, as in so many places in the dwindling colonial world today, such new values focus upon a meaning of overwhelming "badness" in the colonial political structure, certainly that will come within the sphere of change, in one way or another.

But the restructuring comes from within. It is in a sense the by-product. Responsible allegiance to God within any human cultural framework will show up in culture change, sometimes enormous change. It is, however, the allegiance, not the change, which is ultimately significant, and which it is the missionary's role to foster.

Sometimes culture change can be enforced on such a large scale that it becomes permanent. Headhunting, scarification, polygamy, or human sacrifice have been eliminated from several cultures by the police-reinforced diligence of an alien administration. I am not necessarily opposed to all such activity on the part of administrators, but it is very clear that resulting change has no moral value whatsoever. The meanings expressed by these cultural forms are preserved in some other way, and as long as the same meanings are preserved nothing of moral value has been accomplished.

Some individuals may have been saved from suffering or death, and from a Western viewpoint this is of enormous value, but within the local culture it may have no significance whatsoever. It is only when a sense of respect for the personality of other individuals, for their physical welfare, and above all, for them as actual or potential brothers in Christ, gets reflected in a change of behavior toward reducing suffering and death within the culture that such change has moral significance.

## The Role of the Church

Who is to do this restructuring of the value system? The government? No. It cannot. Neither can the lawyer, the anthropologist, or the missionary. No alien can, although new ideas, stimulus for change, awareness of new horizons, alternative forms of behavior, may all well come from these outside sources.

It is precisely the community itself, including the Christian community, which has the principal though generally quite unconscious role in the change of values and habits. For the Christian community there is yet another force, and that is God in culture, the Holy Spirit dwelling within the children of God. It is interesting, though, that God seems more willing to work through the existing forms of culture than many of His more intellectual followers want to admit.

The missionary, no matter how complete his identification with the local community, remains an alien. I have discussed his role in culture change elsewhere.[1] If he honestly and perceptively faces up to the issue of leading men to God, to total commitment to Christ, to an awareness of Christian life in culture, *their* cultures, stimulating them to find the structures which will best express their new faith, he has fulfilled his role. He may then well "let history take its course" because he has "concerned himself with more important issues."

[1] William A. Smalley, "The Missionary and Culture Change," PRACTICAL ANTHROPOLOGY, Vol. 4, No. 6 (Nov.-Dec., 1957), pp. 231-237. See also, William A. Smalley, "Cultural Implications of an Indigenous Church," PRACTICAL ANTHROPOLOGY, Vol. 5, No. 2 (March-April, 1958), pp. 51-65, **and in this volume.**

*Dale W. Kietzman*

**Reprinted from Vol. 5, No. 5 (1958), pp. 203-210.**

# Conversion and Culture Change

*In his analysis of the process of culture change, Mr. Kietzman reduces the problem basically to a series of interactions of various kinds between individuals. These individuals represent the local culture, and the West (in the case of the missionary) in their ways of behaving. The interaction is not only between the two different cultural groups, but also within them, among individuals with varying predispositions, backgrounds, and points of view. The agents of conversion are the Holy Spirit and the Word of God. These also bring about culture change by working through individuals to whom they have spoken.*

THE application of the science of anthropology to the cultural problems involved in missionary activity has yet to be precisely defined. Many practical applications have been reported on the pages of PRACTICAL ANTHROPOLOGY, and an occasional attempt has also been made to discuss its essential usefulness in relation to basic missionary principles.[1] But there seems to be no unanimity of opinion on this point on the part of either Christian anthropologists or missionaries.

To some, anthropology has its major usefulness in permitting the missionary to understand more completely the motives of the people with whom he works. Others add to this the thought of successful communication of the Gospel message. There are many who favor a policy of "action" with regard to cultural forces which must be "molded" or "disciplined" to fit more exactly their concept of "Christian morality." Opposing the latter view are those who assert that our knowledge of cultures given us no right to institute or further any cultural modifications, however desirable they may seem.

Which of these (or other) viewpoints is correct? A definitive answer to this question would be important both for current missionary work and for the training of new missionaries. It is the purpose of this paper to seek a simple answer to this problem from among the complexities of the mission field of today.

## Two Basic Factors in Missions

The factors which confuse our view of mission field problems are not primarily those of differing cultures and widely divergent religious systems. It is

[1] As for instance, the three-point statement of missionary aims given by Barney, PRACTICAL ANTHROPOLOGY, Vol. 4, pp. 48-49.

**Dale W. Kietzman is director of the work of the Summer Institute of Linguistics in Brazil. He has written two previous articles for PRACTICAL ANTHROPOLOGY. They are "Folklore: A Tool for the Missionary" (1955), and "The Missionary's Role in Culture Change" (1954).**

not to be denied that these features demand modifications in our approach and methods, but these should be changes only in detail of application, not in basic principle. Rather, the complexity originates in two factors: the history of missionary work on a given field, and the variation in approximation of indigenous groups to Westernized "Christian" culture.

With regard to the missionary effort on a field, the determining factor of difference is best stated in terms of the relative degree of success with which cultural problems have been met. Some fields represent very old works which have been crowned with good success, as demonstrated by the deep spiritual understanding and judgment of the Christians, particularly toward their own conduct and witness in the society. Other fields, equally old, display results only in terms of overt cultural changes or statistical factors, with little evidence of real understanding or permanence of decision in the hearts of the people. Then there are newer fields. On one there is remarkable success, with many conversions; on others consecrated missionaries have worked unsuccessfully toward the establishment of a vital witness within the society.

The approximation of the native culture to our civilization is noted because it largely determines the ease with which our purposes and our presentation of the Gospel may be understood. It also affects, both in quantity and in kind, the cultural changes which may result from missionary activity. The degree and ease of approximation is, in turn, determined by such factors as the size and homogeneity of the native population and the nature of and reaction to cultural contacts in which it has participated. There are groups like the Terena of southern Mato Grosso in Brazil, who display a real drive toward the achievement of equality with, and eventual integration into, the neo-Brazilian population that surrounds them. Surely here a missionary would be justified in helping to prepare these people for what seems to be the only possible solution for their future. But there are other, usually larger groups, which, although they may have the same degree of contact with Western civilization, may nevertheless preserve their ethnic and cultural identities for generations to come. In contrast to these are the very small groups, some tending toward extinction, some already caught in the cross-currents of Westernization, some untouched cultural islands.

We may restate these two factors as being our presentation of the Gospel and the resistance of the native culture to it. These are the essential features also of the problem of the indigenous church, which is the presumed goal for most missionary activity today. We normally think of our particular presentation of Christianity as being placed in direct opposition to specific features of the pagan culture. The success of our program will be demonstrated by the establishment of a church, ideally a self-maintaining institution which will remain in permanent and visible contrast to the institutions of the pagan religion and culture. The problem of initiating such an indigenous church has been stated as that of making our message relevant to, or in, the culture; then, of transforming the culture, insofar as the Christian community is concerned, so that the church can maintain a suitable standard of Christian morality, and thus a witness to the non-Christians of the society.

**The Individual**

This particular presentation of the problem is a completely impersonal one. It represents the conflict as between two systems or institutions, each presupposing a way of life that is intrinsically antagonistic to the other. This consequently divides the society into two opposing groups, each with its own standards of conduct and, in a real sense, its own culture.

But this viewpoint completely ignores one important factor. That is the individuality of the bearer of the culture and of the believer in the church. We need not elaborate on the fact that the conversion of a Christian is a completely individual decision, and that he assumes, through the new birth, a personal relationship with God, his Father. The reality of the church institution can never be permitted to obscure this essentially individual character of Christian responsibility.

In the same way, while we speak of cultures and corresponding societies, we must not lose sight of the fact that individuals are bearers of the culture. They individually and deliberately may choose between alternatives of conduct or decide to depart from traditional ways. True, most individuals never examine critically their reasons for action, and even when they do, they probably seldom undergo a crisis experience equal to conversion. Yet this does not nullify the individuality and personality of the bearer of the culture. Thus, just as the spiritual vitality of an indigenous church is determined by the depth of personal experience of its members, so the validity of a cultural item is determined by the acceptance or lack of acceptance accorded it by the individual members of the society.

**Interactions Between Individuals**

We can now reduce the problem of the mission field to a series of interactions between individuals, some of one culture and some of another. The first such interaction is between the missionary, a representative of one culture but with a standard of obedience that is not entirely bound by that culture, and individuals of another culture whose standard of obedience is culturally determined. The missionary hopes that this interaction will result in the conversion of the pagan. The anthropological problem involved is that of communicating the Gospel, but in such a way that it is comprehensible entirely within the thought patterns and other bounds imposed by the pagan culture.

The next type of interaction observable in missionary activity brings together these same individuals, and they are still within their original cultural groupings. This time, however, the missionary is attempting to "perfect" the new believer, or to help him to become mature in his Christian faith. This he does by imparting to his convert the same standard of obedience that he himself follows. The anthropological problem involved is that of encouraging this growth through teaching that is based neither on the culture of the convert nor on the culture of the teacher, because this standard does not spring from either culture. "Be not conformed to this world, but be ye transformed by the renewing of your mind, that ye may prove what is that good, and acceptable, and perfect will of God."[2] It is the mind of the convert, and not his culture, that is here transformed.

The third instance of personal interaction does not include the foreign mis-

[2] Romans 12: 2.

sionary and is basically apart from his activity. It is the interaction of the transformed Christian and a non-Christian of the same society. Both are bearers of the same culture, but they now have divergent lines of obedience and, therefore, may make different choices of conduct within the culture. The convert has matured, as one of those who "by reason of use have their senses exercised to discern both good and evil."[3] It is precisely his wisdom of choice of the ethical "good" within his own culture that constitutes his witness to the non-Christian. The choice of a foreign pattern of conduct could never represent such a culturally pertinent testimony.

This is the stage at which cultural change will occur as the result of the acceptance of the Gospel. But initially, barring outside pressures, it will be in terms of a change in the frequency of choice of a particular behavior pattern — generally a choice that was already possible within the culture. The anthropological problem for the missionary is one of nullifying effectively the cultural influence of his own physical presence on the scene of such an event. The change must come as the result of a discipleship of obedience to God on the part of the native Christian, and not as the result of any obedience or allegiance to the missionary as such.[4]

This series of personal interactions, while sketchy, serves to define the role of anthropology on the mission field. This role can be stated in a twofold principle:[5] (1) to make it possible to communicate adequately the complete Gospel message across cultural barriers; and (2) to prevent the missionary's cultural background[6] and interpretations of Christianity from affecting the development of the native Christian pattern of obedience to God within the aboriginal culture.[7]

## Culture Changes

This presentation of the problem of the mission field leaves a number of areas on which further discussion is required. Foremost of these is the question as to whether we can be sure that an obviously needed change in the conduct of new Christians will come about without the direct or indirect guidance and leadership of the missionary. The answer to this needs to be sought in two directions, first that of the normal processes of change within a culture, and then of the peculiar power which is at the disposal of the native Christian as he continues to live within his society.

Several aspects of culture change have importance for us. We need to realize that, in any culture, there are frequent alternative patterns of conduct, of many of which we are completely unaware.

[3] Hebrews 5: 14.

[4] Note the comment of Fredrickson, PRACTICAL ANTHROPOLOGY, Vol. 4, p. 221: "If by the skilled use of natural group pressures the missionary-teacher obtains conformity from the disciple-student, the missionary-teacher is guilty of substituting an arbitrary law of a religious culture for the law of God, and thus he has replaced God with an idol."

[5] I consider this to be a positive and a negative statement of the same proposition.

[6] Here "our cultural background" can be taken to include academically learned alternatives of behavior, which we many not practise but which we may be tempted to introduce into a third culture. They are just as foreign in that culture as they are in ours.

[7] I have used terms which may seem to limit these comments to the so-called primitive mission fields. That is not the intention. I believe these same principles apply to the "native" Christian in America who must make his witness to the "pagans" around him in terms of the "aboriginal" culture.

Except as the result of intensive and perceptive study, we do not observe more than the grosser patterns of conduct, those practised by the majority. The percentage of deviations from the norm will be small, and furthermore these deviations are apt to be shielded from the view of the outsider, either deliberately, or simply because "rebels" do not represent the leadership of the tribe which is in the van of contact with the outside world. It is also possible that these differing patterns of conduct are not practised at all at the present time, but are remembered and honored only through the historical influence of the folklore. Such a native pattern of conduct, if compatible with Christian life and witness, would obviously be more meaningful to Christian and non-Christian alike, than would a completely foreign item. It is the native Christian, and not the missionary, who is in a position to know of this possibility and to make the decision to utilize it.

Along this same line we should mention the fact that such minor patterns of conduct are not infrequently widely recognized as "good," even though the majority of the people do otherwise, with perhaps no sense of "badness" about their actual conduct. Barney, for example, cities the fact that among the Meo of Laos there was a "conscience" within the pre-contact culture which presented a "better" norm of conduct than that usually followed with regard to trial marriage and the use of opium. It was precisely these things which the native Christians first spontaneously "changed," although in reality they were only actualizing a standard at least partially existing within their own culture.[8]

[8] Barney, PRACTICAL ANTHROPOLOGY, Vol. 4, pp. 33, 39, 40, and in this volume.

Another feature which we often overlook is that cultures are in a constant process of change, both as a result of internal pressures difficult to analyze, and as a result of pressures from without. This means that there are many facets of a culture which, at any given moment, are either in the process of change or on the verge of an overt change. Even after the introduction of Christianity, Christianity is not the only force at work causing or shaping culture change. In fact it probably results in a good deal less disturbance than many of the "civilizing" features which often accompany its introduction. In all such situations of change, regardless of the cause, there are natural forces at work which, if given time, will adequately shape and stabilize the modified culture. For our purposes, we need to analyze accurately the pressures both toward change and toward stabilization, so that we can be sure which changes are really the result of the introduction of Christianity, which are incidentally shaped by it, and which have no vital connection whatever.

## Change Resulting from Conversion

Then we need to recognize what are the true agents, or motivating forces, of such changes as do result from conversion. These I would limit to the Holy Spirit and the written Word of God. Whether these forces are to be permitted to operate in freedom and fulness is, in a real sense, within the control of the missionary. The arena in which they can work is the heart and mind of the native Christian. As a product of his society, he is acutely aware of the drives and pressures of the culture. As a born-again child of God, he becomes also the temple of the Holy Spirit. If the written Word of God is available to him, we have brought these forces which determine behavior into their natural area of interaction, counteracting as effectively as we can the second culture problem present in the missionary, and leaving the message with the irreducible minimum of cultural problems inherent in the Bible itself. We can be certain that there are present all the necessary potentialities for the right kind of cultural change. To answer the question, then, of whether desired cultural change can be brought about without the action of the missionary, we have suggested both the power of the Holy Spirit to change cultures when allowed to do so, and the power of any culture free from external and contradictory pressures to accommodate such change.

It could be objected that following this policy presents the possibility that, by ineptness or an overabundance of zeal, the native Christian may somehow disrupt his own culture and cause irremediable damage. Again we need to emphasize that the living force of Christianity will not destroy a culture.[9] Christianity brings, rather, a reexamination of religious tenets and related institutions, which causes, not destruction, but new life to be brought to each item thus examined. It would be a dead faith indeed that could not bring life, even on a cultural level.

Now such reexaminations, by native Christians, of culturally determined beliefs will take time. It may be that change will proceed too slowly to suit the observer, then appear to spurt far beyond any practical limits, considering the result to be obtained. Or it may take a most unusual, and to our eyes, "unchristian" turn. But as Buchwalter very pointedly observes, "this has also forced me to accept as of the Spirit of God, Scripture interpretations which in some respects differ from my own"; and "if we really believe we should be founders of indigenous churches, we dare not entertain any illusions as to the form they will take."[10] These same facts are emphasized by anthropologists who speak in general terms of culture change, apart from the specific problems associated with the introduction of Christianity.[11]

### The Presence of the Missionary

This brings us then to the problem of the physical presence of the missionary on the field while these changes are taking place. Will he not be regarded as an example for believers, and, actually, should he not be so regarded? Will he not be consulted on these problems? How can he avoid the responsibility of teaching that which he knows is applicable to the moral problems being worked out? Again we need to approach these questions from various angles.

The really serious problem here is that the missionary is seldom aware of the many ways in which he is affecting native life, completely apart from so-called "missionary" work. His very presence as a foreigner, even though living in modified Western style, can at times have a greater disruptive effect than his preach-

9 Note the contentions of Reyburn, PRACTICAL ANTHROPOLOGY, Vol. 4, p. 166; and Barney, pp. 49-50.

10 Buchwalter, PRACTICAL ANTHROPOLOGY, Vol. 3, pp. 94, 102.

11 As for instance A. P. Elkins, in *Social Anthropology in Melanesia,* Oxford University Press, London, 1953, p. 148: "The new objects . . . moral standards and religious beliefs must be introduced through native authority and acceptance, so that natives themselves can work out the consequent changes or cultural and social adjustments. They alone can do this, and it takes time, experience, and experiment."

ing of the Gospel. Even where we may, to outward appearances, adapt ourselves to native patterns, our subconscious habits and our attitudes and questions, betray our "otherness."[12] We may be accepted, but the native population has had to make a conscious adjustment to accommodate us. Thus our problem is greater if we are concerned with not being an example in non-essentials, than if we want to be an example toward some particular item of moral practice.[13]

On the other hand, the missionary may feel that he can overcome this barrier and present a true witness within another culture, by following a participative role in that culture. In may ways there is greater danger along this line of reasoning than in frankly realizing that the matter of culture change is outside the scope of the missionary task.

The question could be put, "How indigenous can the missionary become?" The missionary's participative role is always limited. It is impossible for him to cut loose completely from his own cultural moorings and adopt wholesale those of another people, submerging himself completely in the moral orientations of a different culture.[14] As long as the missionary remains, in any respect, a foreign element, it is not within his power to demonstrate by his life how the practices of a native culture are to be "transvaluated." This is the job of the native Christian. We are and will remain different, and the problem is to make our message, and not ourselves, culturally relevant.[15]

The correct understanding of the missionary's role in molding Christian conduct is of extreme importance in laying the foundation for an effective and continuing witness within a culture. Our most important witness will always be the Word of God in the language of the people. But there must also be a witness that is within the specific framework of the culture. If that witness is

12 One of the most disturbing of these "foreign" attitudes, which can have a profund effect on native peoples, is strikingly phrased in the article by Taylor, reprinted in PRACTICAL ANTHROPOLOGY, Vol. 3, pp. 116-117: "It is surprizing how many white people . . . imagine that an educated African should be a replica of themselves. It is far more tragic when Africans come to share this view. . . . The source of much of the desperate frustration of Africa is a fundamental lack of faith in the contribution of the coloured people, not only on the part of the white folk, but among the Africans themselves. The fantastical technical success of modern Western man seems to so dazzle the eyes of blacks and whites alike that the European easily assumes a similar superiority in all other spheres of life, and the African, bedeviled with self-mistrust, seeks only to play a resentful second fiddle to the white man's tune."

13 We do not refer to the social service type program which many missions carry on. While these missions may find their motivation in Christian love, or in the more pragmatic view that these programs are the means of attracting people to the spiritual purposes of the missionary, these same programs nevertheless can be, and are, carried on effectively by agencies of a-religious governments. We have in view the conscious spiritual and moral objectives of the missionaries. Only as these other programs may affect the moral judgments of native Christians are they in question here.

14 Note particularly the argument of G. A. deLaguna in "Cultural Relativism and Science," *Philosophical Review*, Vol. LI, 1942, pp. 141-66, in which she approaches the problem from a philosophical viewpoint and demonstrates that a theoretical relativism involving an exchange of cultural standards is impossible.

15 This is not to deny the effectiveness of participation as an anthropological technique for winning the confidence of the people and for giving unusual insights into their thought patterns. The reference here is to participation with the expectation that it will be possible to demonstrate Christian values of conduct to those of another culture.

to be basically one of conduct, then the conduct must be such that it is understandable to everyone who is within the culture. This cannot be established by the example of a foreign missionary or by the introduction of foreign elements. To be effective it must come from within, it must be an indigenous reinterpretation of cultural values.

This is not a *laissez-faire* outlook upon the missionary's role in culture change. It is a practical realization of our deficiencies and of the power of the Holy Spirit to revitalize and "cleanse" a culture through the agency of native Christians. It still requires the careful training of missionaries in the problems of culture in order that they may adequately meet this extremely delicate problem on the field.

*John Beekman*

# A Culturally Relevant Witness

ONE of the important duties of the missionary is to learn the culture of the people among whom he serves so as to be able to select those Scriptural truths which will have the greatest relevance to their particular needs and concerns. These are usually not the same as those which have appealed to the missionary in his own culture. While the basic need of man and the basic message is the same everywhere, the most effective presentation of the gospel is that which takes into account the cultural beliefs and fears of the people. The rapid growth of the church among the Chol Indians of southern Mexico may, in part, be attributed to a culturally relevant witness.

The Chols believe in the sun and the moon as beneficent deities. These have been equated with God the Father and Mary, the mother of Jesus, as the result of the influence of Catholicism. In their churches an idol of Jesus has also become an object of their belief. The devil, however, occupies a greater place in their thinking than the aforementioned. Since the Father, Mary, and the Son pity mankind and all their activity is directed toward the well-being of man, they need never be appeased. In contrast, the devil, who is considered the owner of the world and the ruler of the spirits in the realm of nature and in the animal kingdom, is the one who causes the hardships of life and who must be satisfied with sacrifices. When angered, he steals part of a person's spirit and locks it in a cave. It is important to avoid his anger. Belief in his malevolent avariciousness for spirits has given to him a greater importance than the deities of their more formal religious life.

When a baby boy or girl is born among the Chol Indians, the midwife may take the baby to the cave where the devil is supposed to live. After sweeping the inside of the cave and making an animal sacrifice to the devil, the midwife will request the privilege of asking for additional spirits for the new baby. The devil supposedly answers giving permission, and the midwife will proceed to ask for the spirits of a tiger, an earth mole, a humming bird, a fox, of the lightning, of the wind, and of fire. Seven spirits are requested. Only in infancy and in this manner can a person be indwelt with extra spirits. With these extra spirits the baby will grow strong with little sickness. After such a child has grown and has been taught the chants, he becomes a full-fledged witch doctor with the power to commune with the devil and to work black magic on others.

All sickness among the Chols is believed to come from either of two sources. The devil, who is considered to be the owner of the world, may become angry and steal part of one's spirit. Sickness then follows. For example, if a baby in learn-

---

**Reprinted from Vol. 4, No. 6 (1957), pp. 83-88. Mr. John Beekman is director of the work of the Wycliffe Bible Translators in Guatemala. He was formerly a member of the committee which translated the New Testament into Chol.**

ing to walk falls upon the ground, the devil may become angered because the baby fell on his property. In his anger he will steal part of the baby's spirit and the child will become ill. Or, when a corn field is made, large trees are felled and finally burned in preparation for the planting of corn. The devil may become angered with this use of his property and cause sickness. Or when a new home is built, holes are dug for the four corner posts. Logs are taken from the forest and grass from the lowlands. This use of the devil's property may arouse his anger and bring sickness to the residents of such a house.

The second source of sickness is the curse of a neighbor or the witch doctor, through which one may become indwelt with an evil spirit. For example, the spirit of frogs causes a bloated stomach; the spirit of wasps causes boils; the spirit of an earth mole digging away at the roots of a tooth causes a toothache. The cure for these, as the cure of all sickness, requires a consultation with the witch doctor. For a toothache he will prescribe the trapping of an earth mole. After this has been trapped, he will begin his chants and ceremony, moving the dead mole over the aching tooth. As he does this the spirit at work in the aching tooth is supposed to pass out into the dead earth mole.

When one's spirit has been stolen by the devil and imprisoned in his cave, the witch doctor must be consulted also. He will first commune with the devil to find out what sacrifice will appease his anger. It may be a pig, turkey, or chicken along with a designated quantity of liquor. When the sick person or a member of his family has secured these items, the witch doctor will come into the home of the patient. The animal is stuck and the blood caught in a gourd. Then the ceremony begins. The blood is mixed with liquor and herbs. The witch doctor takes these into his mouth and then spits them out in a stream upon the sick person. Then the patient may be given some to drink. The chanting and the playing of the violin accompany this ceremony, which may last a day and a night or several days and nights.

Sickness may be prevented by anticipating the anger of the devil. When a corn field is made, a sacrifice can be given to the devil in advance of any sickness. Thus, before any corn is planted, parts of a chicken are planted in the four corners of the field. Likewise, when a new home is finished, before the family moves in, the witch doctor is called to make a sacrifice to the devil. He spits the blood of an animal on the walls, then climbs up into the rafters and spits the blood into the grass roof. Parts of the sacrifice are buried under each of the corner posts. The house is thus dedicated to the devil. Therefore, if a child in learning to walk should fall within the house, no sickness follows. For this same reason, until recently the pagans buried their dead within the home.

How would you present the gospel to a pagan people whose faith and fear in this system was such that it entered their daily thinking? In times of crisis the new believers would seek out the services of the witch doctor. It was evident that he was the unifying factor in the culture. He was the only one who could commune with the devil to determine what sacrifice would be acceptable to regain one's health. He was the one through whom one could get revenge on a stronger neighbor who had done one evil. He was the one to be feared because of his extra spirits. Could he not cause corn to be blown down with his wind spirit? Could he not go great distances and spy on one's deeds with his humming bird spirit? Could he not cause one's house to be struck with his lightning spirit? Did he not have extraordinary powers with seven extra spirits?

The gospel was not presented in terms of salvation from hell, not that this is not an important truth, but because it was not the most important in the thinking of the Chols. Everyone expected to go to hell for a certain number of years and to escape it entirely seemed presumptuous and not especially necessary. To be sure, Scriptural truth was brought to bear on the belief that one would be given a term of years to serve in hell.

The gospel was presented in terms of gaining a Spirit more powerful than all the spirits of the witch doctor. Those who were contacted on the trails or in other places were told that the witch doctor was not altogether wrong. It is true that we can be indwelt with other spirits. They were then told of the Holy Spirit, who not only the witch doctor could have, but anyone at any age of life could have through simple faith in the shed blood of God's Son. The blood was specifically mentioned because of their cultural belief in the efficacy of animal blood, as already pointed out. They were told that the witch doctor was powerful, but that the Holy Spirit had more power than he. In fact, he had more power than the devil himself. It was God who created the world. It was the Holy Spirit who moved upon the face of the water bringing order out of chaos. The devil, after all, is not the landowner. The ceremonies made for the devil as the landowner should, therefore, be made to God, who is the real owner.

The animal sacrifices made by the witch doctor were not directly condemned. The question was asked: Who started animal sacrifices? The answer varied between the devil and the first witch doctor. It was then pointed out that the Old Testament pictures animal sacrifices. But today, since Jesus has come and has shed his blood, the sacrifice of animals has no further purpose. The very core of their pagan belief was thus dealt with in a manner that each one could understand and was replaced with the heart of the gospel.

This, however, was not enough, as we have already intimated. Something has to take the place of the ceremonies. Cultural substitutes arose, some naturally by the believers themselves, some introduced by the missionary. When a corn field is to be planted, prayers for rain and a good yield are made. When the corn is harvested, a special service is held during the week to praise God for his provision. One congregation is now returning one ear of corn out of ten as a harvest offering. When a new house is finished, believers are invited to the new home to have a soft drink and cookies and to sing and pray for the blessings of God upon the new home and its occupants. When sickness comes, medicines are purchased. Instead of the witch doctor's chants, the missionary prayed for the effectiveness of the medicines and provided a phonograph with gospel records to be played throughout the night. Now, in case of serious illness, those who own a phonograph of their own follow this practice, while others will call in friends to pray and sing throughout the night. The empowering of the herbs and blood by the chants and music of the witch doctor has been replaced with medicines empowered by the prayers and hymns of the family. When children fall at play, no fear grips the heart of an onlooking mother. The simple truth presented in relation to their cultural beliefs and fears has indeed set them free.

---

*Eugene A. Nida*

# The Role of Language in Contemporary Africa

THERE is no doubt but what the limelight of publicity has been turned on the Dark Continent, which, of course, is no longer dark, except in the imaginations of those addicted to movie thrillers. This limelight of concern is promoted primarily by the fact that this huge continent, almost four times the size of the United States, is the greatest relatively untapped treasure of natural resources still available to the industrial world of western Europe and North America. But this focusing of attention upon Africa is not only characteristic of the secular press, the short-story magazine, and the leaders in industry; it is also characteristic of the attitudes of many foreign missions, which see in Africa not only a great challenge for the future, but one of the strategic areas for consecrated effort, especially in view of the pressures of materialism, Communism, nationalism, and Islam.

## Rapidity of Cultural Changes

It is almost a truism to state that Africa is rapidly changing, but the truth is that the rate of change is almost breathless. It would seem as though two thousand years of human development were being squeezed into the space of fifty years. What the ultimate results will be one cannot predict with certainty, but of the rapidity of change there is no doubt. Perhaps something of the incredible differences in present-day Africa, in contrast with the past, may be understood better by illustration than by statistics — as impressive as the latter may be. For example, several years ago we arrived in Ougadougou, in West Africa, at the time when a young African was being sent off to Paris to be a member of the National Assembly. He was bid farewell by all the French and African officials, given full military honors, and feted more lavishly than any resident of France who was ever elected to that office. In contrast with this, several of this young man's own relatives had only twenty years before been subjected to severe humiliation and torture for not having paid the assessed taxes required of their district — a policy

**Reprinted from Vol. 3, No. 3 (1956), pp. 122-137.**

which the French government is understandably anxious to have forgotten.

In Elizabethville, in the Belgian Congo, a part of what in the maps of one hundred years ago was only a black blob, a tourist lands on an all-concrete airstrip, is received at a beautiful airport, and may put up at any one of several strictly modern hotels, can visit a lovely museum, attend any one of a number of imposing churches, or visit some thriving night clubs. In this rapidly growing urban center there are over 100,000 Africans, representing at least twenty important different languages. It is no wonder that in the Methodist Church they have had eleven different Sunday school "departments," each for a different language group and each using its own New Testament or Bible.

Another aspect of African life is well illustrated by the leader of the Mau Mau movement, Mr. Jomo Kenyatta. Mr. Kenyatta was no ordinary native nationalistic enthusiast who "dreamed up" a nativistic movement because of some unrecognized frustration. He had studied anthropology in England and had had further training in sociology in Moscow. He was thoroughly acquainted with the best techniques of social dynamics, and only overwhelming military force has crushed for the time being a very well worked out plan for revolution.

In all these fascinating aspects of a continent rapidly breaking out of its "neolithic chrysalis" we must not lose sight of the fundamental cultural factors: rapid urbanization, concentrated industrialization, widespread education (following European patterns), the rise of an African elite, the potent forces for nationalism in Central and West Africa, the struggle for white supremacy in areas of permanent white settlement, and the increasing self-awareness of Africans on every level. However, in and through all these factors at work in transforming the life of Africa is one very important ingredient, language. And to understand what is happening today, we must take full note of language (and languages) as the mechanisms for social action, the symbols of prestige, and the technique for social structuring.

## Fundamental Aspects of Language

Before we can deal with some of the specific ways in which languages are playing an important role in contemporary Africa, we need to clarify certain fundamental facts about African languages and their significance. In the first place, we must recognize that in all probability there is more multilingualism in Africa than in any other equivalent area in the world. It is not at all uncommon to find people who speak three and four languages. Many are able to communicate in five or six. Furthermore, Africans have an unusual capacity for learning foreign languages — a trait which has been recognized and emphasized by almost all who have come in contact with this phase of African life.

In the second place, one must reckon with four functionally distinct kinds of languages: tribal, trade, colonial, and national. Of the tribal languages, there are probably at least 800 mutually unintelligible varieties. Fortunately, in a number of areas there is an overlayer of trade languages, which are often strictly for commerce. That is to say, they do not possess many of the richer refinements of large vocabularies, subtle grammatical categories, or widespread idiomatic usages. On the other hand, a number of "trade languages" like Swahili, Hausa, Yaounde, and Bambara do possess just such qualities, for in their trade usage these are only extensions of highly organized linguistic systems — tribal languages.

National languages include Arabic in the Sudan (involving certain special problems which we shall treat below), Amharic in Ethiopia (although it is meeting strong opposition from non-Amharic tribes), and English in Liberia. (English can scarcely be regarded as a colonial language in Liberia, for it was the language of the returning slaves from the United States, who "took over" Liberia not as a colony, but as an African home, with the purpose of developing a distinctly African nation.)

Colonial languages include French, English, Portuguese, and Spanish, with some residues of German and Italian from earlier periods of colonialization.

In the third place, language must be regarded as more than simply a technique of communication, for as in all societies, it is much more than that. Languages in Africa are important symbols of prestige, of social status, and of religious association. Unless we recognize these essential factors right from the beginning, we will fail to appreciate the function of language in African life, either in its contemporary setting or in its future role.

It is, of course, quite impossible in an article of this type to attempt to summarize all the developments with regard to languages in Africa, especially since the situations are so diverse in various parts of the continent. However, we do wish to call attention to certain specific developments as being typical of what is happening in various areas, and on the basis of these suggest some of the lines of development and the possible role of language in the future. To do much more than this would require a book dedicated to the various special problems.

## The Development of a Trade Language

Trade languages develop from "regular languages" by the simple process of being extended in their usage. However, they may (1) retain a major part of their original vocabulary and grammatical structure intact, or (2) be very much simplified. The spread of Swahili, Hausa, and Tshiluba has taken place largely along the first lines. The spread of "Pidgin English" in Southeast Asia and on the west coast of Africa and the development of Haitian Creole illustrate the second type of trade language. In these latter instances it was the European who tended to "speak down" to the indigenous peoples. However, in the development of Kituba, one of the four important trade languages of the Belgian Congo, the roles were reversed, but the process of simplification was similar. What evidently happened in the development of Kituba, spoken now by approximately three million people in the southwest part of Congo and in the southern portion of French Equatorial Africa, was that the Kikongo-speaking people in the lower Congo found that, in order to communicate effectively with the incoming white traders, government officials, and plantation and mine owners, they needed to employ a very much simplified form of their own language. The traditional forms of Kikongo proved to be entirely too complex for the linguistically inept whites. Undoubtedly, some similar form of simple language had been used in certain intertribal contacts before, but with the coming of the whites this very much simplified form of Kikongo was rapidly promoted, not only by the Africans, but especially by the whites, who found it ever so much easier to learn and to use.

This ultrasimple form of Kikongo, known as Kituba, Kikwango, Commercial Kikongo, and Kibulamatadi (Bulamatadi, meaning "stone-breakers," was the name given to white men in the lower Congo), was recognized by the Belgian colonial government as the official language of the native law courts and was employed throughout the southwestern area of the Congo in stores, mines, and factories, on plantations, and along the major arteries of communication and transportation.

There was some strong opposition to the use of Kituba, especially by missionaries who regarded it as utterly unsatisfactory for the purposes of evangelism and instruction. To an extent they were quite right, for it would not only be absurd, but quite wrong, to try to employ such a language in communicating to Kikongo-speaking people. However, in contacts with a multiplicity of small tribes on the fringe of the Kikongo area, it is easily understandable how missionaries soon began to use the Kituba, despite its many limitations.

## The Turning Point in Kituba Development

During all this time, however, Kituba was rapidly growing in vocabulary and was acquiring certain additional grammatical refinements, but still it remained essentially a second language until within the last ten to fifteen years, when it has become the only language for a considerable sector of people, who have lived all their lives in urban centers, on mining compounds, or in plantation areas. Young people have grown up to speak only Kituba, and many others, though they do know another tribal language, find that they can express themselves more adequately in Kituba than in any other. In the meantime, the government has published laws, chauffeurs' manuals, and formal notices in Kituba. It is used over the radio in broadcasts from Leopoldville, and is even employed in popular recordings of music. It has now passed the crisis stage in the development of a language, for it is a full-fledged language and is growing rapidly, not only in the size of vocabulary and idiomatic richness, but in the number of speakers.

We must not assume that Kituba will largely supplant the tribal languages, certainly not in the rural areas, nor will it ever be able to compete with French, for it has neither the long tradition nor the world usefulness, but Kituba is here to stay — at least for a good long while — and now, like every other language, will compete as a means of communication in an increasingly more complex area of African life.

## Extension of a National Language

Rather than deal with the spread of English in Liberia (where the people of the hinterland are only too anxious to learn it), or the development of Amharic (were there is a kind of stalemate in some areas, due to injudicious means of encouraging Amharic), it would seem best to mention some of the special problems related to the spread of Arabic in the Sudan, for here the various ethnolinguistic problems are exceedingly complex and the consequences particularly important for missionary work.

In the first place, it must be recognized that the artificial carving out of the Sudan as one unit might have been geographically justified, but it certainly was not ethnically valid. Almost from the start the British government recognized this fact and set about an undeclared policy to alienate the south from the north. This was not, of course, very difficult, for there have been thousands of years of animosity between the peoples of the north and of the south. Moreover, the Islamic culture of the north is entirely different from the Nilotic pagan culture of the south.

In the second place, it was only natural that, as a part of the over-all policy in the southern Sudan, the British government should emphasize training the south Sudanese in English. This was not only easier for the British officials, but more in keeping with the larger policy of division and the oft-expressed hope that the south Sudan might possibly be united to Uganda rather than to the north.

There was, however, a very special difficulty encountered by missionaries working with the Nilotic languages, namely, the extremely complicated phonemic systems. Not only did such languages have a great many vowels, but different units of length, breathiness and nonbreathiness, plus extremely complex systems of tone. English-speaking missionaries and educational officials were generally opposed to the phonemic representation of the various significant features of sound, for they insisted that this would require the use of diacritical marks, and it was the almost unanimous conviction of missionaries and British officials that Africans could not learn such diacritics. (It is not without interest that in French- and Portuguese-speaking areas of Africa education officials have no such attitudes concerning the use of diacritics and the Africans seem perfectly able to learn the French and Portuguese orthographic systems.) The results of this policy were that, despite some quite good orthographies in some of the languages in the extreme south of the Sudan, the systems of writing the Nilotic languages were highly unsatisfactory. Furthermore, the Nilotic peoples were never very enthusiastic about education, and as a result English did not spread as fast as colonial officials would have liked.

## The Spread of Arabic

During all this time Arabic was of course the language of the north and as increasing numbers of people from the south went north to work they learned Arabic. Furthermore, traders from the north penetrated farther and farther south, and with Egyptian sponsorship some imposing mosques were built in the south, as for example, in Malakal.

Christian missionaries strongly resisted the spread of Arabic, for they rightly saw in it the threat of the extension of Islam. However, rather than meet the issue head-on, with an emphasis upon the fact that not all Arabic-speaking people are Muslims, they tried to brace up the program of teaching in the indigenous languages, while many of the people themselves, especially after the removal of British officials, were keen to learn the Arabic and take advantage of the economic advantages involved.

On the other hand, there was a strong outward opposition to Arabic on the part of many young people of the south Sudan. They boycotted Arabic classes in school and ostensibly refused to learn Arabic. However, it is interesting to note that a number of those same persons were taking a keen interest in listening to the Arabic radio and, for all practical purposes, were trying hard to learn the language, even though ostensibly denouncing its use.

With the collapse of the military revolt in the south and the inevitable imposition of Arabic upon the country as the basic language of education, official communication, and economic and social opportunities, missions have had to rethink their educational programs. Moreover, they have had to give consideration to the writing of the Nilotic languages with Arabic script. The irony of it all is that, whereas a few years ago most missionaries insisted that it was totally impracticable to use a few diacritics with the Roman alphabet, they will have to use a multiplicity of diacritics with the Arabic alphabet, even in the most simplified adaptation to the Nilotic languages.

One thing is certain, the future of the educational program of missions in the southern part of the Sudan is definitely tied to the necessity of working with, not against, the dynamic drive to nationalism. Here is another instance in which it is almost too late to get on the bandwagon.

## The Distinctive Role of Colonial Languages

For the Africans the learning of the colonial language of the area in question has always been of prime importance, for it has been requisite for a good position, advancement within the government bureaucracy, or employment in a white-collar job, and essential for further education outside Africa. Furthermore, the knowledge of a colonial language brought great prestige. In fact, it has been one of the primary elements in the formation of a special African elite: the government clerks in British areas, the *évolués* in French and Belgian areas, and the *assimilados* in Portuguese colonies. In each country, whether by direct government planning or by the very socio-economic structure, these special classes of African elite have grown up. They are the ones who are promoting nationalism and taking over leadership in some of the newly freed areas (as in Ghana) and who in the future will control the destinies of the various countries.

At present such groups in most areas are only second-class elite. That is to say the European "rulers" are the first-class elite and the Africans the second-class. However, a number of countries in Africa will inevitably be given complete freedom, or at least a high measure of self-government; and almost inevitably these second-class elite will form the first-class elite. In other words, they will change from being "number-two boy" to being "number-one boy." The European technicians may very well stay on, as they have in many instances in India, but in terms of the indigenous social structure they will form either a second-class elite or, more likely, they will be more or less completely isolated from the social structure of the nation.

There is no doubt but what the present colonial language will continue as the "national language" of the respective countries. It may be that some of the countries will attempt to establish one of the African tongues as an official national language, in much the same manner as the Philippine Islands have proclaimed Tagalog as the national language. However, this is essentially only a nationalistic fiction, for English is the *de facto* national language of the Philippines. On the other hand, it may very well be the case that the colonial language will continue primarily as a language of the elite. For example, this is precisely what has happened in Haiti, where the elite and some of the middle class employ French in official contacts, but the entire populace, including all levels of society, use Haitian Creole (a development from a Pidgin French) in all daily contacts. A not altogether different situation exists in Paraguay, where the official language is Spanish, but the vast majority of the people use Guarani more than Spanish.

Even though some of the African leadership may advocate the promoting of indigenous languages, even in programs of universal education within the countries, there is no doubt but what the colonial languages will continue to be the mechanism by which the ruling elite will manage affairs and maintain their status. This is strikingly illustrated in Liberia, where English, in its characteristic developments within the country, is not only the instrument of government but the technique by which certain groups are excluded from the governing class. Furthermore, any contacts which such countries may have with the outside world will of necessity be by means of the colonial languages. This means that participation in the United Nations or any other such international body must be through one of the world languages — another reason for the continuance of the colonial languages.

There are some who think that there may occur in Africa what has happened in Vietnam, namely, a repudiation of French by the people. Not only is the repudiation of French more or less an official fact in Vietnam, but even those who at one time learned to speak French very fluently sometimes prefer to speak it badly so as not to be thought guilty of too close an identification with a repudiated class. However, the situation in Vietnam is quite different from what exists in Negro Africa (excluding for the time being North Africa). In the first place, there is a veritable welter of languages in all French-speaking areas of Africa, and it is very unlikely that any one group would be sufficiently strong to identify the national cause with its own language. Since, moreover, the leadership of most geographical segments is drawn from a number of different tribes, the almost inevitable result will be the retention of French in those segments. In North Africa, on the other hand, the identification of nationalism with Islam will inevitably produce the same situation as has developed in Vietnam, namely the almost complete repudiation of French, unless by some miracle, the moderates in North Africa win out.

## Rebirth of Tribalism

One would think that with the spectacular strides which so many countries in Central and West Africa are making toward nationalism (the problem is no longer as to whether they will be independent, but how soon), there would be little or no concern for the tribal languages. That is to say, we would expect people to forget about their own petty allegiances in the struggle for national unity. The truth of the matter is that right in the midst of the seething rise of nationalism there is an almost unprecedented concern for local tribal recognition.

The essential reason for this rise in tribal feeling is the fact that during the process of acquiring a national outlook all people become increasingly more self-aware. The result has been that the people have recognized not only the larger unit, but have become more keenly conscious of their own roles. For example, in the French Cameroun, where the movement for independence is far advanced as compared with many other areas, the people are not content with the Presbyterian mission educational policy of training them first in Bulu (one of the trade languages) and then in French. They are demanding education in their own tribal language *and* in French. Whereas in earlier days a small tribe regarded the acceptance of Bulu as more or less inevitable, now many of the people have strong reactions against what seems an unnecessary impediment in their acquiring a proper education. Of course, the real desire of the people is for a French education, for this opens up to them all the material and social advantages of the rapidly developing country. However, if they have to take less, then they want something in their own language, but not a halfway measure.

Though the details of this process of making people aware of themselves are different from one area to another, nevertheless the fundamental reaction of the people still remains. They are not only aware of the national destiny of their people; they are also increasingly conscious of the tribal unit of which they are members. For this unit they are demanding recognition. Part of this recognition is the possession of a literature in their own language — the most important symbol of the ethnic unity of a people.

## Languages in the Urban Centers

In the huge urban centers which are growing up all over Africa, it is inevitable that languages will not only influence, but be influenced. For one thing, in such multilingual regions the spread of trade languages is inevitable, for communication cannot settle in linguistically defined tribal lines.

On the other hand, in such urban centers the people do tend to congregate, wherever possible, according to linguistic groupings. However, even when the people cannot settle in linguistically defined areas, they tend to form all kinds of societies, of which a common language is the most important factor determining membership. Even when most of the people speak a trade or colonial language, they still tend to form their social clubs along older tribal lines, and hence language lines. Interestingly enough, whereas in the rural areas the clan organization was the dominant factor in social grouping, in the large urban areas the identity of language is the fundamental feature.

As the people drift more and more into the urban centers, they tend to give up older tribal "markings": e.g. distinctive scarification, filing of teeth, extraction of certain teeth, designs painted on the body, and characteristic tribal ornaments. These more readily visible symbols are rapidly being supplanted by the almost sole distinction of language. In previous times language was only one of several evident symbols designating one's tribal relationship. At present, language is becoming a relatively more and more significant symbol.

## What of the Future?

In view of the many diverse developments in contemporary African society, especially in Central and West Africa, can we make any valid predictions as to the shape of things to come, as far as language is concerned? We have already suggested some of these in our treatments of trade, colonial, and national languages. However, there is a very special sense in which language will be an important fact in the social structure of African societies, especially in the independent countries.

In the first place, in these independent

countries the elite will in all likelihood be trilingual. That is to say, they will speak the colonial language (which in one way or another will function as the national language), at least one trade language (for they will have to carry on affairs with those who do not speak the colonial language), and in most instances a tribal language (that is to say, the language of their parents or home community).

The middle class will be predominantly bilingual. They will speak at least one trade language, usually the dominant trade language of the area, and their own tribal tongue. Of course, the more progressive of the middle class will seek to acquire the national language, and will find that its acquisition is one of the most important means as well as requisites for entrance into the elite group.

The lower class will be predominantly monolingual. These will be the villagers, living in rural areas and speaking their own tribal tongue. Almost inevitably, however, they will have to learn something of a trade language, especially if they become day laborers in the mines, factories, or on the plantations. The acquisition of certain technical skills, plus ability to communicate in the trade language, will make them eligible for the upper lower class or lower middle class, and these persons are likely to want their children educated in the national language in order to acquire upper middle class membership, and if at all possible, a place among the elite.

There is a real sense, of course, in which this is an oversimplification. In the first place, in a relatively short time many people in the upper class are likely to cease speaking a tribal language, unless it is important for social grouping or for "identification with the masses." Moreover, the middle class will increasingly learn more of the national language in order to share in the greater material benefits. The lower class will be compelled to learn a trade language as urbanization and industrialization increases. Accordingly, within a generation or so the upper class is likely to be predominantly speakers of the colonial language and a trade language; the middle class will vary between those who speak the colonial and the trade language and those who speak a trade language and a tribal language,[1] with those in the latter category becoming increasingly fewer. In the meanwhile, the lower class will be increasingly more bilingual.

We would not want to exaggerate the role of language in the emerging social structure, for there are many other factors, such as education, technical competence, capacity for leadership, wealth, and ability to communicate. Note, however, that these "sanctions" in the new social structure are not the old ones (clan membership, hereditary privileges, religious prerogatives, etc.). On the other hand, it would be equally wrong to overlook the significance of language, not only as an important mechanism in the formation and maintenance of the new social structure, but as important symbols of social status.

---

[1] It is important to note, however, in speaking of trade languages we do not include only those whose structure is a highly simplified one. We mean any important tribal language which because of its commercial significance has become extended beyond the immediate tribal boundaries and is thus a significant means of fairly wide communication. To this extent it is possible that a man's own tribal language would also be a trade language.

# Christianity in Human Cultures

*William A. Smalley*

# Cultural Implications of an Indigenous Church

OVER the past generation, a large amount of thought concerning the strategy of modern missions has gone into the question of the relation of the new churches (which have resulted from missionary work) to the missionary body and to the society (the non-Christian culture) around them. It is not my purpose here to go into the extensive literature dealing with this subject, but a classic work, often referred to and widely read, is Roland Allen's *Missionary Methods, St. Paul's or Ours?*[1] The burden of a great deal of this discussion has been the well-taken observation that modern missions have all too often resulted in churches which are tied to the supporting home church in the West, protected by the mother denomination, and unable to stand alone in their society. This is an oversimplification, but I am in substantial agreement with a great deal of it. There are some anthropological problems which have not always been faced in such discussions, however, although many writers have at points touched upon them and Roland Allen seems well aware of many of them.

## A False Diagnosis

It seems to have become axiomatic in much missionary thinking that a church which is "self-governing, self-supporting, and self-propagating" is by definition an "indigenous church." It further seems to follow in the thinking of many people that such an indigenous church (and so defined) is the goal of modern missions. There are some very serious reservations which may be made to this point of view, however, and it is a point of view which may be very misleading as it molds policy for the development of a church, if we look at some of its cultural implications.

It seems to me, first of all, that the criteria of "self-governing, self-supporting, and self-propagating" are not necessarily diagnostic of an indigenous movement. The definition of such a movement has to be sought elsewhere, and, although these three "self" elements may be present in such a movement, they are essentially independent variables. The three "selfs" seem to have become catch phrases which can be stamped without any particular understanding on one church or on another. Yet it is evident on an examination of the facts that they are not necessarily relevant at all.

## Misinterpretation of Self-government

It may be very easy to have a self-governing church which is not indigenous. Many presently self-governing churches are not. All that is necessary to do is to indoctrinate a few leaders in Western

[1] Roland Allen, *Missionary Methods, St. Paul's or Ours?* (Chicago: Moody Press, 1956).

**Reprinted from Vol. 5, No. 2 (1958), pp. 51-65.**

patterns of church government, and let them take over. The result will be a church governed in a slavishly foreign manner (although probably modified at points in the direction of local government patterns), but by no stretch of imagination can it be called an indigenous ment patterns), but by no stretch of of mission fields today under the misguided assumption that an "indigenous" church has been founded.

It is further possible for a genuinely indigenous Christian movement to be "governed" to a degree by foreigners. Even in the large-scale Christward movements which have taken place in the world, movements which have been so extensive that the foreign body has had more difficulty in controlling them than what it has had in most of its mission work, the mission body has often exerted its governing influence upon the upper level of the society, at least, where it was related in any way to the movement. This may have been by the direct action of missionaries or by the action of church leaders who were trained in the foreign patterns of government. Although such government may be unfortunate in many cases, it does not in the least detract from the indigenous nature of such a Christward movement on the part of a group of people.

## Misapplication of Self-support

It is unlikely that there would be any disagreement with the idea that the Jerusalem church in the first century was an indigenous church. The Jerusalem Christians were so strongly Jewish in their attitudes that they resented the conversion of Gentiles unless they joined the Jewish ritualistic performance of the law. That church, however, in its time of need received gifts from abroad, from Europe — in modern-day terminology, from the West. Paul himself carried some of those gifts to Jerusalem. No one would argue that the receiving of such gifts infringed upon the indigenous nature of the Jewish church.

Neither can one argue, I believe, that the receiving of such gifts by the younger churches today will necessarily infringe upon their indigenous character. This is true in spite of the very real dangers which exist in the subsidy of the younger churches by the mission bodies.

I was in Indo-China as a missionary during some of the years of civil war. Those were days when the whole country was badly upset, when church congregations could be cut off from the mission without more than a few hours notice as the battle line shifted, when groups which had been under mission subsidy could suddenly lose their mission help and be placed in a fearful economic position. Together with most of my colleagues, I felt the tremendous weakness of a missionary program which was based upon the foreign financing of its national workers. In a time of crisis such as that we worked hard to see to it that the church was placed on a footing of self-support.

Self-support is, wherever possible, really the soundest method of church economics. It is healthy for the church and for the mission, but there certainly are situations in which it is not possible, or where it is not advisable, where self-support can make church growth nearly impossible, and in such situations its presence does not necessarily imply the lack of an indigenous church. It is an independent variable within the pattern of the mission and church. All depends on how the problems are handled, and how the temptation to control church life through the manipulation of funds is resisted by the mission body. If foreign funds are handled in an indigenous way, they may still have their dangers, but they do not preclude an indigenous church.

Examples of areas in which the younger churches can usually not be expected to be self-supporting are publication, Bible translation, education, health and medicine, and many other fields entirely outside the range of their economy. These are not indigenous activities, but they are valuable activities for many churches in the modern world. Whether or not such things enter into the life of a church in an "indigenous manner" is entirely dependent upon the way in which the changes take place, not the source of income. If the changes in the younger church society take place as the result of the fulfillment of a strongly felt need, and in a manner planned and executed by them for their own purposes and in their own way, the simple presence of foreign funds in the project does not destroy its indigenous character.

The richness of Western economy makes it possible for many Western church groups not to need to seek for funds elsewhere. However, even in the rich West many groups have to seek for funds from foundations or other institutions. This does not destroy their indigenous character in the least; it is simply a part of the Western economic scene. Such economic possibilities are usually not open to the younger churches except as they seek their help from the mission body. It is the way the funds are administered, the way the decisions are made, and the purposes to which they are put, that are diagnostic of an indigenous church, not the presence or absence of such foreign funds.

It would be hard to think of any more fiercely or self-consciously independent country than India today, yet it receives large sums from abroad to bolster its economy and to do things which badly need to be done for its people. On the other hand, it would be very easy to find many examples of self-supporting churches in which the basic indigenous character is not present. There is, for example, a church which is advertised by its founding mission as a great indigenous church, where its pastors are completely supported by the local church members, yet the mission behind the scenes pulls the strings and the church does its bidding like the puppets of the "independent" iron curtain countries. This colonial manipulation may even be quite unconscious on the part of the missionaries. If the church makes its own decisions, without outside interference, as to how its funds shall be used, and does so on the basis of economic patterns natural to it in its own cultural setting, this church may be considered indigenous, even if funds are provided by an outside source.

### Misunderstanding of Self-propagation

Of the three "selfs," it seems to me that that of self-propagating is the most nearly diagnostic of an indigenous church, but here again the correlation is by no means complete. In a few areas of the world it may be precisely the foreignness of the church which is the source of attraction to unbelievers. There are parts of the world where aspirations of people lead them toward wanting to identify themselves with the strong and powerful West, and where the church provides such an avenue of identification.[2] Self-propagation in such a case may be nothing more than a road to a nonindigenous relationship.

I very strongly suspect that the three "selfs" are really projections of our American value systems into the idealization of the church, that they are in their very nature Western concepts based upon Western ideas of individualism and power. By forcing them on other people we may at times have been making it impossible for a truly indigenous pattern to develop. We have been Westernizing with all our talk about indigenizing.

## The Nature of an Indigenous Church

What, then, is an indigenous church? It is a group of believers who live out their life, including their socialized Christian activity, in the patterns of the local society, and for whom any transformation of that society comes out of their felt needs under the guidance of the Holy Spirit and the Scriptures. There are several basic elements in this tentative formulation. For one thing, the church is a *society*. As society it has its patterns of interaction among people. If it is an indigenous society, an indigenous church, those patterns of reaction will be based upon such patterns existing in the local society. This is true simply because people learn to react with each other in their normal process of enculturation, of growing up, and those normal habits are carried over into church structure. If other patterns are forced upon a church by missionaries, consciously or unconsciously, such a church will not be an indigenous one.

The presence of the Holy Spirit, however, is another basic factor in the indigenous church, and the presence of the Holy Spirit implies transformation both of individual lives and of society. But, as I have tried to point out in another article on the nature of culture change,[3] such transformation occurs differently in different societies, depending on the meaning which people attach to their behavior and the needs which they feel in their lives. Missionaries generally approve of and strive for culture change which makes people more like themselves in form (and this is true even though they may overlook the meaning of this form). An indigenous church is precisely one in which the changes which take place under the guidance of the Holy Spirit meet the needs and fulfill the meanings of that society and not of any outside group.

Many have said things like this, and such a statement should and could be elaborated considerably to provide a more adequate description of the nature of an indigenous church. Sometimes in our search for an understanding of the nature of the church we turn to the New Testament (as we rightly should) and seek for it there. But it is not in the formal structure and operation of the churches in the New Testament that we find our answer. As a matter of fact, the church of Jerusalem was apparently different even in operational matters from the churches in Europe, and it was certainly different in the outlook on the basic cultural issues which were so important to the Jews. In the New Testament we do find the picture of the indigenous church. It is that of a church in which the Holy Spirit has

[2] William D. Reyburn, "Conflicts and Contradictions in African Christianity," in this volume.

[3] William A. Smalley, "*The Missionary and Culture Change*," PRACTICAL ANTHROPOLOGY, Vol. 4, No. 5 (1957), pp. 231-237.

worked its transformation within the society. And where that society differs from another (as the Greek world is different from the Jewish world) the church resulting is different.

## Missionaries Do Not Like It

But having said this much, we would now like to stress some of the implications of an "indigenous church," implications which have often not been realized. One is that missionaries often do not like the product. Often a truly indigenous church is a source of concern and embarrassment to the mission bodies in the area.

An example of this which every reader of PRACTICAL ANTHROPOLOGY should study is that of the Toba Indians as reported by Dr. William D. Reyburn.[4] The mission was disturbed and unhappy about the indigenous church which spread so rapidly among the Toba people because it assumed a form so different from that of the mission group. It was not until they saw something of the nature of the church in the sense in which we are discussing it here and of the working of the Holy Spirit in societies other than their own, that the missionaries not only became reconciled to the indigenous church's existence, but sought to harmonize their program with it, to the strengthening of that church and to the greater glory of God.

There have been indigenous movements which missionaries have approved of. This approval was sometimes due to the unusual insight and perception of the missionaries who saw beyond the limitations of their own cultural forms and recognized the movement of the Holy Spirit among other people. At other times the general value systems of the new church group so nearly coincided with our own that the result was a church which reflected many of the things that we hold very valuable. Movements in China such as the Jesus Family[5] displayed outstanding personal qualities of frugality, cleanliness, thrift, and other virtues which rate so highly in our own society and which were considered to be the fruits of the Christian movement. These are, however, ideals present in non-Christian Chinese life. A transformed life in such a case resulted in the perfection of such value systems already in existence in the culture. But that was not the case among the Tobas, where the giving away of possessions, the sharing with one's relatives and neighbors, and the joining in of emotional expressions of religion characterized the group because it was in these ways that their values were expressed.

However, as Dr. William D. Reyburn put it some time ago, most of us want to join in the jury as God is making his judgments upon people and cultures, yet we don't even understand the meaning of the trial. We are quick to make our evaluations and quick to decide what course the new church should follow or what course a new Christian individual should take, but we simply are neither competent nor qualified to make such decisions, having little or no real knowledge of the cultural background of the people or individual.

It is our work first of all to see the Bible in its cultural perspective, to see

[4] William D. Reyburn, *The Toba Indians of the Argentine Chaco* (Elkhart, Indiana: The Mennonite Board of Missions and Charities, 1954).

[5] D. Vaughan Rees, *The "Jesus Family" in Communist China* (Chicago: Moody Press, 1956).

God dealing with men through different cultural situations. It is our responsibility to see him change in his dealings with men as the cultural history of the Jews changes, to recognize that God has always, everywhere, dealt with men in terms of their culture. It is next our responsibility to take new Christians to the Bible and to help them see in the Bible God interacting with other people, people whose emotions and problems were very similar to their own so far as their fundamental nature is concerned, but also at times very different from their own in the specific objective or working of their forms of life. It is our responsibility to lead them in prayer to find what God would have them do as they study his Word and seek the interpretation and leadership of the Holy Spirit.

It is the missionary's task, if he believes in "the indigenous principle," to preach that God is in Christ Jesus, reconciling the world unto himself. *That* message is supercultural.[6] It applies to all cultures and all places. The faith it engenders is supercultural, but the medium of its communication and the outworking of its faith in individual lives is not supercultural, it is bound in with the habits and values of every people. It is to deliver that message, the message that turned the world upside down and continues to do so, that the missionary is called.

It is, furthermore, the missionary's responsibility to be a source of cultural alternatives for people to select if they want and need them. The missionary, with his knowledge of history, his understanding of the Scriptures, and his knowledge of the church in his own land and in other missionary areas, can often suggest to local groups that there are ways out of their dilemma, that there are ways of a better life in Christ than what they are now living. This is certainly a legitimate function of the missionary and this is his role in culture change. But if genuine change is to take place, the decision, the selection, has to be made by the people themselves, and if the church is to be an indigenous one, we can know that the selection will be made in the light of the needs and problems, the values and outlooks, those people have.

It is the church which will have to decide whether boiling water, abstinence from alcohol, the wearing of clothes, and monogamy are the proper expressions of a Christian in that society. It is the church under the leadership of the Holy Spirit which will have to determine the best ways of fostering its own growth, spreading its own witness, and supporting its own formal leadership (if it should have any formal leadership at all).

As we have already suggested the problem of the implications of the indigenous church are as old as the Judaizers of Jerusalem. Those Judaizers saw Greek Christianity through Hebrew eyes. They are like many missionaries in that, if they were content that any Gentile should be converted at all, they saw conversion in the light of filling of a formal mold.

The New Testament, however, clearly repudiated that view and sets up the church as a group of believers within its own society, working a chemical change within the society like salt in a dish, rather than cutting the society to pieces as the Judaizers would. This is not to

---

[6] William A. Smalley, "Culture and Superculture," PA, Vol. 2, No. 3 (1955), pp. 58-71; William. A. Smalley and Marie Fetzer, "A Christian View of Anthropology," *Modern Science and Christian Faith,* (Wheaton, Ill.: Van Kampen Press, 1950).

gainsay the exclusiveness of Christianity. The church is a separate group, but it is separate in spiritual kind, in relationship to God. It is in the indigenous church that the relationship between the Holy Spirit and society comes into being. This is the New Testament church.

The converts of an indigenous movement are not necessarily cleaner than their neighbors, not necessarily more healthy, not necessarily better educated. It is, furthermore, often the moment at which they become cleaner, more healthy, more educated that the barrier begins to grow which makes their indigenous interaction with their neighbors less likely and the growth of the movement begins to taper off. As Dr. McGavran has pointed out in his tremendously significant book *The Bridges of God,*[7] missions have traditionally poured their funds not into the people's movements but into the station churches, into the huge mission compounds, into the churches which are their satellites, rather than into the grass roots growing development of an embarrassing indigenous church.

Not only do many missionaries not like some of the outstanding examples of indigenous church movements, but to an even greater degree their supporting home constituencies are likely not to approve of them. Our cultural values as applied to our churches are so strong that we feel that a corporate structure, a profit motive, individualism, and thrift are *ipso facto* the expressions of Christianity. That God should work his will in any other forms than our own is inconceivable to most of us.

An implication of the indigenous church which I think is very unwelcome to many missionaries is that the missionary can make no cultural decisions for the Christians. By this I do not mean that the missionary does not make value judgments. As an individual he cannot help doing so, nor should he wish not to do so.[8] His value judgments, if they are to be worth while, have to be cross-culturally oriented, but they will be there. Neither do I mean by this that the missionary cannot exercise an important measure of guidance, of suggestion, on the younger church as he fulfills his functions of teaching and preaching and, in many respects, advising.

## An Indigenous Church Cannot be "Founded"

The next implication which has often not fully penetrated into the thinking of missionaries who discuss indigenous movements is that it is impossible to "found" an indigenous church. The Biblical figure of planting and harvesting is far more realistic than our American figure based on our American values and expressed in the idea of the "establishment" or "founding" of a church. At one time I had the opportunity to observe the effort of a group of missionaries as they very sincerely were concerned about the "founding" of an indigenous church where up to that time they recognized that the believers were heavily dependent upon the mission for their sustenance. The procedure followed by the mission was to establish a constitutional committee which contained three tribesmen and two missionaries. The mission considered that they were extremely generous in their outlook by putting more tribesmen than missionaries on the committee.

When the committee met, the mission-

---

[7] Donald McGavran, *The Bridges of God* (London: World Dominion Press, 1955).

[8] William D. Reyburn, "The Missionary and the Evaluation of Culture," in this volume.

aries asked the tribesmen what they wanted in their constitution. The tribesmen, of course, did not know what they wanted in their constitution. They had not even known that they wanted a constitution until they had been told so. The missionaries suggested some of the possibilities for a constitution and the tribesmen readily agreed to most or all of them. The result, worked out in good faith by both the missionaries and the tribesmen, was a replica of the denominational constitution of the mission body. To this day no one seems to have sensed the fact a tribal church with a constitution is no more an indigenous church than a tribal church without one, as the existence of a constitution is entirely irrelevant to the relation of the church to God and to surrounding human life.

In any honestly indigenous work a true constitution (if there were any at all) would be one which would describe the structure of the church society in its workings. This does not mean that those culture changes which are needed to move toward a greater church action than is possible in the original local pattern should not take place. A constitution, if it is truly the expression of forward-looking church leaders, may guide the group in that direction, but it will only do so if it is an expression of such internally felt needs or vision.

Some missions have legislated the gradual withdrawal of financial subsidy from younger churches. This is done in order to put the younger church on its "self-supporting" feet. It is a step toward the day when the church will be indigenous, as the mission sees it, but the withdrawal of subsidy by the mission is a foreign act and not in the most remote sense indigenous.

No, indigenous churches cannot be founded. They can only be planted, and the mission is usually surprised at which seeds grow. Often they have the tendency to consider the seeds which do grow in any proliferation to be weeds, a nuisance, a hindrance in their carefully cultivated foreign mission garden, and all the time the carefully cultivated hothouse plants of the mission "founded" church are unable to spread roots and to derive their nurture either from the soil of their own life or from the Word of God in the root-confining pots of the mission organization and culture.

### Indigenous Churches Start Apart from Missions

Another implication of the whole idea of an indigenous church is that the great indigenous movements are often not the result of foreign work in any direct way. Sometimes they are the result of the witness of someone who was converted by the efforts of foreign missionaries, but usually it is not the foreign missionary himself whose witness brings about the establishment or beginning of an indigenous movement. Saint Paul was not a foreigner to the Greek world. He was a bi-cultural individual, one who was as much at home in the Greek world as he was in the Hebrew world and whose preaching carried to the Greek world the message which came to him from the Christians of the Hebrew world.

Prophet Harris, who wandered along the west coast of Africa preaching about the men who would come with a Book, was not a foreign missionary. The men from whom the Tobas heard the gospel as it came to them in its pentecostal form were not foreigners. True, they were not Tobas, but they were the poorer-class

Latin-Americans and mixed Spanish-Indian inhabitants of the areas where the Tobas lived. They were very much a part of the cultural picture in which the Tobas found themselves; they were not foreign missionaries. The people's movements in China were usually the result of the energetic faithful work of a Chinese Christian, not the result of foreign missionary evangelism except as he may have been a convert of missionaries.

The Meo movement described by G. Linwood Barney[9] was not brought about through the preaching of a missionary, but through the cooperative work of a Meo shaman who had been converted (under a missionary) and who took another tribesman of the area with whom the Meo were very familiar from village to village, preaching from town to town. Our distance from most other culture is so great, the cultural specialization of the West is so extreme, that there are almost no avenues of approach whereby the work which we do can normally result in anything of an indigenous nature. It is an ironical thing that the West, which is most concerned with the spread of Christianity in the world today, and which is financially best able to undertake the task of world-wide evangelism, is culturally the least suited for its task because of the way in which it has specialized itself to a point where it is very difficult for it to have an adequate understanding of other peoples.

## The New Testament Indigenous Churches

Of many quotations which could have been taken from Roland Allen, the following has been selected to conclude this article. The significant thing, as Allen points out, is that the Apostle Paul did not approve of much of the behavior of either of these churches, but neither did he legislate to either one. He did not even stay around and spoon-feed them. He wrote to Corinth, persuaded, entreated, advised, addressing them always as the "church of God."

> The Church began in Jerusalem as a body of Jews who carefully maintained their Jewish tradition and observed the custom of their fathers. The Church in the Four Provinces consisted almost entirely of Gentiles ignorant of that tradition. Consequently, if a Christian from Macedonia or Achaia went up to Judea he must have found himself in a strange atmosphere, in a community as unlike that to which he was accustomed as it is possible to imagine. Circumcision was practiced, Sabbaths were kept, meats avoided as unclean, the Law was the practical rule of every-day life. There was a strictness and a reserve which must have oppressed and dismayed him. Christianity in Jerusalem must have seemed to him a thing of rules hardly distinguishable from pure Judaism. Many of the Christians shrank from a Gentile, or tolerated him only as a sort of proselyte. In the meetings of the Church the prayers were modeled on Jewish patterns and expressed Jewish thought in Jewish speech with which he was not familiar. The only point of real contact was a common devotion to the Person of Jesus, a common recognition of the same Apostles, and a common observance of the same rites of baptism and the Lord's Supper.
>
> On the other hand, when a Christian from Jerusalem went down to Corinth the shock must have been

[9] "The Meo — An Incipient Culture," in this volume.

even more severe. The Corinthian in Jerusalem found himself in a society stiff, uncouth, severe, formal, pedantic. The Jewish Christian in Corinth must have thought the Church there given over to unbridled license. Uncircumcised Christians attended the feasts of their pagan friends in heathen temples. Every letter of the ceremonial law was apparently broken every day without rebuke. Even in the meetings of the Church, preachings and prayers were built on a strange system of thought which could hardly be called Christian, and there was a most undignified freedom of conduct. He must have welcomed the presence in the Church of a party led by men from his own city who argued that in dealing with a people like this it was useless to compromise matters: the only possible course was to enforce the observance of the whole Law throughout the whole Church. To omit anything would simply be to admit the thin end of a wedge which would split Christian morals into fragments. If a man wanted to be saved he must keep the law.[10]

Denominationalism is in many cases a result of the development of more or less indigenous churches in various subgroups or social levels of Western society. Usually they start in the lower brackets, fossilizing in their cultural forms as they move up in society and on through time. Until we are willing for the church to have its different manifestations in different cultures as between the Jewish Christians and the various kinds of Greeks, rather than export the denominational patterns rooted in our history and often irrelevant to the rest of the world, we will not have indigenous churches, whether they are "self-governing, self-supporting, and self-propagating" or not. It is not until we are willing to let churches grow also that we have learned to trust the Holy Spirit with society. We are treating him as a small child with a new toy too complicated and dangerous for him to handle. Our paternalism is not only a paternalism toward other peoples; it is also a paternalism towards God.

---

[10] Op. cit. pp. 166-167.

*William A. Smalley*

**Reprinted from Vol. 6, No. 3 (1959), pp. 135-139.**

# What Are Indigenous Churches Like?

*It seems that the only optimism that can be generated with respect to reaching the millions without Christ is not to be found in the number of missionaries who go to the field, but in the rapid multiplication of Christianity among nationals reached by nationals. How effective are indigenous churches? How free are indigenous churches? How numerous are they? Is the use of the term "indigenous church" simply lip service to a concept? [Question by Frank E. Houser, Jr.]*

"THE indigenous church" is an expression on the lips of almost everyone (especially in non-denominational missionary circles) who wants to sound up-to-date in his missionary thinking. Some of the denominations do not use the term so much, but their work and vocabulary reflect a similar kind of outlook in their shift to boards of "ecumenical relations" instead of mission boards and to "fraternal workers" instead of missionaries. There are some fundamental differences between the "indigenous church" thinking and "ecumenical mission" thinking, but they both represent ways of trying to deal with the same basic problem, the same historical mistake in missionary activity, and the same difficult world situation in which the Christian witness in non-Western lands finds itself.

The problem with which this whole missionary emphasis is trying to deal is that of the traditional colonial paternalism with which Western missions have historically approached their task. I will not go into a description of that traditional missionary behavior here. The literature is full of missionary breast-beating on that subject — some of it a bit Pharisaical, I fear, but much of it sincerely and thoughtfully recognizing and analyzing a difficult problem.[1]

The direction of this modern missionary emphasis is to place greater responsibility on the younger churches, to delegate authority to them, to encourage their participation in evangelism and other means of the extension of the gospel, and to expect of them a greater economic responsibility in paying their own way. Unquestionably there has been enormous gain almost everywhere in this direction. In some areas it has been greatly stimulated by political developments, by increasing feelings of nationalism, by the demands of an increasingly more vocal and educated church leadership. In other cases, changes just as extensive have been made arising out of the conviction and the troubled conscience of the missionary group.

[1] See, for example, many articles in the *International Review of Missions*, and such books as Donald McGavaran, *The Bridges of God* (published by the World Dominion Press and distributed in the U.S. by Friendship Press, 1955), and the classic work by Roland Allen, *Missionary Methods, St. Paul's or Ours?* (reprinted by Moody Press, Chicago, 1956).

### Example 1: Within the Ecumenical Movement

In order to illustrate the two kinds of approach which seem to be developing, I would like to describe briefly, as examples of these trends, the recent behavior of "missions" (one of which no longer calls itself that) in Thailand. The first is an enthusiastic participant in the ecumenical movement. Its board at home is now a "Commission on Ecumenical Missions and Relations." Recently its missionaries became "fraternal workers." Its properties in Thailand, worth a great deal, were turned over to a local board. Its large budget is channeled through the church administration. The net effect is that the Thai and Americans are now trying to do jointly what the Americans usually did more nearly alone before.

In spite of some remarks which I shall make, I believe this is progress. It is a step away from an increasingly intolerable situation. It tries to eliminate such problems as the word "missionary," which for all of the richness of its theological implications, is weighted with bad emotional overtones of cultural imperialism to many peoples of the world. It tries to reverse the status arrangements between Thai and Westerners by rearranging the organization, to put Thai into places of equal prestige with Americans. It gives Thai leadership increased opportunity for experience and responsibility.

### Example 2: Outside the Ecumenical Movement

The second group has followed a different course of action in trying to respond to some of the same problems. It maintains a distinction between "mission" (consisting of foreigners) and "church" (consisting of Thai). Over a period it has set about to "indigenize" the church by encouraging it to assume full financial responsibility for its own affairs, to govern itself, and to engage in vigorous evangelism independently of the efforts of the "mission" in this line. This group conceives of an "indigenous church" as being "self-governing, self-supporting, and self-propagating." It has studiously, with great care, engaged in restructuring the Thai church to which it is related, to make it fit this pattern. It has withdrawn outside financial support from the Thai ministry, and has insisted that business affairs within the Thai church be carried on by them.

Again, I believe this is progress. Clearly, the Thai church has taken more initiative, has shown more life, is growing somewhat faster than it did before in this area. Thai leadership is given the opportunity of more experience and responsibility.

### The Joker

In neither of these situations, however, have things changed as much as the participants think they have. There have been shifts and adjustments, but the differences are not necessarily very fundamental. In both cases the missionaries (whether they are called by that name or not) who previously had political power within the church still have that power. It is exercised in less direct fashion, but it is there. Paternalism in missions is in danger of changing to puppeteering. The fathers have become brothers, but they are brothers who pull strings. A foreigner cannot make a "native person" become "indigenous." The cards are stacked. Both mission programs, over a period of many years, taught an ecclesiastical structure, a pattern of government, a system of relationships which amounts to an ecclesiastical culture. The newly elevated churches have little imagination or liberty to depart sharply therefrom.

I have discussed some of the cultural implications of an indigenous church before. I will not go into them now. The term is, of course, relative. There is no such thing as an absolutely indigenous church in any culture, because Christianity is always intrusive to a certain degree. However, some churches more nearly than others approximate a group of people "living out their lives, including their socialized activity, in the patterns of the local society, and for whom any transformation of that society comes out of their felt needs under the guidance of the Holy Spirit and the Scriptures."[2]

### What are Indigenous Churches Like?

In a most interesting article J. W. C. Dougall has described and discussed the significance of some of the indigenous church movements in Africa.

> There are certain features common to African separatist churches in East, West, or South Africa. There is a characteristic love of color in the adoption of hoods, purple cassocks, chasubles and white robes with blue, red, or purple sashes. There is also an emphasis on ritual different from that of many Western churches. African churches of the separatist type find and afford an outlet for religious feeling in movement, hand-clapping, and dancing. The Western form of worship practiced in many mission churches is felt as an unnatural strait jacket.[3]

Dougall goes on to describe other typical characteristics of these separatist churches (and indigenous churches everywhere tend to be separatist). There is emphasis on baptism by immersion, confession as a real purgation (delivery of the body from evil matter), healing by prayer, and survival of belief in magic.

The African sects normally forbid their members to use Western medicines.

> Why does this teaching appeal so strongly to the African if it is not because Western medicine has so largely neglected the spiritual issues inherent in health and disease? It has given a mechanistic view of the body. African thinking is completely opposed to this. It looks for a spiritual cause and spiritual cure. African thinking is closer to Biblical thinking because it recognizes the whole man.[4]

We cannot generalize from these African churches to indigenous churches in other parts of the world, but people who have seen them elsewhere will be struck by some similarities.

I am not meaning to imply that all splinter movements and synchretistic religious developments are Christian. No matter how "indigenous" they may be, they may also not be "church." The dividing line, of course, lies in their relation by faith to God through Christ. This is a supercultural matter.[5] It lies outside of culture, although it must have cultural expression. I think it is clear, however, that a very large number of such groups are "church" in this fundamental sense. The missions, and the mission churches

[2] "Cultural Implications of an Indigenous Church," PRACTICAL ANTHROPOLOGY, Vol. 5, No. 2 (March-April, 1958), p. 55.

[3] "African Separatist Churches," *The International Review of Missions,* July 1956, p. 259.

[4] Ibid., p. 261.

[5] William A. Smalley, "Culture and Superculture," PRACTICAL ANTHROPOLOGY, Vol. 2, No. 3 (May-June, 1955), pp. 58-71; G. Linwood Barney, "The Meo — An Incipient Church," PRACTICAL ANTHROPOLOGY, Vol. 4, No. 2 (March-April, 1957), pp. 31-50.

(including the "indigenized" ones and the "fraternalized" ones) usually do not know quite what to think of them or do about them.

### How Effective Are Indigenous Churches?

Judged in terms of reaching men for Christ, many indigenous churches are marvelously effective. The rapidly spreading Pentecostal-type indigenous movements in Latin America simply cannot be matched by the churches which belong more closely to the Euro-American Protestant tradition. These groups often grow by splintering. They worship by participating. God is alive. He speaks to them. He heals them. Theirs is a highly emotional religion, but it has enormous vitality.

Ben Elson wrote the following in a letter after his visit to the Tzeltal church, which shows many signs of being an "indigenous" church in spite of the fact that it was sparked through the work of Marianna Slocum, of the Wycliffe Bible Translators:

> The preacher took his text from Matthew 13, proudly reading from the Tzeltal New Testament which they have had since last August. The sermon was an expository one. When he finished making a point he would ask the congregation, "Did that reach your heart?" And they would reply, "It did." Once, however, a young man said, "No, it didn't reach." So the preacher went over the point again. The sermon lasted until 12:40 p.m. If anyone got sleepy he stood up, to stay awake. After the sermon there was pray, during which the congregation knelt.
>
> At 2:00 everyone again gathered in the church for the announcements. These consisted of recognizing those who had come from a distance to the meeting, of reporting on evangelistic trips, and of announcing the names of those who were to meet with the elders for discipline, and of announcing the discipline meted out to those who had met with the elders during the week. One reason for the success of the Tzeltal Church is the strict church discipline: "sin is not allowed in the Camp." Discipline consists in being excluded from the church building — though one can listen at the window — and offenders are not to be treated as brothers by the rest of the congregation — they do not greet them, they do not visit them, they do not wish them well, they do not pray for them except that they will repent. Those who do repent ask forgiveness before the congregation and are thus reinstated into fellowship.
>
> The thing that impressed us most was that the church was a Tzeltal church. Though it is now affiliated with the National Presbyterian Church in Mexico, it is not an American church, nor a Mexican church; it is a distinctively Tzeltal Indian church. Almost no money from the outside has ever been used to help the people; all the church buildings have been built by the Indians themselves and with their own money (the metal roof was given). There are no paid workers — elders and preacher-boys donate their time. If they spend a lot of time in evangelistic work the others may help them with their cornfields. The Tzeltal Church sends money out to other missionary projects!

On the other hand, some indigenous churches die out. Through lack of leadership, lack of spiritual force, inability to solve some perplexing cultural problem which makes existence as a group impossible, or for some other reason, they stagnate and disappear. Sometimes the mission-related churches, or the mission itself, helps to squelch them. If not, they are often relieved, at least, to see them go.

### The Church in Culture

In this modern day it seems inevitable that church forms will move somewhat in the direction of Western forms. This is the direction of most culture change. In many places older economic and social structures are becoming obsolete. The weary procession of churches with ecclesiastical structures which ape their Western teachers will not diminish. In time even some of the separatist groups which survive will take on more of this "respectable" Westernness. This will happen because life around the world, for better or for worse, is moving in that direction. Education is weighted toward the West. However, no group will go all the way. No group will, or can, become fully Americanized. There will develop in each group a synthesis between the old and the new. Each group, if we know anything at all about human nature, will look upon its own synthesis as a more perfect expression of the gospel than any other, no matter how tolerant its outlook.

In the lands of the younger churches probably they will continue the process already begun in so many places, a trend so universally exemplified in Western Protestantism. This is the tendency for the church to move up in social class and away from the masses.[6] When that happens, if there is any spiritual vitality at all, there will be new mass movements, new splinter groups, new "indigenous churches," if you like, which will speak to the humbler folk of the new generation. It will be by such signs as these, perhaps, that we will know that the power of the gospel has already taken root, that the Holy Spirit has found another cultural vehicle. Thus reads the history of the church in culture.

[6] Eugene A. Nida, "The Relationship of Social Structure to the Problem of Evangelism in Latin America," PRACTICAL ANTHROPOLOGY, Vol. 5, No. 3 (May-June 1958), pp. 101-123.

*William D. Reyburn*

# Conflicts and Contradictions in African Christianity

IN MANY discussions of the gospel in African society, the fundamental and most basic question has been avoided. This is the question of the roots of Christianity in this society, for if we are attempting to bolster systems whose roots have never penetrated, we labor in vain.

It is the desire of some mission boards, for example, to subsidize high-level theological education in order that the church will have the leadership which this rapidly evolving society will need. However, a symptom of a very real problem may be seen in the fact that African pastors of the Presbyterian Church in the Cameroun have unanimously favored a higher intellectual training, but they are demanding a solid Presbyterian doctrine, with no desire to bring in anything which is not of the Calvinistic tradition and Westminster Confession. In other words, they fear a seminary which is open to argumentation from other than Presbyterian doctrinal lines. This fear is due to the insecurity of a weak establishment of Christianity in African society.

## The Conflicts in African Thinking

It is true that a few African leaders have already been thoroughly instructed in a solid Calvinistic position, and this for them is extremely important. It is important for any Presbyterian. However, consider the sociological fact that Africa is in search of a unity of thought and action. Africans everywhere are being asked by modern industrial and colonizing societies to pass from nonliterate, primitive economies and ideologies directly to modernization and technological ideas. This has not been the normal course of history. On the contrary, the history of the development of modern societies is radically and fundamentally opposed to such rapid and rootless transitions. Our own European society proceeded through the long and tedious evolution from peasantry in a feudal world to the rise and fall of independent states and then to the gradual unity of national states accompanied by a slowly developing system of political ideologies and economic power blocks.

We may question whether such an evolution is necessary for nonliterate forest societies which have shown such a vast capacity to import and adopt Western ideas and materials. Since this appropriation of Western culture has been accomplished so quickly and so easily, one is prone to ask if it has been personally and individually appropriated. Or is the real power of acceptance and innovation not contained in an all-embracing orientation which may be the real motivating force

**Reprinted from Vol. 4, No. 5 (1957), pp. 161-169. This article is based on an address to the annual mission meeting of the West Africa Mission of the Presbyterian Church, U.S.A., in August, 1956.**

and power. This merely displays itself in a temporal mass adaptation to outward circumstances, in this case Western ideas and material culture.

Africans have been set upon by conflicting ideologies as colonization has developed. The increase of these answers to man's problems have come in the form of imperialism, colonialism, Communism, Christianity both Roman and Protestant, technology, foreign educational systems, new political structures, new desires and opportunities for giving the individual a meaningful role in a strained and breaking society. These oppositions and contradictions cannot be adjusted indefinitely by even the most impressionable and adjustable personality. There is a limit to the opposition of categories with which a human mind can contend.

## The Roots of Western Ideology

Now it is quite easy for Westerners to sit together and disagree theologically, politically, socially, and in many other ways. The reason we can do so is that we are fairly sure and secure in our ideological base. Any change of opinion we can be fairly sure will not be an upsetting of our entire tradition. Also, we must, as Europeans and Americans, think back and remember that the right to "agree to disagree" was purchased for us in wars and struggles across Europe in which numerous men and women were sacrificed for their ideas. To agree to disagree and to remain friends (Christianity requires nothing less than love) is one of the greatest accomplishments of our history and the one which when lost leads always to the rise of a totalitarian system. The two best cases in our day are hierarchical Catholicism and Communism. The roots of the antitotalitarian attitude rest in the social realization of our Christian faith. The only alternative to the denial of the Christian faith expressed in social democracy is toward some form of totalitarianism.

Unfortunately, it was not the reformers of our faith who grasped this idea (John Calvin had a theologian who disagreed with him on the matter of baptism put to death). It was rather the human cry for justice which we know best in the French Revolution. However, we must remember that Roger Williams, in the Constitution of the State of Rhode Island, preceded and aided the ideological impulses of the French Revolution when he as a Protestant declared that all men were free to worship God as they wished. This came as a matter of fact in America after thousands of Europeans had died in the conflict in which such a revolutionary idea was seeking for a root. This idea was not born of Catholicism, nor is it supported by any totalitariam system. Hence I ask if it is a small matter that African pastors fail to find in their lives and in their system of values any root for such an orientation to theological discussions.

## Development of African Leadership

It is with genuine honesty and goodhearted Christian concern that mission boards should wish to finance a high-level academic seminary. However, the idea must be carefully thought through. African pastors must decide whether it would be better to have a core of Ph.D.'s and D.D.'s within the present mass constituency of the church, or to have a lower level of academic pastors and a more enlightened and rooted congregation. This they must decide. The money required to produce a dozen Ph.D.'s could prepare a hundred well-trained leaders *if* churches are ready to admit that they can have no transformation of their society and social problems unless Christianity finds its roots in the life of *this* human environment. By this I mean that the perplexing problems of lack of confidence and mutual trust, dependability, human responsibility, and a tolerable ordering of human justice cannot be achieved in the churches unless the people in those churches bring themselves and their alleged Christian faith to grips with the menacing problems contained in their attitudes and values.

Much of the problem, admittedly, lies in the weaknesses created in the social and economic crises brought on by the attempt to become Europeans. However, it has not become evident that the two sets of values are in contradiction. The movement for independence reflects and should reflect the fact that there is a basic inequality between those opposing and unadjustable ideologies. Nationalism is not a solution to the African problem. It is merely an awareness of a problem. Nationalism does not even define the problem. From nationalism to independence is a fairly sure move at this time. However, the crux of the problems lies beyond independence. This applies to the churches as well as to the territory. When an African pastor, the moderator of a synod, stands in this meeting and says his synod has not paid him for nine months, I am forced to ask myself if the Christians in that synod have taken Christianity seriously or if they have merely adopted the form. The point to be taken seriously here is that allegiance to Christ, responsibility to God, personal relation to man's eternal destiny involve the deepest revolution in the ideological history of mankind. If this Christian conversion of the self remains an idea without confronting a human reality, it finds no *raison d'etre*, no living human witness to its truth, and it becomes another contradiction which must be discarded with the rest.

## The Roots of Christianity in African Society

The gospel is a living testimony which must seek its roots in the lives of those who profess it both in their social structure and in their ideals and hopes. The roots of Christianity cannot go down far in any society without confronting in a truly startling fashion human traditions. If Christianity finds its roots, it does so because it challenges and questions every aspect of the soil in which it seeks its rooting. This in no way implies that Christianity is merely a sociological institution, but it does imply very strongly that a Christian lives and witnesses to his conversion in terms of a society and cultural form. This is the medium of his communication. This is the area of *his* Christian responsibility. He does not perform the task of the Holy Spirit. He witnesses through his living conversion to the power of the Spirit of God in Christian words and deeds.

One cannot live and communicate Christian conversion without becoming sharply aware of a contradiction between being eternally related to God and temporarily related to man. Also, the Protestant conception of the Christian faith faces man with a personal responsibility to God. When a man assumes individually his responsibility to face his guilt (confess his sin) before God, and when two men have undergone this reorientation toward the individuality of sin and accompanying responsibility for personal decision and action, responsibility to one's fellow men must follow. It is possible for a half-Christian to conceive of a God-directed individuality that escapes the accompanying responsibility to man. However, this is a development in the loss of Christianity. Where there is love there is responsibility. True conversion means a concern for one's fellow men. This is the beginning place for the roots of Christianity. The destruction of a society and the loss of a living force caused by responsible Christianity is an illusion. True love and concern cannot destroy meaning for a society. It must, however, come to grips within its own societal setting and bring about a truly Christian (this always means love and concern) orientation to societal forms and ideals. An individual who claims to have experienced God's love in Christian conversion and who does not require therefore the accompanying conversion of his ideology is the most superficial kind of Christian. The roots of personal conversion grow from the *totality* of conversion.

### The Transformation of Society

This does not mean that there is an evolution of conversion from a Christian in a primitive society to one in modern society. The lamentable decline of Christianity in America is adequate proof of this. The weakening of Christianity as a living force always carries along numerous "Christians" by its sheer inertia. Too often these people live upon the dying echoes of a Christianized tradition. The rise of Christianity is always faced by an equally dangerous problem in which church institutions replace or usurp domains of authority and control that were never intended for them in the New Testament idea. Hence, many men in these situations find justification for their conversion in the fact that it is a thing which great numbers in their society are doing or have done. The sociological imperative overrides the divine imperative, and faith is maintained in the expression of societal need. Since the roots of Christianity are set down by individuals dealing with themselves before God, there is only a societal foundation for Christianity when some individuals have done this and witnessed in love to this complete conversion. The transformation of society can follow only in the wake of a truly transformed individual.

We ask ourselves why a Christian church is beset with such contradictions and problems as the Cameroun churches are. We must remember that God revealed his love in Christ without consideration for a particular form of society or system of cultural values. God confronts men in Jesus Christ where they are in their most human reality. Whether the society is monogamous or polygynous is a cultural fact and is not a determinant of God's love toward man. The Christian faith believes that God in his absolute will has reserved in every human individual a possibility (the image of God) for faith. This potential of faith cannot be touched by history or culture. It is God's possession which he has kept unto himself and through which he brings man unto himself. This relation with God is the dimension of humanity which cannot be known by science, but only by faith itself.

The anthropologist who sees this is the one whose anthropology has been converted along with his person. When this dimension of faith is opened up and realized in man, it results in the comprehension of what is the most basic and real aspect of his existence. Faith in this religious sense may be directed in numerous ways, even back into society itself. However, it is only the Christian faith which recognizes the source and the motivation of God's love to bring about conversion. The mass acceptance of Christianity in Africa and in certain other parts of the world has too often been little more than an importation of a conqueror's religious form. Western Christians with honest enthusiasm have paid evangelists, built church buildings, and underwritten schools to keep up the rush of people into the church. Now that these churches are asked to move under their own power, they show that they are largely incapable of independent action.

## The Church's Western Orientation

In the rapid rise of churches and mass conversions in which these people have been readjusting to an innovation orientation, they have not been given an opportunity, nor have they needed, to come to grips with their own human reality. As long as Christianity in the Cameroun was another imported item from Europe and America, it was treated like many other exterior and superficial accretions. African societies undergoing vast undermining of their social structure by Westernization found the church a genuine social replacement, and its value for them has been largely a filler for holes knocked out of a former way of life. The church often serves, therefore, as a kind of cultural buffer to the sociological shock of Westernization. The church is often an institution whose line of communication runs between the African and the new Western forms of life. Hence the church seeks its roots in a foreign ideology and in so doing fails entirely to see the relation of Christianity to its own cultural base. Since Westernization has only the thinnest kind of veneer established in African societies, it is impossible to hope that African Christianity can become rooted and meaningful as long as it looks to Western cultural forms for its meaning.

The present climaxing rise of nationalism and independence does not at all guarantee that the Cameroun churches will become independent and strong churches. What it does mean is that the church must move to the level of its own sociological reality. When it can see (as individuals) that what it has preached for so long can and must be applied in living witness to African values and social structures, it will find the frontier along which it must battle for its true existence. This church might easily become unrecognizable in a few years. It may even split into numerous factions under old tribal affiliations. While this would be a shocking spectacle as the result of fifty years of missionary labors, it must be said that the church of the Cameroun cannot begin to set down its Christian roots until it plants them in its own human soil. It may take many years before these roots can produce the fruits of a vital Christianity. However, without such a foundation there is little hope for an African church, a transformation of African society, and a living witness of Christianity in Africa.

*William D. Reyburn*

# Motivations for Christianity: An African Conversation

How does a missionary anthropologist get information? Does the fact that he is associated with a mission cripple his ability to get at the facts? Whatever may be his disadvantages, the missionary anthropologist must always work with the people in their own language, and he must have an abiding desire to identify himself with the people he serves. His anthropological advantage is that of securing his data from the normal situations of native life rather than from informant interviews only. He is different from his colleagues in that he must be free to question things which other missionaries take for granted. He must be ready to offer explanations of a people's response and interpretation of Christianity as he ferrets these out through investigation.

Such study may be accomplished in a number of ways. The brief account that is given below is intended to provide a small example of the missionary anthropologist's work at his laboratory, attempting to find the answer to a problem which has come to his attention. In this case the question concerns the high motivation which exists among the Kaka of the Camerouns for being "written in the church."

### The Problem Appears

"We were written in the mission because we are afraid of our own power," exclaimed an African village chief to me recently. On a previous occasion I had noted that the mission had "written" the names of 164 adults in the Kaka village of Lolo in the subdivision of Batouri, French Cameroun. However, only a handful of women and fewer men ever attended the services regularly.

I tried talking with the local catechist to find out the motivation for "being written," but without success. His reasons were not comprehensive and did not accord with some of the major aspects of Kaka culture. His replies that the women liked to go to church on Sunday and that the men wanted to drink wine were insufficient. I determined to investigate, and what I found out proved the catechist wrong, both in his replies and in his ministry.

Lolo is one of those villages where Christianity in the missionary view has been almost totally unsuccessful. It is a village of some four hundred souls where the leading men must have several wives to be accorded status. On the one hand, Lolo is quite primitive. They scarify their children's bodies, perform circumcision rites and chip their teeth, practice numerous taboos related to birth, death, and the hunt. Their economy is divided between hunting and gardening. Their food is almost exclusively manioc flour which they boil into a gelatinous mush and eat with their hands.

**Reprinted from Vol. 5, No. 1 (1958), pp. 27-32.**

On the other score, Lolo is quite modern. It boasts a Christian church with a paid catechist, a French school (first and second grades) subsidized by the government, and a year-round automobile road which cuts through the heart of the village. Tuesday and Wednesday, as regularly as clockwork, a four-engine plane drones through the clouds high over Lolo. The weekly G-string is covered on Sunday by a flowery print dress, a flowing Hausa robe, or occasionally a tattered European overcoat. A small bus is available several days a week for the eighty-kilometer bounce to the regional center at Batouri. In spite of all this, the power of a dead panther is vastly more significant in the Lolo way of thinking than the airplanes which fly overhead.

## Where to Begin?

The problem I wanted to investigate was not complex, but how I would approach it would determine largely the kind of information I would obtain. I could choose to sit at the catechist's house and invite informants to come and visit with me, or I could go into Lolo and live with the people and seek the answers to my problem from the normal conversations of the day and in more subtle ways than asking direct questions. I chose the latter. Taking my regular assistant, a Kaka tribesman who knew many of the men in the village, we moved in with no food and as little gear as we could possibly get by with. It took two weeks to convince the people that a white man could really want to live like the people. Their constant remarks were, "The other tribes don't like our food and say we are dirty. We are so surprised that a white man eats with us, and we thank you." During this two weeks, I did not push for answers to questions but merely listened to others talk and only talked when I was addressed.

Later our talks often ran well into the night as I was riddled with questions about the strange world of the whites. I even had to attempt to explain about Sputnik, and that in a language that has no words for *rounds, gravity,* or *space.* I wondered often why in all of their incessant questioning they never seemed to want to inquire about the mission. I thought this was perhaps because I was connected with the mission and they did not want to bring up a subject which they were tired of hearing about from the catechist.

## The Natural Occasion Ripens

Finally one night, as a group of village elders and I were sitting in the chief's courtyard, the old chief puffed slowly on his clay pipe, blew a gust of smoke against his hand, handed the pipe to the man beside him, and turning to me said, "White man Kaka, what is your name?" I told him my first name. "No," he exclaimed, "that's your pagan name. What is your mission name?" Fortunately my middle name is also good in French, so I told him, and he sighed, "Aha, we will call you Davidi now."

At last it began to look like they were going to start talking toward my subject. I asked him in turn if he had a "mission name." "No," he blurted, "I can't have a mission name." "Why?" I asked. "Look around you," he exclaimed, pointing to six thatched-roof kitchens in his enclosure. "The mission refuses us because we have wives."

I thought to myself, "Shall I unload a long discourse on polygamy as I view it, or shall I see what develops here?"

I sat quietly. There was a long silent pause. The stars were twinkling brightly in the cool night sky. I did not want to lose the thread of this conversation, as I was determined to find out what I was after only by avoiding the traditional informant kind of artificial situation.

I went back to the question of "mission" names. "Mboundjeliko, do you have a mission name?" I asked a bearded man wearing a Hausa covering. "Yes, God knows me," was his reply. "Would God know a Kaka name?" he asked, looking at his colleagues. A low grunt of "No" drifted across the courtyard from some of the chief's wives who were listening at a distance. Now they were beginning to expose their thinking, as I wanted.

I thought I'd better probe a bit while they were thinking about this. "All right," I said, "suppose you have got a mission name and now God knows you, is that all God is good for? If God knows your mission name, Satan must know it too." Their faces turned toward me. "God can read, can't he?" asked one man. "Yes, I should think so," I replied. "Can Satan read?" two men asked as they rocked forth toward me. "Why not? Even children learn to read." Then again silence fell over us. "Who is stronger, God or Satan?" asked the chief. "God is, of course," I replied. A sigh of relief arose from the men. Turning to the chief, I asked, "Tell me, what do you care about the strength of Satan? Are you a child that you should cry because of Satan?"

### The Pay Load Arrives

The chief stood up and pointed a long bony finger at me and said, "We all cry because of *lémbo* that Satan puts in us." I knew that *lémbo* was a supernatural power which enters a human and causes him to kill and perform sorcery. The individual may be treated by a shaman and be cured. Sorcerers are people who are possessed by *lémbo* but will not submit to exorcism and have their *lémbo* removed. At last they had touched on the vital source that was underlying their motivation for being written in the mission. "Tell me," I said, "are you afraid of *lémbo?*" The chief replied, "Yes. All men are afraid of the power of *lémbo.* With *lémbo* you kill people without wanting to do so; you never touch them, but it is your *lémbo* inside of you that has killed them. The mission taught us that God would punish killers. We are all killers and we fear God's punishment. We believe that God can stop our *lémbo* from growing inside of us. Our *lémbo* will stay small and quiet. God will read the names and know whose *lémbo* to arrest."

"But," I objected, "how should that affect you men? Most of you are polygamists and the mission won't write your names." "Oh," he laughed, "we have sent our first wives. This is to show our good heart to God. Would God forget a man who has given him his first wife? The mission will accept only one wife, so we all have put our first wives into God's hands and she will work for us and take care of us in heaven."

I looked about me, and every man in the group was nodding his head in assent to the chief's words. Some of the men started to get up to go home. "Wait," I said, "one more question. What about your *lémbo?* If you are not written in the mission. . . ." The chief cut me short this time. "No, I'm not written, but I have told others to get their names written. Less chance of me getting killed by their *lémbo* that way." "That's the way it is," added the group of village elders as they arose and began to depart into the night. I stood up, stretched, called out, "Sleep well," and picked my way through sleeping goats and sheep until I reached my shack. With the aid of my flashlight, I wrote up my notes for this night's interview.

## Questions

1. Why had the local catechist, the one literate man in Lolo, been unable to provide an answer to the questions concerned? Was he not aware that the people of Lolo were living under considerable stress created by witchcraft assumptions? Yes, he was very much aware of it, but missionaries had always relegated witchcraft to the trash can and the trained catechist's training and contact with missionaries had taught him to be naive about the most dynamic forces in his own life. His education was formed in the categories of the missionaries' experience only, and this had imposed upon him a sophisticated atmosphere which was irrelevant to the task of presenting the gospel in Lolo.

2. If the Kaka belief in witchcraft and its understanding of the male and female roles had been made an integral part of the catechist's training, would the preaching in Lolo be as irrelevant as it is presently? There can be no doubt of the matter. The catechists are trained by the mission to play hide and seek with their own beliefs. They themselves have been successful in their learning of the missionary teaching only by accepting an additional set of assumptions. There is no evidence that they have replaced earlier ones. The people of Lolo must interpret the teaching within their own categories of cultural thought. Had the catechist dealt with the gospel in the light of the people's belief in *lémbo* and in terms of the male and female relations, the function of the church and their relation to God would have been both intelligible and true. As it is, they have been left to interpret it blindly. His teaching left completely untouched the areas of their thinking which were to them the ones related to the subjects which the catechist spoke on, viz. man and his religious world.

3. Is it possible to merely announce the "good news" in the language of the people? Definitely not. Announcing new ideas concerning man and his religious thoughts must compete with the preexisting understanding that is already formed in his life. He must associate ideas, interpret, select, and discard in the light of his comprehension and preexisting belief. It is the task of missionary anthropologists to point up this problem in communication and suggest concrete ways for more effective communication.

*William D. Reyburn*

# Meaning and Restructuring: A Cultural Process

IN the foregoing article, "Motivations for Christianity," we discussed the problem of reinterpreting the meaning of "being written in the church." The discussion will now be continued a bit more in detail, with an attempt to state some of the aspects of this general process, which will be referred to as *restructuring*. Restructuring is the process whereby an individual receives some information, interprets it out of his personal and cultural background, and then responds to it in terms of its restructured meaning. This aspect of communication enters into the praclamation of the gospel and must be closely observed by missionaries who are usually attempting to communicate across widely divergent backgrounds.

As is indicated here, restructuring occurs at two levels, that of the individual at any particular moment, and that of the total stock of experiences which the individual shares with other members of his group. While individual differences are important, we shall be concerned here with the restructuring which is largely determined by the cultural background.

To illustrate, I cite an incident which occurred as I was writing the first lines of this paragraph. Seated at a nearby table writing was my assistant, an educated Kaka tribesman. A villager known to both of us appeared suddenly at the window and said, "Are you awake?" We both returned the greeting, "Yes, are you also awake?" At this point the verbalization of the conventional greeting called for no special interpretation because there was so little information contained in it. The villager replied, "Yes, I am awake."

There was a short pause, then he began again. "Your nephew fell from his bicycle and is being treated at the dispensary." At the same instant my African assistant and I reacted with two different remarks. I asked whether he was hurt badly, and my assistant merely said, "Huh," took from his pocket a small soiled notebook, and jotted down the nephew's name and the date, then launched into a diatribe with the visitor on how awful the mission is for not allowing goats to be kept on the mission property. In the cultural categories of my assistant's thinking a wounded nephew is equated with a payment in cash or animal to the nearest maternal uncle. Our restructuring of the information was determined by the cultural nexus of wounded nephews in each of our backgrounds.

Seizing upon the occasion for further reactions, I reached into my desk drawer and broke in on the pro-goat palaver to announce to the two men that I had in my hand a letter saying that my wealthy maternal uncle had just died. The villager grinned and inquired, "How many wives

**Reprinted from Vol. 5, No. 2 (1958), pp. 79-82.**

did he marry?" This is an example of how we are constantly reading meanings into things out of the cultural experiences which serve to make the world meaningful to us.

## Restructuring at Lolo

In the case at Lolo (locale of the foregoing article), we saw how the act of being written in the mission was restructured to serve as a defensive mechanism against witchcraft. It was also pointed out that the first wives of polygamists were induced by their husbands to become church members. The restructuring of this situation was that wife-lending to God calls for reciprocity in some way, in this case admittance to God's eternal bliss. The possession of a mission French name was seen to be a further defensive mechanism against witchcraft.

The sacrament of communion is also restructured by the village Kaka to fit into previously made assumptions. Missionaries in the Kaka area have often remarked that the communion may strike the people as a kind of magic, and of this there is no doubt. However, this does not appear to be the real reason why the communion Sunday is the only one which is attended in force. It should be noted that the mission plays a sort of police role between *Ndjambie* (God) and the people. Failure to pay one's weekly pledge, to attend the services, or to keep the mission laws concerning adultery, stealing, or killing are faults for which the offender is severed from the mission and therefore from *Ndjambie*.

In Kaka culture, when a grave offense has been committed, one goes to his older brother who prepares food with the offended party and these two eat this food in a purification rite which dissolves the enmity between both parties. Usually it is the eating of two chickens. The restructuring of the communion appears to be associated with this ceremonial eating which is called *sataka*. The mission session judges the faults of the baptized members and refuses communion to those who are believed to be guilty of some church violation. However, the missionary and catechist cannot possibly know the extent of these violations. For those who are allowed to take communion the meaning is that of *sataka* "removing the sin." Interestingly enough, if a church member is removed for a violation, there will often be another kin who will take communion and thereby "remove the sin" in a way analogous to the pagan *sataka*.

## The Missionary and Restructuring

The problem of restructured meaning is obviously many-sided and beset by numerous problems. However, considering this problem from the point of view of cultures, we may state a premise, namely, that the orientations, organizations, and values, as well as the stresses, that are inherent in a particular culture tend to provide the basis for the restructuring of new meanings in ways which are compatible with these cultural determinants.

In so far as we are willing to allow for individual variation and other variables, the way in which a people will restructure meanings of new forms should be in some degree predictable.

In some degree, I say, because the social acceptance of a restructured meaning may be difficult to account for. The role of the innovator, the stress under which the acceptance is made, and many other factors are important in determining how a given form is going to be restructured. People living on a mission station are exposed to a wider variety of innovations and are less conservative than their village brothers whose outside contacts are very limited. Consequently, the villager's more frequent contact with *sataḳa* appears to make him more dependent upon it, and his understanding of communion in the framework of *sataḳa* is more evident.

It is a missionary's responsibility to know how and when restructuring will most likely occur. The juxtaposition of similar ideas does not always provide a neat bridge to the differences, but more often provides a framework for reinterpreting from the one to the other. It is exceedingly discouraging to a missionary among the Kaka who preaches, teaches, and translates, only to find out that no small portion of his listeners were happily satisfied because they were lending God their wives and expecting salvation in return. By the same process, some of the Mazatec people in Mexico have reinterpreted the missionaries' message as referring to the mushroom. The missionary must constantly ask himself, "What would this mean to me if I assumed the world to be as these people assume it to be?" The missionary can only know what the people assume about the world by digging it out through painstaking effort, patience, and participation.

*William D. Reyburn*

**Reprinted from Vol. 6, No. 2 (1959), pp. 78-83.**

# The Spiritual, the Material, and the Western Reaction in Africa

"My father, an African tribal chief, had six wives and three children. Two were boys and one was a girl. Then one of my mothers gave birth to a son whose hair and skin were very light in color. He was not an albino, but a light colored baby. From the day of his birth it was generally believed in the village that his life was delicately hanging in a balance. He was a weak baby and did not have a loud cry. My father and his brothers all feared for the child's precarious life and sought out which taboos must be kept in order to protect the child's life. The one day an old uncle came to my father and said that he had dreamed that someone killed a goat in my father's house. He added that no one in the family should kill a goat or shed any blood before the new baby should be old enough to walk. The child became sick after several weeks and was taken to a mission hospital. His stool was black and formed like a goat's. Another uncle, a catechist, searched through the Bible trying to find something to do for the child. Then one day an animal was killed in the forest by one member of the family. At the very instant the animal was killed the baby screamed and died."

The above account was related, not by a pagan African with no knowledge of Christianity or civilization, but by a highly educated Christian. Another example cited to me by a college graduate in Africa:

"Mr. —, a well trained gentleman whom you know, was told by his sick wife before she died that if he should remarry after her death she would reappear to him and tell him the name of the girl he should marry. Mr. —'s wife died, as you know, and within a few days Mr. — was sitting alone in his house when suddenly his wife appeared to him and announced in a clear voice the name of the girl she wanted her husband to marry. Mr. — went immediately and made the arrangements and married this girl."

Recently while lecturing to classes of Cameroun college students on the relation of African pagan religious beliefs to Christianity and Islam, I asked them to write out for me at least one mysterious incident which had happened in their lives, and which they felt was totally without rational explanation. These college students had no trouble filling up pages with accounts of personal encounters with the world of mysterious events such as the two cited above.

## Integration of the Pagan View

The pagan view of life expressed in most of Africa south of the Sahara does not make a rigid distinction between the religious and the secular life as found in European society. It goes without saying that the pagan African does not make medicine and throw it into the forest expecting to return tomorrow to find a garden growing. His secular world exists in the sense that he reckons with nature with his iron tools in so far as he can. He sharpens his cutlass and hacks down the forest and plants his seeds and does everything he knows to cooperate with nature in the production of his food. In the hunt he uses his highly trained sense of perception in studying animal tracks and moves in to the kill according to the movements of the wind in order to take his prey by surprise. The integration of the religious and the secular is expressed in the way in which the religious feeling for things is carried out in social life and exists to give social relations a sense of the holy. The intrusion of the West into the African's socio-religious life has created a tendency to separate the two into several distinct spheres into what is often called the secularization of African life.

This secularization of African life or the separation of religious sanctions and values from other aspects of tribal life has been partially produced from contact with colonization and Christianity. This subject is an entire study in itself and we can but indicate the nature of it by giving a few examples. These may be taken from the area of law and authority, economic, as well as from many other phases of life. However, we will part with the view that this secularization is as complete as some are inclined to think.

Prior to the arrival of the German military conquest of what is now the Cameroun, many tribes held adultery to be a very serious offense. Adultery was conceived as a violation of family or clan rights of ownership and was punishable by death or by declaration of war on the family or clan of the guilty man. In this way adultery was not thought of as an act between two individuals, but between two large family groups, clans or villages, depending upon the nature of the social relations involved. If the guilty man were apprehended he was killed outright, or if he succeeded in escaping some other member of his family was killed. This blood vengeance is expressed in Kaka by a commonly heard proverb: "The chimpanzee goes up one tree and comes down another." The man who commits the crime is not always the one who will pay. In addition to this offense being considered a group affair, there was the further belief that such a sin produced an impurity in the village and in the family which had to be removed by religious ritual. This consisted mainly in a rite requiring the sprinkling of chicken blood on the house of the offended party and ritual bathing to remove the personal impurity.

Into this picture came the French colonial machine which simply codified adultery along with many other offenses. Cases of adultery along with dozens of other infractions of the law were placed into the hands of the tribunal. There a fixed penalty in the form of imprisonment or fine was levied and the entire matter was soon removed from the area of the religious and stuffed into the world of economics. The matter was righted in the sight of authorities by paying the fine or spending the time in jail. Since only the guilty party could be sentenced under the law, only one man was required (or allowed) to go to jail. This had the further consequence of conceiving the adulterous act as being entirely personal and no longer the offense between two socially stable groups. However, even though the act of adultery was placed upon a private and individual basis, there was not, and perhaps still is not, produced a personal and individual sense of guilt. Money to pay the fine was and is secured from the clan or family group and the individual is fortified in the sense of a collective act which tends to remove any one individual from blame. Since most any offense can now be arranged by the payment of a fine, the need for righting of the wrong has a material rather than a spiritual dimension. This partial substitution of the material for the spiritual and the individual for the group is a basic process which underlies most of the developing commercial centers of West Africa.

The hunt in the Cameroun is another example of this materialization of religious experience. Under more primitive conditions in the open savanna or jungles, the hunter with his crude implements such as bows, spears and traps hunted the ferocious elephant, gorilla, bush cow and lion with a very real sense of potential failure. All of his hunt was prepared and carried out with the very precise execution of rites and ceremonies. With the gradual introduction of effective and accurate firearms and the obvious superiority of these over local methods, there was a tendency to replace the spiritual concern in the hunt for a material concern for the possession of the firearm and ammunition. However, it is here that one must be careful not to despiritualize the materialism. *There was little reason to seek the aid of spiritual forces if these forces were obviously already contained in the magical firearm.*

It is just at this point that we must inquire briefly into the nature of what is referred to in French areas as "*le matérialisme des noirs.*"

## African Materialism

Is the desire for the material, wealth and its rewards, really a mechanical materialism as understood by many writers who see Africa shifting from pagan magic and sorcery into a crass materialism devoid of ethical, moral and spiritual values? Or is there not a conception of the material as containing the spiritual? When I once was told by a group of African school boys that the white man possessed *lémbo* (magic power) because of his inventions, I asked them how they could know whether it were *lémbo* or not. They answered that it is not something which you know in itself. Instead you see the things which *lémbo* can provide for its owner. This is expressed in the words of one writer as: "Ye shall know them by their fruits" (Matt. 7: 16). Regardless of what name is attached to it, the African is concerned that the fruits of his power or being show their presence and guarantee their force by bringing to him material rewards. The lack of such rewards is a poor man, lacking in spirit and therefore in goods.

The manifestation of the material witnessing to the abiding presence of one's *force* plays its role in the social world also. The man who is poor has few friends. This is expressed in another Kaka proverb which says: "The birds roost long in the trees with the leaves." That is, a man whose material possessions witness to the quantity of his personal force, his quantity of life, attracts many others who, basking in his presence, hope that his power will be transferred to them.

Again, the possession of the material transfers a person's status in his group. Upper mobility depends upon the presence of power. If one has no such power he cannot be granted authority over others. If he has such possessions it is generally held that his power will grant him the ability to lead and to decide tribal questions.

Our discussion to this point has brought us to say that the meaning of the materialism of modern Africa has many aspects to it and that the African even in his *search to acquire* is perhaps not primarily moved by the possession of the object as an end in itself as often is the case with Europeans. He is rather attempting to prove to himself and to his world that the presence of *spiritual forces* are at his service and that he stands in good with these. The thick façade of the material is then merely covering this desire to let himself know that all is spiritually well.

Under these conditions Christianity often becomes, not the spiritual reality underlying his behavior, but rather a manifestation that the spiritual reality exists.

## The Spiritual Reality

What then is this spiritual reality? We have referred to it here as a force or power. It is best expressed in African languages with the word *life*. In many of the languages of the Cameroun the Christian terms for "salvation" and "to be saved" are "life" and "to live." Now if life or something similar to it is the essence of this spiritual existence, it is most clearly characterized by its relation to time and space which reveal many aspects in African behavior. Life as conceived in the western world is a series of timed events which come and go, and to all things there is a point of beginning and of ending. Time in this view is a sense of experience as running down and ending. Life in the African view does not have these fixed points of beginning and ending. The past is not historically conceived and does not flow out from a starting point. The end of life on this world is not the end because of the very real spirit world which continues to ever exist. Life is not that span which adds up to the time units counted between birth and death. The constant appearances of the dead to the living both among Christians and pagans reflect the fact that life is not a dwindling to zero, but a change in space without reference to time. A careful study of this concept of life and time could throw light on many bewildering practical aspects of African life. One should not be deceived by the possession of the ubiquitous wrist watch in Africa. Counting time units in a day and a concept of time are two different things. To the African there is simply no sense in the statement that "life is a race with time."

Christianity proclaims a view of life which is eternal, and it is this which the African grasps and makes of it an authoritarian expression of his own belief. In saying this it should be emphasized that I do not refer to "African" and "Africans" as individuals or even as groups of tribes or nations, but am rather equating the word African with the view of life and time as I have described it. Of course Christianity also conflicts with many of his beliefs and practices. However, it is precisely here that we return to the original point of our discussion, the relation of African religious beliefs to Christianity.

### Western Christian Reaction

The problem is great due to the fact that African beliefs are a bewildering variety and Christianity, like Islam, has a complicated set of expressions. However, we are concerned here only with certain implications of the African view of life described above and the reaction to it by Christian missionaries. This greatly simplifies the problem and makes it possible to come to a few conclusions.

Missions in Africa were often founded upon the principle that the lost heathen had nothing in his life and that his religious mind was totally void of any revelation. He was a *tabla rasa* on to which religion was to be engraved for the first time. All his beliefs fell into the missionary's category of the superstitious. Fetishism, magic, sorcery and the more underlying religious beliefs for their existence were too often discounted. The European or American missionary who approached his work in Africa with this attitude did so partly because his own history had proved for him that, given enough scientific knowledge and rational thought, all nonrational phenomena could be disposed of as simply superstition or the work of Satan. It did not require much time for the African Christians to become aware that their own world of mysterious phenomena was discounted by the missionary as devilish or not valid at all.

The consequences of this attitude on the part of the western Christian churches caused the African spirit world to go underground. The official position of the church was merely to deny the African reality or to hand out church discipline to the member who delved in this realm. Since missionaries preferred to deny their reality rather than work with the African in appreciation of these phenomena, the African has in many areas of Africa held his Christian faith in one hand and his belief in the mysterious world of his pre-Christian days in the other.

I have never talked confidentially with an African Christian who would deny that the dead appear to the living and affect them in their plans and activities in this life. However, these same Christians are quick to admit that those things are never mentioned in church and that they are not supposed to occur, according to the church.

The attitude of the western missionary toward the African spirit phenomena struck the African at the same time as the invasion of the European secular and material world. The acceptance of clothes, tables, and a wide assortment of European merchandise helped conceal the spiritual gap that existed between the African and the western missionary. The African became aware that the real separation could be covered over by adaptation through the material means made available to him by European industrialization. However, this meeting of two worlds on the material plane has not been a true meeting at all. The underlying orientation for the African view is essentially spiritual, and the grasp for the material has not been entirely what it appears to be on the surface.

This is the nature of a conflict in African Christianity. The conflict is not the fault of the African church but rather the closed attitude with which it was approached by the western church missionaries. This attitude was formed largely out of our secular western world and not out of a true attempt to understand Biblically the nature and validity of the African's "superstitions."

The task which lay before Christian missions in Africa at the beginning still remains largely the same. However, at this time the problem is even more complex, due to the fact that so many social and religious changes have been produced. The African Christian tends to withdraw from the western missionary and to maintain his beliefs in isolation. It is not that the African is any less a Christian believer for this. It is rather that he does not wish to share with outsiders that which brings on ridicule and misbelief.

If the churches of the West are to prepare and work with African Christianity in the face of Islamic advance, there must be an entire rethinking of the deeper reality of nonrational phenomena. Beside this formidable task, all the other problems of Christianity in Africa are of secondary importance. The Western churches and Western cultures are not producing a satisfactory interpretation of religious phenomena. Unless they do, the result for Christianity in Africa is going to be felt soon. A great hope lies in the developing theological education in Africa, provided the lines of inquiry are formulated by African thought open to discussion and sensitive to Christian truth.

*John C. Messenger, Jr.*

**Reprinted from Vol. 6, No. 3 (1959), pp. 97-103.**

# The Christian Concept of Forgiveness and Anang Morality

*This paper examines the major causes underlying the spread of what African elders and Westerners alike regard as immoral behavior among Anang youth in Southeastern Nigeria. The Anang have experienced profound cultural change since World War I, at which time they were finally pacified by the British and the first trading post and Christian mission were established among them. When this change is assessed, it is apparent that most of the forces contributing to immorality among young people in other African societies are also operative in Anang society, namely the breakdown of traditional political, religious, and kinship forms and the adoption of Western values, especially those in the economic realm.[1] This paper treats these common causal factors, but emphasizes one in particular which is important in producing immorality among Anang youth: their acceptance of the Christian concept of forgiveness. Probably this new doctrine is affecting the behavior of other African peoples in a similar manner, but, if so, it has not received adequate attention in acculturation studies.*

CERTAIN beliefs embodied in the indigenous Anang religion partially explain why the adoption of a new conception of divine intervention in human affairs has so strongly influenced the conduct of youth. The Anang are monotheistic, the central theme of their religion being the worship of a sky deity, named *abassi,* who rules the universe and mankind. He is assisted by numerous spirits residing on earth in shrines, and by souls of the dead awaiting reincarnation in the underworld. Although he is considered both omniscient and omnipresent, he lacks ultimate omnipotence, for ghosts, witches, and the

John C. Messenger, Jr., is **Assistant Professor in the Departments of Social Science and Sociology and Anthropology of Michigan State University. He has the Ph.D. in Anthropology from Northwestern University, and in addition to the field work represented in this article he has done general ethnographic research among the Arran Islanders of Western Ireland. He is author of several previous publications on the Anang. The present paper was delivered before the American Anthropological Association in 1958, and is based on research conducted in Nigeria during 1952.**

[1] For a general account of culture change in Anang society, I refer you to my *Anang Acculturation: A Study of Shifting Cultural Focus,* Ann Arbor, University Microfilms, Pub. No. 23525, 1957, pp. 196-290; also to my "Religious Acculturation Among the Anang-Ibibio," in *Continuity and Change in African Cultures,* ed. by W. Bascom and M. Herskovits, Chicago, University of Chicago Press, 1959.

spirit of evil magic possess powers over which he sometimes exerts no control. The Anang do not know where these malevolent powers originate, so they must be combatted with preventive magic.

Fate as ordained by *abassi* directs the course of each human life, but rather than remaining immutable following assignment at conception, it may be modified within narrow limits through the exercise of free will by the individual. A divinely enunciated moral code embracing every aspect of human behavior forms the basis for evaluating acts transcending fate. Should these acts conform to his code, the deity will alter a person's fate so that future misfortunes are canceled. On the contrary, should the freely perpetrated deeds of an individual transgress against this code, *abassi* will compound predestined misfortunes.

Supernatural retribution takes many forms, from the extreme of causing an object of little value to be misplaced to that of transforming a soul into a ghost at death. The severity of the sanction depends upon the nature of the misdeed and the predilection of the deity. The most favored sanctions, however, are to have a person be found guilty of a crime in court and be subjected to judicial punishment, or to have the oath spirit attack one who has sworn an oath falsely or who has committed one of several other specific crimes.

The recognition of a divine moral code and the ability of *abassi* to punish any divergence from its tenets constitute the most powerful mechanisms of social control. The Anang individual is far more sensitive to external controls, most of which are ultimately religious, than he is to internal ones, and there is little evidence of a well-formed conscience that evokes feelings of guilt for a socially disapproved act.[2]

## Anang Response to Christianity

The foregoing features of Anang religion provide a framework for appraising the impact of Christianity and other aspects of Western culture. The first mission in the region was founded in 1919 by the Wesleyan Methodists. Seven other Christian bodies, two of them African in origin, were installed between 1919 and 1948,[3] and today all maintain churches, some schools, and several hospitals. Most of the denominations have had marked success in gaining converts during recent years, and slightly more than half the people now profess the Christian faith.

The Anang have reacted to religious acculturation differentially according to sex and age groups. Women as a whole have embraced Christianity,[4] whereas

[2] The relationship between internal and external controls in personality and its consequences is discussed in R. Benedict, *The Chrysanthemum and the Sword*, Boston, Houghton Mifflin Co., 1946, pp. 222-227; F. Hsu, "Suppression vs. Repression," *Psychiatry*, Vol. 12, 1949, pp. 223-242; D. Riesman, *The Lonely Crowd*, New Haven, Yale University Press, 1950, pp. 10-31. The Anang culture is a "shame culture" rather than a "guilt culture," "suppression" rather than "repression" is the basic mechanism of socialization, and the Anang personality is predominately "tradition-directed" rather than "inner-directed" or "other-directed."

[3] These are the Kwa Ibo (English interdenominational) established in 1920, the Roman Catholic (Holy Ghost Order) in 1925, the Lutheran (Missouri Synod) in 1936, the African Apostolic (nativist) in 1936, the Christ Army (nativist) in 1940, the Assemblies of God in 1946, and the Seventh Day Adventist in 1948.

[4] The major reason for their acceptance is their belief that the Christian God affords them greater protection in child bearing than does

only boys and young men among the males have done so. Old men are either antagonistic or indifferent toward the encroachment of Christianity and, almost without exception, are attempting to preserve traditional beliefs. Incapable of arresting emergent change, since they no longer possess the political and kinship authority they once did, the old men spend much of their time together extolling the past and criticizing Western innovations. In particular, they remonstrate against the immorality displayed by youth, holding that the assorted political, economic, and social ills which have befallen the Anang during the past three decades have been perpetrated by *abassi,* who is angry with young people for disobeying his moral mandates.

Middle-aged men, on the other hand, have been much more susceptible to conversion, but among those declaring themselves Christian, few are orthodox in their beliefs, according to mission reports.[5] They tend to reinterpret and syncretize Anang and Christian dogmas while preserving many traditional forms of worship. The two nativist denominations are supported almost entirely by men in this age category and by women.

The strongest supporters of Christianity among the Anang are those who were born after religious proselytizing commenced. Many were reared as Christians, and most claim to be Christians whether or not they are members of a denomination. They tend to join missionary churches, mainly because only these can finance well-equipped schools and hospitals. Formal education is highly prized, since it is a prerequisite to positions that bring high income and prestige, such as medicine, law, business, teaching, and the civil service. Young people express admiration for most things European, and the person who adopts Western customs, including religious ones, gains recognition as a result. The nativist denominations are denigrated in the urban centers, as they are financially incapable of sponsoring schools and hospitals, and are severely criticized by missionaries for their pseudo-Christian doctrines. Belonging to either of the African churches means "losing face" in the estimation of Westernized Anang youth.

## Ignorance of Anang Religion

Young people tend to have only a vague understanding of the indigenous religion. Systematic probing of the religious knowledge of numerous children and young adults revealed that they were either ignorant of or misunderstood such basic Anang beliefs as the role of fate in guiding human affairs, the nature of the nether world, and the functions of numerous shrines and sacred groves. They

*abassi.* One of the principal prestige symbols for both men and women is offspring, and prior to the introduction of Western medicine the infant mortality rate was over forty per cent. Women soon learned that care by European-trained midwives and delivery in mission or government hospitals ensured increased success in child bearing. European medical specialists are believed to gain their abilities through manipulation of supernatural power emanating from the Christian God, just as indigenous workers of magic and diviners are thought to control power bestowed by *abassi.* The reduction of infant mortality following the use of Western medical techniques convinced women that God is superior to the traditional deity.

[5] Lutheran statistics indicate that although fifty per cent of the Anang and neighboring Ibibio have been converted to Christianity, only an estimated ten per cent are "true believers." See H. Nau, *We Move Into Africa,* St. Louis, Concordia Publishing House, 1945, p. 161. It is my opinion that the author has considerably overestimated the latter percentage.

betrayed an even greater ignorance of sacred rituals. Only in the areas of magic, witchcraft, and oath administration did they reveal extensive knowledge of traditional customs.

One of the important reasons for this ignorance is that teachers in both government and mission schools inculcate Christian doctrines and denounce Anang religion. In government institutions this is done by instructors who, for the most part, have received their education in mission schools. Nigerian law limits formal religious instruction to fifteen minutes each day, but since many of these institutions offer room and board facilities, there is ample time outside the classroom for students to be proselytized. Those children who do not attend schools and express an interest in the indigenous religion are held up to ridicule by friends who are students.

Another reason for the vagueness of religious belief among youth is that many of them leave home at an early age to pursue occupations in urban communities, and thus never receive adequate religious instruction from their parents and other kin. Even when living at home, children spend much of their time away from adults as members of organized gangs, and the adults themselves are frequently absent while engaged in farming, trading, and political activities.

In addition, it has been noted that women have accepted Christianity to a greater degree than their husbands. Most of them object to having their children taught what they consider false beliefs. Family quarrels often center about whether or not younger members should be allowed to attend traditional religious ceremonies, join secret associations having religious functions, or become members of a Christian church.

Finally, with the loss of authority as a result of acculturation, older men are no longer in a position to command the obedience and respect of youth, and thus are unable to impart religious knowledge to them effectively. Indigenous governmental and judicial forms have been abolished in large measure by the British, and new leaders have arisen who serve as models for young people, men who are educated, financially successful, and Christian.

### Spread of Immorality

Theft, bribery, fraud, perjury, adultery, murder, and many other infractions of Anang and Western morality are committed on a broad scale by Anang youth, largely in pursuit of wealth and prestige. The spread of immorality is attested by the rapid increase during recent years in offenses tried by Native and Magistrates' Courts and by traditional judicial bodies which, although illegal, continue to meet in a few villages. Prison capacities are overtaxed as well, with youth making up the bulk of the prison population. Village life is disrupted because of the deep schisms between young people and their elders. The latter bitterly resent the adoption of Western customs by the former and are, as indicated above, especially critical of deviations from Anang morality. They place the primary blame for this condition on Christianity, in particular on the concept of God and salvation embodied in Christian dogma.

Protestantism, by preaching an "intellectual" gospel emphasizing salvation through faith, and Roman Catholicism, by introducing the sacrament of confession, have fostered, however unintentionally, the widespread belief among young people that the Christian God forgives all sins. The youth tend to accept Christian morality as expounded by the missionaries, largely because of its similarity to Anang morality, and they understand that it is divinely sanctioned, yet the opinion is widely held that its tenets may be disregarded without fear of spiritual punishment if belief is maintained or if sins are confessed and absolved.

Sermons by Protestant ministers stress the extreme sinfulness of man and the possibility of salvation through faith, seldom urging the practice of good works as a principal means of expressing faith. Lutheran and Methodist missionaries, as far as could be determined, are unaware of the powerful impact of this doctrine on young people, although several Catholic priests who were interviewed recognize, to some extent, what is transpiring and admitted stressing punishment in hell for sinful acts when instructing youth.

Many young persons wear Christian crosses because they believe that this will assure God's forgiveness for an immoral deed, as well as protect them against the machinations of evil spiritual forces. They also believe that the Holy Spirit is especially capable of obtaining the forgiveness of God, and they direct prayers and sacrifices to this being. A favorite song among the youth reveals the attitude of this age group when criticized for misdeeds. It has the following words: "I don't care. I will tell the Holy Spirit. He will tell my Father. All will be well."

Few converted Anang comprehend the nature of the Trinity. Most believe that three distinct entities exist: God, the creator of the universe; Jesus, his human son, who was sent by him to spread the Christian doctrine to the peoples of the world; and the Holy Spirit, whose major tasks are to heal the sick and injured, to foretell future events, and to gain from God forgiveness for sins. Seldom were Anang able to explain the significance of Jesus' dying on the cross to atone for the sins of mankind, although most realized that belief in this act must be maintained to ensure salvation. It is not an exaggeration to say that worship of the Holy Spirit dominates the belief system of young Christians, even though God is known to possess ultimate power.

The nativist denominations, whose chief support comes from women, middle-aged men, and youth from rural villages, owe their considerable success to the emphasis they place on the Holy Spirit and salvation through faith and confession. "Evangelists" assigned to each nativist prayer house are able to become possessed by the Holy Spirit and heal and prognosticate, much in the manner of traditional workers of magic and diviners. When foretelling the future, the evangelist speaks in a jargon purported to be the voice of God interjected into his mouth by the Holy Spirit, and only the specialist can translate what he has uttered once the state of possession is terminated. These denominations are known as "spiritualist" ones, and their dogmas are based upon various Biblical verses stressing the nature of the Holy Spirit, healing, prophesying, and speaking in diverse tongues.[6] Christ Army "catechists" instruct their communicants that *abassi* will forgive all sins so long as belief is held in Christ as Savior and these sins are confessed in a ceremony resembling that of the Catholic Church. Thus this body has incorporated into its doctrine elements of both Protestant and Catholic dogma.

[6] For example, the Christ Army Church bases its legitimacy on the following Biblical excerpts: Joel 2: 28-32, Matthew 10: 1-14, Mark 16: 17, Luke 9: 1-6, Acts, 2: 17, and I Corinthians 12: 4-11.

Whereas *abassi* is conceived in the indigenous religion as one who is largely unforgiving and will punish all misdemeanors, the Christian God is regarded as a forgiving deity. We saw that belief in a divine moral code and the ability of *abassi* to punish any deviations from its strictures are the most potent social control devices in Anang society. The acceptance by youth of the concept of a forgiving deity has greatly reduced the efficacy of supernatural sanctions and has actually fostered immorality. Lacking well-developed internal controls and freed from important external restraints, the Christian can deviate from prescribed ways of behaving with impunity.[7]

### Effect of Legal Sanctions

The major regulator of conduct now is the threat of legal punishment for civil and criminal offenses. However, the British-introduced judiciary is viewed with contempt, and the Native Courts, in which most cases are tried, are notoriously corrupt. As a result of missionary influence, oath swearing before indigenous practitioners was discontinued in Native Courts in 1947 and swearing on the Bible substituted. Since young people believe that the Christian God will forgive perjury, and they are no longer forced to take the dreaded oath spirit into their bodies, there is no compulsion for them to speak truthfully. This eventuality has slowed judicial procedure, placed undue emphasis on circumstantial evidence, and caused many unfair verdicts. Persons wronged in court usually resort to sorcery in order to obtain redress, and as a result the practice of "black magic" has increased rapidly during the past few years.

Even though accepting Christian doctrines on a broad scale, most youth maintain indigenous beliefs concerning the power of the evil magic and oath spirits, witches, and ghosts. Despite attempts by most missionaries to discount the reality of these supernatural entities, traditional attitudes persist, or else these beings are collectively regarded as manifestations of the Devil, a view some missionaries support. Young people are fearful of the attacks of sorcerers, ghosts, and witches, and they employ preventive magic as frequently as do their elders to defend themselves. The only success traditional leaders have had in exerting any measure of authority over many recalcitrant youths is by resorting to the use of the oath spirit, who, in addition to castigating those who have sworn oaths falsely, is also able to punish other forms of immoral conduct.

It is important to note that immorality is more prevalent among young men than among young women. The latter are prone to be less honest in their trading affairs than in the past, and husbands generally claim that their young wives are more quarrelsome and adulterous than their counterparts thirty years ago. The Anang consider women to be more strongly motivated sexually than men, and the problem of adultery on the part of wives, especially those living in large polygynous households, was regarded as

[7] It would appear that the nature of the personality controls of a people being converted to Christianity is an important factor explaining the success or failure of the proselyting effort. Roman Catholic missionaries are often more successful than their Protestant counterparts in converting Nigerians because of their willingness to employ strong external religious sanctions, which often involves modifications of Catholic dogma and rituals. This willingness to reinterpret Catholic and traditional religious forms, supplemented by a greater emphasis on ceremonialism and the use of icons, appeals to the Nigerians.

a rather serious one before the advent of the British. Many women when interviewed admitted that Anang wives are more adulterous today, but asserted that the Christian God forgives this offense. Most wives refuse to swear an oath when first married that they will not commit adultery, as was customary before the introduction of Christianity.

In conclusion, let it once again be pointed out that acceptance by youth of the Christian doctrine of a forgiving deity is only one among a number of major causes of immorality. The importance of non-religious forces, referred to only briefly and tangentially above, cannot be overemphasized in accounting for this phenomenon, so it is hoped that the accusation of "religious determinism" will not be directed against the paper.

*Mahlon M. Hess*

# Political Systems and African Church Polity

A MISSIONARY to India was recently describing the experience of his mission in organizing the young national church in their district. The congregations were divided into districts under district councils, district councils sent representatives to regional councils, and regional councils chose representatives which constituted a national council. It was a comparatively simple democratic arrangement, but they are not finding it to work too well at the present time. The people of that area have a temperament of dependence and subservience, are accustomed to the servant-master relationship, and in the judgment of this missionary would perhaps respond better to some system which provides strong central leadership.

In another area of India, some Indian nationals were conversing with their missionary leaders and expressed deep appreciation for the fact that the missionaries had brought the gospel to them. Then they asked that the missionaries not require them to adopt in their churches a Western type of worship and organization, and appealed for liberty to follow a pattern of church life adapted to their own Eastern way of life.

The author has had one term of service on a mission field in East Africa where there is a growing national church that is just at the point where it needs a more definite organizational form for the sake of its own development. The first pastors were only recently ordained, after the churches had prayed until they had achieved unanimous discernment as to the men of God's choice. This experience has been a great factor in making the national Christians realize that they are a church under God, and not entirely dependent upon the foreign missionaries who brought them the gospel. Experiences along the way have indicated that the organizational patterns of our Western churches are not entirely relevant to East Africa. We now face the problem of the degree to which we shall transplant some American polity, or if not, how to discover what type of polity will be relevant to the life and needs of our brethren in East Africa.

The writer is keenly aware of the warning sounded by Radcliffe-Brown that "we cannot hope to pass directly from empirical observations to a knowledge of general sociological laws or principles"; that, as Bacon warned, this would lead "only to a false appearance of knowledge." However, having the benefit of surveys of representative African tribes made by recognized anthropologists, as well as having access to comparative studies made by scholars and the conclusions drawn therefrom, the author feels encouraged to believe that the ideas hereafter set forth have some validity.

---

**Reprinted from Vol. 4, No. 5 (1957), pp. 170-184. Rev. Mahlon M. Hess is a Mennonite missionary in Tanganyika.**

## Systems in the Whole of Life

While Westerners tend to compartmentalize their lives, to the Oriental and to primitives life is a unified whole. Providing the material necessities of life, social relations with one's own group and with those outside the group, perpetuating the family and the culture, and relations with the supernatural are regarded as being, as indeed they are, intertwined and interdependent.

Every society has "mechanisms for the regulation of affairs that concern the group as a whole."[1] We commonly term these mechanisms political systems, and they serve to regulate both behavior within the group and relations with outside groups. The purpose of such political institutions is to make possible the harmonious functioning of the society and the perpetuation of the group and its culture.

In order to assure the perpetuity of the group, the whole of life is therefore regulated: marriage, family and community relationships, economic activities, religious activities, etc. This close regulation of the whole of life is also related to the communal viewpoint of primitive societies and Eastern peoples. They have a keen sense that a man does not live unto himself, and that what each individual man does involves his whole clan; in fact, not only those who are living, but even his deceased ancestors.

In a society which regards life as a unified whole, the social system regulates the whole of life and may even combine the totality of leadership functions in a single official.

In Africa it is often hardly possible to separate, even in thought, political office from ritual or religious office. Thus in some societies it may be said that the king is the executive head, the legislator, the supreme judge, the commander-in-chief of the army, the chief priest or supreme ritual head, and even perhaps the principal capitalist of the whole community. But it is erroneous to think of him as combining in himself a number of separate and distinct offices. There is a single office, that of king, and its various duties and activities, and its rights, prerogatives, and privileges make up a single unified whole.[2]

## Life Oriented from a Religious Standpoint

In most of the non-Christian societies, not only is life regarded as a unitary whole, but it is oriented from a religious standpoint. Not only can it be said, as Ruth Benedict comments, that "a much greater area of life is commonly handled by religious means among primitives than among any civilized peoples,"[3] but one also notes that religion is intimately related to the most ordinary duties and is in some respects almost an unconscious habit of life.

The powers that rule the universe are known, and the ways in which they are approached are part of the routine of living. To make a token offering of food to gods or ancestors before eating, to murmur a formula before the arrow leaves the bow, or

---

[1] Fortes, M., and Evans-Pritchard, E. E., editors: *African Political Systems.* Published for International African Institutes by Oxford University Press, London, 1940. p. xi.

[2] Ibid., p. xxi.

[3] Boas, Franz, editor: *General Anthropology.* D. C. Heath and Co., New York, 1938. p. 648.

to strengthen the power of a charm by sprinkling it with palm-wine, takes no more thought, and occurs as frequently as our conventional "Excuse me" or "Thank you"[4]

Just as life as a whole is religiously oriented, so the political systems are frequently regarded as of religious origin and having mystical authority. "An African ruler's . . . credentials are mystical and are derived from antiquity."[5]

In his chapter on political systems, Herskovits calls attention to the wide range of political forms found throughout the world; later he calls attention to the fact that such range is likewise found in Africa, but that Africa has more of the complex type of governmental forms than are to be found elsewhere.[6]

One observes that among some of the African peoples, basic authority is vested in the local unit of society; elsewhere in a larger regional unit; elsewhere in the tribal or territorial unit. This classification is somewhat arbitrary, for there are so many variations and interrelations that clear-cut classification is not possible. However, each system has a major focus which can be classified in one of these categories, so we will use them to facilitate discussion. Where the local unit is basic, the political organization tends to be nonformal; however, there are recognized and authoritative patterns to be followed. The regional and territorial types of government are in some cases highly centralized. Below are examples of the three forms.

### Local Government

Pygmy government, as described by Patrick Putnam, is entirely in local hands.

> There are no chiefs, councils, or any other formal governing bodies in a pygmy camp. In making any decisions concerning the whole camp, two factors are involved. The first of these is respect for older people. . . . Secondly, while the opinions of most of the old men are respected, every man in the camp is entitled to state his own views on any subject. Thus during the evening talking time the pygmies will discuss whether to move camp; where to and why; or whether to go net hunting, and where to hunt. The discussion has no leader and may go on for several evenings. Finally the men who are shouting out different opinions will come to an agreement and the decision will be acted upon.
>
> In general it is the older and more experienced men who make the decision, but as some of the old men are considered eccentrics and freaks, little attention is paid to them. Rather, it is an oligarchy of the more respected among the old men, a body with no formal membership or specific composition. In their decisions the pungent remarks of the women also have a considerable influence.[7]

One notes that peoples who are primarily governed locally, such as the above, also have certain ties to the larger groupings of their society and to the tribe as a whole, ties which may derive from kinship, age-set groupings, religion, or common needs such as defense. Nuer

---

[4] Herskovits, Melville J.: *Man and His Works: The Science of Cultural Anthropology*. Alfred A. Knopf, New York, 1949. p. 362.

[5] Fortes and Evans-Pritchard, p. 16.

[6] Herskovits, pp. 327, 332.

[7] Coon, Carleton S.: *A Reader in General Anthropology*. Henry Holt and Co., New York, 1948. p. 334.

society has an interesting system of segmentation which provides that in every intratribal conflict the defending group will always be as large as the aggressive group; against an external foe the whole tribe will unite. Apart from these extraordinary circumstances, their life is regulated on a local basis.

## Regional Government

On the basis of the data available, this type is the most difficult to identify. It would appear that those tribes in which the clan is the significant political unit tend to have a parallel series of independent regional units. Wagner describes the Bantu of Kavirondo as follows:

> As regards submission to political leadership, the largest groups, both among the Logoli and the Vugusu, are the exogamous, patrilineal clans, or clan grouping consisting of one larger and several smaller clans, but not the whole tribal society. The tribal unit is marked by the belief in the descent of all clans from one remote tribal ancestor, Murogoli and Muvugusu, respectively, and by the occupation of a continuous stretch of territory. In addition, there are numerous institutionalized forms of cooperation and interdependencies between the different clans of the tribal group which distinguish interclan relations from intertribal relations, but there is no tribal authority which overrules clan authority, either in its dealings with foreign tribes or in the management of its internal affairs. In terms of the the definition given above, the clan would thus have to regarded as the only political unit.[8]

Hailey describes the Musoma District of Tanganyika as an area "where . . . the clan unit is still the most significant feature in the indigenous structure." Their political structure consists of subsidiary councils of subclan heads (Igiha) which form a clan council (Kizaku) and each clan council sends representatives to a tribal council.[9]

## Territorial Government

Oberg describes how in Uganda the pastoralist Bahima intruded into the country and overcame the agriculturist Bairu, and how they then established themselves as the rulers of the country, setting up a centralized government.

> The king, or Mugabe, we observed, formed the centre of this system of relationships. The exercise of power demanded still further developments. A system of government grew up around the king's person, consisting of office holders, the military bands, and the host of servants and specialists to uphold the king's dignity and authority and to carry out his orders as the leader of the politically organized Bahima ruling caste.[10]

## Localization of Authority and Democracy

Though the Ashanti[11] have a highly developed centralized government, in many matters the local units are autonomous. The Ngwato likewise have a hierarchy, but local matters are handled locally among them.

> In certain respects each section, district, community, village, ward, and family-group is independent of the rest, managing its own affairs

---

[8] Fortes and Evans-Pritchard, p. 200.

[9] Hailey, Lord: *Native Administration in the British African Territories.* His Majesty's Stationery Office, London, 1950. Part I, p. 235.

[10] Fortes and Evans-Pritchard, p. 136.

[11] Herskovits, pp. 333-334.

under the direction of a recognized head whose authority extends over almost every sphere of public life.[12]

It appears also to be a common tendency for African tribal units to split into two groups rather than become too large. This is significant, for local government seems to be most effective only when the group is not too large.

The democratic nature of African society functions in two particular ways. In some cases every person is allowed to participate directly in discussions, and we noted in the instance of the pygmies that the counsel of the women is also regarded. The centralized types of government frequently make provision for the principle of representation.

## Centralized Government

One notices at least two factors that gave rise to the development of centralized forms of government. Perhaps the most frequent is that of conquest. When a tribe brings under its dominion peoples of other cultures and economic pursuits, some form of centralized government is almost invariably developed. However, in the case of a tribe of homogeneous peoples, the very size of the tribe may call for some form of centralized control.

In centralized governments the checks and balances are provided by giving every group representation. The conflicts of interest thus serve to balance eaah other. There is the balance between the central administration and the people's interests, the balance between the central and regional interests, and the balance between authority and responsibility.[13]

In the noncentralized governments the equilibrium grows out of the conflict between local interests, which tend to segment the tribe, and lineage and ritual interests, which tend to consolidate it.

## Conservatism of Political Systems

African societies tend to be small and homogeneous, living largely in isolation from other groups and having accurate knowledge of only the recent past. Their chief sources of knowledge are observation and absorption of tradition. In such a society, therefore, the older people are those who have the greatest understanding of life in terms of the tribal culture. They are, as a result, most influential in guiding the life of the group.

There is also in African temperament what one writer calls a slavish conservatism, a dull acceptance of what is with no effort to change the situation. As an illustration of this, I have observed that when a branch falls across a native path, rather than trouble to move it out of the way, every person walks around it, and the path develops one more crook in it.

While African societies tend to be conservative, they are not static. Crisis experiences such as famine, pestilence, etc., may cause cultural and political modifications in a society, as will also the influence of surrounding groups. Regarding the Sukuma tribe of Tanganyika, East Africa, Hailey writes that the old men's societies may modify custom. He also calls attention to the fact that the young men's societies have on occasion been able to check the arbitrary powers of chiefs. Here then are two channels which the social structure itself provides as instruments of cultural change.[14]

---

12 Fortes and Evans-Pritchard, p. 63.

13 Ibid., pp. 11-13.

14 Hailey, p. 225.

## Qualifications for Leadership

Schapera, in describing the Ngwato of Bechuanaland, indicates that a headman is the leader in each local district, and that this position is hereditary.

> ... During his absence, or after his death, the man next to him in line of succession, normally his eldest son by his first wife, automatically takes his place.
>
> This hereditary principle runs right through the Ngwato political system. It means in effect that the administration of any group is vested not so much in one particular person as in the whole family of which he is the head; and that the leading member of this family present on any occasion when action must be taken is able, by virtue of his birthright, to exercise authority over the other people of the group.[15]

Among some of the Bantu peoples, also, authority is based on descent.[16] One notes numerous other instances in which a given office is hereditary within a family group as a whole; in such cases choice between the possible candidates is made by a group of elders representing the people. Regarding the Ashanti, Herskovits writes that the paramount chief, "like all other officers, was selected by the elders from possible candidates in the matrilineal line."[17]

In some of the simple societies, ability is the only qualification for office.

> Among the Bushmen, some of the larger bands have a chief, but in most of them the "common affairs," such as migration and hunting, are under the direction of men whose skill alone earns them the respect and obedience of their fellows. . . . This "official" is thus a leader with authority only as he demosstrates his ability to use it.[18]

Guntner, in discussing the Bantu of Kavirondo, points out a number of factors by which individual persons could attain prominence and become recognized as leaders: primogeniture, wealth, qualities of personality, reputation as a warrior, possession of magico-religious virtues, and age. By way of summary he says: "The more qualities of leadership came together in one person, the higher was his authority and the wider the group that recognized it."[19]

## Political Systems and Economic Level

Many societies of the world produce more material goods than are required to maintain their existence. This economic surplus makes it possible to release, to a varying degree, certain persons from subsistence activities to specialize in such activities as will further the interests of the group as a whole. These specialists are usually of two types: those who direct the affairs of the tribe in an administrative capacity, and those who serve the tribe in a religious capacity. Where there is no economic surplus, there can be no specialists. The Bushmen, who have no economic surplus, and the Hottentots, who have, are excellent examples, living as they do contiguously and in similar situations.

Because their religious and political life is always geared to their economic level, it appears that nonliterate peoples

15 Fortes and Evans-Pritchard, p. 60.

16 Ibid., p. 83.

17 Herskovits, p. 334.

18 Ibid., p. 338.

19 Fortes and Evans-Pritchard, p. 235.

are generally able to support their religious institutions. It may not be easy for them to do so, but these obligations always take precedence over personal comfort and needs. These societies also have mechanisms for sharing between those who have and those who have not. For example, in a time of food shortage a man may ask and receive help from his relatives who yet have a supply. When there are not sufficient resources in a family to provide the bride-price for a young man whose marriage has been long delayed, help may again be solicited and expected from relatives.

## Headman and Council of Elders

Two of the most common political institutions of Africa are those of headman and a council of elders. Each of these is found in the local unit of society; both may be found in the same society. Their exact form and functioning varies from tribe to tribe. The functions of the council of elders is well described by Wagner. Note, too, that the elders of all subclans formed a clan council.

> When disputes or quarrels could not be settled by self-help, the person who believed himself wronged appealed to the old men of his subclan, and the accused person, if he belonged to the same subclan, was called by them, or he came on his own account, to defend his case. The old men then listened to the case as presented by the two disputants and any witness. The decision could be announced by any of the elders present as, with the facts ascertained, there was only one possible judgment which was common knowledge to all.[20]

---

[20] Ibid., pp. 220-221.

## Conclusion

The nature and characteristics of African political systems as outlined above reveal to us something of what Africans value and of their life and thought patterns. They also reveal to us what are to them familiar patterns for the control of individual and group life. For these reasons the structure of African political systems provides us some guidance as to what might be a church polity relevant to African cultures. Elements that are universally true must be universally recognized in African church polity; factors that are of local incidence are relevant for that particular area. In skeleton fashion we will list below some of the directions in which the above study seems to lead us.

1. Since African life is a unified whole, we must make Christianity relevant to the whole of life. Just as political systems provide leadership for the whole of life, so should the total church organization provide leadership in integrating Christianity to the whole of life. This wholeness of indigenous life also points up the need to bring the gospel to bear on the group as a whole, and to avoid detaching individual converts from their tribal and family group.

2. Since non-Christian Africans orient their lives from a religious standpoint, it will seem natural to believers that one's relationship to God must be central in life and that the rest of life must conform to the demands of that relationship, unless we spoil them by our Western secularized type of Christianity. Religious sanctions can often be used as a factor of church discipline rather than external force as such.

3. Because African political systems place basic authority in either the local

unit of society, or the regional unit, or the territorial unit, the form of church polity followed in a given place should follow the political pattern of the given tribe. Where the indigenous government is basically local, a congregational form of church life will be more familiar and appreciated; where the nationals are used to regional government, they will prefer a presbyterian type of polity; where they have a king, some episcopal form will probably serve best.

4. Just as African political systems tend to keep authority in local hands and allow for a large degree of democracy, so also in church life the churches should be given as much local autonomy as possible.

5. In the same way that African cultures have some institutional patterns by which to work together as an entire tribal group, varying according to the type of political structure, so should the Christian church in Africa have channels for mutual consultation and cooperation. While this suggestion as given relates first of all to churches of a common origin and polity, it should also apply to relations betwen the families of churches.

6. African political systems provide checks and balances between the various interests within the group by giving each group some representation in the governmental functions and by maintaining a balance between position and responsibility; both these means may be used by the church as factors to hinder the development of authoritarian control, but they will be effective only to the degree that the spiritual life of the church is maintained.

7. As African political systems tend to be conservative, the church will want to stand for what is stable and trustworthy; just as the governmental scheme allows for growth and development, so likewise the church must be alert to the changing demands of a growing society.

8. Just as African systems of government frequently provide that those of demonstrated ability become leaders, so should the church find ways to discover and utilize such. Spiritual qualifications must be paramount, coupled with the type of personality insisted upon by Bantus, i.e., "men who talk gently and wisely and who can make the people listen and return to reason when they want to quarrel or fight."[21]

9. Just as Africans keep their cultural institutions on a level that the indigenous economic system can support, so must the church be geared to the economic level of the people. However, the church has in her hands the tools to improve the economic situation. She must teach principles of stewardship, industry, and thrift, and the older churches must share their know-how techniques.

10. The responsibilities of the African headman are very like the responsibilities of a Christian pastor, which suggests that the pastoral office will be familiar to and appreciated by African Christians. It will seem natural to them to look to him to be their leader in spiritual matters and in all phases of life, as their disciplinarian and protector, and as the one who ministers to the newborn, the sick, and the dying. In other areas some of these responsibilities are carried by a council of elders. Just as some African societies use both of these institutions, the Christian church will likely find both of them useful in most situations.

---

[21] Ibid., p. 232.

This study is obviously incomplete, for there are other factors which should be included, particularly something of the communal nature of African life and its religious backgrounds. Some of the inductions are likely naive and immature, but if they stimulate thought and investigation they will have been of value. In brief, from a survey of the literature regarding African societies and political systems, we have attempted to discover their basic factors and characteristics, and have attempted to evaluate their significance for African church polity.

---

*William D. Reyburn*

# The Church, Male and Female

AN OBSERVER may readily gather the impression the world over that the Christian church is more attended by women and more earnestly followed by females in general than by males. In Latin American society the role of the female cannot be understood apart from her identification with her parish group and her symbol identification with the Virgin. Every society presents its male and female roles in different contexts, and consequently their relatedness to a single institution such as the Christian church is thereby radically affected. Missionaries are often content to dismiss the disproportionate female-male church membership with such statements as "the men are too worldly minded." However, a closer look at such female predominances reflects other cultural and societal factors which produce these effects much more than the males' worldly outlook.

The case presented here is a brief discussion of some of the factors contributing to female preponderance in the Christian churches of the south Cameroun. First we shall state what may be said to be rather generally claimed as self-evident. Then we shall proceed with a set of factors which are specifically part of these cultures and need not be true of others.

The outlook of females in most of the world probably exhibits more dependency than that of males. Her very biological make-up prepares her for being subjected to stronger fellow beings and grants her a place of less secure standing. Her more limited outside experience, foreign contacts, education perhaps tend to produce a certain naiveté which makes it easy for her to believe what she is told. Her

Reprinted from Vol. 4, No. 4 (1957), pp. 140-145.

credulous personality is tightly tied into the activities in a limited area where she must identify herself. She may be under greater pressure to belong to someone or something. Many other propositions could be listed which might be said to contribute to the female attachment to Christianity or any institution which appeals to some of these female qualities. These generalized conditions in themselves are *post facto* explanations, however, and do not tell us why a certain innovation such as Christianity was rejected in a given case. They do not help as they stand to explain why in the Cameroun it is not all ages of females that identify themselves with and seek membership in the Christian mission churches. Neither are they sufficient evidence to assist us in understanding the dynamic fashion in which a group of females begin to experiment with their traditional forms of life after the coming of the church. In order to probe into these latter problems we need a more specific look into the particular circumstances of several of the societies involved in this case.

## The Woman in Cameroun Society

The most important base line for understanding the predominantly female reception of the Christian church lies in the social organization of the tribes considered here (Bulu, Yaoundé, Bafia, Meka, Gbaya, Kaka). A village consists of a number of males who represent several distinct families and who claim to have issued from a common legendary ancestor. These males all belong to the village they inhabit and they are members of their father's family, their paternal grandfather's family, and so on ascending the male line. They will select their mates from outside their paternal village group and in certain patterns of avoidance such as taking no mate from their mother's clan. Their future lives will be lived at least eventually in their father's village. They will in turn expect their sons to do likewise. They will be preeminently concerned for the continuation of their family male line, which is a continuum with the real and the mythological. The respect due each ascending male is reinforced by a complex of behavior, and every male's position is well ascribed by age, relatedness, and wealth. The males have a sense of *belonging* to the village of their fathers in which they were born.

On the other hand, the world of the female is greatly contrasted. The female is born with the sure knowledge of *not belonging* to her village permanently. She will be married into another village where she will raise children, all of whom will belong to her husband's family. In the case of her husband's death she will not be free to take her children and go to another marriage. She will be remarried by her husband's relatives if possible, and if not she will be exchanged for cash and kind to another village, leaving her offspring behind, to begin all over again another family which she may in turn lose through another husband's death. The discontinuity of her life is great and she is constantly faced with the fact of not belonging. She is greatly loved by her children and often by her husband, but she is forever a stranger in a foreign village.

The stability of her marriage is fixed by the dowry, which assures that she remain with her husband, for if she returns to her parents' village, her husband has the right to demand reimbursement of the dowry. However, the dowry received has usually been spent to bring into her village a wife for her younger brother, thus keeping a balance in gains and losses.

A village, then, seen from the male-female division on the level of its social organization, presents a solid front of males very much at home; a group of young females not knowing where home will be eventually, although very much related to their temporary paternal village; and finally an agglomeration of foreign females, often from numerous diverse areas, who must get acquainted, work, and live together in their newly adopted village. In a sense, the adult females are a group of immigrants finding a relative here and there in their new surroundings, but even with occasional or frequent meetings with such relatives there is no sense of permanency or of belonging.

We might be justified to conclude at this point and say that "therefore the Christian mission will find ready response from the dislocated females." While this is partly true, it is by no means an adequate accounting of the facts. How do we account for the fact that the church member females are not young brides but women who have inhabited their husbands' village for some years, or who are middle-aged, elderly, or even senile females?

## The Role of the Young Bride

The answer to this question involves various considerations. The young bride's first function in the village is sexual fertility. Her worth cannot be counted until she has had children. She is not psychologically free to form "free associations" until she has provided the village with a contribution of children. She is likewise in a period of severe strain and adjustment, seeking to be accepted through traditional modes of behavior such as childbearing, planting, harvesting, fishing, cooking, and taking care of her husband's wants. The church association is more properly the property of those who have either gained sufficient status in the village to be granted the freedom of outside life or who have proved over the years that they are of little productive value anyway. Where African village life has undergone city or town transformation, or where girls have been able to pursue education, new factors have arisen which enable the younger females to make the church identification or to reject it. In some areas, such as among the Gbaya and Kaka of the eastern Cameroun, young female are conspicuously absent from church, since they perform a vital function in dance medicine which is held to be contrary to Christian practices. Consequently, a mother and older sisters may be members of the church, whereas a dancing girl's function is respected and she does not consider church membership until she is older and has ceased to be a medicine dancer. She will view both Christian church and medicine making as vital aspects of village life but will separate them only in the role she plays in each. It is to her more like a boy on the basketball team who cannot be on the wrestling team at the same time.

## The Function of Church Society

The Christian church (another formalized institution would serve the same purpose) serves as the nucleus for the formation of a grouping for the females in a village. The one thing which they all have in common is the fact that they are foreigners. The church in a sociological sense brings the females into a common bond which they feel as necessary for the satisfactory ongoing of village life. Actually the formation of the female church group serves to smooth out many of the differences and fights which take place among the village women. However, it is not primarily Christian theology that penetrates and enables them to solve their differences. This factor does display itself in certain rather unexpected ways. The real pacifying function of the woman's church affiliation is found in its own social structuring of the group. The women, like the men, arrange themselves in a hierarchy where each knows pretty well where she stands, and disputes are settled quickly by a recognition of status in the "women's company," the church organization. This is merely one indication of the African's flare for political organization and is to him (and her) an essential means for facing the world.

In the development of this process there appear to be certain characteristic steps which tend to be rather generalized in the areas concerned. First, there is more male curiosity than female. Soon the males learn that Christianity appears to favor females, since the wives of a polygamist may be admitted to membership whereas the husband may not. Soon the complexities of Christian theology and the Trinity impress the males as something for school boys to bother their heads about. (Following a brief explanation of the Trinity — the term for God in Kaka is *Ndjambie,* which also means 'spider' — an elderly village savant turned away and remarked, "Everybody knows that Ndjambie is a spider. How could he have had a son?") Next, a school is started and the whole proposition of Christianity is relegated to the school children. The women have in the meantime found something other than Christian doctrine which appears to serve for them a genuinely felt need. This status of the women's church company and the school teaching Christian doctrine continues for a full generation. Added the impact of Westernization, a breakdown in traditional values due far more to the inroads of government and industry than to missionaries, one arrives at a period when the males begin to enter the church as members. It is not until this time or some years following this that one sees the beginning effect of Christian doctrine.

### Needs Satisfied In Church Membership

During the pre-male period in the eastern Cameroun (today) the female member finds other satisfactions in her new group — the possession of a name card by catechumens, the recognition granted by a white missionary, the opportunity to display husband's status and wealth with a brightly colored print dress on Sunday, or the privilege of belonging to the select group who dress in white following the passing of the pastor's examination and baptism. For many females the church organization is a protection mechanism. Women, especially older females, seek the church, the catechist, and the white missionary as a protection from sex-seeking males. Most males view the church as antisexual and hence fear to make advances toward women who are protected by the church. In the less acculturated areas the idea prevails that a baptized woman could cause serious illness to a man who committed adultery with her. Hence, in order to protect their wives from adultery, some men are known to openly encourage their wives to seek baptism. In the more modern areas this idea breaks down entirely and adultery palavers are the main occupation of church sessions.

*Joseph E. and Barbara Grimes*

# Individualism and the Huichol Church

THE Huichol Indians who inhabit the southern Sierra Madre Occidental in the states of Nayarit and Jalisco, Mexico, are markedly individualistic. This means that the Huichol manifest a type of behavior which has wide cultural limits of acceptable variation, and consequent to the wide range of variation a low predictability of specific actions. Some of the more obvious elements of the individualistic complex as they occur in Huichol culture have their effect on practices of the Christian community. These features will be taken up one by one; their cultural manifestation will be discussed first; then their effect on the Huichol church.

Individualism should not be interpreted as implying full freedom from cultural restraint. As in all cultures, there are important limits to Huichol individualism. The kinship group, for example, is one of the factors which limit individual action. In theory the kinship group consists of all people who have any common ancestor up to the fifth ascending generation. In practice, however, only people who know of some common ancestor consider themselves of the same kinship group. Customarily, only people belonging to the same kinship group marry each other or settle on the same ranch.

Age is a second limiting factor. Most civil and religious leaders are over forty years of age. Younger men show reticence to tell stories or sing in the presence of their elders, though if they are performing and an older person joins the group they do not stop performing on his account. Older relatives frequently command the services of younger relatives.

Correlate to both kinship group and age limiting factors is the structure of the immediate family. Children live with their parents until they marry. A man then lives with his father-in-law's family after marriage unless he is an eldest son, in which case he eventually moves back to his father's. A son prefers not to move very far away from his father as long as his father is alive. These three factors in the culture tend to limit individual action.

## Freedom of Movement

In residence pattern the Huichols consider themselves free to move wherever they like within a wide area, subject, of course, to the restrictions already mentioned. Partly because of the poor soil and the necessity for changing maize fields each year, and partly by inclination, some families move as often as once every two or three years. In 1941 there were eleven Huichol families living at the ranch, La Piedra Gorda. In 1954 there

**Reprinted from Vol. 1, No. 8 (1954), pp. 127-134.** **Joseph and Barbara Grimes are missionary linguistics and Bible translators with the Wycliffe Bible Translators among the Huichol Indians of Mexico. Dr. Grimes has the Ph.D. degree from Cornell University.**

was only one family on the ranch, and all of the families living there in 1941 had moved elsewhere. Most moved to another ranch after two or three intermediate steps made independently. The father of one of the Christians moved three times during 1953. On one ranch the Huichol families each year moved farther up the mountain on which the ranch is situated. They considered themselves as living on the same ranch as formerly though one family of Huichols which remained at the foot of the mountain lived closer to the ranch where the authors lived than it did to some of the families on its own ranch.

Until 1954 the Huichol Christians showed no tendency to group themselves apart into a Christian community, but retained this pattern of freedom of movement. However, two of the Christians made plans to build their houses together on the same ranch in 1954, although they were not related to each other in such a way that they normally would have done so. Due to subsequent developments they were not able to carry out their plan. In this case it seemed that their relationship in Christ took precedence over their relationship — or rather lack of it — in the kinship group.

Visiting between persons or families is frequent and, especially near harvest time, is sporadically accompanied by gifts of food brought by the person visiting, though there is no rigid custom regarding exchange of gifts. Visits normally last less than a day. However, a person who feels inclined to prolong his visit may stay for several days. One family came to visit the authors for medical treatment and stayed for approximately two months. They built themselves a shelter and helped with the work of other families on the ranch. Other visitors stayed for two and three days. None gave indication of how long he planned to stay or when he planned to leave until he was ready to go.

Through this pattern of visiting the gospel has been carried to other areas within the tribe. Whenever the oldest believer has time or feels inclined, he goes on a visit to a town two days by trail from his ranch. There he stays with his relatives, plays records in Huichol made by Gospel Recordings, Inc., reads portions of the Scriptures, and discusses the gospel at length with his relatives and other visitors. He also witnesses to visitors who come to his ranch. There is no way of predicting who will come to visit, or when they will arrive or leave, but the irregular visiting pattern has been the main channel of evangelization within the culture.

### Story-Telling Patterns

Story telling is fairly well developed in Huichol culture. Individualism in story telling takes the form of unpredictability of repetition. Stories are never told the same way twice. There is an over-all pattern of folk-tale structure which involves the use of paragraph introducing morphemes and the narrative mode. Actions are frequently repeated by five characters in sequence, instead of three as in European tales. However, innovations are made on the spur of the moment, with the result that the exact words used are never predictable. At times even the identity of principal characters is changed between tellings of the story, as when different species of grasshoppers are substituted for each other or the wolf in one telling becomes a coyote in the next.

When the Gospel of Mark and the Epistles of John were translated into

Huichol and made available to the Christians, it was at first expected that the Christians should memorize portions of Scripture as part of their instruction. However, due to the influence of individualism in the story-telling pattern, such attempts failed; a verse was never repeated the same way twice. Synonyms were introduced in the repetition for words in the original; equivalent grammatical constructions of various kinds were substituted (for example, substitution of the narrative mode for the affirmative and vice versa); the order of words was changed. These changes were not of the same order as corrections of the accuracy or style of the translation, though such corrections, happily, came to light in the process as well. They were the same type of changes as occurred between different tellings of the same story and seemed to be made purely for variety.

After several attempts to introduce Scripture memorization it was found that those who regularly read the Scriptures, especially the Epistles of John, were perfectly familiar with the content of these portions. In the songs they composed the Scripture text appeared, though of course not in the same form in which the translation had been cast. The oldest believer, who was trying to improve his facility in writing, made up writing exercises for himself without reference to the Scripture text. However, they contained such a high proportion of quotations and allusions that it was evident that he had, in effect, rethought and reuttered the Scripture message in detail. So, no further effort was made to promote the verbatim recitation of Scripture passages, and emphasis was put on the verse-by-verse understanding and exposition of passages, usually a paragraph or more at a time.

### Singing

Songs for amusement or dancing are sung to the accompaniment of violin or guitar or both. Some people are recognized as more proficient than others in composing songs, which they make up on occasion to commemorate or lampoon something or often merely to provide amusement.

Songs are not sung the same way twice. However, as distinct from stories, the words remain relatively unchanged from singing to singing, through one singer's version of a song frequently differs from that of another singer. The characteristic treatment of songs is the rearrangement of lines in a verse. A quatrain may be sung one time *abab, aab, abcd, cdaa, dcdd*, with instrumental interludes between stanzas as marked by commas. The next time the same song may be sung *abcd, abcc, aacc, a, ddccdd, cd, ad*, etc. Songs of more complex structure or more lines are varied in analogous ways. Only one person sings at a time. He may or may not play an instrument or dance as he sings; or he may do both.

The three older Christians have all composed songs about the gospel. The first believer, 54 years old, has composed several. His wife composed one which was sung only a few times. His son composed two, one of which is sung frequently. The other was sung only a few times. These songs are of the same form as those used for amusement and are accompanied on instruments but are expressions of Christian truth or portions of Scripture set to music. Their Huichol character is attested by the observation that most unbelievers in the area also know the songs, and that one song was even learned and used for side amusement in a Huichol ceremony in another area.

When the first believer heard his son's song, he made extensive additions and modifications of the words. Probably because of the factors of age and family relationship, the son now sings more or less his father's version of his own song.

The only Western song which was introduced into the Christian hymnody is "Jesus Loves Me." Not much attention was paid to the song, and not much emphasis was put on it. However, the oldest believer's four-year-old granddaugther picked it up, changed the rhythm and the tune to Huichol patterns, and sang it while playing. It is not sung at gatherings of Christians.

An attempt was made to encourage congregational singing as practiced in most Christian communities. It was expected that congregational singing would help unify the Christians and encourage others to join them as it has elsewhere. However, after a few tries, the uniform response of the Christians was unenthusiastic, and they continued with their pattern of having one person sing to the accompaniment of instruments. One difficulty with congregational singing was that with no set form for the order of lines in a stanza and much repetition no one knew how anyone else was going to sing the same song. As a result the basic Huichol pattern of one singer at a time has been retained in all gatherings of Christians. Sometimes one person continues on with the singing of a song when a previous singer stops.

In summary, the Christian Huichol community has retained regular Huichol patterns in regard to visiting, learning the Scriptures, and singing. The restrictions of the kinship group on the dwelling pattern have shown signs of reshaping to include the Christian community. The restrictions of age and immediate family relationship have given a place of prominence and respect to the older members of the Christian community, but have been modified in that younger members have shown no hesitation to pray in public in the presence of their elders, or to help in the instrumental accompaniment of songs.

## Huichol Culture Change

The rate of acculturation of the Huichol tribe has in general been extremely slow. Certain features of the culture have tended to limit the incursion of features from other cultures. One such factor is the kinship organization and the concomitant endogamy within the kinship group. Marriages outside the kinship group are rare enough; marriages with non-Huichols are extremely rare though Huichols occasionally marry members of the neighboring Cora tribe.

Another feature is the integration of religious, social, and civic organization to provide maximum participation and coverage of all areas of life, with a resultant high stability. Roman Catholicism, to the degree in which it has been accepted, has been regarded as an accretion added to the basic Huichol framework — in effect, a few more deities to be added to the list — so that a certain amount of Catholic forms are observable in the culture. Catholic influence is, however, superficial, and the Huichols apparently do not feel that it is inimical to cultural integrity.

Evangelical Christianity, on the other hand, has among its implications for the Huichols the destruction of the integrity of their religion. Pressure has been brought to bear on the Christians from time to time for this reason. However, paradoxical as it may seem, the older Christians are respected members of the culture. Their advice is sought on personal and civic matters. Some pressure on the younger ones continues.

It is not easy to understand why the strong acculturative influence of evangelical Christianity, with its destructive implications for a significant portion of the activity carried on within the culture, should be at all tolerated by a people noted for their successful resistance of Western influence over a long period of time. One reason so little resistance has been met may lie in the type of tolerance demanded by a complex of permitted individualistic behavior in diverse areas of cultural activity. After a period of initial disapproval, members of the culture have observed that the Christians continue to participate fully in the social and civic activity of the group. Coupled with this is the recognition, heard from many sources, that the Huichol religion does not completely fulfill its aims of providing health for people and livestock and insuring good crop yields. The Christian are not yet fully instructed in the Scriptures, but their experience points toward an eventual integration and completeness of their Christian lives, which in the thinking of the non-Christians may be regarded as a satisfactory and permissible substitute for the abandoned religion. Because of the retention of social and civic ties, the life of the Christian community remains firmly rooted within the Huichol culture. The gospel has been propagated within the culture rather than from outside the culture in that the missionaries have concentrated their work on a few who have told the gospel message to many more. Therefore, it is possible that Christianity may be accepted as a valid substitute within the culture for the Huichol religion, rather than as a destructive influence from outside the culture.

*William A. Smalley*

# The Gospel and the Cultures of Laos

IN northern Laos, which lies on the southern border of China between North Vietnam and Burma, three different ethnic groups have been particularly subject to missionary effort. There are other ethnic groups in the country as well, local tribes and migrant minority populations like the Chinese, Indians, and Pakistanese, but their contact with the gospel in North Laos has been more sporadic, and missionary work with them less systematic. The three groups which have had intensive evangelization present a very important problem in missionary anthropology, for in spite of the fact that in many cases the same individual missionaries work among the three groups, that some of the same mission stations serve them all, and that the same mission policies apply, the differences in the response of the three groups to the Christian message are striking. And what is more, some of the usual assumptions about missionary work do not apply, at least on the surface. The only one of the three groups which has the Scriptures in its language is the least responsive. The one with the shortest contact with missionaries is the most responsive. The best results have been achieved in the cases where the misionaries did not know the language, where they used interpreters, or where preaching was in a language foreign to the listeners.

As Christians we feel that God does inject himself into history and perform what we call "miracles." As anthropologists we are also aware that there are cultural reasons (complex though they may be) for differences between peoples. We want to study those cultural problems whether we consider them to be instruments of God's dealing with men or whether we consider them independent of or contrary to God's purpose for man. Although the problem of these three groups plagued me throughout my term as a missionary in Laos, I could not give detailed, systematic attention to it. There are some observations of a more general nature which can be made about them, and perhaps that will help to point up something of the magnitude of the problem of presenting the gospel to peoples of all cultures in such a way that it is relevant to the problems of each.

## Culture A: The Lao

The *Lao* are the politically predominant people of Laos. They are of a general Thai pattern, and differ little in speech or culture from those Thai (Siamese) who live across the Mekong River or any other part of their mutual political border. The Lao live principally in the river valleys and cultivate both irrigated rice (in the general manner familiar for East Asia) and non-irrigated mountain rice by a slash-and-burn technique. Lao communities are loosely structured politically and socially, but there is a deep-lying consist-

---

**Reprinted from Vol. 3, No. 3 (1956), pp. 47-57.**

ency to their patterns. Centuries of influence from other cultures have resulted in a thoroughly syncretic pattern with historical roots in India and China as well as in Southeast Asia. But whatever the roots, it is thoroughly Lao now.

The Lao are devout Buddhists, but they are great fish and meat eaters, and they see no inconsistency there. Rituals stemming from the local animism are intermingled with rituals from India with no embarrassment. The resulting religious culture is a most fundamental part of Lao life, and most men spent a part of their boyhood in a monastery or pagoda where they were students or apprentice priests.

More modern influences from the West are not so fully assimilated. Western artifacts (flashlights, lamps, watches, cigarette lighters, some clothing, etc.) which fill a Lao need are assimilated and are to be found everywhere. (The Lao need for watches is often a desire for jewelry, not for telling time.) Western forms of government, business, education have been adopted by only a small segment of the population, the elite in the cities. Chinese people and Indians do most of the business; until the present independence, Vietnamese office workers were often imported by the French because the Lao were so uninterested in government employment; education is traditionally in the hands of the Buddhist monks, but government schools are increasingly more important.

Christianity has made no impact whatsoever on the Lao, and this goes for Catholicism as well as Protestant Christianity. The handful of Lao converts consists almost entirely of marginal people — someone whose mother was Vietnamese, or someone who has been rejected by the Laos as being possessed by a *Phi Poop*, a spirit which is declared to enter some individuals and control them. (Some of these cases of *Phi Poop* are obviously pathological. In other cases the accused is the victim of witch-hunting. But in any event he is usually driven out of his community and is cut off from normal social intercourse.)

The Lao temperament shows very little anxiety, very little stress. Westerners consider the Lao improvident. When Point-Four aid was trying to set up a pilot program on the use of fertilizer, Lao farmers were much impressed with the yield of adequately fertilized crops. Orders for fertilizer were below expectations, however. The Lao had estimated how much acreage it would take to produce the same amount of fertilized rice as they had previously produced without more than haphazard fertilization, and were reducing their area under cultivation to produce the same crop rather than increase their yield. From the standpoint of their lack of anxiety, they are the closest to the old stereotype of the idyllic simple life of the "primitive" of any group I have seen. The Lao are, of course, by no means "primitive." Their culture level is more that of a folk culture.

### Culture B: The Khmu

In contrast to the Lao, the Khmu are a minority group of mountain-dwelling people with no political importance. Their culture is more that of a tribal "primitive" culture although they have learned a great deal from the Lao. They are not Buddhists. They are poorer than the Lao, and have traditionally been considered slaves of the latter. They put up little resistance, although the Lao take every possible advantage of them.

Whereas the Lao show a high degree of internal integration in their culture, the Khmu show signs of deterioration and disintegration. The gongs and jars of tremendous value which are characteristic of tribal peoples in southeast Asia and which are remembered as a part of Khmu culture of the past, are virtually gone. In all af southeast Asia these gongs and jars are a focal point of interest in the culture. They are symbols of prestige and wealth. The fact they have disappeared among the Khmu, and that apparently nothing has replaced them, is certainly of significance.

I cannot state for certain the causes of the deterioration of Khmu culture. I suspect that generations of pressure and domination by the Lao is a factor. Some of the results, however, are very obvious. There is less zest for life among the Khmu than among other peoples of similar culture in the area. Their general attitudes is one of resignation, of apathy. They have a collective feeling of inferiority to the Lao and to the West. These remarks are possibly more true of the Khmu in the western than in the eastern part of the country.

The first Khmu converts to Christianity were made a generation ago by the same missionaries who were itinerating among the Lao. Through the years, particularly since the last war, the number of Khmu converts has grown appreciably. They were reached through the Loatian language and through their own student preachers who preached in Khmu but studied in Lao. Latest figures are not available to me, but an estimate of two thousand Khmu Christians is probably a safe one.

The tradition of the mission in the area has been strongly paternalistic, and the Christian Khmu have accepted that paternalism with real gratitude. They look on both God and the missionary as powerful protection aginst an unfair and capricious world of the Lao, sickness, and even the elements. Some of the missionaries have been disturbed over the fact that Khmu Christians were so dependent on the mission, and have made changes to enforce more independence and self-reliance on the church in the more superficial respects of finance and internal government. These changes have been a real source of anxiety to the Khmu. The big problem remains: how to present the gospel to the Khmu in a way that will be relevant to their need for security in their dying culture, and yet build for a "responsible Christianity"[1] among them.

## Culture C: The Meo

The third ethnic group to be mentioned here is a relative newcomer to Laos. The Meo (called Miao in China and Thailand) are moving by the thousands out of south China into northern Vietnam and Laos, and on into Thailand. In contrast to the easy-going Lao, and the apathetic Khmu, the Meo are vigorous, aggressive, and purposeful. New things which they meet through culture contact they meet with amusement, wonder, and delight. I have repeatedly observed both Meo and Khmu people as they come in contact with a sample of the West — a missionary home, the missionary plane, a missionary and his air mattress, clothes, etc., or missionary children. The Khmu stand at respect-

---

[1] On "responsible Christianity" see William D. Reyburn, *The Toba Indians of the Argentine Chaco* (Mennonite Board of Missions and Charities, 1711 Prairie St., Elkhart, Indiana; 1954), p. 58.

ful distance and look. The Meo exclaim and laugh, poke and ask questions and make comments, their faces beaming with delight.

The Meo women do excellent needlework, which is lavished on their costume. The folklore is rich, though material culture in most other things than clothing is poorer than that of the Lao and just as poor as that of the Khmu. Many Meo have wealth through opium growing, and many would rather buy their rice than grow it. As a rule several people in a village are addicted to opium smoking.

There are signs that Meo culture is undergoing transition, and in a state of stress. For one thing, they have changed within just a few years from being an exclusive group, one which avoided contact with other peoples, one which stayed on its mountain peaks and never came into the valleys where the Lao are, to a people which, though it does not like the valleys, moves freely through them, trades freely in Lao towns, and has even taken an important commercial place in the town of Xieng Khouang.

The biggest sign of change in the Meo, however, is in relation to its response to Christianity. For years the Christian witness made no impression on the Meo. Then, suddenly, in the space of a month in 1949 about a thousand converts were made. Today there are several thousand Meo Christians. Furthermore, occasionally "prophets" declare themselves to be Jesus. So far none of these splinter movements has become widespread, but they are symptomatic of the fact that the Meo are undergoing a period of cultural reformulation which was triggered and given its particular form by the Christian gospel.

The Meo revival is discussed by Barney elsewhere in this book. In reference to the subject of this paper, however, there are some observations which should be made. The relation between the mission and Meo Christians has never been as paternalistic as in the Khmu case. This is partly because of the good sense of some missionaries who disliked the paternalistic role, but it is also due to the fact that the Meo do not feel so strongly the need for such complete supervision. When given half a chance, they take the initiative.

Once they are Christians, the Meo are vigorous, aggressive witnesses. The missionaries (their communication problem compounded by the distances and the ruggedness of the mountain trails) can never quite keep up with the new converts. It is not unusual for a whole village of 50 to 100 people, or the major portion of a village, to "enter Jesus" at the same time and send a messenger to the missionary to ask, "What do we do next?"

## "Revitalization" of Culture

Wallace[2] has spoken of five stages which comprise the cycle of a "revitalization process" in culture — that is, the stages in a culture transformation which is not of the slow, "normal" chain-reaction type in which new element A is introduced and is gradually assimilated, causing changes in C and D, which in turn affect E and F and G, but rather a culture transformation which affects a whole system or an important part of a cultural system rather suddenly and rather completely. Some of the different types of such "revitalization processes" are "nativistic movements,"

---

[2] Anthony F. C. Wallace, "Revitalization Movements," *American Anthropologist* 58.264-275.

"reform movements," "cargo cult," "religious revival," "messianic movement," "utopian community," "sect formation," "mass movement," "social movement," "revolution," etc.[3]

Wallace's five stages are: (1) Steady State, (2) Period of Individual Stress, (3) Period of Cultural Distortion, (4) Period of Revitalization, and (5) New Steady State. The Lao are clearly in a steady state. Needs are satisfied by present patterns on the whole. Stresses are not severe. Innovations have not produced bad dislocations. Potentially a danger point will be the growth of a city such as Vientiane. The stresses between an essentially rural culture and an urban development may cause trouble but they are at present met without serious difficulty.

The Khmu, it seems to me, represent a period of cultural distortion, in terms of Wallace's formulation. The distortion is of long standing, I believe, and it is manifested now in what he characterizes as "disillusionment with the mazeway [traditional patterns of reaction as perceived by the individual member of the society] and apathy towards problems of adaptation." This is a different way from which other peoples will react to distortion. In some groups it may mean violence, in others a disregard for traditional mores, in others irresponsibility. To the Khmu it means an uneasy resignation. There is no sign of the beginning of a period of revitalization among the Khmu. Some individual Khmu have been assimilated to Lao life. Khmu villages nearest the Lao centers have adapted somewhat to Lao patterns. Christians have sought escape through dependency on a mission and on God.

[3] Ibid., p. 264.

Whether present developments among the Meo represent completely a period of cultural distortion, or whether there may be in the Christian movement something of a revitalization tendency, would be an evaluation which someone who knows the situation better than I would have to make. It seems to me that there are signs of both. The sudden and widespread acceptance of Christianity certainly has produced disparities with former habits, and presents inconsistencies. As Barney's article on the Meo points out, however, in a large percentage of cases, these conflicts have been settled on the basis of what the individual Christians felt the Christian reaction should be. This was, in many cases, influenced by the direct and indirect teaching of missionaries and their students.

Wallace maintains that a period of revitalization almost always begins with a particular prophet or leader from whom the major ideas of the new reformulation stem. There is no such figure in the Meo Christian community. As offshoots of it some have started up (often calling themselves Jesus, as was remarked above), but they have been abortive. I am not convinced that revitalization of such a community could not occur in a Christian context without such a local prophet.[4]

The Meo movement could easily develop nativistic tendencies as happened with the Karen of Burma, so many of whom are Christians. Meo Christians do feel a sense of solidarity. They want their language in written form but the Lao government has been opposed to such a development. The Meo have revolted before. They have an increasing self-consciousness.

[4] Reyburn, op. cit., p. 46.

That, sketchily and imperfectly, is the picture of three cultures among whom one mission is working, usually through one language (Lao) and interpreters. The Scriptures and some (very little) Christian literature exist in Lao. The translation of the Bible is poor, and is in the process of revision.

## The Church and the Cultures of Laos

Because of these vastly different pictures, the problems which remain for church and mission working together are vastly different in the three cases. In the Lao case the problem is still one of basic communication. Apparently the gospel has never been made to seem relevant to the Lao. I feel deeply that a careful study should be made of the communication of the gospel in relation to the Lao culture in the way that the Reyburns have been pioneering in South America and Africa.[5] How can the Good News be made to seem good — to be something that people will really *want* — in this culture which does not, on the whole, see other needs than those met by its normal experience? Here the problem is not primarily one of language mastery. The missionaries are no worse than the average, and some are much better than the average, for missionary language learning. The communication problems here are cultural ones. They are doubtless the same problems as the ones which face Christianity in Thailand, where the people are much the same, and where results in terms of response to the gospel have been meager.

For the Khmu a part of the problem is to encourage them to find the security they need in God without an unhealthy dependency on the mission. A few individual Khmu (but not the Christian Khmu community as a whole) have found a new purpose in life in their Christian faith. We would like to see a revitalization of Khmu culture, centered in a faith in Christ as Lord. There is danger that the mission might fight any such revitalization, because inevitably it would not take the form which missionaries unthinkingly would feel it should take. A vital Khmu Christianity, rooted in Khmu culture, cannot be anything but strikingly different from imported American Christianity in its form, although its dedication to its Lord may be just as significant, if not more so, than ours.

The great problem of missionary anthropology among the Khmu, then, is to so understand the Khmu that the mission can adapt to, cooperate with, and stimulate Khmu forms of growth. Of course the Khmu need the Scriptures in their own language. Of course they need missionary teaching in their tongue. But the Khmu language is not enough. Christianity, if it is to become truly significant among the Khmu must find a significant place in Khmu life. Perhaps the terms "self-support" and "self-government" should not be used with the Khmu, for they promote stress and anxiety, but some Khmu way must be found to divert the Khmu dependency on the mission.

For the Meo a major part of the problem is to guide tactfully, and to provide the bases for greater growth in non-autocratic teaching, the development of literacy and literature, the encouragement of Meo forms of worship, and of a Meo Christian culture. One tremendous

---

[5] Ibid. See also the articles by Dr. and Mrs. Reyburn in this issue and othe s of PRACTICAL ANTHROPOLOGY.

problem is the training of Meo leadership in a way that will be compatible with Meo leadership patterns, but still be strongly oriented Biblically and in the broader Christian tradition.

As God injects himself into human history — in the Incarnation, in the revelation of the Bible, in the redemption of any individual — he uses human culture as his means of revelation, and human beings respond to him in their own cultural manner. As cultures differ, responses differ, and a man is no more at home in a culture form which does not meet his needs than he is in a language which is foreign to him. Christian anthropology can do much to help the missionary watch the Khmu or the Meo, or even the Lao, respond to redemption in his own way, to worship God in his own way, to participate in the church in his own way, and watch them with sympathy, understanding, and encouragement.

This article is not an example of such an "understanding." It is merely a statement of some of the more obvious problems in one particular situation. Understanding of this kind is not arrived at without careful, perceptive, and sympathetic study of each of the cultural situations involved — the particular missionary culture, and the particular cultures in which the church is being planted.

*G. Linwood Barney*

# The Meo — an Incipient Church

Of the 45,000 Meo in the area around Xieng Khouang Province, in Laos (Indochina), about 4,500 have become professing Christians since May 1950. During this same period, about 1,500 Khmu, a neighboring group of different culture, have also accepted Christianity. They had heard of it, but never in a comprehensive manner. How has Christianity spread as an innovation in Meo culture?

The Meo people of Xieng Khouang represent part of the great numbers who have drifted southward from China, where they are known as Miao, into Northern Indochina and Thailand. Roux, who has followed their development for four decades, feels that the trail of their "slash and burn" clearings and other changes that they have wrought in the land would indicate that they first entered Laos and Vietnam about 120 to 140 years ago.[1] According to my informants, their ancestors first entered Xieng Khouang Province about a century ago. They located, as is their custom, in the highlands and on mountain ridges, where the elevation runs from 4,000 to 8,000 feet. The Meo still reflect their influence from China by many loan words from Chinese.

A Protestant mission had been in operation in North Laos for about fifteen years when the first missionaries entered Xieng Khouang in 1940. The ministry of these new missionaries was abruptly interrupted by World War II. At this initial entry, little or no contact was made with the general Meo population, which was seldom to be seen in town (a Lao community). It was not until late 1949 that a young missionary couple again took up residence in Xieng Khouang and began a study of the Lao language, the language of the culturally dominant group and of the government of Laos. Catholic missionaries also had some contact with the Meo, with little if any response.

Xieng Khouang town, with a population of about 1,500, is the administrative center for the province and serves as the home of Tubi, the highest Meo official in all Laos. Tubi is appointed by the federal government to be representative for the Meo population of Laos to the Laotian government.

We will use May 1950 as the time of initial contact between the Meo and Christianity. As background for understanding its entry among them, we give a description of the cultural setting at the time of contact, but limit the description to those factors which are relevant to the introduction of Christianity. An account

[1] Roux, Henri: "Quelques Minorités Ethniques du Nord-Indochine," *France-Asie*, No. 92-93, p. 388.

**Reprinted from Vol. 4, No. 2 (1957), pp. 31-50. Rev. G. Linwood Barney, a former missionary in Laos under the Christian and Missionary Alliance, is studying for the Ph.D. in Anthropology from the University of Minnesota and is teaching Missions at Bethel Seminary and St. Paul Bible College in St. Paul, Minnesota.**

of the early dissemination of Christianity will follow. In this connection we shall see the early beginnings of church development until the time of the evacuation of the missionaries because of Viet Minh (Communist) war action in 1953. Next, the church as it existed after eighteen months of Communist occupation is described and its further development during the next twelve months is indicated. Finally, this data will be interpreted in the light of anthropological theory, with a projection of developments into the future.

## Meo Culture at the Time of Contact: May 1950

Rice is the basic food staple for the Meo, although corn is grown and used when necessary. The Meo are the only people in the whole Xieng Khouang area to grind corn in rotating stone corn mills. They are famous for their horses, which are usually somewhat larger than the typical horse in Southeast Asia. They are proud of these animals, care for them fondly, train them well, and produce a beast of burden whose sure-footedness and stamina on the steep rugged trails is amazing. Cattle, goats, pigs, chickens, and dogs make up the remainder of the livestock common in a Meo village.

A village may number from one large household (I visited one with thirty-five members) to a village with as many as forty households. Usually a household consists of the conjugal family with occasional additional elderly members or a married son who remains temporarily until his own house is built.

Clan members do not marry within the clan, and usually several clans will be represented in one village. Polygyny is practiced, usually as the result of adding the widow of a deceased brother. One case of polygyny was observed in which a man had married sisters. Wealthier men, like Tubi, may have several wives, but the "big wife" is considered most important and accompanies him at public functions. Trial marriage, a normal practice, is carried on with a semblance of disapproval by the girl's parents. Marriage is contracted through intermediaries but is not actualized until the young man has earned and paid the agreed bride-price. Thus girls may get married soon after puberty, but men are often eighteen to twenty years old before they have sufficient funds to meet the contract price.

Every Meo household has an opium poppy field. This provides the cash income. French administrators declared that an estimated sixty to seventy percent of the Meo adult male population had been addicted to the opium habit. The women seldom use it except in severe illness and suffering. Boys may be introduced to it, but their frequent use of it is frowned upon until after marriage.

The village chief is the most powerful political figure in a village and, although not commonly a dictator, he is highly respected; when he gives an explicit command it is obeyed. His house is usually large enough to accommodate the entire village when a meeting is called.

The shaman, who probably holds status below that of the chief, is considered necessary in any Meo village. Indeed, many villages have any number of them. Their duties take much of their time, and they are reimbursed considerably. The shaman and the chief seem to operate in different phases of life and thus have little cause for conflict. The shaman is expected to serve the people. Some of his functions are: (1) protecting the newborn child from evil spirits by placing fetish bands on his neck and limbs; (2) performing rituals at funeral and marriage ceremonies and reciting long dirges at the former; (3) securing protection for a rice field at planting time; (4) securing protection for trail and hunting expeditions; and (5) performing extensive rituals for the sick, including the sacrificing of a chicken or some animal offered by the family of the sick person.

The Meo culture is rich in a folklore which is handed down in couplet form and may be recited for days. The folklore and present day practices reflect their deep belief in a spirit world. They believe in a supreme deity, Fua-Tai, who created everything but who has become uninterested in mankind. The Meo are left at the mercy of the spirits who make constant demands on them for offerings and sacrifices. They even set up the specifications for the home, requiring them to be made of hand-hewn boards erected in vertical position. Board shingles form the roof. A central part of the house contains an altar for the spirits.

Another factor which has bearing on the subject of this paper is the relationship between the Meo and another tribal people, the Khmu. The latter live in the foothills and have adopted much of the Lao culture, but are animistic much like the Meo. Their relationship with the Meo is one of mutual respect with no marked friendship or hostility.

## Patterns of Culture Change

In the ten years that had passed since the brief stay of missionaries in Xieng Khouang before World War II and the re-entry of new missionaries in 1949, circumstances had changed. Trends of culture change were evident among the Meo. Reasons are only speculative. Perhaps newer generations were breaking from older traditions due to the migrations. Perhaps Japanese control had given temporary equal status to Meo and Lao alike. Perhaps the personality characteristics of the Meo, their aggressiveness, alertness, inquisitiveness, etc., built up until internal combustion revealed itself in an external manner.

Today the Meo descend in large numbers upon the market. They have little produce to trade, but they make their purchases with opium and silver. (Seldom will the Meo offer or accept any form of paper currency.) The Meo who, ten years before, were seldom seen in town now not only attend market but occasionally take up residence near town and obtain employment there. Many Meo youth, with Tubi's encouragement, have enrolled in the town school, where they can acquire the equivalent of an eighth-grade education. Few actually remain in school for more than a couple of years, but some have completed this schooling and are now in attendance in the *lycée* at Vientiane, and one Meo, a Christian, is in college in Saigon.

Meanwhile, in some Meo villages, education is considered a real attainment and some Laotian teachers have been paid wages above that of the Laotian school to open school in the Meo villages for the local youth. Such schools are rather unorganized, but they have helped toward some literacy in the Lao language. Mission records show that approximately three or four per cent of the Meo are literate. This percentage would increase with closer proximity to town. Learning Lao is considered by the Meo as a necessary evil in order to gain prestige and advancement. (Many are now obtaining semiofficial positions with the government.) Already the Lao, who have dominated the economic and political scene, sense the rising tide of the Meo society. Regardless of what may have triggered these new developments in the Meo culture, they must be considered along with the more static cultural traits described above as part of the over-all setting into which Christianity was introduced. Certain elements were conducive to its acceptance, while others were in direct opposition to it.

## Introduction of Christianity

In May of 1950 the missionary family residing in Xieng Khouang left to attend a conference of missionaries in Vietnam. A young Khmu tribesman from the province of Luang Prabang came to the mission station to watch the property and also to let the local population realize that the missionary had left only temporarily. This young man, Nai Kheng, went about town telling of his Christian faith. One who listened intently was Po Si, an old Meo shaman who lived close to town. He stated that a female shaman had prophesied two years before that in two years someone would come to tell them about the true God, Fua-Tai. Po Si was convinced that Nai Kheng was telling him about the same God and became a professing Christian. He took Nai Kheng to his own village, where the chief led his entire group in expressing faith in Fua-Tai-Yesu, as Jesus came to be called in Meo. Kheng was then taken to the village of the female shaman who had made the prediction mentioned above. After listening to Nai Kheng's message, she stated firmly that she was convinced that this was the one of whom she had spoken, and she led her village in placing faith in Fua-Tai-Yesu.

With this, other villages in the area sent for Nai Kheng, who traveled almost constantly relating the simple events of Christ's life and the means of salvation through faith in him. After being delayed weeks by a typhoon, the missionary returned and was amazed to find nearly 1,000 Meo tribespeople who had announced their faith in Christ.

The missionary then accompanied Nai Kheng and Po Si to the villages of the new Christians where, by request of some and consent of others, he removed and destroyed all fetishes from their bodies, homes, fields, etc. This became an expected ritual on the part of any new convert. The Christians refer very frequently to their freedom from the spirits, explaining that the evil spirit, Tlan, is more powerful than man but less powerful than Fua-Tai, who through his Son, Yesu, has again become intensely interested in man and thus liberates him from the power and effects of the evil spirits. This faith in Fua-Tai-Yesu is very real, as is evidenced by the manner in which the Meo, with no exhortation from the missionary, travel widely in the area telling others about their newly found faith.

At this time another missionary fluent in the Lao language came to Xieng Khouang to teach in a hastily formed catechist Bible school. (No missionary spoke Meo; all communication was carried on through interpreters.) The first session was attended by about thirty-five students. Every village having Christians sent at least one representative who could understand Lao and who was respected by the members of the village. Some of these individuals had attended one to six years in the public school.

Church services were conducted in Xieng Khouang at one o'clock every Sunday afternoon and were attended by 200 to 300 people. A temporary structure of bamboo and thatch was erected for these services.

## Beginning Linguistic Analysis

In 1951 my family and I arrived in Kieng Khouang to undertake reduction of the Meo language to writing. I used a monolingual approach as I knew no Lao and therefore had no intermediary language. Gradually I learned not only the language but many of the underlying facets of the Meo culture. In early 1952 the other missionaries left for furlough and I was left in charge of the work. Sharing the responsibility was Pastor Sali, an ordained Lao clergyman (actually he was of Lao and Vietnamese descent), who quickly picked up a practical knowledge of Meo and was a great help in ministering to the church. All missionary-national communication was carried on in Meo. Only the Bible school, now taught by Sali, continued in Lao, and this because of a ruling by the federal government.

Almost exclusive use of the Meo language broke down barriers and brought to light Meo practices which were in contradiction to American Christianity and some which seemed to oppose the Judeo-Christian tradition everywhere. However, the main concern at this stage was to establish the Meo in the Christian faith, which in its essential element is a God-man relationship apart from cultural factors of any particular society.

Just prior to my arrival in Xieng Khouang, another event of considerable importance took place. Tubi, the Meo leader, became intensely interested in Christianity and attended the services regularly with his family. He called the missionary and the catechists to his home and stated his intention of having a Christian home. He did not want to go on record as having become a Christian himself because of the Buddhist government, but his entire family, including his several wives and all the children, expressed their faith, and Tubi requested that all fetishes be destroyed. His principal wife has been a faithful adherent and supporter of the local church and was in the first group to be baptized. This led to even greater receptiveness among the Meo population and was directly responsible for the conversion of a Meo district chief, Sai Pao, who was responsible for many villages and has himself been instrumental in guiding a large number of those under him into the Christian faith.

Like the expanding ripples caused by a stone thrown into water, the dissemination of Christianity began to spread out from Xieng Khouang and continues today. By March of 1953, about 2,000 Meo and 1,000 Khmu had become Christians. One could travel about four days from Xieng Khouang before he reached the periphery of the movement.

At this juncture, the Viet Minh Communists struck from across the border. Xieng Khouang was one of the first places to fall into Red hands. No time was allowed for preparing the Meo for the sudden forced departure of the missionaries and Sali. Left behind were fourteen catechists who had had training for about two years and six others who had received training for six months. It must be noted that there were also several strong lay Christian leaders who were very earnest in their Christian conduct and witness.

Upon my departure, I was greatly disturbed about the future of this young church, fearing that it was not too well established, wondering whether I should have pushed the Meo into a system of Christian ethics, and questioning the real stability of the faith of the Meo.

Before moving to a description of the situation eighteen months later, when missionaries could again make residence in Xieng Khouang, I should like to recount three personal experiences which illustrate developments in the thinking of the Meo. Each of these situations arose spontaneously, although one might legitimately ask, "Did these concepts arise within these individuals, or did they result from their associations with the missionaries?" It would be nice to think that the former was the case.

### The Marriage Ceremony

Tua Pao, a twenty-year-old catechist, was engaged to be married. He had paid the bride-price and approached me as to the manner in which he should get married, since he did not wish to follow the traditional form completely. After discussion, elements of the Meo culture which were not related to the spirits were retained and a simple Christian ritual was added to produce an over-all ceremony which the Meo have followed with enthusiasm. In substance the entire procedure includes the usual overtures to the girl's parents by an intermediary of the young man, an agreed amount of bride-price, reciprocal feasts by both families, and then the brief ceremony at the bride's home when neck bands are exchanged and a local pastor or catechist asks God's seal of blessing on this new home. Then the couple go to live in the young man's village. Tua Pao's wedding was the first Christian Meo wedding, but many others have followed.

### Trial Marriage

Ntrua, an informant sixteen years old, raised the question of trial marriage. He had been a Christian for two years. Now he was approaching the age when young men practiced trial marriage. The Meo parents offer only a semblance of disapproval when the young man spends the night with their daughter. Actually she is allowed to sleep on a platform apart from the rest of the family and the young male intruder is expected to come and go surreptitiously between the time that family retires and arises. This may continue for some time until the young couple decides that it does or does not want to become recognized by the community as husband and wife. If they do not want to continue, then each looks elsewhere for another partner. Apparently the Meo have frowned upon a repeated change of partners, considering this to be immoral and not for the real purpose of securing a wife. Ntrua questioned the practice in either form for the Christian. I discussed the problem with him without making any ruling. Ntrua drew his own conclusion that he could better follow Christ by not following this practice. He became quite influential in encouraging other youths to do the same.

### Opium as a Source of Income

A Meo tribesman of about forty years of age, who had achieved wealth according to Meo standards, approached me. He had enough rice fields to keep his household but had been very successful in the production of opium. He was not addicted to it himself, but stated that he felt it was improper for a Christian to use opium and therefore questioned whether he should even grow it. He stated that the opium hindered the Meo from working the way he should, eventually making him a "murky" thinker, and kept him in a state of poverty. I discussed other possibilities for cash income. Finally, of his own volition, the man turned to raising market produce instead of opium and reported that he was doing well.

Other cases could be related, but these brief accounts give some indication of the alert Meo mind, his intense persuasion of the Christian faith, and perhaps some of the reasons for the content in the next section of this paper.

### After the Occupation

On our return, it seemed that everyone had some experience to relate in which his faith had proven effective during the difficult and meager days of the occupation. Space does not permit giving these accounts. Except for two abbreviated contacts, the Christians had been separated from the missionaries during this entire period of eighteen months. Perhaps a little comparison will give a quick glimpse of what transpired.

In March of 1953, there were about 2,000 Christian Meo living in fifty-six scattered villages which were located from an hour to four days' travel from Xieng Khouang. Ten villages had chapels. Catechists were supported, the mission and the Christians sharing equally. Most of the Christians came to the missionary for advice and counsel. In September 1954, the Meo Christians numbered between 3,000 and 3,500 and seventy-three villages had Christians. They extended to six days' travel from Xieng Khouang. The church had continued without mission funds. There was a matured Christian concept among many of the Christians, as was evidenced by their ability to make decisions concerning the interpretation of Christianity in their own conduct. The catechists were often sought out for counsel. Some of the catechists had not been too effective as leaders but others had developed splendidly. We were deeply impressed by the strides made by the Christians of Xieng Khouang.

The movement continues. Later reports number the Meo Christians over 4,000. These live in some ninety-six villages, with forty-two villages professing to be one hundred per cent Christian.

Organizational developments have also appeared. Lay leaders are selected from each village by the Christians in that village. Generally, these men have the combined qualities of being typically Meo so as to be respected by the Meo population and also meet what the Meo understand to be the Scriptural requirements of a deacon. The Meo are very ethnocentric and have grown to assume Christianity is as much Meo as it is American. Often a village has not expressed an interest in Christianity until its members are convinced that it is not just Western culture.

The school for catechists is taught by a missionary and by Sali, with forty catechists attending. A new development has been short-term schools conducted for the deacons and slanted to help them in discharging effectively their spiritual responsibilities. Special conferences at Christmas and Easter are attended by groups numbering 1,200 to 1,800. A national church organization has been formed with an executive board consisting of Sali as president, a catechist as secretary, a group of laymen as keepers of the treasury, and representatives from the Lao, Meo, and Khmu ethnic groups. The missionary is adviser.

Along with this progress there remain factors which present and will continue to present problems for some time. Some of these have developed from mission programs; others have been a natural development caused by the contact of Meo culture with Christianity; still others are the fault of neither, but the result of extraneous circumstances.

As natural result of the culture contact there are such issues as follow: (1) the used and production of opium; (2) the practice of polygamy, by choice and by inheritance; (3) the practice of trial marriage; and (4) misconceptions and misinterpretations occurring most commonly at the periphery of the Christian community. For example, at one time a Meo trinity developed with three men representing God as Father, Son, and Holy Spirit. They had quite a following until Holy Spirit died in trying to fly, as a dove, from a high elevation.

Some problems have arisen as a result of mission administration. The time element here has not always been made clear in mission reports, and much improvement has been made, as will be indicated in the next section. Included among these problems are those arising from the following procedures: (1) despite eighteen months of self-support, the mission again became engaged in giving a subsidy to the catechists; (2) the mission has contributed largely to the planning and erection of a permanent church building in Xieng Khouang, and likewise of school buildings; (3) the curriculum and teaching in the Bible school is under mission domination; (4) the church constitution began to be formulated by a committee consisting of three missionaries and only two nationals, both Lao; (5) allocations and assignments of catechists have been made by the missionaries; (6) the missionaries have performed most of the church ordinances; (7) the missionary handled all funds, both mission and local offerings; and (8) the Christians have had the concept that somehow the missionary had greater influence with God than did the catechists.

The constant threat of renewal of Communist aggression and the soaring inflational trend are further factors that create new problems and add to some of those just listed.

## Analysis and Evaluation

Despite many mistakes by commission and omission on the part of the missionaries, I do not feel presumptuous in concluding that Christianity has been well received by the Meo and that the process of acculturation has been much more than a superficial one. A cynic might add, "And this in spite of missionaries."

I should like to attempt an analysis of the data which has been given above in light of conclusions and principles that anthropologists have postulated in other studies of culture contact.

First, in reference to the introduction of Christianity to the Meo, the missionary is an indirect factor. Nai Kheng, a Khmu, might be considered the innovator in that he was the carrier. However, more important is the fact that Po Si, a well-known shaman, became the first convert and in a very real sense was the innovator. It was Po Si who arranged for Nai Kheng to visit the Meo villages and accompanied him on these visits, giving personal testimony to the reality of his newly found faith and urging the Meo to give audience to this Khmu catechist. Following this pattern, in village after village, it has been the chiefs and shamans who have led their people in an acceptance of Christianity. This was given further support by Tubi, the Meo leader, and very active support by Sai Pao, the district chief. Though Po Si was the innovator in the first instance, one might say that there have been many innovators in different villages and districts, and nearly always a prominent person has been the initiator. Christianity has benefited from the prestige derived from these respected individuals. "With respect to prestige, the relation between the innovator and his innovations is a reciprocal one. The fact that he introduced it reflects some glory on him, but the new thing becomes associated with him in the minds of the group and gains or loses its potentialities for conferring prestige upon those who accept it later according to what his status may be."[2]

The acceptance of Christianity throughout the Meo population bears out Linton's further comment in this connection, that a new innovation will filter down in a culture from those of high status to those of a lower status, but seldom does it climb from a low status group to a high status group.[3]

A second factor which is very important in this study is the manner in which the innovation was introduced. Nai Kheng was himself a young convert. He recounted only his faith in Christ, the procedure for attaining this faith, and finally could give, in simple story form, some of the episodes from the life of Christ. He knew little or nothing of ecclesiasticism. Therefore his message did what the missionary's usually does not. It dealt with matters which point more directly to Christian faith without the cultural trappings inherent in the missionary's presentation. It seems that Nai Kheng unwittingly established a pattern which the misionary followed and by which Christianity spread rapidly in Xieng Khouang. Emile Cailliet asserts, "...We should realize that no Christian approach to culture is safe which does not begin by disengaging Christian truth from the cultural forms in which it has been embedded."[4]

A third factor closely related to the one just mentioned is the splendid rapport between the missionary and the Meo in the Xieng Khouang area. There was a marked hesitancy on the part of the missionaries to pressurize the Christians to abandon all their practices, since the former were not sure of the significance of the practices to the Meo themselves. If contact with Christianity resulted in some conflict with the Meo culture, it became apparent to the Meo himself and he struggled with the problem, as in the three cases studied above.

> The new objects . . . moral standards and religious beliefs must be introduced through native authority and acceptance, so that natives themselves can work out the consequent changes or cultural and social adjustments. They alone can do this, and it takes time, experience, and experiment.
>
> Of course, this may seem frustrat-

[2] Linton, Ralph: *Acculturation in Seven American Indian Tribes.* D. Appleton Century Co., New York, 1940. p. 473.

[3] Ibid., p. 474.

[4] Cailliet, Emile: *The Christian Approach to Culture.* D. Appleton Century Co., New York, 1940. p. 15.

ing to the efficient administrator or zealous missionary, but the development of a people in culture has no meaning apart from their continuing as a people with an integrated social and cultural system. A people cannot be preserved by authority, and no people is willing to be "preserved." A people lives from within or dies without.[5]

It seems possible . . . to support the following generalization: people resist changes that threaten basic securities; they resist proposed changes they do not understand; they resist being forced to change.[6]

The first strong action by the missionary in the destruction of the fetishes met with the approval of the Christians and the function of these items was substituted for through Christian practices, often nothing more than simple prayer. Thus there appeared to be little conflict within the culture as a result of taking away the fetishes and the cessation of the shaman's practices. There is only one case known to me in which a village reverted to its powerful drum fetish. This village was located at the periphery of the Christian movement and perhaps had not received sufficient teaching and thereby as clear an understanding of Christian faith.

Some of the problems which are given above in three classifications have been greatly reduced or solved in very recent months. Allocations and assignments of catechists are now made by the executive committee of the recently formed national church. Rites are now performed by Sali and licensed Meo catechists. Baptism and communion are extended to those who are approved by local church committees in conference with the catechist responsible for the group. Delegation of authority to the catechists has resulted in the Christians' placing more confidence in them and going to them for counsel where they would probably have gone to the missionary.

Mission funds are handled by the missionary and are generally used for mission expense, while church funds are handled and administered by the national church. Other measures in progress include a three-year program whereby a third of the subsidy to the catechists will be removed each year and will be replaced by local church support. Thus by 1958 the church should be self-supporting.

Inflation has made the cutting of the subsidy difficult, but it has had its benefits. It has prevented the erection of a rather elaborate church in Xieng Khouang, although the structure will still not seem natural to the tribespeople. One questions whether they themselves would even have the technology for repairs.

Thus far, polygamy, the use of opium, and trial marriage have been considered difficult problems which will have to be handled within the society in time and as their faith takes on clearer manifestation within the framework of the Meo culture. I believe these problems can be worked out if the missionary does not insist on enforcing the attitudes of his own culture toward these items.

Bride-price, frowned upon by many missionaries, has not been considered evil by the missionaries in Xieng Khouang, since it is a cultural trait which gives a measure of solidarity to the Meo marriage. It functions as a proof of the young

---

[5] Elkin, A. P.: *Social Anthropology in Melanesia.* Oxford University Press, London, 1953. p. 148.

[6] Spicer, Edward H.: *Human Problems in Technological Change.* Russell Sage Foundation, New York, 1952. p. 18.

man's worth and his esteem for the girl. At the same time, it serves to discourage divorce, which would necessitate a financial adjustment. Bride-price to the Meo does not mean female slavery or a purchase of a piece of property. Hence it should be retained because of its function in giving stability to the family and thus to the culture.

Missionaries commonly refer to the concept of an "indigenous church" as though it were some magical formula consisting of three ingredients: self-support, self-government, and self-propagation.

In Xieng Khouang self-propagation has developed naturally. Self-support was practically established during the Communist occupation but was partially undermined by the new mission subsidy. It is now being reintroduced with difficulty, by the three-year plan. The committee of three missionaries and two nationals working on the constitution has been dissolved, but self-government is far from a reality. There needs to be a definite program put into action whereby the nationals will be given experience in administration of church and school in order that they may be adequately prepared to take over an ever-increasing amount of the administrative responsibilities.

I had opportunity to observe missionary work in other parts of Laos, in Vietnam, and in Thailand. There are certain principles which I believe should be basic in missionary work. There is not space to draw comparisons from other areas, although such would be most helpful in giving more support to these principles. I have seen groups who have been Christian for twenty years but are not as rooted in local culture as the church in Xieng Khouang. Other groups are completely in operation without missionary supervision. Thus drawing on personal observation and the wealth of anthropological material available, I would make the following summary statement.

The missionary's goal should be: (1) to present Christianity apart from the implications of the missionary's own culture, since he recognizes the latter to be entirely relative and not essential to the establishment of a God-man relationship for the individual who is the recipient of Christian faith; (2) not to be satisfied with the threefold standard traditionally used to indicate an indigenous church, but to be satisfied only as essential Christian faith takes root deep in a culture and the resulting Christian society makes outward manifestation and takes organizational form within the framework of the local culture; and (3) to become, thereby, dispensable to the continuance of the local church and yet be in such a place of rapport with the local church that he shall be welcomed as a guide and stimulus in the growth of the church.

To accomplish this the missionary must be convinced that the nationals — the Meo for the sake of illustration — are not to become American church puppets but rather strong Christians although still Meo. He must be convinced that the Meo can be one hundred per cent Meo and still one hundred per cent Christian.[7]

I would propose that any culture, any society, and any member within a society may become Christian without losing the majority of its distinctive characteristics.

---

[7] Diasuke Kitagawa expresses this concept in his paper: "Racial and Cultural Relations in the Ministry to American Indians." National Council, New York, 1954.

The missionary introduces Christianity. Given time, its real essence will find its level in the depths of a culture, and when it has been accepted wholeheartedly on the level of basic values, acculturation will be possible and the necessary changes will be made from within. "A basic reformation of personality takes place in the acculturation process only when people and values of the dominant culture are successfully attained."[8]

Efforts on the part of a missionary to bring about conformity to his denominational background or even traditional American concepts will bring about, at best, a superficial church which will fade away should the missionary leave and which will not be likely to grow or spread beyond the area which the missionary himself is able to reach.

[8] Spindler, George, and Goldschmidt, Walter: "Experimental Design in the Study of Cultural Change," *American Anthropologist,* Vol. 58, p. 80.

Christianity, as an innovation in any culture, will cause changes, but when properly introduced and cultivated it will produce a Christian ethic within the configuration of the pre-existing culture without having caused a disintegration of that culture.

> With my people, it is not so much what you say as how you say it, and who does the saying.
>
> To my people, one "let us do" is worth more than a thousand "you must do's." Africa is a child, but our paternalists fail to observe that this child is growing. They also forget that in many instances it is more important to work *with* than to work for.[9]

The African clergyman and scholar who uttered those words re-echoes the thoughts of national Christians on most any mission field in the world.

[9] Smith, Edwin W.: *Aggrey in Africa.* A study in black and white. Doubleday, Doran and Co., Inc., New York, 1929. p. 2.

*Eugene A. Nida*

**Reprinted from Vol. 6, No. 2 (1959), pp. 49-54.**

# Are We Really Monotheists?

*The Christian doctrine of the Trinity is a puzzling one for missionaries who try to explain it — or understand it, for that matter. In this article Dr. Nida discusses the mental images of the Trinity which we often carry around with us and try to teach to others. The response in those "others," if they are Muslims, should well give us pause and make us stop to consider just what we do say and think.*

IT usually comes as a surprise to the average missionary in Muslim lands to learn that Christians are consistently accused of being polytheists, not monotheists. To the Muslim, the very idea of God having a son is repugnant, for he immediately thinks in terms of sexual relations, and to associate such with Allah is nothing less than blasphemy. Moreover, the Christian's insistence that Jesus was not only the Son of God but "very God of very God" leaves the Mohammedan all the more convinced that the Christians have no right whatsoever to call themselves monotheists.

Most people set aside the Islamic reaction to Christianity as being based upon ignorance and prejudice. But if they make a serious attempt to study Christians' untutored reactions to the doctrine of the Trinity, they find that the accusation of being basically polytheists seems to adhere tenaciously in the minds of converts, especially those whose Christian experience and training is limited.

### Mental Pictures of God

If a missionary dares to approach the problem realistically, he will probably get the shock of his life. If he asks who God is, the answers often cluster about the concepts revealed in such phrases as "the old man in the sky," "the Father in the sky," "the one who made us," etc. When asked about Jesus Christ, the same people will describe many features of His life and presumed appearance, but almost never do they speak of Jesus Christ as being God. In fact, Jesus Christ is more often than not a kind of culture hero, frequently somewhat in opposition to God, but always standing up for the people. The Holy Spirit is often conceived of as just another, and more powerful, benevolent spirit.

Some missionaries are inclined to think that this is more or less the way people should think of God, for in a sense this echoes their own concepts. The image which is the "mental reflex" of the word symbol "God" does exist for many mature Christians as an "old fatherly person in heaven." The Son, if He is not thought of in terms of the historical Jesus, is "a youthful figure at the right hand of the Father." And the Holy Spirit is a kind of nebulous, "foggy" substance that is supposed to be the "Third Person," but just how this is true remains a readily confessed mystery to most persons. Certainly these mental images suggest three separate entities much more than one.

What is more, some Christians tend to add to the Biblical imagery in such a way that the "three persons" are not only separate in form and function, but diverse in apparent purpose. For example, as an explanation of the theological basis of substitutionary atonement, some people say that God the Father insisted that His holiness and righteousness must not be stained by the presence of human sinners. Accordingly, to satisfy the demands of an infinitely holy and righteous God, Jesus Christ volunteered to go to earth to die in man's place, that God could maintain His inviolate character and still admit into His presence sinful mortals. Such explanations do, in a sense, contain a kernel of Biblical truth, but in some ways they introduce more error than valid clarification, for they tend to conform to pagan views about the standoffishness of God and the function of a culture hero (in this case Jesus Christ), not primarily as a mediator, but as a defender against the demands of God. Furthermore, these explanations implicitly contradict the initiative of God in redeeming man (i.e., His being in Christ Jesus reconciling the world to Himself) and His essential mercy and love.

If, as seems well attested by a careful study of believers' mental images, the results of our teaching, not only on the mission fields but also in our own culture, produce more of a sense of three different entities than one God, what are we really to say to our critics who accuse us of being basically polytheists? Of course, our first line of defense (and a justified one) is to insist that we believe in the Trinity (three in one). This is all very well, but when we are asked to explain what we mean, we find we can only repeat a definition. Search as we may, we cannot find any finite symbol which corresponds to our verbal description of the Trinity. Some people have attempted to describe the Trinity as a circle divided into three parts, but to this the theologians object, for they insist that God is not divisible into parts. Others try to explain the Trinity on the analogy of body, soul, and spirit, but this type of trichotomy breaks down immediately. Still others have spoken of Jesus as "God with a face" and the Spirit as "the heart of God." But whatever we attempt to do by way of finding appropriate symbols in our finite experience finally leaves us without any satisfactory analogy. However, in following the Biblical symbols which grant full attributes of personality to all three persons of the Trinity, we almost immediately lead people to conceive of God, Christ, and the Holy Spirit more as three than as one. What, then, are we to do? We can scarcely admit the Muslim contention that we are really polytheists, for we *really* are not. On the other hand, for all *practical* purposes we certainly appear to be polytheists to the devotees of other religions.

If, as is so obviously the case, we tend to give an impression of being polytheists, by virtue of the verbal symbols which we use, what can we do about it? Is there any way of correcting this difficulty? Or must we go on perpetuating the same views and implied errors?

### Finite Language and Infinite Faith

I believe that we can, at least in some measure, correct our mental concepts so as to be essentially more in keeping with

God's revelation of Himself. In the first place, however, we must come to grips with the problem of Biblical symbolism, and to do this is not easy, for we are instantly involved in the fundamental problem of revelation and communication. However, if we are willing to do some radical thinking on this problem, we may discover something of what God wants to reveal to us.

In discussing the basic problem of God's communication to man, it seems essential, as a basic axiom, to recognize that infinite truth cannot be absolutely revealed in finite language. This does not mean that human language cannot reveal truth, but by virtue of its being tied to finite cultures (with all their human limitations), it cannot perfectly represent the ultimate reality. Paul speaks of this as "seeing through a glass darkly." This glass not only serves to reveal, but also to hide — and so with language.

In order for God to reveal Himself as a thinking, loving, creative "being," He caused Himself to be spoken of in terms of human experience, e.g., as having hands, a heart, feet, as being a Father, as feeling jealousy, pity, and compassion, as repenting, calling, and leading. God becomes located in heaven, surrounded by angels, seated on a throne and with His Son at His right hand. Many people will dismiss many of these expressions as anthropomorphisms, symbols with a nonliteralist significance. But just how far do most people go in this process of assigning Biblical figures to the status of anthropomorphic symbols? Some will say that God does not have hands and feet, and yet they cannot dismiss the concept of a throne in heaven. Others will eliminate a literal throne, but not the surrounding angels. All of these figures, however, are made even more puzzling to the average person by Jesus' statement, "God is a spirit." Does the recognition of God as a spirit completely invalidate all the other symbols? Should we accordingly cast them all out as primitive modes of perception? Frankly, I do not think so, despite what some theologians, such as Bultmann and Tillich, would advocate. God's revelation of Himself in the Scriptures does not hesitate to use such figures, and why should we? Furthermore, there is no evidence that we can come any closer to the truth by rejecting such symbols — the only means by which human language can describe nonhuman realities. Nevertheless, all this seems to imply a contradiction, for we have argued that these figures lead to a misconception as to the person of God, while at the same time the requirements of human language necessitate the use of such figures. Is there any solution to the apparently irreconcilable dilemma?

### Revelation of God's Activity

The solution to the basic difficulty seems to lie in the recognition that *all* these anthropomorphic figures refer not to God's person, but to His activity. The Bible is filled with the revelation of an acting, creative, speaking, revealing God. In so far as we know God, it is *only* on the basis of what He has done. Even in the case of Jesus Christ we have no authentic description of what He looked like, but we have abundant information as to what He did. All this is in direct contrast to the gods of the pagans, who are always described in vivid detail.

If, however, we are to keep people from substituting a Christian "threesome" for a pagan trio, we must interpret the Biblical figures in terms of functions and not form. Since the Scriptures do not explicitly indicate the real nature of God, in terms of substance or form (evidently a fact not communicable in human language), we should be thoroughly Biblical by not presuming to know more than God has chosen to reveal. This means that we must emphasize the essentially functional character of Biblical metaphors and symbols. This approach toward Biblical symbolism may seem a little strange at first, but it squares with the requirements of any linguistic expression and the evidence of the Scriptures. "At God's right hand" is then only a symbol of a functional relationship, i.e., "in closest and honored union with." The "throne" is a functional symbol of governing, and God's jealousy, pity, and compassion are aspects of His breaking through to man in "redeeming love." (Here, as so often, we can only explain one functional figure by another.)

The recognition of (1) the essentially symbolic character of all words (whether so-called concrete terms such as "hands," "feet," and "throne," or the more abstract expressions such as "love," "pity," and "mercy"), and (2) the special functional significance which they have in the Scriptures can go a long way toward helping people avoid the error of being "polytheists." Though we cannot find Biblical symbols which "picture" the unity of God, Jesus Christ, and the Holy Spirit, we do find abundant evidence of the identity of function. Even Jesus, in His statement of His oneness with the Father, made this relationship explicit by indicating that whatsoever the Father did, He did likewise. Even the believer's being in Christ and Christ in the believer is primarily a relationship of function, not of form or space. Certainly, when Jesus insisted that "he who has seen me has seen the Father," he evidently was not referring to bodily, but to functional identity.

**Temptation to Literalism**

It is not difficult to explain the fact that people consistently tend to misread the intent of Scriptures in assuming the literal interpretation of symbols referring to form. This tendency exists in all peoples. In the first place, form symbols are more readily picturable by the mind than function symbols. For example, the mental image induced by "throne" is more readily elicited than one corresponding to "govern," or "rule." In terms of Gestalt psychology, we could say that the so-called form symbol offers greater figure contrast in comparison with the "ground." Function symbols, on the other hand, usually involve "eventing" and the movements against the ground provide less impressionable figures.

Most people, however, are not content with merely ideational symbols; they demand objectifications of these in art forms. This development has taken place in Christianity, particularly in Roman Catholicism, but is increasingly a factor in Protestantism. However, not only does the objective image take the place of the mental image (standing for some historical object or event, e.g., the Virgin Mary), but not infrequently the object itself gives rise to a new series of mental images which for many people are completely divorced from the mental image of the historical reality, as in the case of the mother of Jesus, which becomes the Virgin of Guadalupe in Mexico. When an object no longer refers one back to the original referent, but to a new series of mental images, a so-called religious image is no longer psychologically an image, but an idol.

This extreme form of "literalism" in

formal symbols (by which images become idols) is completely parallel to the psychological tendency to be literalistic in interpreting all types of figures. Formal figures always seem so much more real than functional ones. We can see them more readily with "the eyes of the mind." Therefore we give prominence to formal symbols and we tend to describe functions in terms of forms, e.g., governing in terms of thrones, power in terms of "a strong right arm," and recompense in terms of "crowns" or "fire." In keeping with this basic psychological characteristic of mankind, God has revealed Himself in just such meaningful figures, for they reveal truths (certainly to the vast majority of people) which no amount of abstract terminology could ever make known. Such symbols are certainly not untrue, but if they are interpreted by people without due recognition of their true symbolic character, they may give rise to weird theologies.

### The Approach to the Muslim

But now we return to the Mohammedan objection that we are polytheists, not monotheists. First, we must admit that our chances of convincing a Muslim are very slim, for all his canons of interpretation of the Koran are essentially literalist, formal, not functional, which is no doubt the way Mohammed meant his words. However, if we do wish to try to explain to a Mohammedan what is meant by the Christian doctrine of the Trinity, we must say at the very start that the Bible contains neither a description nor an explanation of the Trinity. The identity which we find in Scripture is one of motivation and action, not of spatial diffusion or isolability. The mystery of the real essence of God will remain a mystery, for evidently though we may formulate a word symbol (Trinity), we cannot really explain in finite categories what it means. We can, however, explain what God has done within the stream of human history, and this is the really relevant set of facts which faces man.

This approach may seem to be essentially obscurantist, since it appears to deny the knowability of certain realities. However, rather than being either obscurantist or agnostic (as others might charge), this orientation takes a realistic view of the limitations of human languages as systems for symbolizing humanly perceptible "events." Moreover, this procedure of dealing with symbols recognizes the priority of form symbols and the fundamental psychological tendencies in the shift from function to form and the literalist apprehension of form symbols.

The missionary who discovers that the new believers have a "warped" literalist understanding of form symbols should accordingly not be surprised, for this has been the tendency throughout the history of Christendom, as well as in other religious systems. For example, the function symbol of "faith" (in the Biblical sense of active commitment and trust) was soon changed to mean the specific "objects" of faith, namely, the formulated doctrines. Likewise the "word," especially as "the word of God," gradually lost its meaning of "self-revealing act of Deity" and became only a synonym for the Bible. In the Johannine discourse on the sacramental nature of partaking of Christ's body and blood, there was the obvious tendency for the audience to think in literalist terms, and for this reason the discourse is concluded by a statement designed to relegate the form symbols to their proper functional status: "It is the spirit that gives life, the flesh is of no avail; the words that I have spoken to you are spirit and life."[1]

**Necessity of Form Symbols**

In view of the inherent dangers involved in the use of form symbols, one might justly ask as to whether we should attempt to avoid such symbols altogether and use only function symbols. In the first place, however, we cannot make any clear-cut distinction between form and function symbols, for even function symbols almost always provide the mind with a "figure and ground" from which certain more or less definite forms may be isolable. For example, for the symbol "repentance" there may soon grow up a widely distributed "mental image" (a culturally shared form symbol) of a man beating his breast in contrition of heart, as in the parable of the Publican and the Pharisee. Accordingly, even if we tried to choose only those symbols which were predominantly functional in character, we would have no guarantee that they would remain so. The history of the images in Roman Catholicism, the icons in the Orthodox Church, and the idols in Buddhism are abundant evidence of what almost inevitably happens to symbols.

In the second place, we would not wish to avoid form symbols, even if we could, for they are important means of communication. They were certainly used by Jesus in His teaching — and by every great teacher. However, what is of singular interest in the case of Jesus is His constant emphasis upon the functional character of the forms. His parables tell of events and happenings; they are rarely static images. Even when Jesus spoke of Himself as a "door," "bread," or "water," He had reference to function, not form. Here, then, lies the key to our use of symbols, namely, the constant emphasis upon their relationship to action, not to concrete figures. This serves to teach their relevance to life and history and keeps them from becoming "idols," whether of wood or of words.

If we are to be thoroughly honest about the allegation of our being polytheists, we are obliged to say that in the thinking of many Christians the word symbols by which the Trinity has been revealed have become so identified with isolable and isolated forms that on the level of this symbolism such people are polytheists. This is especially so if they associate any differences of motivation with various persons of the Godhead. However, on the level of the functional character of such symbols there is complete identity, and here lies the valid basis for our claim to monotheism.

[1] John 6: 63.

*William L. Wonderly*

**Reprinted from Vol. 5, No. 5 (1958), pp. 197-202.**

# Pagan and Christian Concepts in a Mexican Indian Culture

*The capacity of many societies to take some of the formal aspects of Christianity without understanding its meaning has disturbed many a missionary as he has watched what seemed to him to be an unholy mixture of pagan and Christian practices develop, or has found it already fully established. In this article Dr. Wonderly discusses some aspects of this problem in relation to Mexican Indian life, and comes to the conclusion that any profund teaching of Christian ethics can be done satisfactorily only through the life of a community of believers, through the application of principles to specific situations in the cultural milieu. The illustrations are derived from Mexico, and have to do with Catholic contact with Aztec life, but the problem is a universal one in the spread of the gospel.*

IN communicating the meaning of the gospel message to Indians of Mexico and Central America, one encounters many factors that are different from those which are found in communicating the same message to city dwellers or even to rural people in general. How shall we speak of one God to people who still retain many of the polytheistic beliefs of pre-conquest times? How shall we preach repentance and pardon for sins to persons whose ideas of morality are centered around outward prohibitions such as the Aztec religion had, and have nothing to do with inward attitudes? How may we get a man to stop mistreating his wife, if he believes that by beating her he is helping her to suffer less in the hereafter? What aspects of the gospel are most directly relevant for those who think of God as one who neither loves nor expects His creatures to love? These and many other questions come to mind as we consider the religious concepts of our Indian groups. Although we cannot give a definitive answer to all of these questions, it is hoped that the present review article may be suggestive of ways whereby some of these problems can be approached.

This article is, for the most part, a review of the recent publication entitled *Christo-Paganism*: *A Study of Mexican Religious Syncretism*, by William Madsen.[1] Madsen has attempted an objective study of the present-day religious concepts of a Mexican Indian village

**William L. Wonderly is the Translations Consultant of the American Bible Society for Mexico and Central America. He was formerly a translator and linguist with the Wycliffe Bible Translators (Summer Institute of Linguistics). His Ph.D. is in linguistics from the University of Michigan.**

[1] New Orleans: Middle American Research Institute, Tulane University, 1957. Preprinted from Publication 19, pages 105-180. $1.50.

against an historical background of Aztec religion and of the content of the message preached by the early Roman Catholic missionaries. Thus it is a publication that is important for anyone interested in working among Indians, especially in Mexico or elsewhere in Latin America. Although pre-Columbian religious patterns were by no means identical in all areas, different Indian groups have enough in common both in the pre-conquest background and in the post-conquest Catholic developments to make Madsen's study widely relevant.

The thesis presented in that the present-day religion of Tecospa, an Aztec village in the Federal District, is the outgrowth of a tendency toward syncretism which can be seen in pre-conquest contacts of the Aztecs with the religions of other Indian tribes and which since the conquest has continued to the point where the result had best be called *Christo-Paganism,* or "the integration of Christian and pagan religions in pagan configurations." With regard to the process of religious acculturation, his study leads him to the conclusion that "the form of an innovation is accepted more readily than its meaning and . . . that the process of acceptance is affected by the communicability, utility, and compatibility of the change with established custom" (p. 172).

Chapter two, "Aztec religious patterns," outlines Aztec supernaturalism at the time of the Spanish conquest under four heads: World view, Concept of supernaturals, Ethics, and Worship. Chapter three, "Patterns of sixteenth-century Christianity," attempts to reconstruct from historical sources the message given by the early Spanish missionaries, using the same four heads as in chapter two. These same heads then form the general framework for the more extensive description of the contemporary religion of Tecospa. In this review we shall comment on certain aspects of this description, with special note of some factors which in the reviewer's opinion have obvious and immediate relevance for the presentation of the Christian message today to Indians whom Madsen classifies as Christo-Pagan.

**World View**

Present-day Tecospa religion "acknowledges the Christian God as the creator deity but still retains the Aztec concept of multiple creations and destructions of the world" (p. 143). The Christian God has become a destroyer as well as a creator; and both God and the Virgin of Guadalupe (whom the people call by the name of the Aztec goddess Tonantzin, who existed before the creation of mankind) are "integrated . . . into the Aztec concept of a universe ordered by the opposition of male and female deities" (p. 174). The Aztec philosophy of fatalism persists, "but today a man's destiny in the universe is decided at birth by a battle between God and the Devil [which] takes place in the flames of a fire built in the room where a birth occurs" (pp. 145-146).

Concepts of heaven and hell have many points in common with ancient beliefs of the different abodes of the dead. As in the ancient Aztec religion, a person's condition in the future life is determined in many situations by the manner of his death; for example, men who die in battle and women who die in childbirth are believed to go to heaven regardless of their sins. Twins and persons who die by violence go to hell, as do murderers, prostitutes, men who beat their wives excessively and without good cause, etc.

(But it is expected that a good husband will beat his wife some, so that she will not have to suffer in the afterworld.)

### Supernatural Beings

"The God of Tecospa is not a god of love but an enemy of mankind who wants to destroy the human beings whom he created. He is feared . . . also because he sends famine, pestilence, and earthquakes, as the major Aztec deities did before him. . . . The Indians do not pray to God because He is too hostile to answer their prayers but they do petition the Christ of Chalma and other Christs for health and prosperity" (p. 152). Various virgins and other saints are included in the pantheon, many of them carrying over certain of the attributes of specific Aztec deities. Christian monotheism was never accepted by the Indians; the position of God became analogous to the pre-conquest creator-god Tloque Nahuaque, whose importance in the popular religion was relatively small. Devils called *pingos* are the most important evil personages; their chief is analogous to, but not identical with, the Christian concept of Satan. Other important supernatural beings are the rain dwarfs, who not only produce rain but cause certain sicknesses.

An important feature of Aztec religion was the belief in a mutual-dependency relationship between gods and mortals, in which the deities had to be nourished with human blood and hearts so that they would survive and provide for the welfare of men. The fact that abolition of human sacrifice did not put an end to sun, rain, and crops has led to abandonment of the belief that the gods needed human blood for their survival. Madsen says that "today Catholic saints depend on the Indians of Tecospa only for fiesta entertainment" (p. 173). However, the present reviewer wonders whether, at least in those Indian areas where sacrifices of animal blood are still practiced, there is not a greater survival of the mutual-dependency belief than Madsen has indicated for Tecospa.

### Worship

Activities of worship largely center around four major religious fiestas of the Catholic calendar. Part of the Candlemas (Feb. 2) ceremonies includes the blessing by the priest of the baskets of seed which the people will plant during the year, and of candles for use in the hour of death. San Francisco, the patron saint, is honored on Oct. 4; he is part of the pantheon of nature gods, and cooperates with the rain dwarfs in bringing rain. Nov. 1-3 celebrates the return of the dead, and is one of the most important religious festivals in the area. Madsen associates the Indians' fascination with death and its symbols (including the crucifix, which to them symbolizes death, not the Savior) with both Aztec background and Spanish Catholicism. The fourth major fiesta is the series of *posadas* in December culminating in the celebration on Christmas Eve.

### Ethics

"Christo-Pagan ethics in Tecospa are virtually the same as Aztec ethics except that today man's primary obligations are to Catholic saints instead of to pagan gods" (p. 170). God, who does not love, is not loved; nor is man under obligation to love his fellow-man. The Aztec code of ethics forbade murder, theft, adultery, and disrespect for the gods; it obliged men and women to provide for their families and rear their children properly; but the emphasis was upon proper behavior rather than upon right thoughts and motives. These features have carried over to the present time. "Meekness, righteousness, and purity of heart are not virtues. Showing mercy to an enemy is a sign of weakness and cowardice" (p. 170). These virtues were absent from the Aztec code and were never adopted in the later religious system.

## Communication of Religious Concepts

Madsen concludes that the Christian concepts that were accepted by the Indians were chiefly limited to (1) those which were similar to or compatible with the established beliefs, (2) those which were readily communicable, (3) those arising from practices which were enforceable, and (4) those which were considered useful in terms of Aztec culture. Catholic baptism, confession, fiestas, dances, use of images, and prohibitions against murder, theft and adultery come under the first of these categories. Christian concepts of heaven, hell and the Devil were communicable, at least to a degree, because of Aztec beliefs that paralleled them and the somewhat concrete language that can be used in teaching these; but many important concepts relating to these were never communicated. Catholic ritual was enforceable. But the concept of monotheism was incompatible with Aztec polytheism; the Christian view of sin was "too abstract to be thoroughly communicated" (p. 173); and the Aztec philosophy of fatalism was incompatible with the Christian doctrine of personal moral responsibility.

One may wish to question, however, whether the truth of the matter lies in the mere incompatibility of certain concepts or even in the actual incommunicability of certain abstract ideas, since in other situations these same concepts have been and are being communicated to non-Christian peoples, including Indians such as the Chol and Tzeltal, whom Madsen would classify as Christo-Pagan. The answer is probably to be sought in a combination of these factors with the way in which the message was presented by the early missionaries—a subject which would merit a more thorough study than Madsen gives it. This reviewer's impression is that the concept which the early Catholic missionaries (at least apart from such men as Fray Bartolomé de las Casas) had of the church and of their own responsibilities was one that led most of them to lay more emphasis upon those aspects of Christianity which would permit the crown and the church to exercise political and ecclesiastical control than upon the discovery of ways to communicate the living message to individuals and to communities. This is of course borne out in subsequent developments in the Catholic church and in its present-day emphasis upon maintaining the loyalty and outward conduct of its adherents more than upon promoting their spiritual growth and enlightenment. Without attempting here to evaluate the general validity of the hypothesis that "the form of an innovation is accepted more readily than its meaning" (p. 172), it should be pointed out that if the missionaries emphasized the form of a religious element more than its meaning the result could be attributed as much to the approach used as to the inherent capacities for acceptance on the part of the culture. Many of the adaptations made to the Indian culture by the Catholic church were no doubt legitimate and commendable in themselves, had they but been followed up by a positive attempt to communicate the inner content of the gospel message. This type of communication is our chief concern in evangelical missions today, but it is an area in which the parallels with Spanish colonial history are unfortunately not very, close.

**Points of Relevance**

Several of the features in Madsen's description indicate points at which certain aspects of the gospel can and should be emphasized in order to make the message relevant to the religious background of the people. The reviewer has noticed on different occasions the emphasis that new evangelical believers with Indian background place upon the love of God; this emphasis is particularly understandable and fitting in situations such as that described for Tecospa. Whatever carry-over there may be of ideas of mutual dependency between gods and men points to the importance of emphasizing the fact that God's love for man is not because he has need of man, but is a disinterested love. God's sovereignty and consequent uniqueness need to be emphasized in a way that will develop a monotheistic concept and teach man's responsibility before his Creator (as opposed to the present concept of fatalistic irresponsibility in the hands of mutually competing supernatural beings).

Teaching of Christian ethics may find its initial point of contact in the standards of overt behavior handed down from pre-conquest times; but even as Jesus laid emphasis upon the inner meaning of the law, it will be necessary to teach the deeper meaning of sin and of righteousness and holiness — in other words, if the real meaning of Christianity is to be conveyed, it is imperative to communicate precisely those ethical concepts which Madsen suggests were too abstract for effective communication. This can be done satisfactorily only as there develops, in the Indian community, a corporate witness —a church made up of men and women in whom there become embodied these ethical principles, not as abstract concepts but as basic attitudes which influence their behavior in concrete situations. To this end, the communication of these concepts will probably best be accomplished not so much by the teaching of abstract principles as by the Biblical method of showing how these principles apply to specific situations.

At the same time, for Indian concepts or practices that are considered incompatible with the gospel message, it is important to provide the background information necessary to bring about a change, and where possible to discover some functional substitute for the objectionable feature. For example, if a Tecospa husband is to be exhorted to quit beating his wife, he must be made to understand that her future welfare depends on factors other than the amount of corporal punishment he gives her in this life. And if the current practice of blessing the baskets of seed corn at the Candlemas ceremonies is not to be encouraged, then there must be found some way in keeping with evangelical Christianity in which the blessing of God may be asked upon the year's planting. This is especially important in view of the intimate relation that exists, in the Indian culture, between maize and many other aspects of life both material and spiritual, and of the anxieties that are always present with respect to planting and the obtaining of the crop for each year's sustenance.

Bible story materials, as well as other Christian literature and teaching materials, should be selected with these factors in mind, and should be prepared in a way that will be relevant not only to the universal spiritual need of man but to the specific beliefs and practices of the Indian group.

### Further Investigation Needed

Madsen's survey is an important contribution. It should now be supplemented by a further study, in the same culture area if possible, of the patterns which emerge when protestant Christianity is accepted by a substantial group of people in a community describable in Madsen's terms as Christo-Pagan.[2] A study of this type would include, among other things, the following: (1) an analysis of the protestant work with reference to its approach to the social groupings in the community, and which of the social groups have been affected and used for further communication of the new ideas within the community; (2) an investigation of the content of the message and the elements of the same that have been emphasized in the specific situation under study; (3) observation of the way in which this message is received and in turn communicated by the members of the culture themselves; (4) a study of the degree to which concepts that were not successfully communicated by the sixteenth-century missionaries are being communicated to Indians in the present-day situation; (5) an investigation of any recent adaptations of Christian concepts and practices which provide functional substitutes for cultural elements found incompatible with evangelical Christianity. In order to avoid, in as far as possible, facile conclusions based on new and untried developments, such a study should take into account the religious attitudes and concepts both of persons who have been converted directly from their traditional religion and of the younger generation who have not known the earlier religion of their parents. One of the acid tests of a community's effective acceptance of protestant Christianity is, of course, its transmission of the new concepts to the younger generation, and whether or not the latter, with their increasing opportunity for contacts with the secularist civilization of the twentieth century, bring Christian concepts to bear upon their own way of life.

[2] The nearest approach to such a study which has come to my attention is that contained in Robert Redfield, *A Village that Chose Progress: Chan Kom Revisited* (Univ. of Chicago Press, 1950; 187 pp.). Redfield discusses at length the factors involved in the growth and decline of protestantism in a Maya village over a period of nearly two decades. If, in addition to the material he presents, he had obtained data direct from the missionaries as to the content and emphases of their message and the form in which it was presented to the people, his valuable study would have been still more useful from the standpoint of illuminating the problems of communication and of acceptance, rejection, or modification of new religious elements in the present-day situation.

*John Beekman*

**Reprinted from Vol. 6, No. 6 (1959), pp. 241-250.**

# Minimizing Religious Syncretism among the Chols

*Syncretism is the tendency for new culture patterns to be combined and intermingled with existing patterns when they are adopted into a society. In one sense syncretism is an inevitable characteristic of any profound culture change, because change does not take place in a vacuum, but is developed on, or out from, or in contrast to an existing way of life. In this article John Beekman discusses some of the dangers of syncretism where the resulting behavior is out of keeping with the gospel. He also discusses the "reorientation" of Chol values and practices in the light of the gospel. This reorientation places the gospel in a framework which seems relevant to the Chol people. In a sense it is a syncretism in which pertinent elements in Chol culture are used to point toward the gospel, or are selected for the way in which they highlight the gospel to the Chol mind. At the same time they avoid the kind of mixture which points essentially toward paganism rather than toward Christ.*

IN his recent book *Christo-Paganism*, William Madsen gives evidence that the present beliefs of the Aztecs living in San Francisco Tecospa are a result of a syncretistic process which began long before the introduction of Catholicism.[1] Morris Siegel, in his article "Cultural Changes in San Miguel Acatán, Guatemala," says that the religion of the Indians of San Miguel Acatán is a fusion of Indian and Catholic beliefs and practices, which does not resemble the Catholic religion in its orthodox form.[2]

William Reyburn introduces his article "The Spiritual, the Material, and the Western Reaction in Africa"[3] with an account of the death of a baby which was told to him by an African Christian. Apparently this man's beliefs concerning health, sickness, and death still admit elements of paganism.

Juan Comas, an outstanding Mexican anthropologist, in a conference held last year in Peru, made the following observation: "Practically the same thing has happened [in Peru] as with Motolinía and the Franciscan friars who arrived in Mexico in the early years of the conquest. They baptized about five thousand at one time. Theoretically these are Catholics. Actually, however, they practice their Indian religion simultaneously with

1 See William Madsen, *Christo-Paganism: A Study of Mexican Religious Syncretism* (New Orleans: Middle American Research Institute, 1957; preprinted from Publication 19, pp. 105-180), and William L. Wonderly's review article "Pagan and Christian Concepts in a Mexican Indian Culture" (PRACTICAL ANTHROPOLOGY, Vol. 5, Nos. 5 & 6, Sept.-Dec. 1958).

2 *Phylon, The Atlanta University Review of Race and Culture*, Vol. 15, No. 2 (1954), pp. 165-176.

3 PRACTICAL ANTHROPOLOGY, Vol. 6, No. 2 (March-April 1959).

Catholicism. This syncretism means that there is a religious factor and primitive superstitions that have not been eliminated."[4]

Missionaries also give wide testimony to the fact that certain concepts or practices of paganism persist for years among their converts and often are found in second and third generation Christians. These concepts become an integral part of their new religion. What can be done by the missionary to avoid unwarranted degrees of this type of syncretism? What can legitimately be done to at least attempt to reorient these cultural beliefs? What can be done to encourage suitable substitutions which are introduced by a new group of converts?

Since there are many factors which enter into possible answers to these questions, the author, who has had no formal study of anthropology, does not intend to answer these questions even as they relate to the Chols among whom he has worked as a missionary-translator for ten years. Selected field experiences are presented in which a certain recurring pattern may be seen. This may suggest an approach or methodology which may be helpful to others. It is not presumed that this is the complete answer to avoiding unwarranted religious syncretism, but merely a method of communicating religious concepts in such a way as to direct or guide the process of change by which pagan belief is reoriented in terms of Christianity. Many predisposing factors in the culture in general or in the experience of the individual are not dealt with in this paper.

In the first years of his work, among the Chols, the missionary often accom-

**John Beekman is a member of the Wycliffe Bible Translators, working among the Chol Indians of Chiapas, Mexico, and one of the translators of the Chol New Testament. He is also Director of the work of this organization in Guatemala.** **The present is the first of two articles which expand and further develop some of the concepts introduced by the same author in "A Culturally Relevant Witness" which appeared in PRACTICAL ANTHROPOLOGY, Vol. 4, No. 3 (May-June 1957).**

---

panied some of the converts in evangelistic trips and noted some of the oft-recurring objections which were raised to the gospel. After there were readers, classes were conducted in the study of the printed portions of the New Testament for groups from different villages. As many as seven different groups were taught independently in the course of each month. Opportunity was given to them to tell of their experiences in witnessing and in strengthening new converts. The problems which had been both seen by the missionary and reported by the Indians were presented to each group who came for Bible study. The discussion was guided for the most part with pertinent questions in the same manner in which the missionary conducted the Bible study classes.[5] Sometimes a conclusion reached by one group would be different from that reached by another. Sometimes that which had been studied from the Old Testament Bible stories or New Testament portions was presented in the course of a discussion as pertinent to a problem.

[4] Unpublished paper, presented August 20. 1958.

[5] One visiting missionary after observing the classes made a criticism which later was reported to the writer: "Anybody could do what he does. All he does is sit there letting the Indians explain the passage. He asks questions but doesn't stand up and lecture."

The author recalls a discussion concerning the problem of young girls who were given in common marriage and after a few weeks or more returned to their homes. While the usual reason given was that the fellow and girl did not like each other, it was suspected that the real reason was that the girl did not work hard enough to please the mother-in-law. The missionary, therefore, suggested that perhaps the girl could live at the home of the groom's parents during the day and return to her own home in the evenings. The marriage state would then begin when the girl's father was asked permission to have his daughter live at the boy's home. This suggestion was not accepted. Rather the Chol Christians insisted that in God's sight a couple entered the marriage state as soon as the promised girl began to live at the fellow's home. A recent tendency has been observed of solving the problem by building a separate house for the new couple. This house is built by the groom's father, usually very close to his own. In view of this procedure, it seems fair to say that the Indians themselves arrived at the conclusions as to how to cope with this problem. On the other hand, without the presence of the missionary to note the problems and to focus the attention of the Indians on them, it is doubtful that some of the solutions presented in this paper would have been discovered. In any case, whether the idea originated primarily with the missionary or with an Indian, they were at complete liberty to try it or to ignore it.

The first example which we shall give of actual syncretism among the Chols exists among those who call themselves Catholics. Except for new forms and symbols introduced among the Chols, their beliefs remain basically pagan. For the lack of a better name reference will be made to this group with the phrase, 'followers of the traditional religion.' Those who have been converted from this group to the evangelical faith will be referred to as the 'converts.'

**Problems of Syncretism in Easter Observances**

The ancient Chols had a feast at corn-planting time which, in part at least, has survived to the present time. Its form may be somewhat modified, but its purpose has probably undergone no change. The Roman Catholic priests apparently tried to substitute the Easter celebration for this, since both occurred at about the same time of year. An image of Christ on the cross was used, and today the Chols follow the practice of covering the image with a black cloth during Holy Week and of removing it on Easter morning to indicate the resurrection. The Chols have accepted this ritual, reinterpreting its significance in the light of their own corn-planting ceremony. With some variations from village to village, the following summary indicates how these new items are reconciled to their purposes. The 'god' is covered so that he will think it is dark and cloudy and remember to send sunshine to dry out the recently felled trees and underbrush so that the fields can be burned. When the cloth is removed, it is to show him the blazing sun in order that he will send rain for the newly planted corn. During this season sacrifices are made in the corners of the fields which have been cut for planting. Fasting is also practiced. The only item which one may drink in any measure is liquor. To encourage the fast the religious leaders explain to the people that eggs eaten at this time are vultures' eggs, black beans are flies, the corn drink is pus, tortillas are dung.

For the converts, on the other hand, the Easter celebrations have become extended love feasts with services from Thursday evening through Sunday; though some villagers attend to their work on Saturday. At these feasts one or two steers are often purchased and cooked in front of the chapel by the women, or each family provides chickens, beans, or other food items much as in American pot-luck suppers except that the food is not brought fully prepared. At first the services included prayers for the crops, but more recently they center almost exclusively around the events of the life of Christ which happened on these days as recorded in Scripture.

This latter development may be due to two causes. The availability of materials relating to the death and resurrection of Christ, along with men who can read and explain these in the services, has contributed to this trend. The second cause originated with the feeling on the part of one or two of the missionaries that such fiestas were an economic burden to the Indians and not a proper observance of Easter. A Mexican worker in his visits to the Chol villages, therefore, discouraged these fiestas which had become a symbol of their very purpose. A feeling of guilt still persists in the minds of some, and as a result communal gatherings of this type in some villages are not as fully attended as before. In view of this some meet this need by holding a family feast, usually of turkey, for the purpose of praying for good crops and protection from falling trees, machete cuts, and snake bites.

These converts had had their beliefs concerning the 'world owner' and the elements of nature reoriented to the beliefs of Christianity. If this had not been so, this prohibition might have resulted in a combination of Christian ideas and the old ceremony with the sacrifices made in the fields. Syncretism could have been produced rather than prevented.

### Abortive Attempts at Syncretism

Among the converts in the village of Tumbalá were those who could read and understand some Spanish. In their reading of the Old Testament and from messages which they heard from Spanish-speaking pastors they became acquainted with the sacrifice of animals as a symbol of the sacrifice of Jesus. They also read that the Israelites were to eat no pork. Their own cultural background reminded them of the importance of animal sacrifices and the central use of blood in the witchcraft ceremonies. These fellows became the proponents of the teaching that the blood of pigs is the blood of our Holy Father. It should not be eaten. Therefore when a pig is killed its blood must be caught in a gourd and ceremonially buried behind the house. This practice was short-lived.

Here is another example of what could have become a peculiar characteristic of Christianity among the Chols. A shaman who continued loyal to the traditional religion attempted to synthesize his ceremony with some of the items connected with Christianity. In a village where more than half of the families had become converts, this enterprising shaman suggested some substitutions in his ceremonies. A shelf was set up, decorated with flowers and satin, on which a Bible was placed. His chants were then directed to the God of the Book and to the land-owning spirit. The convert was permitted to substitute liquor with a soft drink, but was required to provide liquor for the shaman. In questioning some of these believers it became obvious that the reason for the substitutions was very hazy in their thinking. Others felt it removed what God hated in the shaman ceremony, but did not affect its usefulness in regaining health. All still felt that health would be restored when the land-owning spirit had been effectively contacted on their behalf. Even though some items and terms of the Christian faith had been used, the basic pagan idea was unchanged.

Why did these converts accept the modified services of the shaman? Christianity at this point in their experience had been related to only a small part of their basic religious needs. They knew what it meant to be reconciled to the living God, but beyond that Christianity did not yet seem to have any real relevance. Their beliefs as to the cause and cure of sickness had not been changed. The modified ceremony did not seem to them to endanger or overlook the area of their Christian experience and conviction. While some opposed this syncretism, they were unable to explain their stand or to adequately answer the claims of the shaman. When the cultural beliefs concerning sickness were explained in terms of related Christian truths, the shaman received no further calls from the converts.

Up to this point our illustrations refer to actual or aborted attempts at religious syncretism. The following illustrations refer to potential areas of syncretism. This is based on the premise that wherever a group of converts accepts a new idea or practice without a proper understanding of its full significance or meaning, resistance to the new by the followers of the traditional religion tends to result in syncretism. To be sure, other factors limit or provoke this tendency. Some success has been observed among the Chol Indians in eliminating potential areas of syncretism by reorienting cultural beliefs. Five examples follow.

### Reorienting Beliefs concerning Shamanism

The shaman with his chants, guitar, violin, and sacrifices to the land-owning spirit is a real temptation to the evangelical convert and fills a very important role for the followers of the traditional religion. In fact, one of the first questions asked by those who are approached with the gospel is what one does in times of sickness. The chants and music are believed necessary to bring the shaman into communion with the land-owning spirit. This they believe is effective only because he is indwelt with seven extra spirits. Others using these same means would not be able to communicate because of spiritual impotence. The animal sacrifice is the basis of success for his plea on behalf of the sick individual. The land-owning spirit desires other spirits and at times imprisons the spirit of a person which he releases in exchange for an animal spirit. The spirit which is acceptable to him is revealed to the shaman usually in audible communications. Often a shaman is accused of having failed to contact the land-owning spirit if a person does not recover after the prescribed sacrifice has been made. Among at least some of the Chol converts the idea that a spirit being could be contacted through music and by addressing him was not refuted; nor the idea that one must be indwelt with a spirit or spirits in order to commune with spirit beings. At the same time, the belief that a sacrifice was necessary in order to receive any benefits from a spirit being was not only considered worth retaining but worth emphasizing. One can see that many of these pagan practices are motivated with ideas that are in at least some measure compatible with Christianity. These beliefs which parallel Christian truth to be sure will need reorientation, but once they are recognized they become an important point of contact for teaching which should be exploited. The compatible ideas are extracted from the details and given emphasis. Then on this hook of mutual belief are hung the fuller truths of Christianity. One convert in speaking to a follower of the traditional religion during a measles epidemic said in part, "You call us 'monkeys' because you think our singing is like their chatter. We want help from God. You do too. You go to the old men to have them recite for you and to the shaman to have him chant. We pray and sing in our homes and in church. Our children get better; yours die."

Hymns, gospel phonograph records, and prayers are explained as the true means of contacting God. The church leaders who have been entrusted with the phonographs also know the hymns and can pray and read from portions of the New Testament. They were the logical ones to be called upon to minister to the sick instead of the shaman. The teaching that by faith in God's Son God gives us his Spirit to live in our hearts was not difficult for them to accept for it was a reorientation and extension of their belief that the snaman is indwelt. The sacrifice of God's Son (who committed his spirit into God's hands not because he was afraid that the land-owning spirit would imprison it, but to show that God was well pleased with the sacrifice of his Son) could be accepted as a sufficient and better sacrifice, making the sacrifice of animals no longer necessary. In some cases it was necessary to point out that the Old Testament sacrifice of animals and the sacrifice of Christ were not to a spirit-hungry God. The first was a picture of and the latter the actual payment for our sins, so that with nothing written against us God could hear us. Payment for sin as a basis for reconciliation and fellowship was easily understood in view of their experience with ranchers to whom they frequently were heavily indebted.

### Concepts of Sin

The subject of sin is so close a corollary to the sacrifice of God's Son and so closely related to the belief in the land-owning spirit and the shaman, that one is never dealt with without the others. It seems pertinent, therefore, to make the following observations.

Making extractions from stories and comments about sin, we can begin with those ideas which correspond to Christianity. Thus we would say that sin is an offense to a spirit-being or to one's fellow man. To the followers of the traditional religion, nothing is sin unless it involves offense. Drunkenness is therefore not a sin unless it ends with a fight. Theft is not sin unless the owner 'hurts in his heart' over what has been stolen and consults the shaman to find out who stole his goods. Converts lost much of their corn through theft perhaps because it was known that they no longer consulted the shaman. Unless the thief was caught, he was quite certain that even though offense had been caused, the convert had no way of avenging himself. (However, since the converts attended services and never worked in their fields on Sunday, and since most of these thefts occurred on Sunday, this may be the major reason for these thefts.) To the follower of the traditional religion, the physical condition of his family is one of the main factors in determining whether he is guilty of offense. If he offends the land-owning spirit, sickness will fall. If he offends his fellow-man, sickness may fall if a spell of black magic is cast on him or a member of his family through the services of the shaman. Health, then, although never explicitly stated as such, is a measure of one's spiritual relation to others and to the land-owning spirit. (The term 'God' as used by the followers of the traditional religion includes the concept of the land-owning spirit, although there is a separate term used to specifically refer to the latter.)

Converts often made the statement to the followers of the traditional religion that Christ died for their sins and they should believe on him. Invariably the answer received to such a statement was: "I don't have any sin." This was a sincere answer although the author was unable to explain it in his early years among the Chols. The Indian did not mean that he had never lied, stolen, or beaten his wife. He meant that since he and his family were well, there was no unappeased offense in his life. The convert, therefore, developed another set of criteria on which to base his relationship with God. Instead of arguing that he was a sinner and God's Word said so, he pointed to the greater well-being of the converts in general. He compared his shirt and trousers to those worn by the individual to whom he was talking. He compared his shoes to the other's bare feet. He spoke of eating crackers with the family instead of losing money, hat, and machete in drunkenness. He spoke of owning mules and tin-roofed houses instead of carrying firewood on his back and patching up a grass roof. His argument implied that health is not the only criterion of one's relationship to God, and it has been a very effective answer in winning converts. It should be noted that medical work among the Chols is a very effective means of gaining converts. When the followers of the traditional religion come for medicine, it usually indicates that they have tired of the unavailing services of the shaman. They come with a subconscious feeling that all is not right because of sickness in the family. They are ready to listen to culturally related spiritual truths.

### House-Dedication Practices

When a new hut is constructed the shaman is generally called upon to dedicate it to the land-owning spirit whose property (trees, grass, land) has been used in its construction. In his chants he requests protection from fire, the wind, thieves, and spirit manifestations. The drumming and violin-playing and drinking of liquor lasts from one to three days. The converts, however, dedicate their new homes by inviting the church leaders and friends to an evening of refreshments consisting of cookies and soft drinks. Prayer for the occupants of the new home and for the protection of the house, along with singing, characterizes the evening's activities.

The desire for protection from the forces of nature and from thieves is legitimate for any people. The purpose of the shaman's ceremony has been carried over into that which was substituted by the converts. Its focal center, however, has been shifted from the land-owning spirit to a more powerful spirit, i.e. the Holy Spirit. Instead of being based on appeasing the land-owning spirit through the medium of the shaman with his extra spirits, it became based on the indwelling Spirit through whom one had guidance and protection from God. The fact that rattling gourds, whistlings in the grass roofs, dirt throwings, etc. were reported as no longer occurring at the homes of converts was convincing evidence of the power of the Holy Spirit.

## Use of Liquor

It is interesting to note the efforts made by one of the leaders of the convert group in the Tumbalá church to undermine the religious significance attached to the use of liquor. All the shaman's activities as well as all religious observances require the use of liquor, which the followers of the traditional religion believe to be of divine origin. The old men feel it is necessary in their prayers in order to 'get warm in reciting.' The shaman declares that he cannot offer his chants without liquor. Often when speaking to the cross he may order that 'the bottom of the gourd be poured on the cross' in order to cause the Father to be more communicative and less angry. Week-end drunkenness, apart from religious fiestas, has been a long-standing problem in Spanish-speaking cities. In the Indian village drunkenness is almost exclusively related to religious functions. In appealing to his fellow-converts to desist from all use of liquor, the above-mentioned leader made reference to Proverbs 20: 1, 2, which reads, "Strong drink is raging.... The fear of a king is as of the roaring of a lion," and also Luke 13: 1 which speaks of the Galileans whose blood Pilate had mingled with their sacrifices. These verses became the text for a Sunday sermon. The Indian preacher declared that liquor, which causes us to become ferocious like a lion, originated when the blood of people from Galilee was mixed with the blood of a raging lion. While this fellow's intentions were good and the impressions of his message vivid, his understanding of these verses was quite defective.

A more biblical way was found to meet the objection often raised that liquor is necessary for religious expression. Those who raised such objections were told that it is true that some outside stimulant is necessary to man in order to free his inhibitions. It is impossible to pray right without this, and the true God wants us to have it. Then the teaching of Acts 2, where the Pentecostal experience is clearly explained to be the result of the Spirit rather than liquor, is made relevant here. Again it may be seen that the purpose in the use of liquor, i.e. that an outside stimulant or constraining power is necessary in order to worship God properly, is retained but reoriented. It becomes based on the Spirit rather than on liquor. Thus the religious use of liquor with its accompanying drunkenness is no problem among the converts and can no longer be considered an area of potential syncretism.[6]

[6] Would this approach to the emotional experiences connected with the ritual use of mushrooms, as described by Pike and Cowan

### Images

When the converts were asked why their church building contained no images, which the followers of the traditional religion call 'God's image,' the first answer used was the conventional one. The theological reply was given by the convert: "God is a Spirit and we cannot see him; however, he is present in our churches." This answer, however, did not seem to entirely satisfy the inquiring follower of the traditional religion. The statement was often made in ridicule: "All your churches have is a phonograph machine on a table. The saloons in Yajalón have the same." The underlying assumption was that a church, to be more than just a building, had to have in it something visible. To be a place of real worship and not just a place of play, it should contain something sacred, something like God. This assumption was not refuted. It was reoriented by showing that the church building does have in it those whom God himself has declared to be in his own image. The answer now given has been more or less along the following lines: "God's book tells us that he made *man* in his own image. The more we obey his commands the more fully do *we* become his image. What you call '*God's* image' is something made by man. God tells us what really is his image. It is something *he* made, not what we make. It is ourselves, not a wooden idol. He gives his Spirit to all his children. Nowhere does he say that something which *we* make has spirit power. Our churches are full of God's images when a service is held."

in PRACTICAL ANTHROPOLOGY, Vol. 6, No. 4 (July-August 1959), be a fruitful way of showing that the Christian message has an adequate substitute for these chemically-induced 'revelations'? [W.L.W.].

### Candles

The followers of the traditional religion use candles in all religious functions. Prayers conducted in the Catholic church by the older men and women as those conducted by the shaman are accompanied with the burning of candles. The total disappearance of candles in the religious life of the converts has often become a point of ridicule. "You must have candles and sometimes even incense in order to make real prayers" was the answer normally given by the followers of the traditional religion as to why candles were used. A few reports filtered back to the missionary that some converts resorted to the use of candles in times of critical illness and in funeral wakes. It finally became clear that the use of candles was motivated by the idea that light made one's prayers acceptable. The converts now have an answer to queries as to why they do not use candles. They explain that God likes light and all that it represents. He wants us to have a light when we pray to him, but not a small flickering light made by man. He wants to see a great light which he himself sent down from heaven to shine in our hearts. Jesus said that he himself was the light of the world. This is the light God wants to see in our hearts. Here again is an illustration of reorienting a religious motif after one understands its purpose. Whatever in this purpose is compatible with the gospel becomes an equally acceptable starting point to both parties before proceeding to the new and fuller truth or practices of Christianity.

Perhaps all that should be claimed from the foregoing discussion as a method of avoiding religious syncretism is that it has given converts an intelligent understanding of what their new faith embraces and why they desist from certain practices and have adopted substitutes for others. It has removed what would otherwise be temptations into which they would frequently fall. For at least some of the honest inquirers, this approach has contributed much toward removing their fears and doubts concerning the way of the gospel.

Reprinted from Vol. 5, No. 5
(1958), pp. 234-236.

*William A. Smalley*

# The World Is Too Much With Us

ALICJA IWANSKA, a Polish anthropologist, in describing her observations upon an American farming community, made some generalizations which struck me as extremely pertinent as a summary of American value systems.[1] She said that for the farmers on the large Western farms which she had studied the universe was divided up into three different categories. She labeled the first category *landscape*. It included the distant mountains, the trees, the scenery, the environment of the farmers in so far as this environment was not manipulated by them. They looked at it, they enjoyed it in a disinterested sort of way. It had no high emotional content for them.

The second category of life she labeled *machinery*. To these farmers machinery was an important part of their lives. They polished their machines, they cared for them. The machines had high value to them and they rated their machines in terms of their productivity in their farming life. The livestock belonged to this machinery class of the universe. It was important according to its productivity. It was cared for and kept with much the same earnestness and much the same eye to profits that the machinery had. Real affection and interest, and a great deal of value, was placed upon the machinery category.

Finally, the third category was that which she labeled *people*. People were neighbors, individuals who came in for a cup of coffee, folks who cooperated in times of need or emergency. People were human beings with whom one grew up and lived and died, and with whom one had constant relationships on the social and business level.

## Human Beings but not People

The fascinating significance of all this, however, was that not all human beings were people. The Indians, for example, belonged to the landscape class. They were part of the scenery. On a Sunday afternoon one took a drive out to the reservation to look idly and curiously at the Indian communities as one drove by. Mexican migrant workers were machinery. Their value lay in their productivity. Their help was important to the same degree that the help of a cow or the functioning of a fuel pump was important. When their productivity was lessened they would be discarded in much the same way as an old car would be.

Human beings who were people were different in that they had value in and of themselves regardless of their productivity.

[1] Her paper, entitled "Some American Values," was read at the annual meeting of the American Anthropological Association in Chicago, 1957.

As I listened to her talk, I could see myself in her characterization. There have been many times when I have sensed the temptation to look on certain groups of human beings as scenery, as part of a landscape. Once, on a mission station where I was working for several months on an important language project, there were people of a colorful tribal group who passed my door daily. I found myself idly interested in them as anthropological curiosities, as part of the passing scene. Now as I visit from country to country, this temptation is always there.

The temptation to look on human beings as scenery finds one kind of expression in our romanticization of the mission field. It is reflected in the kinds of form letters which we write home to tell about color and glamor on the field — color and glamor of a *National Geographic Magazine* sort but without any real humanity in it.

And how utterly characteristic is the tendency to look on human beings as machinery! We value the preachers in the local church on the basis of the "production" of their weekly quota of sermons and pastoral calls or their converts. It is not that we do not love our machines. We like to take care of them, to keep them in good health; we like to keep them in their proper place, however, like the well-loved dog which is a member of the family so long as it sleeps on the floor. We like to have such human beings come and visit us so long as they keep their place and do not usurp the prerogatives of people, and really expect us to treat them like people.

### The Need for Change

If we are going to deal with people as people in a culture that is vastly different from our own, we have to come to the fundamental realization that people are different from society to society, and to do this *we* are going to have to make the major move to change. If we are going to be persons among people, our privacy, our established patterns of what is convenient and comfortable are going to have to be drastically modified. Our sense of belonging to ourselves will have to be filed away and we will have to develop a sense of belonging to others, which characterizes so many societies in the world.

This sort of experience involves a tremendous emotional drain. It is an extremely difficult attitude to take and position to follow. It means "becoming all things to all men so that by all means we might win some" in the deepest sense, and it means a type of cultural suicide which Paul characterizes as being "crucified with Christ." On the American scene the problem is just as great. It means to count as people, and not simply as machinery, the Negro groups in our communities, so that they enter into the life of people, as people, in our church groups, in our schools, and in our neighborhoods. This requires a transformation of a major sort for the American system of values.

The deep-seated, ingrown values which have been characterized here cannot easily be peeled off. Rather, a change involves an internal restructuring. It involves being remade inside. Jesus called it being reborn. It implies an intellectual and emotional conversion on our part to the point where we can become neighbors with all human beings everywhere.

In all of the discussion about what "worldliness" means in a Biblical sense and all of the examples of various kinds of behavior which have been classified as worldly by one group or another, I think that often has been neglected the very basic fact that the spirit of this world is not easy to identify nor is it easy to shake off. Certainly it lies in the attitude and predispositions of our day more than in any particular thing we do. I believe that an important ingredient in the spirit of the American world is that we so often do not really consider human beings to be people.

*William A. Smalley*

**Reprinted from Vol. 6, No. 4 (1959), pp. 186-189.**

# The World Is Too Much with Us—II

It seems clear that culture patterns have a strong effect on the response which people make to the preaching of the gospel, and on the effect which any conversion to Christ has in the church or in the society as a whole. That Arabs are harder to win than Vietnamese is an obvious kind of illustration, and that a church in central Africa takes on a different ethos or "flavor" from a church in southeast Asia is another.

It is also clear, I think, that Christ's requirements of total commitment are at variance, in differing amounts and in different ways, with all cultures. In saying this I mean *all* cultures, including the religious culture (the approved behavior, the ecclesiastical system) of my denomination and every other denomination or independent church. Such denominational or church groups are individual subcultures within the larger subculture of Western (and world) Christianity. Even our churches stand in the way of that relationship to God for which we were created.

Evidence of this last point can be seen in the fact that occasionally a group which has been only recently evangelized shows a response and a degree of personal loyalty to God that is rare in our own churches. To take a very specific example, the Meo culture of northern Laos seems in some areas to stand less in the way of such a relationship than does the church I attend in White Plains, New York. This is true in spite of a pagan Meo religious system which is replete with an enormous number of spirit beings who are placated, bribed, or appeased, as the situation may warrant. These spirits, beneficial or not, are equated with "demons" by the Christians and by many of their missionary teachers.

This Meo movement in the Xieng Khouang area of northern Laos has been reported in PRACTICAL ANTHROPOLOGY.[1] It is characterized by a rapid turning to Christ on the part of several thousand people, and an intense loyalty and dedication on the part of many. It is the intensity of this faith, the strength of this loyalty, which I am now contrasting with the American groups with which I am familiar.

There is a severe danger of oversimplification here. At least one other major factor enters into the picture, and that is the activity of the Holy Spirit as God works in history and in culture. I think, however, that in spite of this all-important other factor we are justified in making some generalizations on the basis of culture differences.

### Some American Characteristics

If we grant that the Meo are in some ways culturally more "ready" for the

[1] G. Linwood Barney, "The Meo — An Incipient Church," PRACTICAL ANTHROPOLOGY, Vol. 4, No. 2 (Mar.-Apr. 1957), pp. 31-50, and in this volume.

gospel than Americans, and even American Christians, what are the peculiar *American* cultural barriers to a man's relationship to Christ? Some of these will be true of other groups as well, and some will not. Some of the cultural barriers which the Meo will have will not be true of us.

The effect of "secularism" and a mechanistic outlook on life have been cited so often as to need no discussion here. The American characteristic of looking at certain classes of people as "landscape" or "machinery," rather than as "neighbors" and fellow human beings, belongs here too.[2] The tendency to substitute theology or dogma for experiential religion is another of our temptations.

The complexity and sophistication of our life is another very strong deterrent in keeping us from Christ. Our culture shows an amazing genius for organizing our lives into ever more complicated institutions. Even the simplest of our churches are no exception unless they have reached the point of disintegration where there is no life left. Our typical response to a church problem, or to an individual need, is to organize another church group. In a typical busy American church today, if we do not participate actively in many branches of this enormous program this is a sign that we do not love God. If we do participate fully, and at the same time fulfill our obligations to the equally complex business, civic, and social life we must lead to be responsible Americans today, it is impossible to love God as we should.

[2] William A. Smalley, "The World is Too Much With Us," Practical Anthropology, Vol. 5, Nos. 5 & 6 (Sept.-Dec. 1958), pp. 234-236, and in this volume.

## The Dilemma of the Christian in Culture

At one point or another, in every culture, the sensitive Christian is brought up against the inescapable dilemma created by the conflict between culture patterns and his own relationship to God. An Abraham leaves the civilization of Ur to follow God's call into a wandering existence, a promised land, a new understanding of God, and a new course for history. An Amos burns with indignation as he sees the rich crushing the poor, the merchant with the double standards of measure, the indolence of the leisured class (cows of Bashan), and he pronounces in lyric poetry the wrath of God and the destruction of the country at the hand of its enemies. A Martha is busy getting the house and meal ready for her Lord, while a Mary sits and listens at His feet.

The dilemma of the Christian in culture is that he cannot really escape his culture, but he must transcend it, in some measure at least. The pilgrim (or missionary) who like Abraham leaves his city and his culture behind him does not really do so. He carries most of it with him. His habits of life and thought, his social relationships, his sense of values, his language, his mechanical skills, these all come along. But an Abraham is different from the people he left behind, different from the very fact that he left them behind, different from the changes necessitated by the new circumstances of his existence, different by a new developing understanding of God.

Like all prophets, an Amos is also a part of his culture and is limited by its confines — but not completely limited, because the function of the prophet is precisely one of seeing beyond the horizon his culture poses, even though it be only a little. Whether he is a prophet of God or a man with unusual vision for his time and place, he is sometimes able to speak to his culture in such a way that it listens and is changed.

In some of the stages of the history of Christianity there have been Marys who have felt that they could renounce their culture to live a contemplative life. But this, too, is at least partially an illusion. It is true that the hermit and the monk are shielded from selected details of life around them, but there is always the rest of a man's life, his background, his thoughts, his presuppositions. He carries them to the monastery or the hermit's cave. They, too, are of this world's culture.

## Relation of the Christian to His Culture

What can it possibly mean to be "in the world, but not of it"? How can the Christian possibly be part of his culture and yet transcend it? There are at least two dimensions here. One is the dimension of personal ability, insight, "prophetic vision," which can be seen sometimes in non-Christians and is often not seen in Christians. In other words, there are people who by their own abilities step slightly outside the limits of their world. Some of them are Christians, though it is not this insight which makes them so.

The other dimension, one which is profoundly Christian, stems from that supercultural relationship to God which we call faith. Everyone who has that relationship to God which the New Testament speaks of in such vivid language: being brought back (redemption), making friends again (reconciliation), being rescued (salvation), has also transcended his culture. The supercultural fact of God in history, in individual life, is what really makes a Christian "not of this world."

Christians are quick to select elements of behavior from culture around them and to label these as "non-Christian" or "sinful" (like dancing or racial segregation, depending on the American denomination they belong to). In so doing they forget that the real grip of a culture lies in habits, values, and viewpoints which are not so well defined. The very complexity of our life is a case in point. It is not going to do us any good to pass denominational resolutions calling for a simpler American society. We could simplify our denominational and church structures, but I doubt that it would work. We know of no other way to operate in our complex world. The monastic escapism has been shown by history to be a false way out. It seems to me that in this tightening web of organizational activism our only hope of being in this world but not of it is to develop that independence of judgment and spiritual perception which makes it possible for us to refuse to participate when participation is required beyond the point of emotional health and spiritual wisdom.

Refusal to participate, of course, can be an escape, a way out. I am thinking of it here, however, as a creative step, a question of priorities, to make ultimately more worth-while activity possible, to foster intellectual and spiritual growth.

Frequent, and even occasional, refusal to participate in a prolifera of church activities, in a denominational survey, in a mission meeting, in an evangelistic campaign, as well as in selected secular activities ranging from PTA to a collection for the March of Dimes, will certainly be criticized in a culture which places its greatest values on prompt reports, committee attendance, and adding wheels within wheels. But in this day and age, if Martha is to sit at the feet of Jesus, even the dishes may occasionally have to stay dirty.

# The Missionary in an Alien Culture

*William A. Smalley*

# Respect and Ethnocentrism

A MISSIONARY once remarked to me that the reason why his mission had an unusually splendid record for competence in the use of the language of their area of work was that they had a high degree of respect for the local culture. I think it would be possible to point to many cases where respect for local culture correlates with language competence. It would be possible certainly to point to many cases where strong disrespect for local culture correlates with abysmal language use. It may be coincidence, but the one country of the world where, in my experience, the people are most criticized by missionaries serving there is also the country which seems to have the lowest level of missionary language ability.

Our missionary's remark deserves thoughtful consideration. But if we do begin to think about it and to cite cases, we are immediately confronted with the problem of what we mean by "respect." I walked into a church of the same mission. Except for the use of the local language in the singing, preaching, and Scripture reading, what evidences of respect for local culture were there? I found none whatsoever. I did not know the language and could not understand the sermon, but the implication of the form of service was that there was nothing in the local culture worthy of its incorporation in a Christian service.

I talked with some members of the mission concerning dialects of the national language. These dialects were spoken by large percentages of the population of the country, but not by upper-class and educated people. Some missionaries showed respect for these speech differences. Others did not and felt that any use of them in the program of evangelization was a waste of time.

In contrast with this there were missionaries of other missions who concentrated on the use of the "substandard" dialects, showing a much higher degree of respect for them as media of communication with the masses of people. And whereas the first mission often showed a laudable respect for the virtues in the theological system of the religion of the country, the second group paid it little attention but showed high respect for the individual common man and his needs.

By saying this, I do not mean to imply that these attitudes are mutually exclusive in any individual or in any mission group. But they are obvious emphases, patterns of work and attitude, which reflect important differences in the values of the missionary.

Not only do we see such contrasts between missions in the same area, but we see them between the missionary traditions in various areas. Missionaries in Southeast Asia tend to learn their local languages well, while the missionaries in West Africa tend not to. On the other hand, missionaries in Africa tend to have

**Reprinted from Vol. 5, No. 4 (1958), pp. 191-194.**

greater respect for and use of dialect differences than do missionaries in China.

## The Self-centered View of Culture

Ethnocentrism is the term used by anthropologists to represent that point of view which we all have to varying degrees, that our own culture, our own way of doing things, is best. It may lead us to assume that our own way is the only right way. It ranges from the repugnance my wife and I felt when our Khmu houseboy ate a rat we caught in a trap to the uncontrollable laughter that struck a Khmu friend when my wife cried because our pet dog died. I heard ethnocentrism in a prayer recently, when a pastor thanked God that we were privileged to live in a culture so well suited to a Christian way of life. Every missionary, no matter how keenly developed his Christology, finds some of his motivation in his ethnocentrism, and it is a major motivation in our present ideological struggle with Russia.

What we select to be ethnocentric about may vary from person to person. It certainly varies from culture to culture. It undoubtedly is somewhat different from mission to mission. I asked a missionary in Africa once if chewing Kola nut was a sin, and she replied with a twinkle in her eye that that depended on the mission station. This should not be read to imply that Christians should not make value judgments. Every human being does make them, whether he wants to or not, and every Christian is morally obligated to do so. The problem lies in the unthinking ethnocentricity of those judgments. It lies also in our imposition of our judgments on other people.

## Ethnocentrism of "Respect"

A proper basis for value judgments is not the subject of this editorial, however, it is simply that we recognize the ethnocentricity of even our "respect" for other peoples. We tend to respect what we like or lean to like. If we come from a background of advanced education, of emphasis on "correctness" in our language, and on good breeding in our conduct, we tend to respect the high language and upper-class characteristics of another civilization. If we come from a lower stratum of American society, we tend to be more at home with more humble folk in a foreign culture. If we have been trained to a point of view which sees language primarily as an art, we tend to shun the less artistic, less literary forms of the language which we learn in another culture. If we see language primarily as a medium of communication, however, we want to shift our language medium according to our audience. If liturgy and art are important to us, liturgy and art we single out to enjoy in another country. If we prefer the relaxed informality of ordinary individuals, we seek them out.

Certain things which we can select to be ethnocentric about are much more detrimental to the church than others, of course. Linguistic ethnocentrism is disastrous, but so is the ethnocentrism of Methodist or Lutheran or Presbyterian or Pentecostal ritual. And so also can be the forms of education and medicine and agriculture which we employ.

Full cultural objectivity is impossible, but an awareness of the vagaries of our selective ethnocentrism is very helpful. One of the most wholesomely "respectful" of missionaries whom I ever met was a man who worked himself from dawn until bedtime with a discipline and application that very few Americans can match. He confessed that one thing he could never get used to was the African's idea of a day's work. Contrast this reluctant admission which acknowledged an awareness of ethnocentrism with the attitude of another missionary whose every conversation is punctuated with complaints of the "laziness" of people around him.

Without respect, without clear-eyed love, that identification which is essential for the missionary will never be achieved. But before we fall into the temptation of congratulating ourselves on the features which we have selected from the culture to respect, let us take stock of our attitude toward other things as well. Does our work really reflect respect for people of all classes, for the various subcultures of the community, for the church? Do we respect the church by "allowing" it to run "independently" *the way we taught it to run;* or do we respect it by watching it work out its own new society within the matrix of its daily life?

Ethnocentrism will always be with us. The value of an anthropological point of view, which sees customs and institutions in the light of the way they are worked out in many societies, is that it helps us to be aware of our ethnocentrism and to soften it. In a sense, the cross-cultural view which comes through the study of many peoples is an important aid in understanding the relationship between the cultural speck in our brother's eye as opposed to the log in our own.

*William D. Reyburn*

# The Missionary and the Evaluation of Culture

FEW problems facing the missionary are more subtle than those involved in the evaluation of cultural practices. Some missionaries, however, do not take more than a moment's reflection to pigeonhole as good, bad, or indifferent the customs of a group of people. The criterion for this judgment is usually the missionary's own *ideal* background (often not his *real* background). Customs and practices are normally labeled as good if they are agreeable to the "ideal" of Christian living as he understands it. This ideal is, of course, one which is of necessity limited by its own cultural and historical frontiers. In this orientation the good should be cultivated and developed. The bad must be snipped off like a thorny bush, and what is left passes without scrutiny as innocuous.

This threefold categorization of the aspects of a culture contains within itself certain assumptions which lead to unproductive action. It is often assumed that one can encourage the good to grow and thwart the bad. While this may be very true and is basically what all men do who strive for the good in life, it leads one to conceive of a cultural complex as a series of separate plants, each growing independently from its own roots. In reality, any way of life is based on a series of assumptions which are in some way interrelated so that they reinforce each other and cannot be dealt with as isolated phenomena. This does not mean that all are of equal value as seen by the individuals in the society, but they are interacting.

A further misconception which arises from this three-sided evaluation of a culture is that the category of the indifferent is somehow assumed to be static, while the good and the bad are treated as though they were dynamic. However, while one is encouraging the good and deploring the bad, the indifferent cannot so remain. This is so again because of the dynamic and changing nature of culture, which reacts to stimulus more like an organism than like independent cells.

## The Interrelatedness of Behavior

An intelligible view of culture is one which embraces the interrelatedness of a way of life within its evaluation. We may illustrate this briefly from the problem of polygyny. Polygyny in modern Africa has many facets which often compel the missionary to evaluate it with the judgment of bad, due to the economic self-interests which are displayed. (That these are as bad as American competitive self-interests within our modern industrial economic framework is hardly demonstrable.) However, if one wishes to acknowledge the good found in responsibility and devotion to others, this

**Reprinted from Vol. 4, No. 6 (1957), pp. 238-244.**

attribute will also be found within the levirate form of polygyny in which a man takes upon himself the familial care and obligation to deceased relatives with a fraternal devotion reflecting a high sense of responsibility. The "good" and the "bad" in this case are so interlocked as to defy separation.

This discouragement of polygyny as bad does not by any means imply that when polygyny is given up the deep sense of responsibility often found in it will come forth as a distilled bit of residue. This was demonstrated to me rather forcibly recently when I asked a group of Kaka Christian adults what they would do if their older non-Christian brothers were to die and leave them their wives. Their replies, without exception, shook off the very thought of responsibility. "We would sell the women and get the money for ourselves." This they would have the right to do within the culture they claim when it will bring them acceptable rewards. The moral responsibility partially required by the polygynous inheritance is refused for quick personal gain.

## Reinterpretation of Behavior

In addition to the fact of the enmeshing of the aspects of a way of life, there is always the possibility of reinterpreting a form of behavior to answer some new need. When Pentecostal Christianity came to the Toba Indians of the isolated Argentine Chaco, it brought about a popularization of religion. Before this time only the shaman was a spiritual man. When the tribe as a whole became spiritual, they reacted to it in much the same fashion as the individual shaman had formerly. Jumping and dancing became the vehicle of religious expression. This behaviorism which was the symbol of spirit contact used formerly by the shaman has now become fully sanctioned as evidence of the presence of the Holy Spirit in a tribe where the shaman no longer functions.

Some of the most complex issues facing Christian missions arise out of the reinterpretation and change which develops often within the category of the "indifferent." I shall attempt to demonstrate briefly how the dowry in the Cameroun has passed from the stage of indifference to a front-rank social problem as seen by nationals, administration, and missions.

The changes which have come about in the South Cameroun to reinterpret the meaning of bride wealth or dowry have not been concerned with the dowry itself, but with other social, religious, economic, and political aspects of life. The dowry, because of its integral relation to these, has been vastly affected and has in chainlike fashion produced sharp repercussions in these spheres of life.

## Traditional Function of the Dowry

Formerly (and to a certain extent in the villages today) the dowry was an arrangement between two clans in which a marriage union was held such that the groom's clan legalized their claim to the future offspring through payment in goods and animals to the clan of the bride. The extended families involved in the exchange were primarily affected, but decisions as important as bride wealth were the business of the clan elders. Among the Kaka, metal implements were exchanged in bride wealth, and each clan carefully manipulated marriages to gain for itself the desired offspring and a large stock of metal hoes, tools, spearheads, anvils, rings, etc. The word *soumba* in Kaka means 'iron,' 'wealth,' and 'bride price.' It is true to a certain extent that the interclan marriage arrangement through the dowry made divorce difficult, as the desertion of the wife from her dowry-paying husband required the refund of the dowry. That this guaranteed a happy marital status is hardly the case. However, a bride was reluctant to disobey her husband due to her respect for his dowry claim. In earlier times, the price of the dowry was not exorbitant, as exchanges were determined by the whole history of give and take between the clans and families involved rather than being set by an abstract monetary value.

As European settlers and merchants entered seeking gold and rubber, the Africans were induced to exchange their products for money which could only be used in turn to buy goods from the Europeans. Consequently, the Europeans got their gold and rubber and then through commerce got their money back. The advent of a money-based system made the deepest inroad on the dowry, as the African's primary use for wealth was oriented around *soumba,* bride price. As money became more available, and especially as the desire for acceptance from the Europeans grew among the Africans, the role of bride wealth began to be utilized to realize these new ends.

## Dowry Commercialized

The rise of cities and commercial centers, and the introduction of cash crops, brought about a breakdown in the close clan regulation of marriage and the increased desire for European goods. Laws and regulations required that a marriage was not sanctioned by the government unless the civil marriage was recorded. Individual families in the cities had little desire or practical need to regulate interclan marriages, as the clan was breaking up. The life in the city produced a new kind of young person who was no longer under the daily scrutiny of village fathers. The moral taboos which guarded and protected one from adventure were no longer to be found in the city. The emergence of self-awareness and the means of accomplishing self-appointed ends brought a revolt among many young people who had to make decisions for themselves. However, the high cost of city living and the constant indebtedness of a family father caused him to see bride wealth as a source of money which would make city life a little better, at least for himself. Consequently, the bride wealth arranged between a man and his future son-in-law often became a financial intrigue in which the girl went to the highest bidder. These prices in Yaoundé today often reach well above $500 U.S. plus such articles as a sewing machine, phonograph, bicycle, or even an automobile.

Such incredible bride prices have had far-flung social repercussions. In the first place, a young man earning $35 to $50 a month finds in nearly impossible to get married. Young women in the cities who have tasted of the material rewards of European life do not care to see themselves sold to the highest bidder, which is often done with little recognition of the girl's choice. Consequently, many girls prefer to go into prostitution where they will at least get the money for themselves. The young men who cannot afford to pay exorbitant dowries are their primary customers. Consequently, here is a case in which in the cities at least prostitution becomes a form of biological marriage forced upon these young people through the reinterpretation of the traditional dowry which formerly was intended for quite opposite ends.

The government requires the civil marriage certificate in order to apply for the benefits from the workmen's compensation fund. Since the civil marriage certificate is not given by the government until evidence of dowry payment, it means that there are numerous young people who are always "only half married." The churches require the possession of the civil marriage certificate prior to the religious marriage. In the port city of Douala recent statistics have been released which show that in 1937 out of 89,356 Roman Catholics there were a total of 1,510 religious marriages. In 1957 the number of communicants rose to 178,000 with a decline in religious marriages to 1,070 for that year. Similar statistics for Protestant communities are not immediately available, but one can be sure that the trend here is indicative of the present influence exerted by the dowry.

## The Necessity of Value Judgments

Everyone does and should make value judgments. It would be impossible to decide which trousers a man would put on in the morning if he did not make such judgments. The missionary should not be frightened into an impasse because he is convinced of a certain relative nature of value judgments. I have come to feel that much missionary inaction is the result of the category of the indifferent. Judgments of the good and the bad are often too facile, and what is not immediately self-evident is dropped into this class of the indifferent. Rather than avoiding judgments, the missionary should, on the contrary, make thoroughgoing evaluations of every aspect of culture and not allow the innocuous catchall of indifference to rob him of understanding culture.

It is not necessary nor advisable to approach the evaluation of items of a culture with the categories of only good, bad, and indifferent. These evaluations must be conditioned by the concepts of *relatedness* and *change*. There are three questions with which one may approach evaluation:

1. We need to ask how the people perform such judgments themselves and how they scale their own hierarchy of values.

2. What are the kinds of innovations at work both within the society as well as without which tend or will tend toward change of the present conditions?

3. How are such changes working toward or away from generalized Christian moral and spiritual values?

If we make value judgments within this framework, we are less apt to create a static sphere of disinterest and lack of concern. This does not necessarily mean that we can thereby guarantee the development of the good at the expense of the bad. However, we should be in a position to make the values of Christian living more relevant to the changing scene taking place in our areas of work.

*William D. Reyburn*

# The Missionary and Cultural Diffusion

## I

Two Gbaya workmen at Batouri, French Cameroons, had a prolonged and vociferous argument which they finally brought to the missionary to arbitrate. Their stories revealed only that the first man accused the second of stealing his money and the second in turn accused the first of killing his dog. In the missionary's view of the matter it was a question of determining the "truth" of the stealing and the killing. Since the missionary was unable to prove or disprove either story, he refused to listen to further discussion of the case.

The two disputants were at a loss to understand why the white man with his marvelous machines and wealth had no means of discovering the person who was at fault. Consequently the two went to a native medicine doctor who performed a series of magical rites to determine if the man accused of dog killing had the power to kill the dog. The missionary had not bothered to ask how the dog was killed. The native doctor knew that the recognized process was by turning oneself into a snake and biting the dog. The accused dog slayer underwent the rites of the native doctor who "proved" beyond a doubt that the man did not possess the power to transform his body into a snake. The logical conclusion was that he was not guilty. Therefore his accuser was forced by the local African authorities to pay the accused a sum of money plus two goats.

**Reprinted from Vol. 5, Nos. 3, 4, 5 (1958), pp. 139-146, 185-189, 216-221.**

### The Problem of Two Contrasting Views

The argument which is presented here is essentially that the modern missionary's inherited view of the universe is an inseparable part of his own ethos (the distinctive point of view of his culture) with which he comes to terms with Christianity. His thinking and action are cast in a framework which is for him necessary and meaningful but which appears to the folk societies quite often as meaningless. There is therefore an inevitable confusion which arises in these two ways of thinking. The missionary will not forsake his view for what appears to him as superstition, and the folk can only partake in the modern missionary's point of view as they are brought into a systematic contact with it. This usually means formalized education.

It is often remarked in anthropological writings and in the pages of PA that life in the primitive world is viewed as a whole synthesis in which all of life partakes in the religious feeling of things. Whether we agree to this proposition or not depends largely upon the way in which we define the religious. However, there can be little dispute with the observation that the folk societies do not divide the rational and nonrational into separate spheres in the way modern societies do.

Some anthropologists such as the late Lévy-Bruhl attempted unsuccessfully to tell us that primitive man has his own kind of psychology and logic, and that in these lay the essential differences between the folk and modern societies. Anyone who has lived in a folk culture is certainly tempted to make such statements. However, this position fails to see that a set of propositions about any matter can be exceedingly logical and at the same time very untrue. The people of the folk societies differ from moderns in that they have a different ontological perspective, a different sense of the nature of existence. That is, there exists a unity of life in which things are, regardless of their nature, interrelated. Whereas modern man assumes a uniform order of nature which operates within its own fixed laws, the folk man assumes an interrelatedness between man and nature. Therefore man's spiritual activities can effect changes in the natural world simply because they both share in the same metaphysic. In central Africa a parasitic vine growing on a tree is viewed as an indication that the tree has a supernatural power which causes the vine to grow on that particular tree. By the same token, if a man is able to secure material wealth, it is because he partakes in the same endowment as the tree which attracts the vine.

Modern man inherited from Greek culture a way of viewing the world in which uniform order is assumed and sought out. What is not scientific is usually admitted and there is little attempt to placate, cajole, and appeal to nature. Rather, modern man controls nature in so far as he can by employing natural laws to do so. Moderns are the heirs of two vast changes in cultural history. The first is the separation of God from the rest of nature which the Hebrews gave us, and the second is the Greek gift of separating out order in nature as immanent without any reference to God or the gods.[1] These two historical developments, in which the folk societies do not share, serve to drive the deepest imaginable wedge between the thought of a twentieth century missionary and the people of his folk congregation.

A simple illustration is the case of the bush fire hunts in Africa. At the end of a strenuous day's hunt behind leaping walls of flaming grass fires the hunter may wearily trudge home with nothing in his hands but his smoke-stained spears. To the missionary it is obviously the case that the animals escaped or that there were none in the area. To the African there is a reason that goes deeper. Something went wrong with the procedure which is carefully executed in order to assure the kill. The procedure is partly in taboos kept by the women. If a woman has been talking noisily in her compound instead of sitting quietly in the house, she is at fault and will be punished. Perhaps a careless wife has swept the floor of her house. She has thereby caused the animals for miles away to flee. This is due to no lack of logic but rather to the assumption that spirits of dead animals must not be aroused during the hunt. The relatedness is vividly assumed to exist.

---

[1] See Robert Redfield: *The Primitive World and Its Transformation,* Cornell University Press, 1956.

### Confusion over the Missionary's Viewpoint

The missionary's dichotomy of natural and supernatural strikes the folk Christians and non-Christians as an unintelligible confusion. The folk man is in no intellectual position to see this problem nor to appreciate it. He does not have at his disposal the means of knowing how the missionary divides up the universe. Consequently as the missionary flits back and forth in his conversation between his worlds of the religious and natural, the mind of the folk man gets lost in the switches. The missionary doctor may carefully explain microbes to an ailing native and allow him to see them dashing about under the microscope. When the missionary has done that and then from a bottle of medicine he destroys the whole bunch and says, "You see, just take your medicine and you'll be all right," the native is most likely posing other questions to himself. "Admitted that there are such little animals. Where did they come from and why did they come to me and not to someone else? Who put them in me? Who is trying to kill me with these microbes?"

Missionaries discourse on a wide range of subjects, assuming too often that their listeners share in their view of the universe. The villagers at Lolo were intensely interested in the fact that Europeans can make so many iron instruments. However, one of their questions which they continually repeated was, "How does the European blacksmith protect himself?" I always answered this in terms of mechanical protection of the body while smelting, pouring, pounding, etc. But my listeners always appeared dissatisfied with these replies.

Finally I asked how the local blacksmiths did it, and they revealed that they were speaking in terms of protection against the supernatural power contained in the heated metal. Since I did not share their presupposition about the nature of hot metal, I could never give an intelligible reply. When I replied at last that they retire at sixty-five so as not to die on the job they were satisfied that the European blacksmith has sense enough to realize he is dealing with supernatural forces which can harm him. However, the fact that the European blacksmith's family practices no taboos again threw the whole subject into confusion for them.

I use these illustrations to point out the fact that the missionary carries Western culture with him and communicates it whether he wants to or not. This is so even if the communication of Western thought forms comes across as nonsense and confusion to the native. The missionary who disavows being a carrier of Western culture is denying himself the very structure of his thought into which he cradles his presentation of the gospel and life.

The ordered view of the universe means that faith to believe must be placed in something which is not beneath that order but over and above it. The modern Christian, like the Psalmist, in whose debt he must remain — "Oh Lord, thou hast searched me, and known me" (Ps. 139) — places his faith in a transcendant God. He combines a Hebrew view of God and a Greek view of the universe. The modern man does not sacrifice the ordered feeling for the universe when he finds faith to believe. He views his faith as finding its locus in the source of order.

The folk man has no need to express his faith in a God which transcends an ordered universe. He rather finds faith to believe based on considerations quite unrelated to the universe. In the folk view God tends to be part of the cosmos and enmeshed in it. Belief in the Christian God (often to the missionary's dismay) does not separate scientific order from metaphysical reality. It is largely because of this fact that folk Christians often tend to equate God with fate and are at a loss to move against what fate has brought upon them. Among the folk Christians God replaces the former medium for placating and petitioning nature. On one hunt in which I participated I knew the Christians had of their own accord left off the making of medicines in preparation for the hunt. The chief, a non-Christian, also knew this and was very careful to make sure that the Christians petitioned their God before the hunt. These men felt that prayer was automatically needed in place of the medicines.

When the hunt was unsuccessful, none of the Christians felt free to punish their wives for breaking taboos, but they were exceedingly wroth with God, who appeared to have failed them, so they questioned in turn their relation to God and decided that they had not paid their mission pledges as regularly as they should. I attempted to present another alternative to them, but as soon as they saw that I was approaching the hunt failure from a secular point of view (it had rained to the east and the animals were moving that way), they refused to be sympathetic with my reasoning. Their reply: "Sometimes we almost think that God doesn't have a stomach like a man."

## Two Views of Man

A second source of the modern missionary's ethos is his view of man which is historical and abstract. Here again the missionary soon becomes vividly aware that his folk parishoners have a nonhistorical and nonabstracted view of man. We may more properly call the folk man's view as mythological rather than nonhistorical. His origins are set out for him in terms of myths which he seldom reflects upon until they become nonfunctional in the process of passing them along to his offspring. Parents of another generation do not feel much rewarded in attempting to tell their children local folk tales while the latter have one eye in a mathematics or history book.

In the folk world the historicity of Christianity is felt as unnecessary. It is not part of the local myth and the distinctiveness of Christianity as an historical event is not realized in the local church. This fact reduces the historical Jesus to the *kinship son*. The importance of Christ lies in the kin relationship of son which shares with the feeling for family, clan, and village relationships. Here again the folk man is a kin man. He is built into blood and marriage ties which replace the modern man's feeling for historical ties. Modern man's feeling runs in depth to other generations and other historical epochs, while the folk man is really related in space here and now.

Modern man and therefore the modern missonary speaks and thinks in terms of nations, united nations, one world, space, and the universe. Consequently he can if he wishes take a very abstracted view of man. The folk man is seldom if ever conscious of belonging to a worldwide mass of humanity. He is more properly a very well identified member of a certain well identified family within a known clan or village and his belongingness seldom extends beyond these confines. Consequently man as an abstract is not a popular idea with him. He has little feeling for such an impersonalized human idea.

The results of the abstracting of man from men gives the modern a peculiar position from which to see the good and the bad in man. This is especially true in our tradition in which we separate out the evil nature of man and emphasize certain characteristics such as overeating or sexual excess as contrary to the ascetic qualities which Christianity has emphasized in both its personalized and abstract view of man. The folk man does not tend to carry out such an abstraction, and consequently there is little place for the ascetic emphasis. One of the greatest confusions for missions in modern Africa today is the fact that the missionary living in plenty and comfort stresses in his teaching the ascetic aspects of the Christian life. In a relative way he is practicing some aspects of the modern industrial society's idea of the lightly ascetic life. However, the folk man in Africa is neither interested nor prepared intellectually or emotionally to appreciate what value asceticism might have for the Christian life. The African tends rather to view Christianity (depending upon other conditions) as a means for achieving the fruits of modern living, as a part of the new education.

Finally, it is worth mentioning that the modern missionary is culturally prepared to be conscious of contradictions while the folk man tends to embody contradictions without bothering his head about it. Just as has been the case with European Christianity in the seventeenth and eighteenth centuries, when kings and princes bounced the populations back and forth between Catholicism and Protestantism, the folk masses can contain conflicting ideologies without being aware of the contradictions. The citizens of Heidelberg, Germany, found that they could switch back and forth between the dictates of Rome and Luther apparently without being in the least disturbed ideologically. They simply didn't care. Great portions of folk Christianity do not find it contradictory to give lip service to the tenets of the Christian faith and at the same time adhere to pagan practices and presuppositions. It is exceedingly common for the missionary to recoil emotionally when a trusted convert turns up describing in vivid detail how spirits from the spring chased a man into the forest and nearly killed him.

## Conclusion

The contact of modern missionaries with the folk world introduces the latter to the presuppositions of a modern age. However, these assumptions are such a subtle force within the ethos of the missionary that they seldom come in for discussion. When a missionary learns the language of a tribesman and speaks with him, his point of contact is the language, but often not the thought concealed in the meanings which the words have for the folk man. The missionary's view of the world is quite ordered. The physical and the metaphysical are rather well separated. The folk man operates upon the assumption that the two are integrally related and interacting. The modern partakes in a recorded history, the folk man in an unrecorded mythological past. It is impossible for a twentieth century missionary to live a single day in his workaday routine without exposing the assumptions upon which his thought forms are based. Whether it be his preaching, his teaching, or his silent living, he does so within the framework of ideas which are strange and largely unknown to the folk world. It is because of this that the missionary, no matter how he may endeavor to hide his Western material culture, can never hide his long ontological inheritance.

# II

## Impedimenta Americana

"We are here only to present the gospel, not American or Western civilization," remarked a missionary in Africa recently. At the very moment these words were pronounced this individual was sitting in a large brick house covered with a metal roof with rain gutters which carried the water to a cement cistern. A radio was broadcasting in French the news of developments in Algeria. A neatly set table under electric lights was being prepared for the eating of wild buffalo shot in the early morning by a Remington semiautomatic rifle. A polished pickup truck sat in the garage nearby. Children's tricycles and toys lay scattered about on the veranda. Stacks of books, newspapers, and magazines in several European and African languages were neatly arranged against the living room walls. Two *évolués* Africans sat in comfortable leather chairs awaiting dinner, listening to the news, and occasionally asking about buying certain household articles when the missionary went on furlough.

The truth of the matter is that the missionary in Africa seldom opens a barrel from home that he does not introduce some gadget of Western civilization à la twentieth century. There was a time when it was difficult to diffuse these luxuries. Today, however, in the French Camerouns at least, it has become standard practice for the missionary eventually to sell his goods (from kitchen utensils to trucks) to the African who has the cash, i.e. the *évolué* class of Africans who are mainly government employees, private planters, or shop owners.

The introduction of education, largely the work of missions at first, provided the groundwork for the existence of the government employee group. The awakening caused by education aroused the desire for European goods. The introduction of cash crops by missions and government agencies means cash incomes. Cash incomes mean (in this area) acquisition of goods and further education, which in turn make it easier for the upper-class African to acquire European goods and ways and be acceptable to the white population. So great is the value of material culture in our own society that the missionary traveling in the bush will often go a long distance out of his way just to spend the night with an African who can provide a gas-lamp-lighted room with supper on a table and a metal bed to sleep on. Often such a person is sought out and admired by the European, who often prefers to overlook any lack of personal integrity in the individual.

## A New Status to Maintain

Mission activity, with its schools and institutions, almost inevitably creates a social ranking in the local society. In certain parts of Africa today the mission hospitals have created a class of moderately wealthy doctors and nurses, and the schools have created the class of teachers. Industrial schools turn out artisans such as carpenters and masons. The church creates a new social status in the role of the pastors, the elders, and the catechists. These new roles are those which adapt themselves most effectively to European ways and serve as the bilingual link between European and African. They are the object of the mission's efforts and the channel through which the mission diffuses spiritual, technical, and gross material culture. This class is granted in African society a high position by the *non évolués,* and consequently there is a certain amount of pressure exerted to maintain upper status. In some cases this attempt to maintain a gap between upper and lower is costly and in the eyes of the European ludicrous. I have been invited to eat dinner with *évolués* Africans who sit about supressing miserable hunger pains in order not to eat before nine in the evening. This is a way of indicating to me that they are doing things as in French society. But more important is that they are communicating social status to the local Africans.

A postparturent mother at the Batouri mission hospital, the wife of an *évolué,* sat feeding her newborn babe from a baby bottle while her breasts painfully dripped with milk. She was willing to endure the physical pain in order to maintain her social distance from the common village women who would never dare take the privilege of bottle feeding.

The two cases cited above are to these Africans signs of status which they have appropriated from Western culture, having seen it in missionaries and other Europeans.

Another slightly similar case is that of a man in the village of Lolo who was an excellent hunter and tracker until he got hold of an overcoat. Now when we hunt together he insists on wearing this huge moth-eaten overcoat which inhibits his movements, wears him out, and gets tangled in the under brush. If he hunts by himself or with his brothers, he leaves the coat behind, but when I am there he feels the coat is absolutely necessary. The fact that I tell him repeatedly that I do not have an overcoat makes no impression on him, possibly because he sees that I have shoes and he does not.

### The European Social and Ideological Link

The missionary is not there to carry European or American culture, but he inevitably feels a pull toward his European neighbors. I have experienced this gravitation tendency in Quechua Indian villages in the high Andes of Ecuador and in the tropical forests of West Africa. After spending days with Quechua people, it was always a refreshing experience to deviate off the trail and pass the night with a Spanish-speaking rancher whose world of thought was so much closer to my own than the Indians'. In the Camerouns I have spent a few weeks among the Kaka people without seeing another European. Finally when I encounter a French administrator or tobacco planter and we sit down to discuss the news of the day or talk about Africa, there is a common tie in our cultural background which makes the visit extremely enjoyable. One is struck by the ease with which interpersonal relations are established. To my mind, it is much more satisfying to hear a French administrator say, "I will pass by the village at six o'clock and pick you up," than to accustom myself to the Kaka statement, "I will arrive when the sun is about so." When the Frenchman fails to arrive on time, he has the expected excuse, but my Kaka friend has no excuse to offer and leaves me wondering.

The common cultural bond with the European is very obvious to the African and tends to form an association and identification of missionary with administration, whether the missionary cares for it or not. In one Cameroun village where I was staying a French tobacco inspector heard a missionary was living in the village, so he came to visit me. Upon his arrival, an old woman put her head in the door and said, "Your brother has come." I had never seen the man before.

### The Role Is Often Acquired at Birth

The problem we are discussing here is simply that of role identification. It is possible to identify oneself under certain conditions with Africans so that you will be told that your heart is black. This is extremely heartening, especially in view of the political and national events these days. However, the separation is obvious and deep. It stems from birth.

While living in Ecuador in a tiny Quechua village, I asked the men why they called me *patroncito* 'master,' and they replied, "Because you do not work." I immediately went to work with them in all their manual labor, such as planting fields, cultivating, hoeing corn, building a road, and numerous other tasks. After six weeks of hard work, I asked again, "Why do you still call me *patroncito?*" They replied, "Because you go with the white men." I managed to avoid contact with the Spanish-speaking townspeople for a long period. When asked again, they replied, "Because you wear shoes." I put away my shoes and wore homespun fiber sandals like the Indians. This process continued until I did not see how there was any difference left. Then one day a group of men said, "Now, we will really tell you why you are *patroncito*. You were not born of an Indian mother." I was convinced.

New roles created in a society tend to shift the respect and prestige accorded to older roles. In the Cameroun the teaching of girls has tended to increase their dowry value, which the father receives. In a society where the women are expected to be inferior to the men, a highly educated girl such as those at college level do not wish to marry their college classmates who would be their equals. These young ladies insist on marrying a doctor or wealthy African whose status is unquestionably superior to their own. This comes to educators as quite a frustration. The main problem of concern to these educated girls is not just education, but also status, a factor which makes African life intelligible to them.

### Conclusion

It might well be thought that the missionary disrupts culture by disapproving heathen practices and insisting that people wear shoes. My own personal experience is that missionaries do not harp on heathen practices, but they very definitely encourage the wearing of shoes, simply by wearing them themselves. The introduction of education in the forms of schools and churches has wide ramifications which set the machinery rolling for culture change. Even the printing of a book in a folk language is one of many ways in which Christian missionaries begin to feed in information which will accelerate change and make inroads in the old way of life.

The introduction of Christianity in this

century is heavily secularized and institutionalized. The creation of a new class or classes within the old society opens up new channels for the diffusion of Western culture. The process is that of making a copy, an imitation. The copy can only be partial, especially where there are barriers for intimate contact. Strong pressures existing within the local society's values tend to interpret the meaning of the copy and regulate the way this process works.

## III

### The Christian Predicament

High on the wind-swept slopes of Mount Mojanda in the Ecuadorean Andes a group of Quechua Indians knelt silently in the Roman Catholic church and listened with awe as a Spanish priest chanted mechanically through the early dawn funeral mass. Their stares were fixed upon a huge mural depicting the torments of hell which appeared to blaze and then simmer as flickering candles animated this awesome plight of suffering souls. At the last tinkling of the bell, shrouded figures arose, crossed themselves, pulled their woolen ponchos about them and drifted slowly out into the mist-chilled air of the semi-darkness. Casting a hurried glance over their shoulders at the fiery inferno on the wall, they headed for the graveyard burial, and then moved in a body to the liquor shops to blur their minds to the hellish horror that haunted their sober imaginations.

It was late afternoon before bands of drunken Indians staggered homeward followed by their faithful wives who sat beside fallen husbands and redeemed the time by spinning yarn from a distaff of wool. When a husband awoke and arose to continue on the path the wife got up and followed close behind, never ceasing to spin and twist her yarn. The path wound through eucalyptus trees and century plants past the edge of another sight which caused the staggering Indian to stop, rub his bleary eyes, urinate against a wall and then stumble on down the path. On the wall were the words "Misión Protestante." Here a mechanical demon replaced the medieval flames of the church's devil. Cars, trucks, generators, washing machines, saw mills, tractors, and a score of other devices made a thundersome noise that sent the drunken Indian hurrying toward his hut. Finally, sitting in the darkness of his windowless shack, he breathed freely, feeling that he had escaped the fire of the Roman hell and the machines of the mechanized mission.

The above description serves to indicate something of the impression made by the medieval Spanish Catholic and modern Protestant mission upon the Quechua of the Andes. It illustrates what may justly be termed "the predicament of the Christian mission." Here represented were two contrasting forces attempting in very different ways to make claims about Christianity. The Roman Catholic church in the town of Tabacundo, a mile from the Protestant mission, was nestled into the quiet, pious, reflective, selfish atmosphere of medieval Spanish life. The rhythm of this life was symbolized by the slow pealing of the church bells both day and night. The atmosphere was one of maintaining the *status quo*. Life was envisaged as unchanging and lived out in terms of centuries. All of this was evident in the ancient architecture of the buildings, the trade of the small craftsmen, and the gossip and small talk on the lips of those who gathered to pass the time of day on the one cobblestone street of the town.

The Protestant mission was a sharp contrast. Such a contrast, in fact, that it was looked upon by the most liberal of the townspeople as being there to purposely threaten the quiet gossipy life of the little town. The mission's attitude was obviously set for gearing life to another pace. Early-rising, hard-working, time-conscious foreign missionaries were busily up to something which could end in no good in the eyes of the villagers. The mechanical aspect of the mission was in the view of the townspeople a mechanized invasion of their feudal domain. The third side of this peculiar triangle was the Indian who for centuries had adjusted himself to the townsmen and looked upon the bustling mission activity with even more suspicion than did the whites.

It may appear at first unwarranted to place the Protestant mission in this case in the same predicament as the Catholic church of Tabacundo. However, the same process was at work in both. The Catholic church was presenting the Indian with a view of Christianity brought out of the medieval ages in which the pictorial art and the dazzling architecture of that day were the content expression of Christianity. The Protestant mission on the other hand faced the Indian with a technological world which was just as strange and mystifying to him as the former. Each within its own predicament had something to say about Christianity. That they lead to different conclusions is obviously true.

The predicament of the Christian mission referred to here is seen in the diffusion of cultural complexes, medieval art and architecture, twentieth century wealth and technology which enter the Quechua's world as part and parcel of the Christian message which may or may not lie deeply encrusted within. The Quechua Indian of the Andes has adjusted his life to the Catholic complex imported from Spain and has maintained a passive relationship to it for centuries. He appears as yet to be frightened by the Protestant innovation.

## The Role of Colonial Governments

There are two approaches to the problem of the church, its organization, and its activities which may be seen on many mission fields. One is the missionary direction and participation type in which the missionary sets the pattern for church organization and practice until he has successfully trained local leaders to copy his pattern. This is a form that is commonly seen and appears to be the "natural" process of missions. The other mission approach is what we may call the *laissez-faire* doctrine in which the missionary seeks to make individual converts and teaches them, but does not do so in a "church." Under this approach the folk are obliged to form their own church organization and practices along the lines which seen natural to them. The latter is not entirely "indigenous" because it is missionary stimulated and missionaries are teaching and are available for counsel and advice if this asked for.[2]

Both of these approaches are clearly in contrast in the French and British Cam-

[2] Wm. A. Smalley: "Cultural Implications of an Indigenous Church," in this volume.

eroun. In the former the aim has been to create a church entirely along Reformed lines in which the African pastors may often wear robes in the pulpit, well rehearsed choral groups sing the Hallelujah Chorus, and where a European member of the Reformed tradition would be quite at home. A sophisticated atmosphere dominates in the churches in the French Cameroun where there has been considerable education and the availability of cash crops for the acquisition of many aspects of French culture.

The church in reference in the British Cameroun stands in sharp contrast. Here the educated choir singing from the written music score is replaced by native singing with drum beating, hand clapping, and the blowing of native cow horns. The services are conducted along lines which are somewhat spontaneous and outside the direction of missionaries. I am not attempting to say here that one of these is inherently better than the other. The sophisticated people of the French Cameroun would for the most part be shocked (now) to see their northern "British" neighbors at worship in church. Those in British Cameroun would no doubt feel awed by the formality and lack of spontaneity if they witnessed the churches of the French Cameroun.

These two churches exhibit each in its own way a basic difference in French and British colonial policy. The French attitude is that of suppressing native languages and employing the French language from the first year of school. The British usually use the native languages in the first several years of education. The French conceive of the African as potentially Frenchmen while the British look upon the Africans as Africans. The result is that these two colonial points of view greatly influence the kind of mission development that has been possible in British and French territories in Africa.

The influence of colonial patterns on the development of church behavior is at this time deep-seated. This may be illustrated by our experience in getting a song book prepared for the Kaka churches in the French Cameroun. Blind Kaka tribesman "Die-tomorrow" is known throughout the tribe as an ardent troubadour of Christian hymns and one of the most capable drummers in the tribe. After I had watched "Die-tomorrow" beat the drums I asked him to work out words and music to the accompaniment of the drum. He showed no interest but continued to sing the Bulu hymns in Kaka (with American church tunes). More than a hundred of these Kaka-from-Bulu hymns were recorded and a song book prepared. "Die-tomorrow" has consistently rejected the possibility of adapting his words to local music. It is not simply that "Die-tomorrow" is incapable of doing that task. It is rather an awareness that the Christian people would ridicule him for making the people go backwards rather than forwards in their conscious process of becoming more Europeanized. This again illustrates how the church behavior and ritual is affected by the pressure of the colonial power.

The question that naturally arises is whether or not the Africans will feel constrained to continue this European adaptation after full independence is achieved in the French Cameroun.

## New Gods for Old

Life in Africa is conceived of in a way which is often closely parallel to Old Testament life and thought. African life is controlled by a consciousness of law very much on the order of the legalism of the Jews. The African is aware of traditional law which embodies an unwritten code of behavior which when violated brings on impurity, and a cleansing from this impurity must follow a specified ritual. Respect of traditions, the status of the elders, polygamy, the dowry, the desire to multiply the race, a feeling for spiritual causation, are but a few of the kinds of similarities between the modern African and ancient Hebrew cultures.

The predicament for the modern missionary is his separation from much of this point of view. The attempt on the part of missions to make Greek-thinking rationalists out of Africans is often met with strong resistance. The African Christian wants and reads the New Testament, but there is a home-like atmosphere in the Old Testament where he finds a bond that it largely absent in the writings of Paul and the other apostles.

The introduction of Christianity inevitably takes one of two paths in laying a foundation for Christian teaching. Old gods are destroyed and new ones substituted for them, or the old gods undergo a remodeling process in which they are shaped up to fit Biblical statements about God. The Bulu *Zambe* was a creator but he created and then left man with no more concern for him. *Zambe's* job was completed in the creation of the physical world. Christianity recalled *Zambe* out of his oblivion to complete the unfinished task of redemption. The Kaka *Ndjambie,* a cognate word, had also the role of creator but remained in the form of the spider as an impersonal force maintaining the creation in the skies, but man and the earth were largely independent of him. *Ndjambie* has undergone a radical transformation.[3]

The making over of *Zambe* and *Ndjambie* has been possible because they shared something (creation) with the Christian idea of God. In many societies the transformation of God is the selection of one of several available gods who then undergoes the process of being promoted and replaces all lesser gods. In many cases the lesser gods are not, however, forgotten as their function continues in some changed aspect.

It appears to be the case in many primitive and folk cultures that the spirit world here below is of much more concern than some abstract creator or fateful force off in the heavens. The world of the dead, the presence of evil powers, witchcraft and magic are things which to many tribes are here and now, and upset or control the ongoing life of a group. In the cultures of the Cameroun these spirit entities were freely moving things without any organization among themselves.

However, the Christian introduction of the personality and idea of Satan has been grasped much more vividly than have many other infusions of new religious ideas. It was as though the spirit world were waiting for a ruler to whom the erratic behavior of spirits could be subject. Satan has become the reason and excuse for all human frailty. While God was never a personal idea, the introduction of Satan into the realm of the very close personal-spiritual relation has made Satan a great personal force in the lives of church members. Satan entered a realm where people consciously rub shoulders

[3] Wm. D. Reyburn: "The Transformation of God and the Conversion of Man," in this volume.

with spiritual beings. Satan is in the here and now and gets the blame for nearly everything. *Ndjambie,* on the other hand, is in the far away and appears to be still at long range from the Kaka Christian's thought world.

In addition to the God-Satan introduction among the Kaka, the distinction of heaven and hell are received with interesting reactions. Among the Kaka Christians heaven (called Paradise from the Bulu trade language Scriptures) is essentially an extension of this life. However, it is fraught with difficulties because there is "no marriage and giving in marriage."

While preparing a catechism in the Kaka language, we came to the writing of a statement to the effect that those in heaven would *serve* God. In Kaka there is no word to express any difference between hard labor and merely rendering a service. When I suggested the term *ñélo saé,* "to do work," my two assistants threw down their pencils and looked at each other in disgust. "Is that the reward of a good life?" shouted one of the men. We had to seek a better expression.

### The Christian Scriptures

The translation of the Scriptures is an excellent example of the way in which missionaries infuse native cultures with strange and different ideas from Biblical cultures. I handed a student of the Mpompong tribe a French Bible and asked him to read the twentieth chapter of Genesis. I watched his face as he silently lipped through the words. He frowned slightly as he read how Abimelech had taken Sarah the "sister" of Abraham but did not "approach her." Then he continued to verse twelve where Abraham said that Sarah was his half sister. The student stopped, looked at me, and with a stunned expression said, "No, how could he marry his own sister? He would call her 'sister.' How could his family face their shame? If they should have a child it would die." All of this he read into the passage from his own tribal laws governing the relation between children of the same father.

On another occasion I asked a Kaka teacher-catechist to find for me in his Bulu Bible the most difficult to believe passage he could find. He turned immediately to no New Testament miracle, nor to the birth of Christ, but to the 19th chapter of Genesis and with his eyes blinking and bulged he haltingly read the account of Lot and his two daughters who intoxicated their father and conceived children from him. Putting down his Bible he placed his hands on top of his head in a sign of shame and said, "Oh, no, no. Those children would have to be born dead to remove their sin." This was followed by a long series of "Oh, oh, oh, what customs those people had!"

### Conclusion

Many missionaries decry the loss of indigenous arts. Instead of taking time to make a drum an African may prefer to buy a phonograph and become a listener of music rather than a creator of drum rhythm.

Missionaries may remark that it is to be regretted that the women do not make the beautiful clay pots as formerly. However, one is prone to forget that by encouraging monogamy and establishing church structures that are operated on money values, one is also affecting native art.

When I asked some Kaka women

recently why they had bought pans instead of making clay pots, they replied that since they had no co-wives to help in their husband's cocoa gardens, they had no time to make and decorate a pot. The cash crop helps pay the cathechist who has to be paid according to the established mission pattern. The women are the laborers in the market crop gardens and there is little time now for anything else.

The African is asked why he has given up the beautiful decorative work on his upright drum. His workmanship appears to the missionary as sloppy and careless. The reason is that the African wants a guitar or other European musical instrument. His native drum has had no functional role in the church so why should he be motivated to elaborate it and express his creative art in its manufacture. In order to acquire the European instrument he needs money. He is thwarted and frustrated in his attempt to secure the necessary money and is often criticized by the Europeans as having allowed himself to love money unduly.

Mission developments that have taken place since the beginning or middle of the last century have grown at the same time with American industrial power and technical specialization. Many American and European missions tend to be a symbol of the wealth and technology which is the goal of those who share a feeling for a mechanized world. The more the missionary has become *homo faber* (the machine-age species of human being) the more he has separated himself from the ways and thinking of most of the world's population.

While talking to a group of Kaka villagers about the gospel, I paused to ascertain if they followed what I had claimed. "Do you grant it so?" I asked. A village elder sitting in the rear spoke up saying, "Why should we say you don't speak straight? Haven't we seen that you can fly through the skies?" What this old man meant was that if a white man can cause an airplane to fly, why should the African villager doubt his word about such a simple matter as God's love.

Here is precisely the predicament of modern Christianity and missions. What is the motive to believe? To what extent is Africa south of the Sahara today filled with Christian churches promoted by a feeling of inferiority rather than a desire to believe? What has been the effect on the Indians of the Andes exposed for centuries to the medieval artistic impressions of hell? Be it the flaming scenes on a church wall or the magic of modern transportation, the folk man is destined to be on the receiving end of this worldwide promotion. The missionary is forced by the nature of the age in which we live to view critically and carefully the process by which we spread *Christianity in cultures.*

*Dale W. Kietzman and William A. Smalley*

# The Missionary's Role in Culture Change

THAT the missionary has historically been an agent of culture change in non-Western societies, no informed, thinking person would deny. His role of initiating culture change has often been seriously misunderstood, however, in different ways by the missionary himself, his supporters, and his critics. The basic attitude of the missionary on this matter, and fundamental missionary policy in an area with respect to it, will inevitably influence profoundly the successful communication of the gospel and the possible development of an "indigenous" expression of Christianity.

Some critics of the missionary enterprise have grossly exaggerated the missionary's influence in their condemnation of the "rape" of non-Western cultures, with destruction of values, detribalization, apathy, or conflict resulting. There certainly have been some such direct cases of unnecessary and damaging cultural disturbance in missionary history, but for the most part the missionary's part has been very minor relative to the impact of Western business, politics, and education, not to speak of the often unsavory influences of motion pictures and printed matter. There have also been some outstanding cases where the gospel and resulting culture change have provided an opportunity for the reintegration of a segment of a culture already in rapid change.[1]

Many supporters of Christian missions, on the other hand, have gauged the success of their whole program in terms of some overt, symbolic types of culture change. These may be anything from monogamy to haircuts, from attendance at church to the disappearance of scarification, but the missionary sees in them signs that his ministry is taking effect. Missions and missionaries which declare that they are not going out to introduce Western culture, but only to preach the gospel, are no different in this respect from those with whom they contrast themselves. It is usually institutionalism (hospitalization, education, agricultural mission, etc.) which they are rejecting by such statements, not really their roles as agents of Westernization. They, too, are thrilled when Ay Blah learns to bathe with Ivory soap, brush his teeth with Ipana, and cut his hair in "civilized" fashion. And if Ta Plooy does not give up his second and third wives or contribute

**Rewritten to combine the following articles: "The Missionary's Role in Cultural Change," by Dale W. Kietzman, Vol. 1, No. 5 (1954), pp. 71-75, and "The Missionary and Culture Change," by William A. Smalley, Vol. 4, No. 6 (1957), pp. 231-237. Dale W. Kietzman is director of the work of the Wycliffe Bible Translators in Brazil. In addition to his training and field experience as a missionary linguist and Bible translator, he has done graduate study in Anthropology at the University of Chicago.**

[1] For a case study of a problem such as this see G. Linwood Barney, "The Meo — An Incipient Church," in this volume.

to the church treasury, this is a matter for deep concern, for Ta Plooy obviously is not following the "gospel teaching" which he has been getting.

## The Problem

To many a perceptive missionary, sensitive to cultural values, there has been a very real problem, a dilemma, at this point. On the one hand, there is a realization that cultural forms are relative, that the meanings of different kinds of behavior change in time and from society to society, that the Greek Christians were not bound by Jewish ceremonial law, that God did accept as perfectly normal the plural marriages of the patriarchs, that to have uncovered breasts is not immodesty among the hill tribes of Southeast Asia, and many other parts of the world. On the other hand, there is the clear Biblical record that God, through the prophets and the apostles, condemned sin in terms of overt cultural behavior, like that of David arranging for the death of Uriah so that he could marry Bathsheba,[2] or like women talking in church,[3] or like Onan refusing to have sexual intercourse with his dead brother's wife because "the offspring would not be his" (so that God slew him),[4] or like braided hair.[5]

Clearly the preaching of the gospel in New Testament times did "turn the world upside down," and that at least partly in terms of widespread changes in cultural behavior. Culture change has resulted historically from any widespread acceptance of Christ. But what should that change be? Should monogamy result? Should agricultural methods be changed? Should people put on clothes? Should drinking stop? Should romantic love be substituted for family alliances as a basis for marriage? Should the bride-price be dropped? Should all Christians learn to read? Should churches be built? Should Christians kneel to pray if crouching is their position of reverence and respect? How do we know what culture change is for the best and what is not?

And how can we be sure that a needed culture change will come about? If we feel that reading the Scriptures is necessary for Christian life, do we force Christians to learn to read in order to gain church membership? Such a course of action seems theologically untenable, as well as culturally "loaded" in giving an entirely distorted picture of the meaning of the church; but it has been done, and has been considered essential in some areas. Do we set rules of behavior to which Christians have to conform if they are to remain in good standing? If so, how do we decide what the rules are to be? Are these rules to be imported wholesale from the rules which the missionary observes? If so, which missionary? Are they to be imported wholesale from the Bible? If so, will they include levirate? polygyny? washing of feet? reclining at meals? silence in the churches? How will the choice be made?

## The Cultural Orientation of the Missionary

The picture of a culture being reshaped as a necessary accompaniment of gospel preaching, and the unfortunate misarrangements of bygone years, cause many of the present problems on the mission field. They also provide part of the impetus for a scientifically oriented ap-

[2] 2 Samuel 11:2 — 12:23.
[3] 1 Corinthians 14:34.
[4] Genesis 38:7-10.
[5] 1 Timothy 2:9.

proach to the problem of the conflict between the missionary's message and the native culture. In exploiting this new approach there is the evident possibility of making more adroit the manipulations and changes that are brought about in a culture. The chief advantage of doing so is the avoidance of much adverse popular reaction. This more obvious possibility for missionary anthropology hides its more central application, namely to teach the missionary to remove himself, as an individual, as far as possible from the sphere of conflict between the message and power of the gospel and the individual.

One of the biggest handicaps of missionary work in the present generation is the nationality and color of the missionary. Yet on the whole we have not attacked the problem of making our presentation of Christianity less of the "white man's religion." It seems, rather, that we seek only to make the "white man's religion" a little more palatable and a little less disastrous to the native culture.

With many areas of the world already effectively sealed to the reception of the gospel message, missions are making a pointed effort at correcting methods in order to avoid further misunderstanding. But has the situation really been improved simply by turning over to native leaders some of the previous functions of the missionary? Will those leaders whose minds are inflamed with nationalism be able to see the distinction between a foreign institution manned by foreigners and an institution created and regulated by foreigners, and labeled by them indigenous?

Church policy is a case in point. While no one now seemingly opposes the principle of the indigenous church, with its policies of "self-support, self-propagation, and self-government," is such a church really an indigenous one when the form for it is decided upon by the missionary? Even raising the question of how soon the church is to "become indigenous" betrays the fact that the missionary is considered to be the judge of the fitness of a group of believers to cope with the problems presented by their own culture.

A related problem is that of the preparation of the native leaders for the church. Education is generally considered to be the answer for this problem. Can we say that these men are trained for leadership in an indigenous church when the training is not given in the place and at the time prescribed by the culture, when instruction is by teachers not recognized in the culture, often in a language other than the mother tongue? At the same time, any culturally recognized training, harmless or not, is frequently ruled out of the student's life.

## The Motivation for Culture Change

Culture change comes only as an expression of a need felt by individuals within a society. People do not change their behavior unless they feel a need to do so. The need may be trivial, as that for some new excitement or amusement, or it may be profound, as for security in a disintegrating world. Usually it is relatively unconscious. People have not analyzed it or given it a name, but it motivates behavior. Something which no missionary who senses culture change going on around him should ever forget, however, is that the need being satisfied by a change very likely is not the need which the casual observer from our Western culture might see.

Among some of the tribal peoples of Laos and Vietnam, for example, the missionary sees the need for clothing. Many missionaries would feel that people need clothing for reasons of modesty (as in cases where women habitually wear nothing above the waist) or for warmth in the chilly season of the year. The second need is one which is felt by the people themselves to some degree, but it is strongly overshadowed by the other needs which they feel and which will be discussed in a moment. The need for modesty in the use of additional clothing is not felt at all, because people consider themselves adequately dressed from that point of view.

When the missionary barrel arrives and the clothes are given out, or when the missionary gives away an old shirt, or when some individual buys a new piece of clothing, what are the needs which he is meeting? One is the need to look respectable in the sight of outsiders — the need for being accepted by people who have prestige. This is why women will often not wear blouses in the village, but will wear them into town or put them on when the missionary shows up. Thus clothing may be a symbol of acceptance by the missionary, of status and prestige in relation to him. Another is the desire to look well among one's equals, to wear something difficult to obtain, something impossible for one's neighbors to buy.

A case in point is a preacher from one of the tribes of Southeast Asia after he had been given a topcoat out of the missionary barrel. This was the only topcoat in the lot; he was the only tribesman who possessed a topcoat. It never got so cold in the area that a missionary ever wore a topcoat, although a woolen suit was comfortable in the evening for two or three months of the year. On a trip over rather rugged, mountainous jungle, when people in T-shirts and cotton trousers were perspiring profusely because of the heat, our friend with the topcoat was, of course, wearing it. How else would people see him with a topcoat on unless he wore it?

Then there was the woman who wore nothing above the waist but a substantial pink bra . . . .

A man who starts to wash his clothes after his conversion is probably not doing so because of his love for Christ, even though this seems to the missionary to be vindication of the view that cleanliness is next to godliness. What are the needs being expressed in a change from polygamy to monogamy, in church attendance, in church government, in learning to read, in sending children to school? We would be the last to say that the need of man for God is never involved in some of these, in some places, but even then, as in all human situations, motives are mixed.

Clearly, the typical missionary reaction to culture change is to approve of that which makes other peoples more like themselves in *form*, in the outward aspects of behavior, whether the meaning of the behavior is the same or not. It is quite possible to give encouragement to the development of a form which is expressing a meaning, fulfilling a need, which the missionary would seriously deplore.

## The Role of the Church in Culture Change

Culture is constantly changing, and what is vital for our purpose, it is constantly changing from within. While a good bit is said and written about acculturation, seldom has the role of the innovator, the nonconformist, the rebel been described. Yet all societies have them, and they have their place in bringing about the constant change that is characteristic of culture. The important thing for the missionary to note is that change is almost always initiated by someone within the cultural community. Even though the idea may have been sparked by contact with another culture, it still must be introduced from within to be accepted. The alternative to this scheme is change forced upon a people through superior might, whether moral or physical. This is the sort of change that missions have often been responsible for, and that resulted in such unfortunate reaction.

The real agent of the Holy Spirit in any society for the changes in the culture of that society is the church, the body of believers (*not* necessarily the organized church of any particular denomination). The church is the salt working through the whole dish. It is that part of the society which has a new relationship to God — yet it reacts in terms of the attitudes and presuppositions of that society. It understands, in an intuitive, unanalyzed way, motives and meanings as the missionary cannot. It must make the decisions.

## The Missionary's Part

What, then, can the missionary do about culture change? Is he to be only an evangelist preaching a noncultural gospel without making value judgments? This is an impossibility, even if it were desirable. There cannot be preaching except in cultural terms, and no human being can or should try to escape value judgments.[6]

[6] By this statement we are not, of course, condoning the highly ethnocentric preaching and value judgments many missionaries make, nor the mistaken views of culture on which they may be based. See "The Missionary and the Evaluation of Culture," by William D. Reyburn, in this volume.

The missionary cannot legitimately force or enforce any culture change. Nor does he have an adequate basis for advocating specific changes in a culture unless he has a profound knowledge of the culture.

The missionary does, however, have an extremely important function in the tactful, thoughtful, serious presentation of alternate forms of cultural behavior to the Christians in a society. On the basis of his knowledge of history, his understanding of the church elsewhere, and above all, his knowledge of the tremendously varied ways in which God dealt with men, as recorded in the Scriptures, he can make it clear to them that there are alternative ways of behavior to their own, and help them in prayer and study and experiment to select those cultural forms which would be the best expression of their relationship to God in their culture.

The missionary's basic responsibility is to provide the material upon which the native Christian and church can grow "in grace and knowledge" to the point where they can make reliable and Spirit-directed decisions with regard to their own conduct within the existing culture. This involves a complete freedom of access to the Word of God, with such encouragement, instruction and guidance in its use as may be necessary to obtain a healthy and growing Christian community.

The missionary's role in culture change, then, is that of a catalyst and of a source of new ideas, new information. It is the voice of experience, but an experience based on his own culture for the most part and therefore to be used only with care and understanding. Part of the value of anthropological study, of course, is that it gives at least vicarious experience in more than one cultural setting, for by study in this field the missionary can gain awareness of the much wider choice of alternatives than his own culture allows.

It is the church which is the legitimate agency in which the missionary should work. It is the people who must make the decisions based on the new ideas which they have received. It is they who must reinterpret old needs and expressions, examined now in the light of their relationship to God and to their fellow men in Christ Jesus.

Reprinted from Vol. 6, No. 5 (1959), pp. 231-234.

*Ann Beardslee and Eugene A. Nida*

# The Missionary Role in "Marriage Palavers"

## The Problem

To what extent, if any, should a missionary enter into a marriage palaver in order to help a national Christian? The Senoufos of West Africa "farm" for a bride in addition to giving a bride price. The men of the groom's household begin farming for a girl (after arrangements are made with her household) when the girl is about five or six years of age. This farming is continued for a certain number of days each year until the girl reaches "marriageable age" (fifteen to seventeen years). When the time for the marriage arrives there are one or two special days of farming — one day if eighteen men are available, two days if only eight or nine are available. At this time a bride price is paid and the girl goes to live at the household of her husband. This is often in a different town. During a period of two or three weeks one of the men of the groom's family goes to the elders of her household with a gift of kola nuts and seeks the bride's hand in marriage. It is already understood that the marriage will definitely take place.

This custom presents a problem for believers, for if a young man is converted and has had farming done for ten or eleven years for a wife who is not a believer, when the time for the marriage arrives he will enter into the arrangements made by the elders of his household and marry the unbeliever. In some cases the elders will refuse him his wife because he has left the way of his "fathers." If a young man refuses such a wife it is almost impossible for him to get another one. The ideal would be reciprocal farming among Christians but as yet there are very few Christians in this tribe and it is impossible.

About two years ago a young Christian man took a Muslim wife for whom he had farmed in the customary manner. The wife's family soon began encouraging her to leave him for another man because of his Christian profession. The Africans here are all French citizens and according to French law a wife must stay with her legal husband, that is, the one who farmed for her. In such a case, should the missionary step in and remind the elders of the French law or should he let the Christian work out his own problem rather than appear to be exercising the "white man's supremacy"? If the missionary does not step in to remind the elders of the law in the matter, then they take the wife away and give her to another man and the years of farming are lost. The only thing a man can do then is steal a wife from another man or wait until a member of the family dies and he is given the wife of the deceased man. If a missionary enters too often into marriage palavers, he will then be sought out by unbelievers as well as professing Christians whenever a Senoufo feels he is being mistreated and wants a white man to represent him before the law. It is difficult for an African to have a case tried in a fair manner in a law court without the help of a white man because the French authorities usually do not know the trade or tribal language and the interpreter can be bribed.

*Ann Beardslee*

**What Is our Role?**

There are several reasons why the missionary's help is sought in trying to resolve social conflicts, and these reasons must figure largely in our anwers to the question of the missionary's role.

For one thing, a missionary almost inevitably becomes involved in social problems because he has introduced them. If it were not for the radical nature of the Christian message, such problems would not arise. People would not be changing their ideological loyalties, and therefore their social status would not be jeopardized and their traditional patterns of behavior would not be altered. When the missionary, by virtue of his very activity, creates problems, it is understandable enough that both he and the people would feel some responsibility for resolving them, or at least for judging what seems to be the equity of the case.

Even, however, where missionaries do not create problems by their preaching or by the behavior of their converts, people often like to come to the missionary to have their differences judged. Not infrequently non-Christians will agree to seek out the missionary in order to have their case adjudicated, for the missionary usually acquires a reputation for honesty. He certainly is regarded as less corruptible than the local judges and usually he is not surrounded by official interpreters who live off of bribes.

The help of the white missionary is sometimes sought in presenting a case to the colonial judge, for the missionary usually has a measure of prestige which only the rare indigenous person enjoys. The missionary, therefore, becomes the "friend at court."

For these, and a host of other minor reasons, the missionary may soon become involved in a myriad of legal responsibilities for people, and almost imperceptibly he will find his role being radically altered from what he may have first planned. That is to say, he went to the field as a prophet of a new faith, and he ends up as a judge of a new order. Rather than proclaim a new way of life, he acts as a kind of policeman to see that people keep in the straight and narrow path. Such a role seems almost impossible to escape when it is related to church discipline, for he is the one who feels called upon to keep the church "unblemished from the world," and furthermore the indigenous pastors certainly do not want to assume the onus of excommunicating the faithful, when it is so much easier to pass the buck to the white outsider.

**The Missionary Judge**

However, this role of judge, whether within the church or outside of it, is not quite so socially innocent as it seems, for though it may all seem quite reasonable, from our "disinterested standpoint," it certainly is not judged in this light by others. The reasons for this are, of course, not difficult to see, for the judging of the people is the function of the chief and the elders. The medicine man may be responsible for detecting witches, denouncing the violation of taboo, and arranging for an ordeal, but he does not judge civil suits, unless he wishes to vie with the chief and elders for political power. Likewise, the missionary as a kind of religious practitioner, must beware or he will find himself unwittingly a rival chief.

It is because of this fundamental problem involved in judging disputes that many missionaries have utterly refused to be embroiled in such difficulties. But this is not merely because of the practical results of making as many enemies as one ever makes friends — after all, for each one benefitted there must be at least one who is thoroughly alienated by any judicial verdict. Rather, missionaries have felt that they must keep out of such affairs because these activities are inconsistent with their role as prophets. This position is not, however, easy to explain to one's indigenous friends. One missionary, who had recently declared that he would hear absolutely no more marriage palavers, was immediately accosted by a man who declared, "But, Father, what will we do now?" His immediate reply was, "What did you do for the centuries before we missionaries came?" Of course, the people judged themselves by means of their own judicial systems, which though sometimes corrupt and often very different from our own, succeeded in resolving differences on the basis of a code of equity which was acceptable to the African value system.

The missionary's role must be essentially that of the conveyor of information. He is the new source of information about alternative patterns of behavior, and he must constantly explain these in terms of all their ramifications and complications. To gloss over the difficulties is to deceive people cruelly, but to attempt to right wrongs by taking on the executive and judicial functions of the chief and the elders will be even more disastrous.

## To Whom Has the Gospel Been Preached?

Perhaps the real problem posed by this question is more subtle than appears at first glance. Is it possible that the solution to this difficulty lies in the very presentation of the Good News to this constituency? How does it happen that young men are principally involved in this problem? Has the mission sought primarily to reach young men rather than doing something for girls also? (It is quite true, for example, that almost 90 per cent of all the money that has gone into the education of Africans in the past has been for the education of boys and young men.) Has the proclamation of the gospel been directed to the family as a whole, or has the approach had the effect of "de-family-izing" the young convert? Is the young man or the family in question willing to pay damages to the one who has already worked for some girl who has become a Christian? Have any of the older men — the judging elders of the tribe — been consulted on this issue? What is their judgment on the equity of the case? Is it possible that there are no Christian elders in the tribe, no older men who understand the value system of the people and can interpret the way the people understand this relationship? What would be the attitude toward a Senoufo man marrying a girl from another tribe where there might be more Christian girls available?

These questions may undoubtedly seem to be posing more problems, rather than resolving the original one which has been described. However, we must face the facts that (1) solutions to such difficulties often rest on highly local circumstances and rarely if ever can one propose some "blanket solution" (if this were the case such solutions would have been found long ago) and (2) no solution is likely to be valid or have lasting value unless it is worked out in closest cooperation with the people themselves.

It would seem, however, that in this type of face-to-face community, the only valid approach must be something along the line of McGavaran's *Bridges of God*, where the message is communicated to the basic social unit, the family and the clan. Obviously, in this situation the whole matter of marriage is the problem of the family and clan, for it is not the bridegroom but the males of his household who do the work. Now, what is going to be the relationship of this Christian, who wants a bride, to the ongoing system? Will he be willing to work for a wife for his younger male relatives? Is one of the failures of the people to recognize his right a suspicion that he has removed himself as a potential participator in the continuing system? Do the people think of him as so much under the tutelage of the missionary that he is lost to the cause of the clan or tribe? If this is so, then perhaps they have more justice in their position than may appear on the surface, for equity requires not only that he receive a wife for past work, but that he be one who can be counted on to share his responsibility in the future of this betrothal system.

What we have said here is admittedly no pat answer to the question which has been raised, but it is an attempt to explore somewhat more extensively some of the implications of the problem and to suggest that not only is there more in such difficulties than meets the eye but any solution must be reached in the closest of contact with the people who are responsible for making such social decisions among the people. Appeals to the courts may help an individual client but this is not enough to establish a new basis of viable social responsibility.

*William A. Smalley*

**Reprinted from Vol. 6, No. 2 (1959), pp. 90-95.**

# Some Questions about Missionary Medicine

IN this editorial I expect to raise some questions which I cannot answer. Perhaps there are readers who will want to speak to them. In fact, I feel singularly ill-equipped to discuss missionary medicine as it is entirely outside of my experience, and I have no knowledge of its problems. Yet, as I observe it from a distance, I get the same feeling of "unrealness" from it that I get from many missionary activities — the same lack of coming to grips with the realities of society in the less westernized parts of the world.

This uneasiness was forceably brought to my mind again by the reading of a fascinating little book, *The Edge of Tomorrow,* by Thomas A. Dooley, M.D.[1] Not that Dr. Dooley said anything about medical work in relation to Christian missions. He is the doctor who, out of his own pocket, and out of the contributions which he received from other Americans, led a medical team of Americans and Lao on a year-long venture of bringing medical relief to two isolated communities in Northern Laos in Southeast Asia. Dr. Dooley's motives were humanitarian. An Irish Catholic himself, he was driven by the desire to perform medical service to wretched people. He had become familiar with some of the problems of such medical aid through his work in the Navy in Asia, particularly in the evacuation of refugees from Northern Vietnam, when Vietnam was divided at the end of its bloody civil war. The significance of Dooley's book and the work which he did lies not simply in the number of individuals who were treated or healed through his medical skill. So far as the viewpoint represented in PRACTICAL ANTHROPOLOGY is concerned, the significance lies in his attitude toward his work and its relation to the society around him.

Dr. Dooley started out to spend only one year in Laos. That year was spent in two different communities, both relatively isolated: Van Vieng and Nam Tha. He and his men plunged into their work with the facilities available, and utilized the materials at hand. Here is a description of their home in Van Vieng:

> Our living quarters presented a tougher problem. Ojisan's house was a typical Lao hut perched six feet above the ground on stout poles surrounded by a "porch" and reached by a steep ladder. We climbed up, took one look inside, and came out shuddering. The place was filthy.
>
> The boys tore out everything inside the hut including the bamboo partition between the two rooms. They swept the ceiling clear of soot, cobwebs, and rats' nests, then went to work on the walls. When this accumulation of ancient crud had been swept out, they hauled up buckets of river water, broke out

[1] Published in New York by Farrar, Straus and Cudahy, 1958.

boxes of soap-powder and bleach, and swabbed the deck Navy-style.

The villagers presented us with woven bamboo mats for floor covering, and we laid out our bedrolls and hung mosquito netting. Then we installed all the packing-crate bookcases, benches and tables, and placed two cots against the wall as lounges. This would be our "living room."

Pete Kessey insisted that even the poorest white-trash back in Texas wouldn't live in such a place. Maybe so. But, at least, no one could ever say that the men of Operation Laos lived apart from the natives in an air-conditioned American compound.[2]

Their hospital was just as simple. There was no X-ray machine, no elaborate equipment. Everything was designed so that it could be carried on, when Dr. Dooley left, by the Lao individuals who were trained on the spot. Americans in the enormous Economic Aid Mission which has poured millions of dollars into Laos, with almost no grass roots service resulting from that expenditure, accused Dr. Dooley of practicing 19th-Century medicine. They are correct, said Dr. Dooley, "I did practice 19th-Century medicine, and this was just fine. Upon my departure our indigenous personnel would practice 18th-Century medicine. Good, this is progress, since most of the villagers live in the 15th Century."[3]

There lies the significance of Dr. Dooley's work. His cultural instincts are sound.

There were about four practicing mid-wives in Van Vieng when we arrived, and perhaps as many more young girls who aspired to the calling. We won them over to our side, had them help around the hospital, and made them promise to call us for each childbirth. When we went on a call, we would take along one or two of the younger girls. And, always, we carried a bag containing the wonderful midwife's kit prepared and distributed by CARE. Each of these kits contains gowns, gloves, cord ties, basins, bowls, dressings, soaps, towels, etc. — all the essentials for the delivery of twenty-five babies.

We taught the girls the principles of modern, aseptic midwifery, and the importance of post-partum care of the mother, including removal of the placenta. Then, after each one had delivered twenty-five babies under supervision, and had proved her proficiency and dedication, she was "graduated" with appropriate ceremony, climaxed by the presentation of the CARE kit — always the bag that I personally had carried and used. (This was extremely important for "face.")

Just as in America nurses are "capped" at graduation, so we "bagged" our midwives in Van Vieng. It worked. Those wonderful young women, armed with their CARE kits and somewhat dedicated to the aseptic principles we taught them, have removed many of the old horrors from maternity in that part of Laos.[4]

**Participation and Cooperation**

Dr. Dooley and his men participated largely in Lao life and were part of the Lao communities in which they lived. "Participation," as always, is a relative matter. Dr. Dooley calls "lousy stuff" some of Lao food which I consider delicious! They subsisted largely on Navy C-rations. In the evening they provided entertainment for the community with movies supplied by American Information

[2] Pp. 20-30.
[3] P. 54.
[4] Pp. 35-6.

Service, and throughout the day the community watched fascinated as they performed much of their medical work in full view. People never ceased to marvel that injections were given in the patient's "bottom" for a pain in the head!

The local "shamans," the witch doctors or medicine men, were disturbed by the Dooley mission when it came to Nam Tha. Finally they declared the hospital to be taboo by putting up the characteristic woven bamboo sign used all over Southeast Asia. No one, no matter how ill, dared come near the hospital for help. At that point Dooley did the culturally most sensible thing. He made friends and colleagues of the witch doctors.

> One afternoon I returned from an emergency call in the jungle to find Pete holding an earnest professional conference with Old Joe (a medicine man.) Pete gave me the eye, and I squatted down and listened respectfully.
>
> Old Joe had spread out before him a weird assortment of sticks, bamboo slivers, betel nuts, boiled leaves, pig grease, and cow dung, and was explaining the theory behind his *materia medica.* Most of it was fantastic. But here and there I recognized fragments of the universal folk remedies (like the use of spiderwebs in open wounds), the effectiveness of which are acknowledged by modern medicine.
>
> "Well," said Pete, "we just belong to different schools of medicine. We use different drugs, different methods, but we are both working for the same thing — to free the people from the evils of disease and suffering. The important thing is for us to work together. We'll teach you what we know, and you will teach us." That sounded fair enough to Old Joe.
>
> From that time on Old Joe rarely missed a sick call. We would administer a shot of penicillin, Joe would invoke the proper spirits. We would splint a fracture, then permit Old Joe to tie the indispensable red, white and black strings around the splints. If we were paid two coconuts for fee, Old Joe received one. (In America this practice is held in a bad light; they call it "fee splitting.")[5]

**Expendability**

Laos has only one foreign trained doctor, who is the minister of health. There are about fifteen locally trained men, many of them with little more education than would correspond to junior high school in the States. These are the doctors of the larger communities. Dooley deliberately turned his work over to these men at the end of a year's time. He wanted to return again at a later date, but he wanted to start again fresh in a new community and to begin his training work once more. He did not want to build up his own institution.

Here are the details of his final arrangements with the Lao government:

> We had established the hospital at Nam Tha, and wanted to insure that after our departure it would continue to flourish. All the things we had done were so carried out that our departure would not create a void. We installed no X-ray machines, nor any large electrical plant. We had no complicated or extremely delicate instruments. We utilized ten or twelve basic antibiotics and other medicines, so that their exact usage and dosage was well understood by the local nurses. We turned over to midwives the CARE kits, making them completely self-sufficient. The

[5] P. 79.

vaccination program, carried out by the locals themselves, would add a marked degree of immunity to many thousands of people in the high valley. The instructions would make them more cognizant of the relationships between dirt and disease. I did not want these accomplishments lost after our departure. I wanted to make sure that we would leave something real and substantial behind us.

I proposed three points to the Minister. I asked, first, that he give our hospital a charter. This would mean that a specific amount of money would be earmarked for the hospital based on the number of patients treated and hospitalized. This would mean that certain monies would be allotted for upkeep and care of the buildings. Instead of paint and wood being bought with my own money, the hospital would now be administered and financed by the government of Laos, and their medicines would come from the government warehouse.

Second, I asked that he send to Nam Tha two Bangkok-trained nurses to replace my men. These nurses were well trained in Thailand's school of nursing. There were only a few in the whole Kingdom of Laos, but I asked for two for Nam Tha.

Third, I asked that a *médecin indochinois* be sent to replace me. There are no other doctors by international standards in the kingdom, except the Minister himself. There are fifteen men who have had some medical training, though by our standards very little. These men could practice medicine in Laos.

If Dr. Oudom, the Minister of Health, would agree to this, I in turn would agree to leave everything that we had brought to Laos in the hospital at Nam Tha. This meant that absolutely everything would stay there, beds, mosquito nets, linens, drapes, surgical instruments, stethoscopes, house gear, and about $25,000 worth of antibiotics. All these we would turn over to the *médecin indochinois*. Then I would myself return to America.

The Minister immediately agreed, but expressed some surprise that I wanted to become expendable. I told him that in my mind America should not attempt to build a dynasty in a foreign land. We should not attempt to make a foreign land dependent on us for its maintenance.[6]

As a missionary in Laos, I have seen these local poorly trained "doctors" at work. I have seen them literally kick their patients around if those were of the mountain tribe. I know how their offices have been characterized by graft and personal gain. I can imagine what may well happen in that hospital which he left behind. But I insist that Dr. Dooley is right. Medical aid or any other kind of aid that simply results in a permanent dependency of one country upon another is in this age as bad an enslavement as the military colonialization of a past era.

Let us stop all this blather and bleat about the beatitudes of democracy. Let us get out and show, with simple spontaneity and love, our ability to work at the level of the people we aim to aid. Let us stop proclaiming ourselves as the world standard. Democracy, as championed by the United States, does not translate well into Lao. Not yet. We evolved it from 1776 to 1958. Let us be patient with the Asian. The Lao need only time, education, and stimulation.[7]

[6] Pp. 192-193.
[7] P. 203.

**Missionary Medicine**

What is the function of a medical missionary program? It is easy enough to define its humanitarian function, as thousands of the world's most miserable sick pass through the doors of mission clinics and hospitals daily. It is easy enough to define its function in terms of service to mankind as doctors leave valuable practices and excellent incomes for the reward of seeing the world's less fortunate healed of diseases which are scarcely known any longer in the West.

But what is its missionary function? And what is its function in the society within which it operates? What is its motive?

The only true motivation for missions is the extension of the church of Jesus Christ, the redemption of men. Aside from an opportunity to give a witness to a captive audience, what does the typical mission medical program contribute to that end? These are questions which missionary doctors may well be able to answer, and I would like to hear the answer. I frankly do not know what it is. It seems to me, however, that any worthwhile answer will have three ingredients at least: Christ, church, and local culture.

But, dropping the question of missionary motive, what about medical goals? Should we want to practice 20th-Century medicine everywhere? Or should we not, like Dooley, be content with 19th-Century medicine in rural areas, in the hope that some 18th-Century medical practices might be developed and used locally?

Of course 20th-Century hospitals are not out of place in the big cities of Asia, Africa, or Latin America, any more than they are in Europe or North America. For rural areas, however, are they really functional? Would not a decentralized medical program in which a few individuals were taught some elementary skills and a degree of self-reliance and initiative in their use, be better than the full dependence of a mission medical program on a well-qualified foreign staff?

And what about practice? Is it better to take someone who is ill to an antiseptic hospital where he is terribly frightened, or to leave him in his very unantiseptic home where he feels much more secure in the face of illness and death? Many hospitals abroad, it should be noted, are much more humane than American hospitals about allowing the relatives of the ill to camp with him, cook his food, and give him the reassurance of friends about him.

And what of the medicine man? If healing were the only motive, certainly the cooperative use of the medicine man would be all-important. With the antibiotics of modern medicine and the reassurance of traditional remedies, religious and magical, the patient would get a powerful dose. Dr. Dooley gives a lot of credit for success in some of his cases to Old Joe.

Some missionary doctors shy away from such reinforcement of "superstition" and pagan religion. If it is only a matter of "superstition," I feel that they have no right to quibble. Much of their own medical lore will be classified as "superstition" two hundred years from now. If it is true that such cooperation will place a barrier between men and Christ, I would not advocate it. I suspect, however, that this again is more often a problem of the missionary's understanding than we usually think, and that lack of such cooperation may often in itself be that barrier. Here, it seems to me, is an area where some imaginative feeling for the culture could find an effective outlet.

Perhaps in medicine, as in so much of our missionary work, we think of our techniques more highly than we ought to think. Ultimately, it is the missionary doctor or nurse's reflection of Christ which will be important to His cause. Humanitarian healing work can give a splendid lens to brighten that reflection. But little reflection will take place without participation, without empathy. For a man most at home around a smoking fire in a bamboo house, participation and empathy are hard come by within whitewashed walls and bleached sheets.

Dr. Dooley, in a few months' time, succeeded in making friends on a scale which very few missionaries do. With him perhaps the Lao sensed a freedom from contempt, which is one of the most cherished of all freedoms. But what if the work he left behind disintegrates into a political plum, with the unsterile instruments, moldy medicine, and apathetic personnel so characteristics of Lao medical practice? Any answer will depend on what one's goals are, on the absolutism of one's attitudes toward the perfection of 1959 (as opposed to 1958 or 1858), medical fashion, and the realism in one's knowledge of history and of culture change.

My answer is that the type of rural medicine Dr. Dooley undertook, the respect of local culture which he showed, and his insistence on training people to do the medical tasks which they could do independently of him is more realistic for rural areas and more relevant for Christian missions than much of what we are doing. I would like to hear from the doctors on this.

*Albert Buckwalter, Joseph E. Grimes, and William D. Reyburn*

# How Do I Adjust to Giving?

*What missionary will not recognize in his own situation some problems similar to the one recounted below? It is so typical that a variety of different individuals are presenting three answers as a symposium. The name of the writer of the original question is withheld by request.*

IN MATTHEW 5:42, I read, "Give to him that asketh thee, and from him that would borrow of thee, turn not thou away." Certainly this is a statement to be carried out literally, with wisdom. Nevertheless, it confronts me with a practical problem. I am the first residing white person, missionary or otherwise, among these 10,000 more or less people of West Africa. My problem is how to adapt to the customs and culture surrounding me and simultaneously demonstrate Jesus Christ by life in a pertinent way.

### Native Custom

1. Anyone having two or more of the same item, two pair of shoes, for example, will be asked outright for one of the "extra" pair. This is freely practiced among the people. However, there are limits. One going to the extreme in this giving is called "one who has given his legs away and is walking with his head on the ground."

2. When a person comes to salute you, that is an outright visit, not just passing through, one gives the visitor a gift of money or kola nuts. If this is not done, the visitor reminds you as he leaves that he has come to salute you, which interpreted means, "Give."

3. White man has a lot of money, therefore he should give a lot away. He is the one that makes it in the first place.

4. Kola nuts, I believe, are to be reckoned with in the same category as betel nuts. The results of their use seem to be about the same.

5. The chief here is the big chief of all the Busa people in Dahomey. He is well off financially. He would have to be in order to give away money, horses, robes, etc., the way he does. Strangers, mostly Hausas from Nigeria, sing, flatter, and drum in front of his house for a couple of nights and then leave the village with one or more of the above-mentioned items. The chief, a Moslem, supplies the Moslem teachers with meat from his herd.

### My Approach Thus Far

I will here refer to the numbered items under "Native Custom" for my answers, or my approach to them.

1. I have given old shirts or shorts, etc., to those working for me, but not to those who just came up and asked, and

**Reprinted from Vol. 4, Nos. 3 and 4 (1957), pp. 89-99, 147-156. Albert Buckwalter is a missionary among the Toba Indians of Argentina. On Joseph E. Grimes, see his article on "Individualism and the Huichol Church" in this volume.**

on one occasion I gave five boys one T-shirt each. Then, too, I have given tin cans or small gifts of money (tips) to those bringing gifts from the chief.

2. Some have accepted a hearty "thank you" in return for their visit; others have not, but have gone away disturbed. To some I have given a gift of a tin can or money. This has been, however, to those (very few) who have visited me often and whom I have visited often, who have come to salute me for a holiday or festival. Saluting on a holiday really means a gift must be forthcoming.

3. To those asking for money, I have consented to some and refused others. To able-bodied men I have offered work and found out that they always have an excuse for not coming. I have also passed it off by saying I have no work at the present or trying to change the subject. There are two school teachers, a government nurse, and a veterinarian in the village, all of whom make two or three times as much as my allowance. The government publishes the salaries of these African men, so that we know the scale of pay. Naturally, since I am white, I must make more than they do. It would not be feasible, nor would they believe me, to tell them that I received less than those men. I am sure, however, that I have more than the average village native.

4. Kola nuts or their equivalent in money is the standard gift for all holidays. I consider kola nuts, along with betel nuts, as bad. I do not give kola nuts nor the money they ask to buy them. I empty my wallet before going to town now.

5. Before coming to Africa, I was instructed by veteran missionaries: "Never loan money or give anything, even a tin can, to an African." Then I came to Africa and discovered that this is contrary to the customs of Africans. I agree with the first part of the statement, but I am not convinced of the latter part as a blanket rule, especially in light of Matthew 5:42. The people see all that the chief has materially, they see what he gives away, and then they wonder why I do not follow suit. I could not begin to attain equality financially with the chief or these government Africans, therefore the problem has not given me an inferiority complex. Nevertheless, if the time comes when I will be translating this verse in Matthew with one of these "bush" Africans, what will I say to him if he should ask me, "Why don't you obey this command of the Lord Jesus?"?

[NAME WITHHELD]

# Reply I: A Toba Analogy

MY ONLY qualification for making any comments on these problems is that I have for five years faced some problems which are very similar. My work has been among the Toba Indians, who have within the last decades forsaken a life of hunting and fishing and have only poorly adjusted themselves to an agricultural economy — cotton raising. Within their ranks may be found men who raise cotton quite successfully, while at the same time there are those who are, as it were, adrift in an unfriendly world. They cannot settle down long enough to see a cotton crop through from beginning to end.

An important point to remember is that we do our business in an Occidental modern world, while at the same time we are attempting to give a spiritual ministry in another quite distinct world. It is precisely at this point that our biggest unsolved and unsolvable problems lie. The Western world is an individualistic and materialistic world as compared with Toba ideals. We have a highly developed sense of private ownership, while in Toba society it is common to ask and to receive. No Toba can enrich himself over his fellows, for if he does, it is because he has refused to share, and if he refuses to share he is just plain "mean."

When a Toba becomes a Christian, he does not become individualistic and materialistic, as some North American missionaries used to try to make them so they would be *more* Christian, but his sharing complex becomes more accentuated. To the Toba, this is the natural way of expressing what the Lord has done for him in his innermost being. And there are hundreds of Toba Christians!

So, what is the poor missionary going to do? He has a wife and three children who are just ready to begin their grade-school education. If he had no children, he and his wife would establish themselves in a little grass hut out in the country where the Tobas live, and do all possible to approximate the Toba setup, freely giving, freely receiving, and sometimes freely starving, just simply because he knows that his ministry would be more effective. But he cannot do it so completely.

What I am doing is living in town and taking my family out among the Tobas for short periods of several days. The more extended periods of living with the Tobas I do alone, simply because the children do not have the stamina to take things as they come sometimes.

It seems quite obvious to me already that I can never remove all the barriers between me and the Tobas. And I doubt that the Tobas expect me to. They are surrounded by innumerable white people who in many ways act just as I act. But in some ways, only by the grace of God, I am different from them. I will eat and sleep with the Tobas, I will sit with them, and I am learning to speak their language, things which whites do not "stoop" to do here.

Because of the partially self-induced poverty of the Tobas, the typical pattern of relationship between the Toba and the white man is "the beggar and the master." The economic disparity is obvious to all. The Toba has nothing; the white man has everything. So we missionaries must constantly be bumping up against the apparent but probably unconscious Toba desire for the same relationship to obtain between them and the missionaries. You probably know, too, how terribly easy it is for a North American to feel paternalistic, and so much more if he is constrained to share his religious faith. This is all on the negative side of the ledger; it makes it difficult to obtain a brotherly relationship.

But on the positive side, there is that in Christian Toba personality which reaches out and draws to itself the foreign missionary with his Spanish Bible and begs him to teach him the Bible. So, in spite of the seeming impossibilities of our becoming complete brothers, there is something I can do freely which is of far more eternal value than to fill the oft-idle, outstretched hand with bread. This Bible teaching is received as an obvious sign of my concern for them, even though I cannot always comply with the economic demands which Toba brotherhood puts upon itself.

I thank God there are as many Toba Christians as there are, because it has made it impossible for me to force my own particular "convictions" upon them. This has also forced me to accept as of the Spirit of God Scripture interpretations which in some respects differ from my own. And, not least of all, it has relieved me of the "burden" of being their self-appointed moral judge. Instead, I can freely rejoice with them that God has saved them from darkness to light.

You probably wonder whether I will ever comment on your questions. Frankly, I do not know what to say. As to the advice previous missionaries gave you, I might mention that my own uncle, who founded our work here thirteen years ago, and who is now retired after thirty-two years of foreign mission service, still cannot understand how I can be so "complacent" about the native Toba expression of Christianity. But I am convinced that a church must follow native lines from the very beginning or it is nothing but a missionary's delusion of a church. The missionary fools himself and confuses the people.

As to whether it is "wrong" or "right" to use kola nuts, let the Christians tell you that one. If it is a sin to use them, the Holy Spirit will in time make it clear to the believers. Of course, this does not deny to you the privilege of explaining the evil effects of the drug, but the final decision will be between them and God. It might just so happen that in their way of thinking the use of kola nuts will be classed as of relative unimportance as compared to the practice of "giving"! In Toba society the drinking of maté, a very strong tea, is not a moral question, but to refuse to help a needy brother when you obviously have what it takes is to deny by your actions the love of Christ which you have in your heart (or rather, profess to have).

I might add that in Toba society sharing tends strongly to follow family lines; that is, one is not free to ask from a non-relative. Unfortunately for us, everybody claims us as their "brother." Already we are in a category all to ourselves. But if we honestly try to approximate the accepted Christian conduct, the differences which remain will probably not prove to be as big a stumbling block as we might imagine.

Albert Buckwalter

# Reply II: Is Giving an Equalization Process?

Even though I have spent a fair amount of time on Chicago's Skid Row — not as a denizen, however — I have not yet reached the point of growth in grace where even in my own culture I can, with rejoicing, shell out a dime to a bum who touches me for it. Moreover, in an area where at the present time corn is scarce and other things unobtainable due to the crop failure, and where eating even a little more than the bare minimum is looked upon as putting on airs, I am really at a loss to know what to do for or with needy people who ask and not-so-needy people who usually ask more.

I do not think we as missionaries can dodge the question merely by averring that a dole is sheer paternalism — *panem et circenses*. The Lord did not say anything about stockpiling enough things to make a dole possible, and it certainly is possible to give on a small scale within one's means. It is also impossible to give away what one does not have. This puts the relatively mobile missionary at an advantage in that he can do most of his stockpiling in places where the things will not be asked for.

But that leaves the missionary still with a number of things which could be given away, no matter where he is. I notice that very few of us seem to have problems about giving our time; money and things which can be bought with money is usually the place where the squeeze is put on us. In this respct, I find that I am constantly reminded in the Scriptures that I am a citizen of a place where money does not matter; that I am to follow the good example laid down long ago and take cheerfully the plundering of my goods; that God will supply my needs (and he has). Yet it seems to be harder for me to part with a peso than to perform minor surgery on somebody's poor axemanship. I suppose the only way to convince myself that the problem can be solved by taking the bull by the horns and giving is to try it — and I do not know anyone else from my cultural background who has.

In regard to the way of doing things in your tribe, I wonder whether a study of the gift-giving system would not reveal that one who gives a lot away, such as the chief, does not also receive an approximately equal amount. The fact that he remains a rich man and is not reduced to poverty might indicate that he does a rather good amount of visiting himself — or if he is wealthy from some other source, then other rich men receive gifts as well as give them. So gift-giving does not amount to a method of equalizing the wealth of the banker to the level of that of a gravedigger in the manner of the United States income tax. If such is the case, it might be both practical and a furtherance of the work to give in the expected fashion, and also make enough visits to be reimbursed economically, at the same time getting to know a lot more people better.

JOSEPH E. GRIMES

# Reply III: The Nature of Christian Giving

BEFORE making a few comments on your situation, let me say that we have knocked ourselves out since college days trying not to believe in the absolutizing of our own petty ways of doing things. We found that it is much easier to conform to South American Indian practices and do "identification" kinds of things there than it is in Africa. The source of this difference rests precisely on the difference in the concept of the material. To put it briefly, African life is acquisitive life, while American Indian is renunciative life. This basic difference in orientation permeates every aspect of these two great peoples.

In the renunciative posture the outsider looks for a hole to slip in that he may be on the inside. It is like trying to break into a locked house. In the acquisitive society the outsider all of a sudden wakes up to find he has been pushed inside, and he spends his time trying to find out how to keep his head outside where he can breathe. These matters of acquisition and renunciation are selective and relative and would have to be developed in lots of detail to make them valid concepts, but roughly speaking they express my feelings about the contrasts. It is much easier to conform to the renunciative society than to the acquisitive, especially for stingy Americans and Europeans. Incidentally, you will find very marked differences among missionaries in Latin America and Africa due to these very different attitudes expressed by the two native peoples.

## The Biblical Context

First and always is the meaning of the Biblical text which more often than not suggests some kind or degree of identification or attachment to local tradition. This is especially true in the Gospels, where Christ is setting up the attitudes of a new day which are violently opposed to Jewish legalism. Even here it would not take much cultural fossilization to convert these sayings of Christ into a modern moral code of laws, which would defeat the very purpose which Christ is trying to accomplish.

In the fifth chapter of Matthew, we find Christ launching a series of attacks at the basic issues underlying the necessity of the traditional law. We find there his attack on adultery, divorce, oaths, and retaliation and vengeance. In each of these he goes behind the tradition to strike at the motives of men's hearts to show them that their motives and their thoughts are really the thing which makes it necessary for them to be set under law. Hence, if they will truly be free, they must be set free by the Son. Motives which are wrong, hence necessitating rigid laws to make life tolerable, are the subjects of this discourse.

Considering the broader base of this particular verse, one sees how it fits into the larger context. In verses 21-26, the law of murder is good enough for men but not good enough for disciples of Christ. If anger is properly dealt with, there will be no outbursts ending in murder. In verses 27-30 the Mosaic law of adultery will not stand up to the kind of straight and pure thought which Christ expects of disciples. Here is the heart of Christian discipline. Without it there can be no discipleship with Christ. It is admittedly ascetic in certain ways. In verses 31-32 Christ is concerned with the gross excess of loose marriages in his day and again is stating to his disciples that this cannot be a part of the attitudes and practices of discipleship. It negates another central concept of Christianity, responsibility. The guarantee for a truth in the pre-Christian period of the Jews was by an oath sworn to God (33-37). If an oath was sworn to God, it was more binding than one which was not. Hence Christ saw that men's words were resting on a slippery footing and that true responsibility and interpersonal relations among disciples must not be white truth and gray truth. Christian responsibility required each man to stand individually responsible for his own acts. If responsible to God, then responsible to man; this idea got lost between the first pope and the Reformation. The consequences of it are the most important developments in modern history, to my way of thinking.

## Biblical Giving

Finally, in verses 38-42 the matter which you brought up is dealt with. Retaliation and vengeance are under attack. An eye for an eye was good enough for the Old Testament, but not for disciples. In order that true discipleship should distinguish itself from the traditions of the day, Christ has asked these close followers to do more than try to come out ahead or at least even in every deal they make. Charity is born of the spirit of sacrifice and sacrifice is the essence of Christianity. Indiscriminate giving or giving in a sense of competition or rivalry is hardly what Christ could mean here. Christ himself did not heal everyone who came to him. Christianity in its Protestant manifestation has caught the spirit of this verse, and we see it in all kinds of charity. Catholicism obeys it when it is part of a system of control over institutions.

If we were to take the verse absolutely literally, we could invalidate all that Christ is getting at in these discourses. Suppose one of the disciples figures that the rest are going to take this literally and so decides to ask for the loan of another's wife. Since the first man is tempted to want the other man's wife, he now finds that his temptation can be turned into the real thing because the husband is going to obey Christ and give her up. By *refusing to give* his wife he may calm the man's temptation and help the poor brother to work out his problem on a better footing, something which will lead toward a Christian thought (discipline, responsibility, and charitable love) rather than to the moral undoing of the man. Hence, our giving is always done with a purpose which must of necessity be built into a Christian framework. We must have clear-cut categories of Christian thought which we aim at when we give or when we receive. To do otherwise will not lead toward Christianity. But now comes the anthropological aspect of the problem.

## The Meaning of Behavior

Giving is merely an act, a kind of personal transaction which stems out of some more basic and pushing kind of desire. Christian giving to missions, hospitals, and other charities of any kind may arise from any number of desires, some of which may be Christian. I am sure some of them must be. A missionary is out to make some individuals into disciples for Christ, that is, to show them by word and example what discipleship would mean when translated into the local system, culture, values, or whatever you want to call it. The great weakness of being a missionary is that so few ever really know what discipleship means when translated into the local system of things. For here it has to find its meaning or it has none.

The area where I work is that of the Bulu of the south Cameroun. I think it would be no exaggeration to say that the church of this area (and it is huge) is composed of a vast majority whose only conception of being a Christian is one of imitating the white man's religious system without reference to discipleship within the system of Bulu culture. It seems all too evident that few of the Christians in primitive areas ever come to a position where they understand the relation of Christianity to culture. Few missionaries do; therefore it is something that is not communicated except to say "indigenous church," whatever that may mean.

## Discipleship Transvaluated

The missionary cannot know what discipleship transvaluated is unless he understands something of the system into which the new disciple is built, his culture. Great sections of the Bible remain wholly useless to people who are not forced to undergo a certain cultural appropriation of its spiritual message. The institutional (church-missionary) abrogation of polygyny among the Bulu is a case in point. No Bulu was ever given any occasion to come to grips with polygyny as a moral problem because there was none. He was merely told that it was wrong, and therefore to enter into the new institution which everyone was joining (the reasons being many) he went through the perfunctory act of reducing his number of wives. There was no personal appropriation of anything.

I know that under a house near here there used to be a large press which was used exclusively to remove female neck and ankle decorations which were symbols of marriage. As soon as a woman wanted to join the church, she made a trip to this mission house and had her neck taken out of the rings. No Bulu ever came to grips individually and existentially concerning the demands of Christ upon his life in its deepest and most spiritual (therefore moral) sense. His motives were left untouched. His thoughts went unchallenged because those who sought to communicate to him did not know his motives (and still do not). The obvious, rings on the ankles and neck, plural wives, murder, and blood revenge, were all neatly put aside for the institution. Little discrimination was possible. A sterile kind of overt conformity was the requirement for becoming a church member.

And in all of this conformity there was no need (and perhaps no opportunity) to come to grips with the demands of Christ. The mainsprings of cultural behavior were never considered, hence never changed very much except as inertia changes things. The rite is the important thing, and the man who performs the rite is the important man. *Bidi bi Zambe* (God's food) communion is the principal relation between man, God, and the church. This is not surprising, since this is the problem that was never taken care of by the clash of Christianity. A former orientation to religious matters carried over right into the new church. Priests take care of religious matters by their special knowledge. Now pastors (who are seeking an Episcopal form of church government) who have been set up as judges of offenses, take care of these ritual relations with man and God. So distorted are values that affairs about man and his personal relation with God, his personal life, his responsibility, his individuality before God are relegated as nothing important to the masses and are swallowed up in an orientation which tends to replace man by men. The net result of this is a perfect preparation of this big Bulu church for Catholicism.

## Steps to Adaptation

So what? How do I adapt to local traditions? To understand them is worth more than adapting to them. However, if you make a real concerted effort to understand them, I have found the people will usually make a lot of allowances for your ignorance. Then, the more you understand of their motivations the less rigid is the possibility of adapting. The deeper one gets into the life of a people, the easier it becomes to move around comfortably in it. This always involves the defining of one's role in the eyes of the people with whom he lives. When this is clear, a lot of the stress and strain is removed.

In attempting to demonstrate Christ in a particular culture by doing what is usually required by tradition, we run into many problems. I am sure we do not demonstrate Christ simply by conforming to the requirement of a tradition. However, I make it a rule of thumb to do so in so far as I can. The purpose of conforming to some brand of tradition is more to make oneself tolerably acceptable to the people one wants to present Christ to. It is obvious that we must get over onto the side of the other man and talk to him and live in terms of his understanding, if he is to understand our communication. I personally find that there is no attempt among the various groups we have lived among to look at things in terms of *our* cultural background in order to learn what we are trying to communicate. That is just more sophistication than can be asked for. The almost universal trend is to read one's own motives into the other's behavior and to interpret accordingly.

I recently had a long talk with a group of Bulu Christians on this very point. They told me how they interpreted missionary behavior, and it amounted to saying that the assumed missionaries did the way they did because they were motivated the same as Africans. The Africans interpreted their behavior out of an exclusive African or Bulu frame of reference. When I pointed out that they were not justified in doing this, the Bulu replied: "How else can we do it? We don't know their [the missionaries'] customs." You will admit, I am sure, that you interpret the African's motives out of those which were inculcated in you as a child. This makes for the most grotesque interpretations of cross-cultural relations. It is often like two ships signaling each other with their beams directed in such a way that they miss everything except an occasional signal and lots of static. Before one can communicate Christ, one must communicate oneself. This will demand a sacrifice of many traditional ways of doing things. It will often reveal how stingy we really are.

I would suggest that you do two things among the Busas: (1) try to understand the motives behind the gift-giving and (2) ask yourself what role you can fit into in an acceptable manner in Busa culture. Perhaps you should be a *planteur*, a raiser of cattle or horses, a merchant, a tradesman of some kind. Believe me, I do not believe in the role of missionary. It is one which just too often cannot fit. Even by the wildest imagination of the African, the role of "missionary," the man who is paid to come to Africa for three years and ride around in his car, and then go home for a year's rest, is too good to be true. Who would not be a missionary? I am sure we create a new kind of ideal man. It is anything but Christian.

## Pattern of Giving

Who can give to whom? What can men of two different social levels give to each other on these visits? After you have worked out a chart of the "who gives what and how much to whom, and when and why," you will be in a position to pick your niche and get into it and there be understood.

I personally chew kola nuts when I go out and work all day in the plantations with the Bulu men. Some of my colleagues chew kola nuts when they are driving long distances to avoid going to sleep. Kola nuts contain caffeine. I do not think it could be much of a stimulant, as I have found no effects from it at all. I am sure it is not much more than a couple of cups of coffee and perhaps less than a large Coca-Cola. I inquired from our medical staff here, and they said the only bad effect they know of is a slight discoloration of the teeth — shades of Ipana! The Bulu believe it makes men more productive sexually. I personally have found no sexual stimulation in it.

Giving of old clothes and tin cans could turn out to be a very sour apple indeed. I would not give an African something which was not good enough to give to a white man, unless he specifically requests it and I have a Christian purpose in mind in giving it to him. The African, if he is not in a trade area, soon will be in one and will find out that you gave him what the whites do not want any more, and hence you run the chance of being accused of ridicule, a serious charge among many Africans. The Christian idea of giving comes from sacrifice. Short of that there is no giving that is essentially Christian. Stewardship is probably the most difficult of Christian practices to develop in the "acquisitive" society. Indiscriminate giving on your part would not communicate the idea of stewardship, but of prestige most likely.

The Bulu seek a relation called *mvo'e.* This is a liberty for asking for material goods which is established between men who make a kind of gift exchange covenant. I have unwittingly been sucked into this by giving gifts. I did not know that the Bulu were taking it to mean that I sought a *mvo'e* relation with those I gave to. However, they interpreted it that way. Now that I am caught, I am working out ways of dealing with the Christian concepts of sacrifice and stewardship as meaningful concepts in Bulu economics. These *mvo'e* relations must now be used to impart some Christian ideas.

Here is, on a small scale, what I mean by the transvaluation or the interpenetration of Christian ideas into Bulu. The *mvo'e* relation must be put under the scrutiny of Christian thought as any economy must be converted along with the people who practice that economy. Not to do so is to compartmentalize experience. The African Christian is a past master at compartmentalizing his experiences. I do not plan personally to compete with any Bulu chiefs in wealth or gifts. The role assigned me by Bulu culture is so radically different from that of a Bulu chief that I would not think of myself in the same category at all. Since the people do not either, it would be foolish for me to try to compete with him. If I could, what would I have gained? You have also to face the translation of a verse about the poverty of Christ compared with the foxes who have only a hole to sleep in. The Bible is an embarrassing book. It will be interpreted largely out of the stock of experiences of those who read it. Our tradition, which gives us our translation (or interpretation) problems, is our rationalism. The African likewise has his, his mythology, his wealth, and his political organization. His understanding of the Scriptures cannot possibly be separated from these things which have cast the categories of his thought. The real missionary task is to make the Scriptures understandable within the limits set by these traditional categories. To pass beyond these is to move outside the knowable and to fail to communicate. If we missionaries understand the nature of his compartmentalization, we will know the channels into which we can communicate the Scriptural message. This involves restructuring the "truth." I am of the opinion that the "truth" can come in many shapes and sizes. The distortion of the truth arises mostly because we do not operate with the proper categories to receive it in its "distorted" (restructured) form.

WILLIAM D. REYBURN

*William A. Smalley*

# Proximity or Neighborliness?

MISSIONARIES talk about "going out to live among the people" (although anyone who has seen a typical mission compound will not take that cliché too literally), but how many have ever thought of being neighbors to these "people" near by?

In our western world individuals may be thrown into regular contact, even close physical proximity, over long periods of time, and not have more than the most superficial social intercourse, if any at all. This is most true in our large cities where people in adjoining apartments may never meet each other, or if they do, may have no more than a formal and polite social interchange. Even in smaller communities, however, the boss who works daily with his men may have no other contact with them (except for the annual Christmas party), and people who bow together in church may never meet during the week.

It is not until we reach the very small rural community in the United States that we find a high degree of neighborliness between people in close proximity, where everybody knows everybody else. An indication of the fact that in our culture we do not always put high value on such relationships is that we may add to the previous sentence: . . . and where everybody minds everybody else's business.

Reprinted from Vol. 4, No. 3 (1957), pp. 101-104.

In our highly complex society we have built cultural devices for keeping people close by from being neighbors unless for some reason we choose to include them. These barriers provide a protection for us, keep us from having to associate with people who are not compatible, whose race or education or social status is different from ours. We can withdraw within the barriers for security from people and social patterns which conflict with our own.

Some missionaries live in large cities where this urban pattern of proximity without neighborliness may be well developed. If they bring in their insulating mechanism as part of their cultural baggage it is not particularly conspicuous, although even in the urban setting it may be an almost insurmountable barrier to effective communication on an individual level. Such missionaries have to rely on the mechanics of playing church and mass evangelism to do what has historically been most effectively done by the personal contact of one dedicated soul with his neighbor.

It is in the rural mission areas where proximity without neighborliness stands out in such painfully brutal fashion. Typically, the mission builds a compound on a hill a mile outside of the village. A cluster of huts may be built on the least desirable part of the compound for servants and hangers-on. Non-Western school teachers and preachers have their quarter, too. It is hard to imagine a more effective physical way of isolating the missionary from the people "among whom he is living."

But the psychological isolation is far more serious. As one missionary put it, "The Africans know to which missionary door they can go." A conversation which was reported to me is not an extreme case. One missionary had learned that a Bible revision committee which included both Westerners and Africans had refreshments served during the morning, and asked, "What do you do with the Africans?" When he learned that they were served, too, he asked if butter tins were brought in for the African's coffee. When he learned that they were served from cups no differently from anyone else he was horrified, considering it most unsanitary.

Some missionaries protect themselves from the people around them by a host of devices. They may never participate socially either in the local culture or through inviting people into their homes. They may not learn the language really well. They may be contemptuous of the uneducated and revolted by the unclean. They are not interested in the things which interest people. They are therefore remote, distant, and terribly cold.

On a recent trip in Africa I saw two examples of missionary neighborliness which I would like to contrast to the above. One was in the home of Dr. and Mrs. Wesley Sadler, Lutheran missionaries among the Loma people of Liberia. (In their case the "among" is not figurative.) The Sadlers' home is on the edge of a Loma village, just a few yards from the nearest Africans' houses. It is not, however, that close proximity which makes the Sadlers neighbors, it is their spirit.

During each evening while I was there, anywhere from two to five or six of the villagers, men and women, would drop in. They would come individually and stay for just a few minutes. They came naturally, without the embarrassment which marks the entrance of an African tribesman into so many missionary homes. They stopped and chatted for a few minutes and then left. They were at home. The usual barrier was not there. Equally revealing was the Sadlers' reception of their visitors. It was the reception given someone with whom you are on the very friendly relation of frequent contact. The visit was taken for granted, and it was enjoyed.

Sadlers raised their children under that thatched roof in Woozie, the little Loma village. They studied Loma life and language not just as anthropologists and linguists (Dr. Sadler's Ph.D. is in linguistics) but as interested neighbors. They liked their neighbors and wanted to know them better. I have never seen happier missionaries.

The other example of missionary neighborliness which I saw took place when I was visiting Dr. and Mrs. William Reyburn in the Camerouns. We heard drum beats one evening and went to investigate. A group of students was "playing." They had formed a circle, in which they were dancing and singing, while one person danced in the middle. The person in the center tried to perform some antic which was different from what anyone else had done. When he had finished he would point to someone in the circle who would take his place. Reyburn took a few steps so that they would not think he had come to criticize. He made everybody laugh, and then we sat down to watch.

Before long the dancer in the center pointed to Reyburn there on the bench, and he went into the circle to jump up and down. Before long I had been invited too, and we were all jumping up and down to the beat (I was at least trying) for about half an hour. Once I got over beings self-conscious, it was fun.

The next day word of the Africans' appreciation came through to the Reyburns: "It is the first time anyone [meaning missionaries] ever played with us."

# Anthropology: Role and Method

*Eugene A. Nida*

**Reprinted from Vol. 6, No. 3 (1959), pp. 110-116.**

# The Role of Cultural Anthropology in Christian Missions

*After making a survey of some of the different attitudes toward culture and the mission of the church which have stimulated the study of culture and anthropology, Nida suggests that none of them are adequate. He considers the prime service which the study of culture has to offer to be that of a valuable basis for relevant communication, whether it be in the choice of words, in the cultural relevance of the message, or the issues to which the gospel is addressed. He feels that communication based upon a perceptive understanding of a culture can stimulate some members of the culture to make vital decisions for Christ in a responsible way.*

THERE have been a number of quite different concepts as to the role of cultural anthropology in Christian missions. For some the application of anthropological techniques to missions has seemed nothing less than a panacea for all ills, that is to say, the most effective means of transforming the society through newly discovered insights. Such persons have thought that if they could just understand the culture, they could easily set about changing it.[1]

Other missionaries have regarded the study of cultural anthropology as providing the data on which the missionary might build the Christian message. As Edwin W. Smith so strongly advocated, the missionary was to find in the indigenous religious system the equivalent of the Old Testament viewpoint and background, and on this foundation he was to work out a Christian orientation. The equating of the Old Testament experience of the Jewish people with the indigenous religious traditions was thought to provide the essential contact and basis for the proclamation of the Good News.

Still a third point of view, and one not wholly dissimilar from the second, has been that the application of cultural anthropology to missionology would ease the transition from indigenous religious superstitions and practices to Christian beliefs and rites. By a carefully planned series of adjustments the people could be led progressingly toward the acceptance of the gospel, with the least disruption of native cultural values. This view has been vigorously endorsed and followed

[1] Dale W. Kietzman, "Conversion and Culture Change," PRACTICAL ANTHROPOLOGY, Vol. 5, Nos. 5-6 (Sept.-Dec., 1958), pp. 203-210, has suggested those areas of personal interaction in which the application of this subject of cultural anthropology is highly relevant. Our concern is more in the direction of those procedures of acculturation which must be carried out with due concern for the culture of the people if significant or permanent changes are to be realized.

by the Jesuits in their missionary efforts,[2] and not without remarkable success, in terms of Jesuit goals.

Despite the popularity of these applications of cultural anthropology, it would seem that fundamentally none of them is satisfactory. In the first place, the knowledge of cultural anthropology is no panacea in the development of a mission program. Merely knowing how people function within their culture does not provide the answers to how certain aspects of this functioning can be changed. This does not mean that cultural anthropology cannot be highly instructive to the missionary in introducing modifications in the beliefs and practices of a people, but a mere descriptive view of a people's culture is not enough. Moreover, the methods by which the data of cultural anthropology may be effectively applied to a practical problem are not inherent within the facts of cultural study. There is much more involved — and this we shall try to explain below.

The view that the indigenous religious system, regardless of its nature, orientation, or practices, can provide a kind of "Old Testament experience" for the people is the result of a superficial understanding of either the Old Testament or the local religion. There are, of course, many similarities between religious practices recorded in the Old Testament and the so-called animistic features of primitive religions, such as ordeals, sacrifices, seers, mediums, scapegoats, taboo, etc., but there are more important matters which make the fuller religious revelation of the Old Testament unique: (1) monotheism, in contrast with henotheism (i.e. one exclusive God in place of merely one high god), (2) the relationship of moral behavior to religious holiness (i.e. the moral content of taboo), and (3) the initiative of God in loving and redeeming mankind. These three factors (and there are a number of others) set off the theology of the Old Testament from the concepts of animistic religions in such a way as to provide fundamental and basic differences, which can never be reconciled by pointing out superficial similarities and then trying to build a New Testament structure on an indigenous foundation.

## Jesuit Syncretism

The Jesuit system of accommodation did not begin with the Counter Reformation, which brought the Jesuit movement into being. It actually had its start in the year 601 when Pope Gregory VII wrote to the priests attempting at that time to convert the heathen Britons:

> We must refrain from destroying the temples of the idols. It is necessary only to destroy the idols, and to sprinkle holy water in these same temples, to build ourselves altars and place holy relics therein. If the construction of these temples is solid, good, and useful, they will pass from the cult of demons to the service of the true God; because it will come to pass that the nation, seeing the continued existence of its old places of devotion, will be disposed, by a sort of habit, to go there to adore the true God.
>
> It is said that the men of this nation are accustomed to sacrificing oxen. It is necessary that this custom be converted into a Christian rite. On the day of the dedication of the temples thus changed into churches, and similarly for the festivals of the

[2] Peter Duignan, "Early Jesuit Missionaries: A Suggestion for further Study," *American Anthropologist*, Vol. 6, No. 4 (August 1958), pp. 725-32.

saints, whose relics will be placed there, you should allow them, as in the past, to build structures of foliage around these same churches. They shall bring to the churches their animals and kill them, no longer as offerings to the devil, but for Christian banquets in name and honor of God, to whom, after satiating themselves, they will give thanks. Only thus, by preserving for men some of the worldly joys, will you lead them more easily to relish the joys of the spirit.[3]

In the Jesuit development of this principle (and not without opposition from many quarters of the Roman church, especially from the Franciscans and Dominicans) the technique was to assume "a thousand masks," "being all things to all men" and with "holy cunning" to accept the limitations imposed by the local situation. One must not, however, be too severe in one's criticisms of the Jesuit position, for fundamentally they recognized the fact of cultural relativism, namely, that the same practices in different cultures had quite different meanings and values. They rejected the Platonic concept of "idealistic ethics" and endorsed the Aristotelean view of Nichomachean ethics, based on a sense of cultural diversity and practical application.

Moreover, the Jesuit practices were an understandable reaction to the wanton disregard for the indigenous culture, so often practiced by other Roman Catholic orders. (For example, in Mexico the Franciscans by 1531 had pulled down 500 temples, broken 20,000 idols, burned countless manuscripts, and smashed thousands of priceless objects of art.)

Perhaps the greatest irony of the conflict between Jesuit and non-Jesuit efforts on the part of the Roman Catholic missionaries has been the fact that both incorporated such a high degree of syncretism, whether consciously (as in the case of the Jesuits) or as forced by circumstances, that in the end the "converts" became related to a different set of practices, but with very little fundamental change in basic beliefs. What actually happened in so many cases was that Jesuits did not carry through with a total plan for adjustment, and non-Jesuits found that the shortest road to the goals established by the church necessitated adjustments, not dictated by theory, but imposed by force of circumstances.

For example, the early Franciscans destroyed the imposing temple in the ancient religious capital of Mitla, Oaxaca, Mexico. With the stones from the pagan structure they built a church in the valley, but the people continued to worship amid the ruins on the hilltop. At last, the missionaries adjusted to the pressures of the situation, had the churched pulled down, and rebuilt it on the site of the original Zapotec shrine. Of course, if the purpose of any missionary undertaking is to bring the people into the jurisdiction of the church, then a syncretistic approach is both efficient and expedient. However, if the purpose is to bring the people into a new orientation to life through a new relationship to God, as revealed in Jesus Christ, then a system of syncretism tends to cancel out any gains and the distinctiveness of Christianity becomes almost totally lost. In Orura, Bolivia, for example, during the fiesta of the Day of Temptation, not only do the devil dancers utterly fail to depict any Christian themes or motifs (despite their perfunctory blessing by ecclesiastical authorities), but the very concept of the day is perverted, for this day, which is supposed to commemorate

[3] Ibid.

Christ's resistance to the wiles of the Devil, is reinterpreted by many people as a time during which people may yield to temptation without incurring penalties.

**The Basis of Communication**

If, however, as we have suggested, the legitimate role of cultural anthropology is not to be found in reconstructing a base for Christianity in pagan practices or easing the transition by syncretistic adaptations, what then is it? I would like to suggest that basically the study of anthropology provides a means of effective communication. In and of itself cultural anthropology does not provide the answers to how, when, and why certain approaches should be made. But it can and should resolve some of the major problems of communication which are inherent in any missionary undertaking. The implications of such a proposition are naturally very extensive, but in their simplest forms we may say that the knowledge of cultural anthropology, as it applies to the cultures involved in any missionary task (i.e. the cultures of the missionary and the people to be reached — the so-called source and target cultures), provides an orientation as to (1) the relevance of the symbols by which the Good News is communicated and (2) the means by which these symbols may be communicated in a context which is meaningful to the people of the target culture.[4]

We seem to have no difficulty in understanding the phrase "born, not of blood" (John 1: 13) as being some reference to lineage, for we often speak of "royal blood," "a true blue-blood," and "the blood line." However, in many cultures the word "blood" has no such implications. In Apache, for example, such a phrase would be relatively meaningless, but if someone tried to attach meaning to the utterance the only significance it could have would be that a child was born without any blood in his veins or that the mother in question did not bleed at childbirth. A study of cultural anthropology can provide a missionary with a basis for recognizing the differences in the two symbolic systems, and to know that in Apache for example, the English word "blood" in this type of context must be equated with "family" or "clan."

In one area in West Africa missionaries have for years used a word for "spirit" which has quite a different meaning from the Biblical expression. In this region the word actually means "soul stuff," the basic substance which gives life to all animate existence. God Himself is regarded as possessing such a substance, and it is variously distributed throughout the universe, and quantitatively allocated in various degrees on different levels of existence, so that insects have very little, animals have more (depending upon their strength), and man most of all (with corresponding degrees of such power reflecting levels within the socio-economic structure). When in this language missionaries declare that God (whom they designate as Allah) is "soul-stuff," they are expressing nothing more or less than pantheism, and it is not without reason that these Islamicized peoples seem unimpressed, if not downright shocked, by such a heretical message.

Of course, a study of cultural anthropology will not guarantee that a message communicated to any group of people will

[4] It would be a mistake to assume that all the communicative symbols employed by missionaries are words (they actually include much more, e.g. gestures, acts of kindness, art forms, music, etc.), but for the sake of our limited analysis we shall restrict ourselves to verbal forms for they are indicative of the basic problems encountered in other areas of symbol utilization.

be accepted. Far from it! Cultural anthropology only helps to guarantee that when the message is communicated, the people are more likely to understand. And it is this very fact of understanding it which may result in the people's rejecting it! But this is much better than to have them appear to accept it, when they really do not understand its significance. Once, however, the missionary has a thorough understanding of the cultural relevance of the symbols which he must employ in order to communicate, it is very much more likely that he can at least speak with meaning to the people, thus establishing the first and indispensable level for any missionary undertaking.

**Basis for Cultural Relevance**

Any proclamation of the Good News must, however, advance far beyond a mere recognition of the proper equivalence of word symbols. It must be so oriented that the total impact may be evident to the hearers. This means that the gospel should not be presented as one of the accoutrements of Western civilization, as a watered-down compromise with indigenous beliefs, or as merely another and more powerful technique for doing business with the supernatural. (There is no legitimate place for encouraging the view of "this Jesus-God, he strong god too.")

If the communication of the Christian message is to be culturally meaningful, in terms of the total lives of the people, certain features are essential: (1) It must use meaningful indigenous symbols wherever any concepts are crucial and (2) the implications of the message must be explained in concrete terms which are culturally applicable within a given society.

Because of the inadequacy of indigenous symbols, missionaries have often felt that they could best introduce borrowed words. This may be quite all right for terms for *camel, phylacteries, Pharisees,* and *dragon,* for the proper understanding of these terms is not crucial; but in the case of a word for *spirit* or *God,* such borrowings are almost fatal. Certainly much of the effectiveness of the preaching of the gospel to the Navajos through the years has been hampered by the use of the English term *God,* which actually resembles in sound the Navajo term for juniper bush. In Apache, on the other hand, missionaries have employed an indigenous term meaning "by whom life comes into being," in other words the Creator, but also the Sustainer of life. This expression is culturally meaningful and has served, together with other well-chosen expressions, as part of the basis for effective communication.

Communication does not, however, consist merely of strings of utterances, meaningful as they may be within the language in question. Such words must be related to life, or they are nothing more than catechisms to be memorized (as a passport to heaven) rather than as programs for living. One must tackle real issues and in a thoroughly Christian manner. What, for example, is one to do with ritual drunkenness which occurs as a manifestation of many religious celebrations among primitive peoples? It is certainly not adequate to denounce such practices as being "naughty-naughty" or to apply to them the often unthought-out tenets of Protestant Puritanism. Such drunkenness must be treated for what it is, namely, a false kind of religious estasy,[5] a sincere but misguided attempt to find communion with God. But in its place the missionary must be able to

[5] Eugene A. Nida, "Drunkenness in Indigenous Religious Rites," PRACTICAL ANTHROPOLOGY, Vol. 6, No. 1 (Jan.-Feb., 1959).

demonstrate real communion, which lifts men above the drab experiences of the secular humdrum and gives them the thrill of being the children of God.

An emphasis upon moral righteousness may lead the missionary to denounce excessive "bride payment." This should not be done, however, on the basis that there is anything morally wrong in the concept of such transactions, for in their proper application they can do much to stabilize marriage and to consolidate clan relationships. However, in their selfish excesses such bride payments deprive many people of their moral rights, they tend to commercialize the sacred institution of marriage, and they often thwart the expression of genuine love. The proclamation of the Christian way of life must involve one in just such problems, not as a despiser of all indigenous institutions, but as one who sees in all human forms the potentiality of corruption. In other words, one must take seriously "the theology of man," including a realistic evaluation of man's egocentric orientation.

Such an attempt at a realistic view of life will not prevent serious misinterpretations by the sending constituency as to a missionary's message or motivations. For example, he may feel his mission is not justified in refusing to grant communion to sincere believers who are polygamists and who have a high sense of moral responsibility toward obligations incurred before learning of the gospel, or to those living together in common-law arrangements which may not be resolvable because of arbitrary laws about divorce. His judgment may be based on the fact that though such refusal may preserve the sanctity of the church, it prevents the spiritual growth of men and women for whom also Christ died. In other words the spotlessness of the church may not be so important as the spiritual nurture of human souls, who are admittedly bound for heaven because they believe in Jesus Christ but who are kept out of the fellowship of the church.

### Stimulus to Radical Decisions

A study of cultural anthropology makes it possible for one to see life through the eyes of those who participate in it. Hence, the proclamation must challenge men and women where they are. The Good News for poor workers in the slum *barrios* of Lima, Peru, must not be a translation of some sermon framed for a small-town congregation in America's Bible Belt (which this writer once heard delivered). In Congo the message must deal with such matters as *gaza* rites (involving cliterectomy), equal opportunities for girls, the rightful place of education, the correct employment of natural resources, such as land and game (which are being mercilessly exploited), righteous dealings between employers and employees (including everything from joining trade unions to paying decent wages to mission help), plain ordinary honesty, respect for leadership, abuse of power, etc. But all of these themes, which arise out of the Good News as revealed in Jesus Christ, must be related to the crucial issues of each man's life.

If the gospel is to be presented with utter abandon to the claims of God upon men, it will mean that many persons who might go along with a neutral, syncretistic, a "white-man-he-knows-better" presentation of the Christian message, will reject culturally relevant proclamations. They are too hard to take — even as they were rejected by so many who listened to the Master Himself. This means, therefore, that a knowledge of cultural anthropology and the application of these data to the proclamation of the gospel may actually result in fewer responses to the Good News (at least at first). But the point is this: the relevant witness to the revelation of God in Christ will force upon men and women the necessity of making vital decisions. Such a declaration of the full claims of God upon men (for not only their souls but their lives) will make possible an ultimate acceptance of the message which will mean more than adherence to a set of ritualistic observances. It will be nothing less than a rebirth by the power of God, who alone can take this witness to the truth and communicate it to the life and heart of people.

The application of cultural anthropology thus becomes the effective instrument by which men may be pressed (by the Spirit of God) to make radical decisions about life's fundamental crises.

*William L. Wonderly*

**Reprinted from Vol. 6, No. 3 (1959), pp. 55-64.**

# Social Anthropology, Christian Missions, and the Indians of Latin America

*Mexico has been in the vanguard, among the nations of the American continent, with respect to the application of the principles of social anthropology in the secular fields to the problems of indigenous or Indian groups. The present article attempts to summarize for English readers some of the major bases of this movement as it is being carried forward by Mexican social anthropologists of today. It then points out certain of the principles of the movement which are of special significance for the work of Christian missions among the Indian groups of Latin America, and certain points at which the movement, due to its commitment to a secular approach, needs to be supplemented by the development of a parallel Christian movement by groups who can come to closer grips with the specifically religious anxieties of the Indian peoples.*

ONE of the outstanding names among the *indigenistas*[1] of Mexico is that of Dr. Alfonso Caso, director since 1949 of the Instituto Nacional Indigenista and a distinguished scholar in Middle American archaeology, anthropology, and other fields. His recent book (in Spanish) entitled *Indigenismo*[2] is a collection of twenty articles and lectures, mostly published elsewhere, which have the purpose that is stated on the back cover: that of "explaining, in the simplest possible terms, the theory upon which the *indigenista* action in Mexico is based and the results which have been obtained from it."[3]

In the first chapter of the book,[4] Caso attempts to define who and what are to be considered as Indian. He uses a com-

[1] The Spanish term *indigenismo* is frequently translated as "Indianism" and *indigenista* as "Indianist" or "Indian." These translations, however, seem to be quite inept, inasmuch as the English words are not normally used in the same sense as the Spanish terms. Dr. Gonzalo Aguirre Beltrán, in his significant treatment of "Indigenismo y mestizaje" (*Cuadernos Americanos* 15.4, July-August 1956, pp. 35-51), uses *indigenismo* in contrast with *indianismo*, which further complicates the translational difficulties. In the present article we shall regretfully use the terms *indigenismo* and *indigenista* in their Spanish form, without attempting an English equivalent.

[2] Alfonso Caso, *Indigenismo*. Instituto Nacional Indigenista, México, D. F., 1958. Pp. 159; 19 plates. 12.00 Pesos Mex.

[3] All quotations from Caso's book in this article are our own translation. A number in parentheses following the quotation will identify the page in the original.

[4] The book itself, consisting as it does of separate materials published elsewhere, has a great deal of repetition; many of the chapters or articles develop in brief and interesting fashion an overall view of *indigenismo* or of certain of its aspects, but the progression from chapter to chapter is not worked out as it would be if the book had been written as a unit. Hence our presentation will not follow the order of the book's contents, but will attempt to give the materials in a somewhat rearranged form for the sake of continuity.

bination of four criteria: biological, cultural, linguistic, and psychological. The first three are objective and accessible to the outsider; the fourth, the sense of belonging to an Indian community, is subjective and less amenable to outside investigation, but is the most important from the Indian's own point of view. Caso's primary definition is therefore a definition of the INDIAN COMMUNITY; his definition of the individual Indian is in relation to that community. We give the following translation of his definition:

> An Indian is a person who feels that he belongs to an Indian community; and an Indian community is one in which non-European somatic elements predominate, which speaks and prefers an Indian language, which has a large proportion of Indian elements in its material and spiritual culture and, lastly, which possesses a social feeling of being an isolated community among the other communities that surround it, resulting in its considering itself as different from both white and mestizo[5] peoples (pp. 15-16).

Caso insists that the Indian problem be recognized for what it is, and reminds us of the cultural isolation of the Indian groups, especially those who are monolingual:

> The Indian problem is for Mexico a fundamental one, since 1 inhabitant out of 5 is Indian as to his culture and way of life, 3 out of 20 speak Indian languages, and 1 out of 13 speaks only an Indian language[6] and therefore lives outside the culture of Mexico and the Mexican community (21).

The orientation with respect to the Indian community as a whole rather than the individual alone is an important principle, which is discussed again and again in the book. But just as the individual is not to be considered apart from his community, so the Indian community needs to be treated as part of a larger context, the INDIAN REGION, which includes both the Indian communities and the mestizo town or city with which these are in a symbiotic relationship.

> ... We now speak not merely of Indian communities, but of INDIAN REGIONS; that is, of more or less extensive regions that are characterized by being made up of numerous Indian or Indian-mestizo communities which depend economically, culturally, socially and politically upon a mestizo city, which we call the METROPOLIS of the Indian region in question.
>
> This is the case, for example, with Tlaxiaco, in relation to the surrounding region of the High Mixteco, in the State of Oaxaca; and with San Cristóbal Las Casas and the Tzeltal-Tzotzil region in the State of Chiapas. . . .
>
> On the other hand, the Indian communities themselves have a decided influence upon the METROPOLIS, giving it a character which distinguishes it from other mestizo cities of the country. Thus there is an interaction from every point of view. We may say that the METROPOLIS of a region would be unable to live without its surrounding communities, from which it gets raw materials for its sustenance, for its commerce, and for its local industries (usually carried on by small artisans); and

[5] Since the Spanish word *mestizo* has already crept into our English language and dictionaries, we use it. It should be kept in mind that it means "mixed," and is used to refer to the mixture of Indian and Spanish in both the biological and the cultural sense.

[6] On page 52 he says that 1 out of 20 speaks an Indian language only.

> that the Indian communities themselves would be unable to live without the METROPOLIS, where they must go to exchange their surplus domestic produce for objects which they do not themselves produce but which they consume . . . (76-77).

The character of the metropolis, or mestizo center of an Indian region, is thus influenced by its long and intimate contact with the Indian communities, who have contributed to the mestizo population many aspects of their world view, religious outlook, folk medicine, and so on; and whom the mestizos have at the same time looked upon as an inferior group that is to be exploited for their benefit. Hence any valid approach to the Indian community must also take the mestizo center into active consideration.

### Cultural Equilibrium and Acculturation

In a chapter on "Culture and Acculturation," Caso defines culture in the anthropological sense, discusses the various categories of material and spiritual culture, explains acculturation as meaning the transformation of a backward community through contact with the dominant cultural group. He points out that in this transformation the social anthropologist should be called upon to help plan and direct the acculturation process so as to avoid the disorganization of the weaker community and its exploitation by the stronger community.

He insists upon the INTEGRAL CHARACTER and the EQUILIBRIUM of the Indian culture, and the importance of an overall approach to the guidance of the acculturation process.

> We consider it to be impossible to transform a community if only one of the aspects of its life is changed; for we believe that the Indian communities have their own culture, and that every culture is an equilibrium in which one cannot change a given aspect without the other, unchanged, aspects of culture feeling the effect of the action on the one hand, and on the other hand acting as a brake to retard the proposed change. One cannot, for example, change the economy of a community without taking into account its taboos, its ideas of social prestige, and the ways by which it incorporates its children into the community. For this reason the policy which the Instituto Nacional Indigenista has chosen to follow is what may be called an INTEGRAL POLICY — that is, we study and modify the economic aspect and the social organization, and endeavor to accelerate, through public health, education and road construction, the incorporation of the community into the political and cultural life of the nation (65-66).

As we shall discuss below, however, one of the most important of the aspects which serve to integrate an Indian culture is the religious aspect; and it is difficult for us to agree that any approach to acculturation can, in the full sense of the word, be termed an "integral" policy so long as it concerns itself with the transformation of communities "in their economic, hygienic, educational, and political aspects" (35) but does not squarely face the full religious implications of these aspects of the culture change. This statement is not intended as a negative criticism of the *indigenista* movement, but rather as an indication of wherein lie some of its limitations.

### Protection and Help, not Charity

On the matter of official Indian policy, Caso emphasizes time and again the need and justification for protective laws for the benefit of the Indian, rather than simply considering him as having equal rights with others and as being capable of defending these rights. Just as minors, women, and the physically handicapped are possessed of certain biological limitations which prevent them from holding their own as equals with the rest of the population, so the Indian is socially handicapped and needs the protection of special laws. He is the equal of any other member of the human family as far as his racial heritage goes, but is in a position of real inferiority socially, culturally, and economically; therefore to make him the object of supposedly equal treatment for all men is to take an unrealistic attitude toward him and to actually make him the victim of discrimination. Hence the need for protection and aid, not merely for theoretical equality before the law.

But Caso insists that such protective laws, and Indian policies in general, should not be such as to keep the Indian in a perpetual state of inferiority, but that "the Indian communities should be given all the hygienic and cultural elements necessary to speed up their transformation and to bring them into step with the progress of the rest of the communities in the country" (40). In other words, the Indian communities are not to be helped or protected as if they were indigent groups in need of charity, but are to be given such technical aid as will enable them to become true participants in the culture of the nation.

The Indian is to be helped by giving him education as to hygiene, medicine, agricultural techniques, etc.; he is to be given means of communication so as to market his products; he is to be given opportunity, through radio, moving pictures, and other media, to realize that he is part of a larger world and is no longer isolated. But all this must be done in a way that will avoid such a conflict between the Indian culture and modern culture as would disrupt the Indian culture.

> For these reasons, any government action undertaken to better the condition of the Indians of our countries should be based on recommendations made by anthropologists; inasmuch as it is impossible to change one aspect of a culture without at the same time producing an impact upon all other aspects. One cannot, for example, change the economy of a community without at the same time affecting the family and social organization, the attitude of the individual toward his family and his community, and even his concept of life itself (54).

Among the positive values of the Indian culture that are to be conserved wherever possible, special mention is made of the Indian's sense of community solidarity and of responsibility for mutual help within his group, which is a feature that can be a valuable contribution to the national life as the Indian communities become interrelated with it. Emphasis is also placed upon the artistic sense of many of the Indian groups, and the popular art that is produced by them and which should be encouraged. Four chapters of the book are devoted to various aspects of popular art in Mexico, with special reference to the Indian's contribution to it and to ways of protecting and encouraging it.

### The Indigenista Movement in Mexico

In one of the chapters, Caso points out that the "social transformation that is taking place in Mexico today, . . . starting with the Revolution which began in 1910, has manifested itself in every sphere: economic, political, social and cultural" (85). He then relates to this historical development the "experiment in social anthropology" (85) that is being conducted by the Instituto Nacional Indigenista, which was established in 1948 and which has been carrying out extensive pilot projects in five regions (the Tzeltal-Tzotzil, Mazateco, Tarahumara, and two Mixteco regions). In these projects, three basic policies are observed (90): use of demonstration rather than compulsion; enlistment of the cooperation of at least part of the community prior to carrying out any action; and the use of bilingual Indians as employees and PROMOTERS to carry the action to the people and to promote cultural change.

The projects of the Institute include the promotion of economic change through securing of land, teaching of new agricultural techniques, use of better seed, crop rotation, forest conservation and use, establishment of cooperative stores, etc. They include work in public health and hygiene, and in literacy and the teaching of Spanish. With reference to religion, the approach is definitely secular; Caso indicates the policy toward religion when that it is preferable

> ...not to persecute the individual who makes offerings to the gods of the mountains or to the saints so that it may rain and so he may cultivate his maize, but to construct dams and irrigation ditches which will make constant watering possible, as a better way than that of prayers and offerings (81).

These various activities are directed toward the region as a whole and the culture as a whole:

> The mission undertaken by the Institute is regional and integral. It is regional because it attacks not just the problems of one community, but extends to the problems of an entire region that shares a language and other cultural features, and includes in its radius of action the mestizo city as well, which we call the METROPOLIS of the region.... Our action is integral because it has to do with all the aspects of the culture of the community (90).
>
> ...The clear and definite purpose that we have undertaken is that of accelerating the development of the Indian community so as to integrate it as early as possible with the economic, cultural and political life of Mexico, but without producing disorganization in the community itself. That is, our purpose is to speed up the change, which is inevitable anyway, that will lead to the transformation of the Indian community into a Mexican peasant community, and of the Indian region into a Mexican region with all the characteristics of the other regions of the country. Of course this does not mean an attempt to destroy the positive aspects that remain in the Indian cultures, such as the solidarity of the Indian with respect to his community, the use of certain regional costumes, the production of artistic objects, etc.;... but it is useless to conserve outmoded ideas regarding the causes of natural phenomena and the means of utilizing the forces of nature; it is both useless and injurious to conserve the old ideas of the causes and cures of sickness, or to perpetuate backward and unscientific techniques of exploiting land and forest resources, of animal husbandry, etc. (77-78).

### Use of Indian Languages in Education

With reference to the use of the Indian languages in the program of the Institute, Caso writes, without much elaboration:

> In matters of education, our Indian promoters teach the children to read in their own language, as a step toward teaching them to speak, read, and write in Spanish (92).

This of course follows the pedagogical principle of beginning with the known before proceeding to the unknown; i.e. the learner is taught to read in a language that he already knows, and then his knowledge of reading helps him to go on to the learning of Spanish.

However, in the program of most *indigenistas* the teaching to read in the Indian language appears to be thought of as almost solely for this purpose of bridging the gap to Spanish. Very little basic education seems to be carried on in the Indian languages; as soon as the pupil learns to read his own language and then to read Spanish, he is expected to acquire the rest of his education in Spanish. This of course appears in keeping with the overall goal of bringing the Indian into effective contact with the cultural life of the nation, whose chief linguistic vehicle is Spanish. Yet there are two major difficulties which we may mention here, that are not discussed by Caso. (1) The Indian who learns to read Spanish at this early stage is unable to read it with comprehension unless he is already highly bilingual; reading in Spanish therefore becomes a feat whereby the Indian acquires a bit of added prestige, but does not become a tool whereby he can acquire significant information. (2) Even for the bilingual Indian who does learn to read with comprehension, reading materials in the type of Spanish with which he is familiar are sadly lacking. Very few Indians who are literate in Spanish continue as readers after they leave school.

Without belittling the importance of the use of Spanish, it would seem that somewhat more of the basic education program should be carried on in the Indian language, as soon as the initial hurdle of learning to read in the language is passed. By so doing, reading can immediately become a means of acquiring information, thus making it an activity which is satisfying and relevant to life. And the basic information thus acquired should lead to an earlier participation of the Indian in at least certain aspects of the national culture. In terms of the work of Christian missions, it is of course especially important that the message be communicated in a form that will be intelligible to individuals within their linguistic background as well as their cultural background.

## Significance of Indigenismo for Christian Missions

Many aspects of the *indigenista* movement are highly significant in relation to the development of evangelical Christianity among the Indians of Latin America. In a country where there exists this movement to effectively relate the Indian communities to the life of the nation, an obvious corollary is the responsibility for the churches and missions to relate the evangelical Indian congregations to the life of the evangelical church in its national character. If this is not done, the Indian may upon conversion end up as culturally isolated both from his community and from the nation. But just as in all other aspects of the culture the integration process needs to be carried forward, as Caso emphasizes, without disruption of the existing cultural pattern and loss of the positive values in the Indian cultures, so also in the church this integration needs to be accomplished without the cultural disorganization that will result if the Indian congregations are forced into the Procrustean mold of outward conformity to mestizo church patterns.

A significant experiment in integration is now being conducted among the Chol Indian churches of the National Presbyterian Church of Mexico, in which the Chiapas Presbytery has formed a "Chol Institute of Coordination," whereby the elders of the organized Chol churches compose a body authorized to discuss and decide on problems of local nature which do not involve the Presbytery as a whole. For example, cases have arisen regarding marriage of two people who although unrelated have the same surname — a matter that would hardly even be recognized as a problem if brought before the mestizo Presbytery, but which is a very real problem for Indians who carry this prohibition over from an earlier practice of clan exogamy. The Indian coordinating group may also handle problems of how to dispose of the maize received in the harvest offerings, or of how to carry on Christmas and Easter celebrations in a way which, while Christian, will still meet the cultural needs formerly met by semi-pagan *fiestas*. Although it is still too early to evaluate the success of this experiment, this kind of an attempt, within the organizational structure of a national church organization, to provide a way for Indian groups to work out their own special problems would seem to be highly significant.

Caso's concept of the Indian region as a whole, with its mestizo center, has implications that are of great importance for the development of the church in such regions. The writer of the present article spent a number of years in the mestizo-Indian town which serves as a center for part of the Zoque region in Chiapas. He now feels, in retrospect, that one basic reason why no effective evangelical witness resulted from his work there, either among Indians or mestizos, is that almost all his efforts were directed toward the Indian people in isolation. He failed to realize the importance of the interrelationship between the Indian and mestizo people, to whom the former look for much of their leadership and who are the ones through whom the Indians expect cultural innovations to enter the region. (In support of this thesis, it may be said that during the same period the Seventh Day Adventists were successfully developing a work which did include the region as a whole, beginning with Spanish-speaking nuclei and embracing both mestizos and Indians indiscriminately).

The recognition of the Indian community as forming part of the larger mestizo-Indian region has a significant bearing upon the missionary's concept of the indigenous church. Most Indian groups are at some stage or other in the process of becoming peasant groups — i.e. they are no longer primitives living in complete cultural isolation, but are people who, although they conserve basically their own way of life, exist against a background of the mestizo culture and the urban way of life that they know exists "out there." They recognize the outside culture as having certain values to which either they or their children should aspire, and they seek to find points of contact between their own group and the mestizo group. To the degree to which this is true for a given community, the indigenous church goal should not be an isolated Indian church. If the church in an Indian community is to be really indigenous (that is, if it is to truly "belong" in the community), it should in such cases function against a background of the evangelical church in its national character to a degree comparable to that in which the community in general functions against the background of the national scene as a whole. This of course does not mean absorption of the Indian church by the national church to the point that the former loses its identity; but it does mean that the Indian church should be so organized as to be constructively related to the national church. To effect such a relationship will not always be the easiest way of organizing a church; it may involve tensions and problems of leadership personnel and of organizational patterns. But it is important that such problems be faced realistically and not with what Caso terms an "erroneous attitude [of] a false and romantic *indigenismo* [which] considers that it is best to leave the Indians alone and isolated" (100).

A further significance of Caso's concept of the Indian region with its mestizo center is that the evangelical church in the center needs an educational program that will help its own constituency to understand the problems of the Indian churches in the region. The church in the center needs to cease thinking of Indians as second-class brethren and learn to appreciate the Indian culture and the positive values it can bring to the church as a whole. It then needs to seek ways in which it can help in integrating the Indian churches with the national church life, while at the same time maintaining the cultural integrity of the Indian groups and giving them the effective content of the gospel message by using, wherever necessary, the native language for the proclamation and teaching of the Christian message. No project of Christian work among an Indian group can be said to have been adequately undertaken until these aspects of the problems are squarely faced.

There also exists a need for communicating these concepts to the wider protestant constituency in Latin America, and especially to the leaders of the evangelical movement who are responsible for guiding the development of the national churches in their relationships with the Indian groups. Caso's book itself sets an instructive example of a scholar's endeavors, through lectures and journal and magazine articles, to "sell" the generally educated public on the importance of an anthropological approach and to communicate to them something of its basic principles. Similar efforts need to be made to communicate, to the general protestant constituency, the basic principles of social anthropology as applied from a Christian standpoint to the problems of the Indian groups.

## Need for a Christian Indigenismo

As mentioned earlier, *indigenismo* as it is being developed at present in Mexico is committed to a secular approach. This is in part due to the ideologies of the men who are developing it, and is justifiable on the official level because the organizations concerned are connected with a government which, under its national constitution, does not and cannot maintain any connection with religious organizations or movements. But whatever may be the reasons and justification for a secular approach, the fact remains that the Indian outlook on life is not secular but religious. Agriculture, medicine, social organization — all are permeated with religious attitudes; and any attempt to guide acculturation without taking these into consideration is seriously hampered from the outset. It is hardly accurate to say that such an effort "has to do with all the aspects of the culture of the community" (90).

Furthermore, religion is one of the major stabilizing factors in the maintenance of a cultural equilibrium and of the integral quality of an Indian culture. Granted that our western culture, toward which acculturation is directed, is highly secularized; but the Mexican peasant way of life toward which the Indian groups are actually moving is much less secularized than is our urban culture. The Indian in process of culture change needs, perhaps more than ever before, a faith which will enable him to meet the changing situation and around which he can build his new way of life without the moral chaos and social disintegration that can result if he loses faith in his old beliefs but remains unable to cope with the new anxieties that accompany what we call civilization.

Of course we are not hereby suggesting that the government-sponsored agencies, which in Mexico and some other Latin-American countries, even as in the U.S.A., are committed to separation of church and state, try to direct the religious acculturation of the Indian communities. What we are trying to say is (1) that there does exist a process of religious acculturation which, due to the very cultural equilibrium that Caso mentions, inevitably accompanies the changes that take place in other aspects of the culture; (2) that if left unattended this process may lead to loss of confidence in the old values and failure to discover new ones; and (3) that in order to avoid this creation of a moral and religious vacuum it is important that other agencies, which are specifically committed to a religious approach, develop an *indigenismo* that can supplement in a positive way what is being done in the secular field. Such a Christian *indigenismo* need not be in competition with the secular agencies, nor should it get involved politically. Its purpose should be to make the Biblical message relevant in terms of the changing Indian culture, and thereby to give a spiritual basis to the new way of life that the older religion, geared as it is to the older technologies and forms of social organization, is incapable of giving.[7]

A Christian *indigenismo* will seek to discover those aspects of the Biblical message which most directly relate to the anxieties of the Indian group and to the tensions that are created by the process of change. It will endeavor to find the most effective ways of communicating this message, whether by the use of the Indian language or by the cultivation of Christian practices to replace pagan ones; and in either case it will be concerned to put into the message such content as will be meaningful in terms of the cultural situation.

This orientation in Christian work will

[7] Manning Nash (*Machine Age Maya: The Industrialization of a Guatemalan Community;* American Anthropologist Memoir 87, 1958) found that in the industrialization of a Quiché Indian community the people have compartmentalized their thinking, maintaining their older religious practices (with some modification) with respect to their agriculture and family life but not effectively relating their religion to their factory experiences or their labor union organizations. He suggests that the basic religious attitudes have been left unchanged by the advent of the textile factory, but thinks the lack of change may be at least partly because the factory is institutionalized and beyond the immediate control of the Indian, who works as an employee but bears no responsibility for the management of the industry. Hence the situation described by Nash is not entirely parallel to the introduction of modern technologies into the average Indian community.

also give due recognition to the fact that, in many of the Indian groups, the younger generation's ambitions and outlook upon life are no longer limited to the horizons known to their elders. The recognition of this fact will call for the preparation of Christian Indian leaders who not only are oriented toward the Indian cultural background but who are also equipped to face those aspects of the modern world that are even now affecting the life of the young people in their churches. This ability of the Christian leaders to face both ways, as it were, is an especially important qualification in situations where a church has become established and the children of the originally converted group are growing up as "second-generation Christians."

Although there is still much to be desired and much left to accomplish, we believe Caso to be correct when he affirms that "Mexico can be justly cited as the country that has made the greatest effort to solve its Indian problem" (21). But the very fact that this is true in the secular sphere makes it incumbent upon the churches of Mexico to bring their own country's progress to bear upon the problems of the Indian groups for whose spiritual welfare they are responsible, and thereby to help in the establishment of patterns for church development among Indians elsewhere in Latin America as well. In other Latin American countries there is also progress in *indigenismo,* and in each situation the churches and missionary organizations should recognize their responsibility (1) to relate these developments to the growth of the Indian churches and the meaningful proclamation of the Biblical message and (2) to help the Indian groups maintain, in the face of cultural change, a sense of direction and spiritual stability which is necessarily outside the domain of the secular *indigenista* movement, due to the very nature of the latter.[8]

[8] Since this paper was written, there has come to the writer's attention a brief but informative report in English on the work of the Instituto Nacional Indigenista, in the following two articles: Alfonso Caso, "Ideals of an Action Program," *Human Organization* 17, Spring 1958, pp. 27-29; and Julio de la Fuente, "Results of an Action Program," ibid., pp. 30-33.

Reprinted from Vol. 6, No. 6 (1959), pp. 262-272.

*David L. Hamm and Batua A. Macaraya*

# Acculturation Survey of the Dansalan Junior College

*One of the important problems of missionary communication on any level is the need to know what is being understood by the teaching or preaching, and what influence the message is having upon people's thinking and attitudes. Sometimes there are overt responses which can be interpreted, and which give a clue to what is getting across. The authors of this article devised a questionnaire by which they feel that they measured something of the degree of influence which mission schooling has had on two classes of Filipino students.*

A PRIMARY necessity in dealing with acculturation (the assimilation of new cultural elements borrowed from the outside) is an effort to determine the degree of acculturation of students who come to our schools, and to attempt the measurement of the change in attitudes which is effected by the school program. Accordingly, a questionnaire was prepared for the students in Marawi City, Philippines. It is proposed that these questions will be given in at least one other school and, in translation, to a group of persons of relatively small educational attainment. This report is concerned with the results of the survey as it measures attitudes of the first year and fourth year secondary level students at the Dansalan Junior College.[1]

The questions were prepared in the form of a test known to the students as "multiple choice." A small "story" was provided with three, four, or five action endings. The students were asked to choose the action which would seem to them to be the most appropriate. The stories were in four groups. (1) Three stories were prepared to measure the extent to which the students felt it reasonable to appeal to Philippine law as over and against the use of older extra-legal methods of settling disputes. (2) A second series attempted to measure the changes that take place in the students' thinking about marriage and divorce. This proved a difficult area to approach. (3) Three questions attempted to test their attitude when the cultural situation causes tension between honesty and group loyalty, which is an ethical

[1] With respect to the methods employed in this survey, we would like to acknowledge the help given by Dr. Charles Warriner, Associate Professor of Sociology, University of Kansas, whose consultation saved a good deal of labor.

**David L. Hamm is a missionary of the American Board of Commissioners for Foreign Missions, having served two terms in Marawi City, Philippines. Batua A. Macaraya is Acting Director of the Dansalan Junior College.**

problem in some ways more related to Christianity than some of the other problems. (4) There were three questions involving the reaction to the need for medical attention.

The answers were tabulated on a five-point scale and the possible responses were set into the following scheme of categories: (I) traditional response which would correspond with the elements of Islam and the underlying cultural heritage of the group; (II) modified traditional response; (III) a neutral response; (IV) modified acculturated response; (V) acculturated response.

For purposes of this report we will deal with the tabulation of those answers made by the first year and fourth year groups, dividing each of these groups into Muslim and non-Muslim students. Many but not all of the non-Muslim group are Protestant young people in Marawi City. Table One shows the distribution of the answers given by ninety first-year students and forty-one fourth-year students. The number of responses in each category is given with the percentage figures. These figures indicate that the responses of both the first and fourth year groups tend to be rather more strongly in the new culture categories than in the old. This fact is further brought out if the percentages are compared, combining categories I and II into one figure and categories IV and V into one figure. This tabulation is shown in Table Two. In the first-year group more than 50 percent gave a response which indicates orientation away from the old cultural patterns even among the Muslim group. This tabulation may be useful for comparative purposes as we examine the data.

**TABLE TWO**

| 1st year | I and II | IV and V |
|---|---|---|
| Muslim | 349 (36.8%) | 487 (51.5%) |
| non-Muslim | 33 (25.1%) | 88 (66.6%) |
| Total | 382 (35.2%) | 575 (53.2%) |
| **4th year** | | |
| Muslim | 84 (23.3%) | 260 (72.3%) |
| non-Muslim | 12 (9%) | 117 (88.7%) |
| Total | 96 (19.5%) | 377 (76.6%) |

## Law and Order

For purposes of presentation of the questionnaire to the students, the order of the stories was mixed and the possible responses were also scrambled, so that the numbering used here is for convenience in reporting.[2] The three situations involving cooperation with the agencies

[2] The order of presentation to the students may be determined from the numbers and letters in parentheses after each heading or question in the following discussion.

**TABLE ONE**

| 1st year | O No answer | I Traditional | II Modified Traditional | III Neutral | IV Modified Acculturated | V Acculturated |
|---|---|---|---|---|---|---|
| Muslim | 48 (5%) | 163 (17.2%) | 186 (19.6%) | 64 (6.7%) | 104 (11%) | 383 (40.5%) |
| non-Muslim | 7 (5.2%) | 13 (9.9%) | 20 (15.3%) | 4 (3%) | 18 (13.6%) | 70 (53%) |
| Total | 55 (5%) | 176 (16.2%) | 206 (19%) | 68 (6.6%) | 122 (11.2%) | 453 (42%) |
| **4th year** | | | | | | |
| Muslim | 0 | 29 (8%) | 55 (15.3%) | 16 (4.4%) | 51 (14.1%) | 209 (58.2%) |
| non-Muslim | 0 | 6 (4.5%) | 6 (4.5%) | 3 (2.3%) | 10 (7.7%) | 107 (81%) |
| Total | 0 | 35 (7.1%) | 61 (12.4%) | 19 (3.9%) | 61 (12.4%) | 316 (64.2%) |

of the law were a murder case, a land case, and a case of water buffalo rustling. The following are the questions involving law and order:

1. *Murder Case (1).* Two brothers and their friend, who was a Muslim Holy Man, were returing to their village when the enemy of Older Brother jumped out of the bushes and stabbed him. Older Brother struggled for a while and died. *Which of the following actions do you think is best?* I (B) Younger Brother went after the enemy and killed him. II (C) Younger Brother called the head men and informed them. V (A) Younger Brother took Holy Man with him as a witness and reported the incident to the constabulary. O No answer (blank).

**First-year**

| | Muslim | non-Muslim |
|---|---|---|
| I | 7 (8.8%) | 1 (9.1%) |
| II | 27 (34.5%) | 1 (9.1%) |
| V | 44 (55.5%) | 9 (81.8%) |
| O | 1 (1.2%) | 0 |

**Fourth-year**

| | Muslim | non-Muslim |
|---|---|---|
| I | 1 (3.3%) | 0 |
| II | 8 (26.7%) | 2 (18.2%) |
| V | 21 (70%) | 9 (81.8%) |
| O | 0 | 0 |

The expected response in the Maranao culture (Response I) would be that Younger Brother would go after the enemy. Where the issues are clear, the head men would then declare the situation as being satisfied if the enemy were killed. The case would be closed. The percentage of answers involving reporting the incident to the constabulary, therefore, was quite high for the first and fourth years. The non-Muslim does not show the appreciable shift between the first and fourth year that the Muslim group does.

2. *Land Case (6).* Farmer had a land case against Coffee Grower in which he was seeking to retain possession of his inheritance, because Coffee Grower obtained title through false means. The court decided in favor of Coffee Grower. *Which of the following actions do you think is best?* I (B) Farmer attacked Coffee Grower to scare him out of the case. II (A) Farmer went to the head men for help to protect his property against Coffee Grower's occupation. IV (D) Farmer called the head men and with them went to the governor. V (C) Farmer appealed the decision to a higher court. O No answer (blank).

**First-year**

| | Muslim | non-Muslim |
|---|---|---|
| I | 12 (15.2%) | 1 (9.1%) |
| II | 32 (40.5%) | 4 (36.3%) |
| IV | 17 (21.5%) | 3 (27.3%) |
| V | 14 (17.8%) | 3 (27.3%) |
| O | 4 (5%) | 0 |

**Fourth-year**

| | Muslim | non-Muslim |
|---|---|---|
| I | 0 | 1 (9.1%) |
| II | 6 (20%) | 0 |
| IV | 5 (16.5%) | 1 (9.1%) |
| V | 19 (63.5%) | 9 (81.8%) |
| O | 0 | 0 |

The second case involving land requires for a category V response a rather high confidence in the courts of the land, since it involves an appeal of a case already decided. It is therefore not surprising to find a much lower percentage of the group making a choice in category V. The choice in category IV which received a higher response from the first year students is that involving a representation to the governor. This is definitely a modification of the new culture situation, since the governor is an official in the Philippine legal sense. It represents a common modification. The governor, deputy governors, and town mayors frequently act as intermediaries in disputes, sometimes in cases that are already in the courts. In terms of the degree of acculturation this would indicate a shift in authority from the traditional rulers and head men to the mayor and district official complex. The first year group shows the defiant attitude for protecting the property against the order of the court. On this question it seems to us that we have the most significant shifting of attitude between the first and fourth years.

3. *Cattle Rustling Case (9)*. The water buffalo of Rancher was stolen from his ranch in Bayang. He suspected Strongman was the thief. *Which of the following actions do you think is best?* I (C) Rancher made sure it was Strongman before he took property for revenge. II (A) Rancher notified several ranking head men of the loss and asked them to negotiate for the return of his water buffalo. V (B) Rancher reported to the Philippine Constabulary and asked for help in regaining his property. O No answer (blank).

| | **First-year** | |
|---|---|---|
| | Muslim | non-Muslim |
| **I** | 15 (19%) | 2 (18.2%) |
| **II** | 26 (33%) | 2 (18.2%) |
| **V** | 36 (45.5%) | 6 (54.5%) |
| **O** | 2 (2.5%) | 1 (9.1%) |
| | **Fourth-year** | |
| | Muslim | non-Muslim |
| **I** | 7 (23.4%) | 2 (18.2%) |
| **II** | 10 (33.3%) | 0 |
| **V** | 13 (43.3%) | 9 (81.8%) |
| **O** | 0 | 0 |

The third question seems to set us back on our heels because in acculturation terms it shows regression from the first to the fourth years. Cattle rustling is a serious offense. Two things about the preparation of this story complicate the response. In all the other instances we deleted specific place names. Moreover, we asked the students to consider the questions as though they occurred in their own place. It is quite evident that the response we have here is an exception to that rule. Bayang is one of the most remote of the municipal districts bordering Lake Lanao. There are constabulary detachments in Ganassi and Lumbatan on either side, but the road connection with Lumbatan is practically non-existent. The response may indicate that the constabulary cannot operate effectively in Bayang. Response I is not a very well-worded response. It would, of course, constitute a strong temptation in any culture for one to take revenge against a known offender. Considering these facts it seems likely that we have quite a reasonable reaction from the students. It is likely that some of the ethical dimensions involved were apparent to the fourth-year students but not the first-year students. The non-Muslim group answered in more or less the same way. The first-year and fourth-year groups of non-Muslims treated the question more abstractly.

## Marriage and Divorce

In this general area we selected three situations which reveal tension between cultural values: the desire of students for educated spouses, the possibility of registering marriages as an indication of acceptance of Philippine law, and a situation involving divorce.

4. *Educated Wife (2)*. Fourth-Year Student wanted an educated wife, and so he started to court his classmate. His relatives did not think she would make a good wife for him. They suggested that Student marry a girl from his home place who had two grades of schooling. *Which of the following actions do you think is best?* I (B) He did as his parents desired, and married the girl from his home place. II (A) He refused his parents and said he would not marry yet. IV (D) He and his classmate

decided to "live together" so that when the baby was born the parents would be forced to agree. V (C) He refused his parents and asked them to select an "elementary graduate" or "better educated" girl for him. O No answer (blank).

**First-year**

| | Muslim | non-Muslim |
|---|---|---|
| I | 26 (33%) | 0 |
| II | 19 (24%) | 3 (27.3%) |
| IV | 2 (2.5%) | 3 (27.3%) |
| V | 29 (36.5%) | 5 (45.4%) |
| O | 3 (4%) | 0 |

**Fourth-year**

| | Muslim | non-Muslim |
|---|---|---|
| I | 5 (16.7%) | 1 (9.1%) |
| II | 9 (30%) | 1 (9.1%) |
| IV | 3 (10%) | 3 (27.3%) |
| V | 13 (43.3%) | 6 (54.5%) |
| O | 0 | 0 |

The issue is the conflict of the student's desire for an educated wife as over and against his duty to his parents. It was felt that the desire to have an educated wife indicates a strong desire to incorporate new culture values into living. It is commonly felt that educated boys have a hard time marrying the girls from back home, or else they simply revert completely to the old culture patterns. In this series of responses there is a question about which of the responses constitutes the greatest shift. Answer IV (D) would appear to be a more complete defiance of the parental rule than C (V). However, it is more outside of the institutionalized norms of the Maranao community than of the non-Maranao community. We therefore classify this as modification. It certainly is a modification if we think of the new culture in terms of the legal apparatus. There is, of course, a strong question as to whether or not the "no divorce" laws actually function satisfactorily in the Philippines; whether they institutionalize adequately the cultural values. Response II (A) indicates a modification of Maranao culture under pressure. The culture has been sufficiently fluid in recent years that it has not been expected of all young people that they simply do as their parents request in this matter. There is much more flexibility, especially with regards to the woman's place, than is commonly supposed. The indications are, then, that there is a considerable shift in the direction of the insistence upon educated wives. The significant figures for comparison are in Category I. Thirty-three percent of the first year students selected the old cultural response and only 16.7% of the fourth year students selected that response.

5. *Registration of Marriage (10).* A young man, Farmer, very much wanted to marry a neighbor in his community, Lady Weaver. She accepted his courtship, and the relatives approved the match, and all the arrangements that should be made before the marriage were finished. *Which of the following actions do you think is best?* I (B) The couple were married by the local religious leader but did not register the marriage. III (C) The couple lived together. V (A) The couple were married by the religious leader and the marriage was registered with the government. O No answer (blank).

**First-year**

| | Muslim | non-Muslim |
|---|---|---|
| I | 14 (17.8%) | 2 (18.2%) |
| III | 20 (25%) | 0 |
| V | 38 (48.2%) | 7 (63.6%) |
| O | 7 (9%) | 2 (18.2%) |

**Fourth-year**

| | Muslim | non-Muslim |
|---|---|---|
| I | 3 (10%) | 0 |
| III | 2 (6.5%) | 2 (18.2%) |
| V | 25 (83.5%) | 9 (81.8%) |
| O | 0 | 0 |

The issue is the registration of the marriage and has to do with the use of the Philippine legal forms particularly as these are understood to be deterrent to divorce. The C response, which would probably be regarded by the Maranao group as a kind of betrothal situation, could perhaps be appropriately in category II or even category I. It would certainly indicate that the distinctions about registration or non-registration would mean little. The answer that we get shows an increasing appreciation of the form of registration as having cultural value, though the story here is not stated in a way to indicate as much as might be desired with regards to divorce.

6. *Divorce (12)*. Since their marriage, Housewife and Husband were frequently quarreling and fighting, although they really loved each other. In one quarrel, Housewife got a black eye and Husband got a dislocated arm. Housewife went to her parents. *Which of the following actions do you think is best?* I (A) Housewife with her parents' help got the husband to divorce her. II (C) Housewife asked her parents' help in requiring Husband to pay a penalty of not less than $50.00. III (B) Housewife asked the parents to call the head men together. V (D) Housewife goes back to her husband to be reconciled with mutual promises of adjustment. O No answer (blank).

**First-year**

| | Muslim | non-Muslim |
|---|---|---|
| **I** | 18 (22.75%) | 1 (9.1%) |
| **II** | 20 (25%) | 1 (9.1%) |
| **III** | 14 (18%) | 1 (9.1%) |
| **V** | 25 (31.75%) | 7 (63.6%) |
| **O** | 2 (2.5%) | 1 (9.1%) |

**Fourth-year**

| | Muslim | non-Muslim |
|---|---|---|
| **I** | 2 (6.5%) | 0 |
| **II** | 4 (13.3%) | 0 |
| **III** | 8 (26.7%) | 1 (9.1%) |
| **V** | 16 (53.5%) | 10 (90.9%) |
| **O** | 0 | 0 |

Question 6 is specifically aimed to measure the attitudes to divorce. There are several things involved, though we sought to make divorce the important one. The methods in the old culture in dealing with the quarrel situation would tend in the direction of solution I (A), for the wife to go to her parents and get divorced. Response II (C), which is set quite strongly in the Maranao cultural situation, would penalize both Housewife and Husband because the husband would be required to get the money, but the parents of his wife and her relatives would receive it. Response III (B) is set pretty much within the Maranao cultural complex but it leaves the issue somewhat open and for that reason we classify it as neutral. Response V (D) would, we believe, indicate a change of attitude from the Muslim cultural situation inasmuch as it would place a higher value on the continuity of the marriage than is ordinary. This would, of course, be the most Christian response. This question received a rather high percentage of what we have classified as neutral responses and perhaps the question arises as to whether that relatively passive resolution of the situation should have been included. However, it is to be noted that between the first and fourth year groups there is a very marked shift from the I (A) and II (C) responses toward the III (B) and V (D) responses.

The young people answering are many of them in the marriageable age bracket. A further analysis shows that of the 26 Muslim girls in the first-year group, 35% selected category I, the same percentage as selected category V; 19%

selected III. The Muslim fourth-year girls conformed to the school answer pattern, 66.7% selecting category V, the reconciliation solution.

## Honesty vs. Loyalty

The three questions involving the problem of honesty as over against some type of loyalty put special emphasis in each case on the kinship. The moral problem in the nation is illustrated by the case of Senator Cuenco and the move against him involving loyalty to the Nationalist Party. The situations are as follows:

7. *Kerosene Sale (3)*. Merchant bought kerosene from Wholesaler, a Chinese. When the time came to pay, Merchant changed the price and tried to pay a lower price than agreed upon. The associate of Merchant is his townmate, Seller, who was present at the making of the original agreement. Seller was called by the court to be a witness. *Which of the following actions do you think is best?* I (C) Seller testified that his townmate was right. II (A) Seller refused to testify. IV (D) Seller called the mayor to make an amicable settlement. V (B) Seller testified to the truth in spite of the adverse effect it had on his townmate, Merchant. O No answer (blank).

**First-year**

| | Muslim | non-Muslim |
|---|---|---|
| **I** | 21 (26.5%) | 0 |
| **II** | 3 (3.8%) | 0 |
| **IV** | 24 (30.5%) | 6 (54.6%) |
| **V** | 27 (34.2%) | 4 (36.3%) |
| **O** | 4 (5%) | 1 (9.1%) |

**Fourth-year**

| | Muslim | non-Muslim |
|---|---|---|
| **I** | 5 (16.7%) | 1 (9.1%) |
| **II** | 1 (3.3%) | 0 |
| **IV** | 15 (50%) | 1 (9.1%) |
| **V** | 9 (30%) | 9 (81.8%) |
| **O** | 0 | 0 |

In story 7, the group loyalty would probably involve kinship in the Maranao community, inasmuch as one would almost certainly be related to practically everybody in the barrio or municipal district in which one lives. The English term "townmate" would reflect a kind of relationship anywhere in the Philippines and for that reason it was chosen rather than the term "relative." It was intended that the relationship here should be more tenuous than in question 9 where it is indicated as that of cousins. Again, in question 9 the relationship is not as close as American speakers of English might think, since cousin means a considerable number of degrees of relationships.

8. *School Examination (5)*. Fourth-Year Student knew he would have to pass English to graduate. He had 70's in the first, third and fourth grading periods, and 75's in the second and fifth grading periods. He needed a 75 in order to pass. *Which of the following actions do you think is best?* I (B) He prepared his notes so that he could put them under his legs and look at them during the examination. II (A) He took a chicken as a present to the director asking him to influence the teacher. IIa (C) He took the test without extra effort, and pleaded with the teacher to give him a passing grade. V (D) He studied hard for the test, asking help from the teacher. O No answer (blank).

**First-year**

| | Muslim | non-Muslim |
|---|---|---|
| **I** | 10 (12.6%) | 1 (9.1%) |
| **II** | 4 (5.1%) | 1 (9.1%) |
| **IIa** | 6 (7.6%) | 3 (27.3%) |
| **V** | 54 (68.4%) | 6 (54.5%) |
| **O** | 5 (6.3%) | 0 |

**Fourth-year**

| | Muslim | non-Muslim |
|---|---|---|
| **I** | 0 | 0 |
| **II** | 1 (3.3%) | 0 |

| | | |
|---|---|---|
| IIa | 1 (3.3%) | 0 |
| V | 28 (93.4%) | 11 (100%) |
| O | 0 | 0 |

9. *Fraud (8).* Clerk, who worked in a government office, bought a bracelet for wife from Goldsmith. It was mostly silver but Goldsmith said it was solid gold. Goldsmith's Cousin was in the shop when the sale was made and knew that Goldsmith was cheating Clerk. Several weeks later Clerk discovered the fraud and called the head men to help him get his money back. He named Cousin as his witness. *Which of the following actions do you think is best?* I (D) Goldsmith's Cousin testified in favor of Goldsmith against Clerk. II (A) Goldsmith's Cousin refused to testify. IV (C) Goldsmith's Cousin urged Goldsmith to return the money and get the bracelet but refused to testify. V (B) Goldsmith's Cousin testified against Goldsmith. O No answer (blank).

**First-year**

| | Muslim | non-Muslim |
|---|---|---|
| I | 22 (28%) | 1 (9.1%) |
| II | 4 (5%) | 0 |
| IV | 41 (52%) | 4 (36.3%) |
| V | 10 (12.5%) | 5 (45.5%) |
| O | 2 (2.5%) | 1 (9.1%) |

**Fourth-year**

| | Muslim | non-Muslim |
|---|---|---|
| I | 2 (6.5%) | 0 |
| II | 0 | 0 |
| IV | 20 (67%) | 3 (27.3%) |
| V | 8 (26.5%) | 8 (72.7%) |
| O | 0 | 0 |

In question 8 the group loyalty would be the family or kinship group who would be expecting each student to graduate. Failure would be a reflection on the group. The case of the kerosene sale (7) involves again a situation where, from the point of view of ethics, the better result might be category IV than V, although V involves most complete acceptance of the Philippine Westernized modes of dealing with ethical problems. The amicable settlement, as was noted above, is an in-between system which involves settlement out of court. It is probably as good from a Christian point of view as the other.

Question 8 is the one in which we might expect the highest degree of influence of the school situation on the students. These responses indicate that within the school situation students are carried farthest out of the context on which loyalty to the group predominates. However, the category V response can be considered as loyalty to a new group.

In situation 9, there are parallels with 7. In both cases we have a high percentage of responses in categories IV and V, with the question raised as to which of these two is really most desirable. In situation 8, involving school examinations, it is to be noted that we classified all responses except one as either old culture or modification of it. Response category I, which was desirable to a group of our first-year students, involves misconduct in terms of school norms and this fact is, of course, registered in the responses of the fourth-year group, none of whom checked it.

In this area of social relationships we find a higher degree of response in category IV and V, and most of the responses in the other categories are in part due to the fact that modern changes of Islam constitute a pressure more in the direction of what we consider to be Christian responses. It should be here stated that there are movements in the area tending toward a better level of Muslim ethics than was current before.

In question 7, besides having the problem of group loyalty, we have also the problem of the place of Philippine legal apparatus inasmuch as the case is a court case and cooperation with the courts is involved. We have here what indicates honesty but unwillingness to carry it to the court. The difference between our first- and fourth-year groups is an increased desire to achieve an amicable settlement, but actually a less cooperative spirit on the part of the fourth-year group. The question may be raised as to whether the first-year students were confused with the English that so many of them advocated false testimony. The results here indicate that loyalty *vs.* honesty constitutes a real source of tension. Christianity stresses truth in more absolute terms than Islam does.

## Medicine

The fourth type of situation in which the values of the Maranao culture complex in particular and some of the older cultural patterns in the Philippines generally, come into conflict with modern culture are in the field of medicine. We are justified in calling this modern because the development of medical practice is a relatively recent phenomenon. We used three situations involving three types of medical need: illness, a delivery case, and a wound. They are as follows:

10. *Illness with fever (4)*. Fisherman, a middle-aged man from a village on the shore of the lake, came home from his day on the lake with a very high fever, having a headache and feeling very weak. *Which of the following actions do you think is best?* I (D) He pleaded with the ancestors and guardian spirits, and killed an animal to please them. II (A) He sent for the local Medicine Man to treat him. IIa (E) He saused evil-driving portions of the Koran or other writings to be read to cure him. III (C) He contented himself with self and family medication. V (B) He went to the hospital to be treated. O No answer (blank).

**First-year**

| | Muslim | non-Muslim |
|---|---|---|
| I | 6 (7.5%) | 2 (18.2%) |
| II | 10 (12.6%) | 0 |
| IIa | 9 (11.4%) | 0 |
| III | 9 (11.4%) | 1 (9.1%) |
| V | 40 (50.5%) | 7 (63.6%) |
| O | 0 | 1 (9.1%) |

**Fourth-year**

| | Muslim | non-Muslim |
|---|---|---|
| I | 1 (3.3%) | 0 |
| II | 3 (10%) | 2 (18.2%) |
| IIa | 4 (13.2%) | 0 |
| III | 3 (10%) | 0 |
| V | 19 (63.5%) | 9 (81.8%) |
| O | 0 | 0 |

11. *Childbirth (7)*. Young Wife was in travail with her first child. The child started to come out feet first. The local midwife was having trouble delivering the child. *Which of the following actions do you think is best?* I (E) They let the local midwife continue and killed an animal as an offering to the guardian spirits. II (C) They called the best medicine man. III (B) They let the local midwife continue. IV (A) The father went immediately to get an experienced licensed midwife who was well known in the community. V (D) They took Young Wife to the hospital. O No answer (blank).

**First-year**

| | Muslim | non-Muslim |
|---|---|---|
| I | 1 (1.3%) | 0 |
| II | 13 (16.5%) | 0 |
| III | 10 (12.6%) | 2 (18.2%) |
| IV | 20 (25%) | 2 (18.2%) |
| V | 28 (35.6%) | 7 (63.6%) |
| O | 7 (9%) | 0 |

**Fourth-year**

| | Muslim | non-Muslim |
|---|---|---|
| I | 1 (3.3%) | 1 (9.1%) |
| II | 5 (16.5%) | 0 |
| III | 1 (3.3%) | 0 |
| IV | 7 (23.3%) | 2 (18.2%) |
| V | 16 (53.6%) | 8 (72.7%) |
| O | 0 | 0 |

12. *Wound (11)* While chopping a board for a door panel, Carpenter slashed

a deep wound six inches long in his leg. He held his leg to try to stop the blood at first. Then, *which of the following actions do you think is best?* I (A) He caused curing portions of the Koran or other writings to be read, to cure him. II (D) He sent for the local medicine man to treat him. III (C) He contented himself with what he and his family were able to do. V (B) He sent his son to get the physician, who treated the wound. O No answer (blank).

**First-year**

| | Muslim | non-Muslim |
|---|---|---|
| I | 11 (14%) | 2 (18.3%) |
| II | 13 (16.5%) | 4 (36.3%) |
| III | 11 (14%) | 0 |
| V | 38 (48%) | 4 (36.3%) |
| O | 6 (7.5%) | 1 (9.1%) |

**Fourth-year**

| | Muslim | non-Muslim |
|---|---|---|
| I | 2 (6.5%) | 0 |
| II | 3 (10%) | 1 (9.1%) |
| III | 2 (6.5%) | 0 |
| V | 23 (77%) | 10 (90.9%) |
| O | 0 | 0 |

The types of responses provided represent some estimate of what might be expected in the community at large, and the range of responses checked by the student group indicate that the possibilities are by no means fanciful. Here we are somewhat at a loss to provide modified modern responses. We find illness and wound cases are those in which there is a higher degree of confidence in modern medical practice. The shift between the first and fourth-year groups is most noticeable in the case of the wound where there appears to be recognition that the hospital can do things that the older medicine men cannot. The delivery case is a little complicated by the fact that here again categories IV and V tend to merge. Many of our students are aware of the activities of our school nurse who has been carrying on a midwifery practice in the area for many years. She is highly regarded, a fact we knew when we phrased these responses to the situation. If we combine the number of responses to categories IV and V on question 11, we find that there is a high degree of acculturation indicated. The first-year students answered in these two categories 60.6% of the time, and the fourth-year students 76.9%.

## General Observations

The total questionnaire involves 25 possibilities for response in an old culture way and only 17 possibilities of response in a new culture way. If we look back to the tabulation of totals, we find an indication that, in spite of this fact in favor of the old culture, the student responses are over 50% new culture responses when they arrive at the high school level. This proportion of the responses in these categories goes up to 72% in the fourth year, indicating that the processes of cultural change or changing attitudes continues. We must consider that the public schools from which our students come have done a considerable job of molding the minds of the youngsters. It is interesting to notice, however, that the difference between the non-Muslim and Muslim responses is not as marked in the first year of high school as it is in the last.

## Conclusion

When we have made allowances for the fact that this questionnaire was prepared for and used in an academic situation and that some of the responses were influenced by that, there is still remaining an indicator of the attitudes of the student group. A comparison with attitudes of a public school group will give better ground for judgment. There is valid reason for presenting this much of the study to this group both for what it reveals about the attitudes and for the information in it about the culture in which it was made. Such value as it has is more in the detailed analysis of attitudes than in any generalization that we might make, though I think it indicates that our school, and probably all mission schools, do in fact achieve in a very considerable measure the goals they set for themselves in changing the attitudes of their students.

*Marie Fetzer Reyburn*

# Applied Anthropology among the Sierra Quechua of Ecuador

THE purpose of the field work reflected in this article is the systematic analysis of Sierra Quechua culture to seek methods which will lead to more fruitful work on the part of the many missions working among the Indians. Quechua culture analysis was begun shortly after we arrived in Ecuador at an agricultural mission located on a large farm twenty kilometers north of the capital city of Quito. The mission has been established for six years and has a church with ten members, a school of five grades with an approximate enrollment of fifty, an agricultural program, and a clinic staffed by a trained nurse. We were invited to begin our ethnographical and linguistic studies in the area of Llano Grande and to assist the mission in whatever way possible.

The aim of the ethnographic work was to obtain as complete a picture as possible of the total culture of the area with particular emphasis on economic and social problems, and of the changes that were taking place and the direction of these changes.

## Language Study

The initial step, which of course continued throughout, was to gain familiarity with the language. Few of the older people of the community can carry on a conversation in Spanish, and while many of the younger married people can and do use Spanish (because the majority of the men work in Quito), Quechua is the language of the home. Much of the time in the first school year is of necessity taken up with learning Spanish. Our language learning began with an informant, but inevitably it developed more rapidly through attempts to use it while visiting in the community. Fluency in speaking Quechua was not gained in the five months' time but enough was acquired to carry on simple conversations while visiting and to understand much of what was said between Quechuas.

## Personnel Map

The first few weeks were spent in mapping the area, which covered approximately nine square miles. Mapping served a two-fold purpose: it was an excellent means of making ourselves known to the community, and it gave us a graphic picture of the community which served as the basis for gathering much additional information. Mornings were spent walking through the community, hedgerow by hedgerow. All the members of the community saw us, had opportunity to greet us as we passed their houses and to inquire what we were doing; thus the people found out first hand what our purpose

**Reprinted from Vol. 1, No. 2 (1953), pp. 15-22.**

was. Distance was measured by paces. Houses, eucalyptus groves, planted fields, water holes, cabuya rows, and other significant landmarks were recorded on work sheets.

In the afternoons the data were transferred to a large strip of newsprint, using a scale of one inch to one hundred yards. House types were differentiated according to construction materials. Roads, footpaths and cabuya rows were indicated by different symbols. When the map was completed it was marked off into quadrants lettered clockwise A, B, C, and D. From the center point, a series of concentric circles was drawn, and the arcs in each quadrant numbered 1, 2, 3, etc. The houses in each section were then numbered. Thus each house had a three figure designation, e.g. 1A1, 3B10, etc.

This map served as the basis for the Personnel Index File. Taking a section at a time, systematic visitation of each house was begun.[1] During the visiting we engaged in casual conversations with the purpose of introducing ourselves to the people and of obtaining such basic information as number, names, age and relations of occupants of the house, amount of land owned or rented, type of crops, kind and number of animals, etc. This information was unobtrusively recorded in a small field notebook; often we would wait until we left the house to write, out of sight, behind the corn fields. House to house visitation also afforded an opportunity to correct the map by adding houses that we overlooked or deleting those that were recorded twice. The information obtained was later transferred to 4 x 6 cards that were filed according to section and house number. This Personnel Index File yielded information concerning size and type of family, literacy, economic conditions, population mobility, daily routine, etc. This friendly visiting we found to be an excellent means of establishing rapport with the people, and of acquiring a "feel" for their problems and their ways of behavior.

## Ethnographic File

A general ethnographic file was set up, indexed by the categories in the *Outline of Cultural Materials*[2] that were pertinent to the area, plus some further categories we found necessary to add because of the local situation. The physical aspect of the file was similar to that of the Human Relations Area Files. The first information that went into this file was gained by observation wherever we came into contact with the people of the community: workers on the farm, encounters along the paths, visiting at the school and in the homes.

Often visiting would lead to participation in whatever task the members of the family were engaged in, such as picking or shelling corn, or thrashing peas. Through participation in daily activities and casual questioning about things observed, we were able to categorize a number of attitudes and areas of activity that seemed to be uppermost in the lives of the people; we discovered the main foci of interest around which life in Llano Grande revolved: the close-knit kin-group activities exhibiting a strong cohesive force in social as well as economic life, and the prestige-generating fiesta system. From this point we sought the patterning

[1] Visitation of each house was our goal; actually only two or three sections were completely covered in the time at our disposal.

[2] Volume 1 of *Behavior Science Outlines* published by Human Relations Area Files, Inc., New Haven, 1950.

of these interests and their interrelationships.

Informant work was initiated as a further means for obtaining information. Informants of both sexes and of a wide age range were used. For this work, a series of questions was prepared before each session, designed to detail the outline of information secured by observation and to explore categories not directly observable. Sometimes the sessions were held in our house, and at other times in the home of the informant. Thus, through observation, participation, systematic informant work, and long conversations with friends, the ethnographic file expanded.

Information in the files remains just so much raw data until it is systematized and developed into a whole. Then one can see interrelationships and patterns. When we put our data together in the form of a real ethnography it was possible to see some ways in which the mission could direct its activities to fit the cultural patterns of life in Llano Grande. A number of suggestions were made. Some concerned the possibility of the evangelical church incorporating into its framework some of the existing cultural institutions such as the godfather complex, with very little change; some concerned the incorporation of existing cultural institutions such as fiestas; some concerned the creation of new institutions such as a co-operative that would meet existing needs in a manner that was familiar to the people.

All suggestions were made from the point of view that changes brought about by the mission should be made via substitution based on existing functioning cultural forms. It was also made clear that suggestions based on ethnographical study lead to solutions of problems only by trial and error. While from an overall view one's culture is a rigid mold, there are too many independent variables in such a general study to allow one to consider that study as a controlled experiment. There follows a condensed selection from the ethnographic detail and the ensuing suggestions for mission activity.

## Language

The effective utilization of the language and the social structure point to a more effective mission endeavor. To reach the people effectively, it is necessary to use Quechua instead of Spanish. Although a large part of the community is bilingual, Quechua is the language that is used in the home and wherever the people gather together. Spanish finds its main use in Quito business transactions and other instances of white contact. The soul-touching topics of the Christian religion will be comprehended and absorbed only if discussed in the language that reaches the hearts of the people. It was also apparent that the Spanish used in Llano Grande is not the "book" Spanish of educated Quitenians, nor is it Biblical Spanish. Comprehension of Biblical Spanish is so low that it is virtually impossible for even a schooled Llano Grande individual to read the New Testament with understanding. Therefore, until a Quechua New Testament is available, it was suggested that portions to be used in Bible study be translated and mimeographed in "peon" Spanish.

## Social Structure

The kin and socio-religious structures indicate that mission effort should be directed mainly toward adults: heads of families and men of prestige and respect in the community. The nuclear family was found to be a closely knit unit. In working out the kinship terminology and structure of Llano Grande, age gradation was found to be the basic determinant for many terms used and for types of relationships obtaining within the structure. While there is a specific term for an older brother or sister, a younger sibling is simply called by name. Authority and responsibility are not assumed until marriage. Authority radiates from the oldest to the youngest in such a manner that individualism is almost an unknown concept. Each individual fits into a family niche and is secured there by economic, social and religious ties. An individual who withdraws from this highly structured group to align himself with the evangelicals is left without a place in the social and economic structure of the community.

The extended family was also found to be a closely knit unit, all those recognizing consanguineal and affinal relationship feeling a sense of belonging to one functioning group. Here, too, authority rests in the older members. It is this group that forms the basis of the reciprocal work group, and it is mainly from this group that the all-important godparents are chosen.

The godparent complex binds the people together in a network of social, economic, and religious ties. It is largely through it that economic and social security are found and, of course, the ceremonies are controlled by the Catholic Church. When a child is about fifteen days old the father chooses a godfather and godmother for the child's baptism. Usually for the first born grandparents are chosen, and siblings of grandparents for second born; for subsequent children almost any relative may be selected. A relationship is established between godparents and godchild such that the godparents give advice, training, and care when necessary to the godchild, and he in turn is at the disposal of his godparents when help is needed. A stronger relationship obtains between the *compadres* (reciprocal terms used between the parents and the godparents). In times of financial difficulty, sickness, death, or in times of prosperity, one's *compadre* is always ready to share the burden or rejoice in the prosperity. A strong friendship that lasts until death is maintained between *compadres*.

Every young couple also has marriage godparents. The marriage godparent makes arrangements for the wedding and bears the major part of the expense. He is the source of financial and material aid for the couple, and also becomes their counselor and mediator in case of marital difficulties. Thus, each man, woman and child is a member of a large in-group, closely bound together by mutual obligations that insure for each the security that is needed to fulfill his place in community life.

## The Fiesta

The most important activity in community life was found to be the fiesta. The fiesta is the social vehicle upon which rides the news of the community, which gives the opportunity to see and be seen, which provides the chance for young people to learn the basic ways of life, physical and mental release from the daily routine; above all, it is the giver par excellence of respect and prestige. Besides the Church-controlled main fiesta dates falling in the months of January, April, July, September, November and

December, there are numerous secondary ones, and there is scarcely any large gathering of people that is not accompanied by fiesta activity, eating and lavish consumption of intoxicants. *Priostes* appointed by the local priest are financially responsible for the fiestas, with various classes of assistants.

The expense of a fiesta amounts to thousands of *sucres*, as masses have to be paid, and food and music provided for hundreds of people for days at a time. The financial drain is so great that it may take a man fifteen to twenty years to recover from one year's *prioste* duties. Fiestas are the scene of wholesale drunkenness. At their height there is considerable sexual laxity. After marriage any man is eligible to begin to have minor fiesta responsibilities. Through the years a man climbs the ladder to the post of *prioste*. Most respected are men who have reach the *prioste* rung and have retired to the highest position in community life. *Priostes* and ex-*priostes* — these are the men the people look to, whose leadership they will follow.

## Communication Networks

Such a structure of kinship and social units suggests the advisability of adapting the gospel witness to the direction of flow of life in the community with the object in mind of incorporating into the church units which would have a solidarity in Christ as family and kin groups, not as individuals estranged from the very grass roots of their existence. Thus, it was suggested that the mission concentrate most on heads of families and on *priostes* and ex-*priostes*.

Another recommendation was for the evangelical church to incorporate the godfather complex into its framework, substituting infant dedication for infant baptism (according to the theology of the mission) and strengthening the reciprocal ties of the system for the believer by adding to the existing obligations the responsibility of bringing the gospel to the baptized (or dedicated) child, and the responsibility of teaching the newly married couple concerning the Christian home and family.

Concerning fiestas, it was suggested that the mission could use this medium of contact with the people to explain to invited guests who have shown real interest in the gospel what the gospel is and its power to transform lives. It would, of course, be a fiesta with a non-intoxicating drink instead of alcoholic beverage. Bible study and discussion would end the day instead of the customary drunken debauches. (Such a fiesta was given by us with good success. Coca-Cola was consumed by the case!)

Because of the co-operative nature of Llano Grande life, it was recommended that the mission establish an evangelical co-op as the church membership increased. Members would pay specified amounts, and the fund could be bolstered by proceeds from a piece of mission land set aside for the co-op. Funds would be used for such purposes as financial help to a suffering member family, wedding and funeral expenses, sponsoring of a co-op fiesta designed to invite interested relatives and friends to hear the gospel and learn of the work of the co-op, schooling for a future pastor, and support of a local Quechua worker.

Other items may be mentioned even more briefly. The fact that the community employment (the majority of the men work in Quito) is small plot agriculture in the community carried on by the women leads to the suggestion that the mission organize women's training classes in agriculture. These same groups could be instructed by the medical department in simple first aid and sanitation measures such as boiling water. As a concomitant to the suggestion concerning concentrating the evangelistic program on the adults, it would seem advisable for the school to launch an extensive adult literacy campaign.

Although it is not possible here to give more than an indication of the type of recommendations made to the Llano Grande mission there is no doubt that the application of ethnographic technique provides a sound basis for the planning of Christian institutions in primitive as well as urbanized areas.

*William D. Reyburn*

# Don't Learn that Language!

"DON'T learn that language" sounds like a rather pessimistic heading for a set of hints for language learning. This title is used to help contrast the idea of learning about a language with the learning of the utterances one says when he has an urge to speak.

These suggestions are built around the idea that a *language* is a whole construct which no one really employs except in the business of writing grammars and the like. It does little good to attempt to learn what someone has abstracted into a language system. What the "language learner" really needs is to know what specific utterances can go with what specific situations. The task of "learning a language" is, I feel, a psychological barrier to learning to speak. If we cease to think in terms of learning the abstracted language, with all its idiosyncrasies and illogical ways of behaving, and work to learn an utterance for every situation, we will find that we begin to speak with our first simple phrases and the task of speaking is merely that of expanding the situations and the appropriate phrases.

These suggestions are methods which I have personally employed in learning languages. Naturally, I cannot guarantee that they will solve all the language learning difficulties of others. The reader may, in fact, well get the impression that to use them would create more problems. However that may be, I am sure they will work for the person who will take the time and effort to put them into faithful practice. The major task is that of getting used to a method until it becomes quite automatic. From that point on the learner's mind will carry on with the technique. All he has to do then is give it the opportunity. Even if the reader does not find the cure for his language learning ills, he may discover some clue which, if adapted to his own way of doing things, may lead to more efficient language learning and understanding.[1] If the learner can make a habit out of some of the suggestions here, it may well lead him to the habit of speaking a second language.

## Language Learning: Ability, Background, or Motivation?

It is no doubt true that all individuals *do not* come to a problem with the same mental equipment. Some people are quick and some are slow. Some understand things in detail, while others are more capable of making a mental synthesis. While differences in intelligence may affect the learning of a second language, there are many other factors which are also operative. In a few more years it will probably become a standard pro-

**Reprinted from Vol. 5, No. 4 (1958), pp. 151-178.**

[1] These notes are extremely limited in scope and are not intended to explain about languages or how one can analyze languages for learning. An excellent detailed account of these matters should be consulted in Eugene A. Nida, *Learning a Foreign Language*, (New York: Friendship Press, 1957).

cedure in New York for the missionary candidate to take the one-hour language aptitude test developed by a Harvard psychologist. This test as used in the language programs of West Point and in the Air Force shows validation correlations as high as 80 percent between test scores and later language achievement. However, there are serious shortcomings to such tests which the tests cannot handle.

A person who may rank very high on such a test in a classroom might do very poorly in a field language learning program because he was activated to pass the test but could not possibly be motivated to learn the language of a black primitive African. Some societal groups in America and especially England prepare a person psychologically to make a unidirectional identification with only one kind of people speaking only one kind or brand of a language. These unfortunate souls are so narrowly oriented into a tiny in-group, with its peculiarities of speech which all must try to ape to perfection, that they cannot force themselves to gravitate toward any kind of substandard (not to mention peasant or primitive) dialect. In our own general American culture there is a tendency for the younger generation to become more successful and educated than the parent generation, and hence to conform to a "higher" kind of speech.

These are examples of how one's background can and does prepare its speakers to possess mental blocks to acquiring outside or foreign speech. By maintaining a certain dialect of speech one maintains his social status. If this status means a great deal to a person's security, then he will defend the symbols which support that status. In this case it may mean the inability to adapt to any other kind of speech, for as soon as this person hears his own voice making speech noises of another variety he feels a jerk downward. Hence he quits.

Eugene A. Nida cites[2] the case of a motivated and capable person who had an impossible time with a second language. When he began to investigate, Dr. Nida found that the person's parents had spoken a foreign language. The child had made a conscious effort to avoid the foreign language of the parents in order to identify himself with the dominant social element, the English-speaking community of children where he played. This person could no doubt be helped, but he would have to be willing to admit frankly his emotional block and gradually work it out of his feelings.

Dr. Nida also suggests that it is probably necessary to be uncommitted to a local form of speech in order to take on another language. This is only logical. One cannot be a committed Christian and at the same time a Communist. Or one cannot be committed to Communism and at the same time be a Christian. In order to go from one to the other, one must destroy and put away very basic beliefs or the transition simply cannot be made. If you find that your background has caused you to feel that every brand of American speech is detestable and inferior to yours, you are in for language learning troubles. If you are a social climber pushed headlong toward an identification with the upper crust, you will do best to learn to speak "upper crust" instead of Bulu or Basa. If you honestly do not feel bad when someone kids you for your

---

[2] See the editorial by Eugene A. Nida in *The Bible Translator,* Vol. 8, No. 3 (July 1957), pp. 139-143, for a brief discussion of some of the psychological problems and motivation in language learning.

substandard twang or your Southern drawl, and if you can mimic people's speech, you are apt to learn a language. People who have a tendency to side with the underdog have a decided advantage in the matter of learning the language of a simple folk culture. If you are insecure about your first language, you will probably never be secure in a second one. The lack of security in a language means that added consciousness of being a foreigner.

Furthermore, people who have lots of contacts with speakers of the foreign language are apt to learn well *if* they are interested in identifying themselves with the people. Why do you suppose that field geologists working for oil companies in South America learn Spanish better than technical engineers? Simply because the geologist is out in the country with the people, whereas the technical engineer is surrounded by other U.S. technical engineers. The same oil companies find that an engineer of Italian extraction learns Spanish fluently in two years. Why is this? The U.S. Italian looks like and behaves like his Latin American cousin, and consequently he finds it a natural thing to identify himself with the Latins.

We often assume that a missionary, of all people, would be motivated to learn the African language. However, as we have indicated above, the problem of motivation is often complex. It is made even more so due to the fact a missionary may go to France with high motivation to learn French and, having accomplished some degree of success, he next arrives in the Cameroun with his motivation for the African language at a very low ebb. "Oh me, not another language!" The missionary in the French Cameroun accepts a heavy responsibility due to the ethnic complexity of that country, and he must find ways to gird up his language motivation through at least one African language in addition to French.

The task of each individual missionary is to cast up his position before himself in terms of ability, background, and motivation. Then, with this clearly in mind, he must set about language work with a whole heart.

## Language is the Reflection of Customs and Thoughts

The greatest deficiency in any language learning program is the assumption that one can merely learn a language and thereby "communicate" with the speakers of that language. It is true that one can speak on a great variety of subjects and engage people in a serious exchange of words and thoughts without knowing how those thoughts reflected in the language are felt to be true or false by the people. Real communication takes place between two people when each understands the assumptions which lie behind the other's words and phrases. This is an ideal situation, but it can only be approached through an intimate acquaintance with the feeling and thought patterns of the people. This is tantamount to saying that the purpose of language learning is to be able to handle the language in order to find out what the meanings are. The meanings are not just in the English or French equivalents of the African words but, rather, in the total impression these words make on the *African's* thinking.

Take a simple illustration. While in the bookstore in Ebolowa with a non-Christian Bulu friend, I noticed a very attractive Negress on the cover of a French magazine. Pointing it out to my friend, I asked, *Ye w'anye'e minga nyo?*

'Do you like this woman?' His rather astonished reply was, *Ye o ne ngule ya ve ma?* 'You can give her to me?' My question arose out of an American "cover girl" idea about which any number of remarks could be made. My Bulu friend responded out of a Bulu "female" concept. My question, "Do you like this woman?" stimulated a Bulu thought pattern which is sex-productivity-marriage linked in a way in which the English is perhaps only slightly linked. Consequently, my Bulu friend received my message within a framework which I was not prepared for. His reply, accompanied by a very serious and intensely interested facial expression, caused me to see that I must translate my question for myself if I were to understand it as he had. Now it said, "Do you want to have this woman?" My friend later carefully explained how such a question can occur in Bulu society. It is a question which may be asked in the preparation for marriage arrangements. It would have been better to ask whether the cover girl were pretty or not. Even so, the thought pattern of the Bulu mind will not be concerned about bust, hip, and waist, a la "Miss Universe," but of more practical thoughts of child bearing and dowry rights.

We can rightly ask, then, if we really understand what we talk about. The truth is that most of our talk is so pragmatic that we are satisfied if we have evidence for some minimal comprehension passing back and forth.

If you want to find out how disparate American and African thought concepts are, try telling half a dozen of your best knee-slapping American jokes in translated Bulu or Basa. Even if you adjust the material culture items to fit an African setting, you will be surprised to find that they laugh at entirely the wrong place in the story or look at each other with uncomfortable embarrassment at the close of the story, not knowing what to do next. The point in a joke is an aspect of a culture which has its humorous side. The Kaka tell very funny stories about misfortunes that befell someone. These strike Euro-Americans as being pathetic episodes. However, if one observes the Kaka, he will notice how they will laugh hilariously at a person who falls from his bicycle and gets up bleeding from his wounds.

Every word in a language has its own private history, and there are reflections of various feelings and thought patterns at different historical stages of the language. Simply knowing a lot of verbs, nouns, and connectives does not mean that one can use them in the situations which the society prescribes them for. *Language is a fiction.* There are only utterances which are spoken under the stress or relief, pain or joy, of an indefinite number of situations. Fortunately, the "urge to speak" situations are vastly more complex and numerous than the utterances that may be called forth. Hence the same old grumblings are used by the complainer who feels an untold number of complaints.

While all this is true, it is not possible to know "meanings" before you know words. Everyone starts with phrases and words with approximate meanings and develops slowly through intimate contact with the speakers to arrive at the meanings which lie behind the symbols. However, there is a tendency for one to gain a passable speaking and understanding knowledge of an African language and then allow his knowledge to glide along on a level which goes neither up nor down. If one has reached that deadening level of adding nothing new, learning no new words for months, it is simply because one has learned most of the utterances that are spoken in the situations in which he finds himself.

It is because of this that it is valuable to think of *learning utterances suitable for situations* and not in terms of "learning a language." There is a psychological block which the "learner of a language" sets up for himself. When he has learned the rules of the grammar, knows how to form new compounds, and is at home with his noun classes and their concordances, he deludes himself into thinking that he has "learned the language." He has learned *it* because to him the *language* was the learning of those aspects of grammar. He can speak and handle himself in his routine. He has, in spite of the grammar idea, learned by contact the utterances necessary (or at least the substitutional bases) for his daily set of situations. Under missionary specialization this is necessary. But it tends to set the effective limits of communication. The doctor is at home in the hospital ward and in the operating room, the pastor in the pulpit, and the mechanic in the shop. If language learning is approached not as a mountainous mass of material which one must slowly eat away at and digest, but as "*there is an utterance for every situation*," then one seeks out as many situations as possible and associates his utterances with these specific situations.

## The Nature of a "Situation"

Every thought and activity which a human can indulge in is a "situation." One lives in thousands of fleeting situations (some active and others passive) in the space of a day. Take a simple example. It begins to grow dark, so I want light. I go to the generator. While on the way to the generator I remember that there is no gasoline in the tank. This reminds me of the key to the gas house. On the way I must pick up a can. While walking along the path I think of a relative at home, then, like a flash, I am thinking of a piece of work which I did not finish today. I have a problem that is perplexing me, and I rove over it in my mind as I unlock the gas house door. I see a snake on the floor which absorbs my whole attention. I get a stick and kill it. I am emotionally heightened now as I get the gas. I find myself relating under my breath to my little girl the story of the snake. Finally, I leave the gas house and start for the engine. I simply walk along with no thought until I look up and see the starting rope on a branch. I am reminded of a snake again. As I pour in the gas an African approaches and greets me. As I see his face I recall that we have a matter to discuss and the outline of our affair comes to my mind. We begin to talk. This is given to illustrate what I mean by "situations." Situations are the segmented mental images and thoughts which pour constantly through the mind as well as the real live encounters one has with other humans, snakes, engines, and all the variety of interpersonal or person-thing encounters in one's waking hours. After one is asleep, the subconscious continues to cook up these situations, some of them highly bizarre but still a kind of situation.

Given a variety of situations, the language learner asks but one question, *What is an utterance a native speaker could use in this situation?* There may be dozens of possibilities, but the learner is interested in at least one common one at the start.

If the principle of *utterances in situations* is clearly grasped, we may proceed with a more systematic approach. I repeat. If you are out to "learn the language," don't plan to learn the grammar. Prepare yourself mentally by proposing to learn an appropriate utterance (short and simple at first) for a given simple "situation." Remember that *no one speaks a language*. A language is a system which can only be abstracted from utterances people make in real or imaginary situations. Your task is to learn *utterances appropriate to situations.*

### Hearing and Imitation

One must begin at zero with a language. There is no other starting point. The basic fault of language learning is committed precisely at this point. The natural tendency of schooled people is to suppose that one learns from seeing words on paper. It is no doubt true that a college graduate has such a print fixation for learning that he would be emotionally disturbed if his written words were taken from him. Hence, if one has to see words and phrases to learn them, they should be written in such a way as will signal all the phonetic values of the utterances. This is difficult to do either in music or in speech. Although phonetics books purport to approximate this, one cannot represent the exact values of pitch, rhythm, and vowel tone in such a way as would be practical to read. This can come only through careful listening and imitation. One is certainly justified in attempting to write as many distinctive phonetic values as possible if it helps the learner. In tone languages one may find it a great help to mark tones on words whose tone does not readily stick in the mind. However, one cannot learn to pronounce the staccato effect of Spanish speech even by recording it with a satisfactory device. This learning comes through the careful practice of imitating native speakers and overcoming one's own background of language habits.

The first habit to acquire, then, is that of grasping in your ears the African's voice and speech in such a way that you can close your eyes and hear his voice (even unintelligible speech) long after he has gone. To do this it may help to try a little music appreciation. Go to a phonograph and put on a record. Now sit down and listen like you have never listened before. Force yourself to hear the rhythm only. Keep time with the rhythm by tapping the foot on the floor or beating a stick on the table. Where do the accents fall? Are the heavily accented beats regular, irregular, or displaced? Turn off the phonograph and whistle or sing awhile and make up your own rhythm. If you cannot sing or whistle, just say *one*-two-three, *one*-two-three, each time making the *one* pronounced louder and heavier than two and three. Then, instead of stressing the downbeat, mix up the rhythm. Notice the tempo of a piece of music. Is it fast or slow? Compare the length of a whole note with other notes. Just as with music, where rhythm is basic, speech also employs rhythmic movement. Get used to hearing a whole utterance and then imitating it with the strong rhythmic accents at the right intervals. Record utterances on tape, even though you do not understand them, and make the noises with *la la la,* paying particular attention to the stressed and unstressed parts.

Now tune your ears to the melody of your record and note how the scale is used to provide a tune. This tune may repeat itself in a similar fashion as it progresses. Listen to the song, then turn off the phonograph and hum, sing, or whistle something that is similar to the tune you have just heard. If you can do this, you are simply one of those unfortunate souls like the color-blind. Do your best and explain to your critics that you are tone deaf. While listening to the melody of a song, one attempts to follow the melodic line wherever it may go on the scale. It is similar with speech. In the case of speech, it is much easier to catch the melody, as it employs less intervals and repeats itself more frequently than in music. If you can hum or sing the tune you have heard, then you can by the same token cause your speech voice to follow up and down over the melodic line of the native speaker's utterance.

Finally, listen to your musical record for the timbre or tone color. This timbre is analogous to color in a painting. Each kind of instrument in an orchestra has its own peculiar tonal characteristics. A violin could hardly be confused with a tuba. Distinguishing the tone of a clarinet from that of the bass clarinet is not so easy. However, in speech we are interested to note that there is some tendency for the people who speak a language (or dialect in close geographical areas) to give their speech a certain modal tone color. One can verify this by listening to Midwesterners of the same area or Southerners from the same area. There are also tone colors for different speech situations. In English the football announcer on the radio, the energetic but rhetorical preacher, the political orator, and the high school valedictorian all display situational kinds of tone color in their speeches. In learning to hear foreign speech one must be prepared for these tone color modulations which symbolize kinds of situations.

More important, however, is the fact that in hearing foreign speech one should learn to hear and hold in memory the tone color of the voice of a native speaker. Select a person who speaks clearly and listen to his voice until you are able to hear its tone quality long after you have separated. Practice bringing the sound of his voice back into your mental ears. When you speak, attempt to modulate your voice so as to approximate this mental voice picture which you retain. People learning a European language may do this with the voice of the news broadcaster. When you can "hear" his voice at any time you wish to recall it in your mental ears, then practice imitating it until you are convinced that your adjusted voice now sounds like the news broadcaster's. Record his and yours on tape and compare the two. You may find it more practical to fasten on to the voice of some close African associate. Train yourself to hear his voice after you have returned from your work, and when you speak with him attempt to put his voice into your mouth. Voices differ as to tone color, of course, so do not try to imitate everyone you hear. Pick out a good clear one and work to imitate that one.

Anyone can learn to speak just like a native — provided the native is one who only whispers. The precision control of the vocal cords which gives a language its most distinctive quality is lost when one whispers. There is little difference in sound between a Frenchman's whispered voice and that of an ordinary student learning French. The great difference comes the moment the vocal cords are brought into play. Unfortunately, we cannot go around whispering all the time.

When one is thoroughly prepared to hear (phonetic training is a big help), then the problem is how to learn what one hears. The student of a new language requires two things to get started: (1) utterances which will make clear for him what the order of the elements in an utterance are, i.e. where the actor fits, where the action word attaches, and where the word acted upon goes; (2) fundamental vocabulary which is used in the process of getting a day's living. With these two sets the beginner is able to take off on his own at his own pace. Notice that we do not need to know the ten pronouns and which comes first, nor how many noun classes there are and the rules for their use. This is wasted human energy.

### Stage I: The Initial Utterances

Learn by sheer grit of the brain and imagination a stock of utterances which are suitable to imaginary situations. This can often be done with the mission language lessons up to a point. However, in such lessons we may find "read" before we get to "eat." Even in a literate culture one can do more with "eat" than with "read."

The situation we will imagine in Bulu is that I am eating, so we ask the African to say it. We get our first feel for construction as soon as we change the eating to wanting. Now we have a feel for order of the doer and the doing. In this way we keep getting utterances and at the same time we build up our feeling for order of words or parts of words. The first fifty utterances are not difficult because we have not learned enough to confuse our memory.

With each utterance one should *imagine the situation or get into that situation.* If you learn *m'alañe ķalate* 'I read a book' by saying it over in Bulu and then going back and saying or thinking it out in English, you will set yourself way back. *The utterance in the situation* means that you associate the utterance *m'alañe ķalate* with the act of reading a book by actually doing or at least imagining strongly. Consequently, when you hear *m'alañe ķalate* you receive in your brain the situation image of "reading a book" and not the English or French translation of the utterance. If you caught the mental image of the "reading" situation and missed the pronoun, you are far ahead of the person who picked up the raw Bulu words and went through mentally scratching each out and putting in English words, and then coming out with the correct answer. This mental contortion is the first defeat in language learning. Save your mental energy for more useful things.

After you have gotten a good list of utterances in sufficient grammatical variety memorized so that they call up situations or are given in response to situations, you will know enough about the way the grammar works so that you will not have to think too much about it. The initial vocabulary of which these utterances consist should be the ones which signal the most common and fundamental activities in the daily routine of a native person. In Africa this means learning a few kinship terms such as brother and sister, father, etc. Some people, due to the task of running the house, get all the vocabulary necessary for ordering servants and this is their fundamental vocabulary. This may be necessary, but it should never be a goal!

The secret of this first stage in which one uses written lessons or gets the utterances directly from a native speaker is to practice with imitation, using all the powers you can muster for hearing and imitating. Each time you hear the African say the sentence concentrate on some new aspect of his utterance. Always think of the *situation* provoked by the utterance and never of the words as written in Bulu or as translatable into English. You may find it handy to jot these utterances on slips of paper to review, but let me warn you that you are probably wasting your time unless you can discipline yourself to use such slips in the right way.

In the first stage the learning comes quickly and one zooms ahead with great success. Then one reaches that point where it seems nothing more can be digested. Try as you will, you do not seem to be able to take on any more. You sit with an African who goes over with you each utterance you know, and if he gives you a new word you feel like leaving it. You know it will not stick anywhere. You begin to think that you are a sorry apple at learning a language, and soon despair sets in. You have spent one month and now you think you are at road's end.

If you give up now, this will be the end of your road. The malaise that has struck you, however, is normal. Your brain has been working overtime making new neural connections, and it refuses to be pushed any further. You have mental indigestion, and to cure this you need to strengthen the new channels the brain has dug for you and not try to make any more. Since it is a kind of indigestion, you must now get it out of your system. How? By practicing it on anyone who will give you an ear. But your communication value at this point is a little foolish. You just seem to draw grunts of "Yes" or "No" from the African, and he shows no real interest in your attempt to hold his attention. If you know French, you can escape this dilemma, but remember that this is only temporary escape. The African is not a Frenchman and is expecting you to speak more than French. It is time now to learn to employ inner speech.

**Inner Speech**

The use of inner speech is a technique which children between the ages of two and eight use to learn their language in their daily play routine. Observe a child in his play and you will learn the greatest secret in language acquisition. A child talks to himself in endless repetitions about what he is doing and builds a wonderful world of fantasy supported on words and wishes which he scampers into, then tears it down and comes finally exhausted seeking food and sleep. His rich imagination causes him to fly airplanes through closed doors and to ride over the housetop on a magic stick. He has encounters with wild bears and giants and slays them with a shake of his hand. A child structures his imaginary situations out of the fabric of his fertile imagination and feeds reality into it with an endless stream of linguistic symbols.

Adult language learners can do the same. For the child it is a necessary and almost involuntary aspect of his language development. After normal language acquisition, it is difficult to go back and repeat this process. However, it can be done, and if the language learner will discipline himself to do it, the rewards in language learning will be greatly increased.

In the first stage of imaginary situations the learner has forced himself to learn to catch a mental picture in response to one of his utterances when it is spoken by another person and to give the particular utterance when stimulated by the appropriate situational setting. He never thinks through to the meaning via substitute symbols from a second language — *no translation!* He is now to employ his utterances in such a way that they will be incorporated into his inner speech system. In order to do this, each basic utterance will have a spot which is potentially open for inserting another word. If the basic utterance is "I am eating," then one will add to it all of the words for foods which one has and is learning.

I am eating fish
oranges
bananas
bread
I see a woman
man
dog
house
Where is my dog?
hat?
book?
stick?
Are you going to the village?
school?
house?

One cannot sit down and talk this kind of thing and make very good conversation. However, within one's own internal communication system one can change for hours, substituting these items and changing the situational responses. Even as you do this in your inner speech you should be hearing in your mental ears the voice of an African saying these just as you have heard him say them in your teacher-student practice. After having disciplined yourself to employ inner speech, you will be surprised how easy it is to say things in actual conversations.

The use of inner speech develops with your ability to use the language. Soon you can carry on situational conversations, running narratives, etc. For instance, in the case of starting the generator, each situation there can be verbalized in inner speech as it occurs. If you do not know the word for key, gasoline, or snake, stop and ask an African. Jot it down if necessary, but keep talking about the situation. But perhaps you will go crazy doing this. If so, you should find out as soon as possible!

The use of inner speech is a defense against letting your brain drag its wheels. During your daily activities, especially in a language school period, you will be going about doing many things which will require little concentration. Hence, in order to make good use of what you are learning, force yourself to *converse with yourself* in the language.

The end of the first stage (about one month) should then see you with good basic vocabulary about ordinary events with a fairly sure feel for the way to construct sentences. These utterances are associated with situations, i.e. their meaning, and you have begun to use *inner speech* as the mechanism to provide the practice of repetition you need. If you have really employed inner speech consistently, you may find that you cannot turn it off at night and you may have some wild dreams in which everyone is yelling at you in a garbled form of the new language. If you strike this level, take a few days off and give your nerve endings a rest. Remember also that you can acquire vocabulary in meaningful units. If you learn "eat," also learn the associated behaviors of drinking, chewing, etc. When you learn one pronoun, get the others within a week or so. Trees, hills, and grass go together, as do sky, sun, clouds, rain, and wind. When you learn related concepts (or opposites like love-hate), you can make up much better conversations about things.

### Stage II: Real Situations

The first stage consisted of imagining a situation and then saying the appropriate utterance. This was the schoolroom text-book lesson stage. This stage was brought to its highest fruition by the employment of inner speech. The second stage moves the learner out among the people into *real situations*. Now comes the shock for the timid soul who feels like melting when the African villager squints through his eyes at the barely intelligible question or remark. The brave soul who is un-abashed at his lack of the language charges head-on and bowls them over with his attack. Timid or brave, the sad experience that begins to come to light now is the second stage of that feeling "I can't ever remember what word they use." Even if one writes it down, it seems to be of no avail. In the real live situation there are too many new words. They come like a torrent that swamps the learner.

### Sound-meaning Association Links

How to learn vocabulary and make it stick is the question we must try to answer now. Not all of the words of a language are of the same complexity. Some are long, with difficult combinations of sounds, while others may be short and simple phonetically. Not all words are learned or heard under the same emotional situations. The fact is, no two words are heard under exactly the same circum-stances. The emotional feeling of the learner will vary greatly from time to time. At one period he may be very keen-witted and tend to catch everything that is new, while at another time he may be ill-disposed to speak or listen.

As vocabulary building develops, it is advisable to attempt to jot down new words on slips of paper. On one side the new word can be put in a short situational utterance. Following a conver-sational period, one should go immediately and work on these new words in inner speech, making up all kinds of conver-sations about them to fix them in mind. In the process of learning new vocabulary, if you are like me, you will find that words fall into one of three or so classes.

The first class are words which for some unknown reason just simply stick in the mind. Whenever you need that word it is ready. They are the easy ones which require no special effort. These are most commonly the frequently occurring words which you will hear over and over and will use a great deal from the beginning. These words may impress themselves upon your memory because of the emotional situation in which the word was learned; for example, an angry person bawling you out for a mistake you have made. Or they may have strange onomatopoetic sounds like the French word *gargariser* 'to gargle,' which literally sounds like gargling when pronounced by a Frenchman. Such words as these strike one as having a realistic quality in their sound patterns and are easy to recall. If a word gives you no trouble, there is no point in thinking about it. Save your energy for the hard ones.

The second group of words are those which do not readily stick in the mind and need to be hooked into position by some reinforcement. This work-locking task is accomplished through the process of sound-meaning associations. You may find that this method is too abstruse to be of practical value to you. If it is, try working out some other way. If you have a bit of imagination, you may find it valuable to experiment with. However, the ability to form association links depends upon *practice and imagination.* The more languages one may draw association words from, the easier it is to find suitable association links.

To illustrate a simple case of association, let us suppose that we come across the Bulu word *ḳot* meaning 'to dry.' On our slip we write a short utterance such as *éḳop é ngenan teḳot* 'the skin isn't yet dry.' On the back of our slip we write the English word *coat. Coat* in this case is to signal "dry" or "being dry" or "dryness," etc. The sound of *ḳot* and *coat* are nearly the same, and English *coat* has to do with keeping the body dry. You may rightly object that if you think *coat* as an association link for Bulu *ḳot* 'to dry,' you may get your wires crossed and think fur, sleeve, or buttons when you hear Bulu *ḳot.* It is true that you may do just this. But the purpose of an association link is like that of a scaffold which is intended to be discarded when that portion of the building is erected. Thus, if you use the association link in recall, then employ *ḳot* in situational utterances in inner speech a few times, then use it in live situations with an African speaker, you will soon notice that getting at *ḳot* via the association link *coat* is slow and expensive and no longer necessary, so you drop the scaffolding. However, it will have served its purpose by now. In order to show some kinds of association links, I have listed some examples below.

1. *Cognate words.* When we learn French, we find that we have a lot of words in English that are already tailor-made for us. Many of these are academic words which come into English through Norman French: *primitive, problème, difficultés, résurrection, moments, irrésistible, conception, volume, élément, forme.* Such cognates require a slight adjustment of pronunciation, but with many such words we are merely speaking English in French.

The main problem with cognate words in Latin derivative languages is that many cognates are receptive and mean something quite different from their English sound equivalent. For example, French *rester* is not English 'rest,' but 'to remain.' French *remarquer* is not 'to make a remark,' but 'to notice something.'

In the learning of French one needs to learn the deceptive cognates. The non-deceptive ones are no problem, but a case of straight transfer. Cognate words such as *résurrection* and English *resurrection* are a type of association, since all that is required is that one associate the English word *resurrection* with the French language and then pronounce it with French pronunciation. In African languages we will not find many such common cognates. There are, however, English terms which have come into African languages from English, Spanish, Portuguese, French, and German by way of Pidgin English. Such words as *tote* (to carry), *school, book, steamer, money, matches, engine, car* are among them. Here again one associates certain known English words with the vocabulary of the African language.

2. *Words capable of forming strong associations.* In the case of Bulu *ḳot* we associate English *coat* which is *similar in sound and meaning.* In the case of *ḳot-coat* we have an association which is considered a strong reinforcement. One should never

forget the meaning of Bulu *kot* with an association link which is as phonetically similar as *coat* and whose secondary meaning is strong enough to suggest the meaning of *kot*. Bulu *kup* 'chicken' may be associated with *chicken coop* or merely with *coop*. This association is a bit less direct but is still strong on both counts of phonetic and semantic suggestion. If someone learning Bulu found that he could not remember the word for chicken in Bulu when he needed to use it, he would need a booster with the association link such as *coop* provides. If he finds himself talking about chickens with no trouble, he can let the *chicken coop* support fall away.

As was stated earlier, the more languages one knows, the easier it is to form associations. Bulu *kalate* 'book' or 'letter' probably comes from Spanish *carta* 'letter.' *R* and *l* are frequently substituted for each other across language boundaries, hence if we know Spanish *carta* it is but a slight shift to Bulu *kalate*. The association *carta-kalate* in this case gives us a strong phonetic-semantic association.

Strong associations (as well as weak ones) may not all be equally direct in their phonetic-semantic symbolism. If I cannot remember the Bulu word *jo* 'to talk' and cannot find a good association, I may recall a person by the name of *Joe* who is a big talker. Each time I come across this slip of paper with *Joe* Smith's name on it, I know that on the other side is a sentence such as *w'ate jo aya?* 'What did you say?' I simply have to picture *Joe* Smith as a talkative person. There are many possibilities open for some words and practically none for others. For *jo* 'to say' may grasp at *joke*, as joking is often in *saying* something; or *choke* (he chokes off his words), or I might think of the prophet *Joel* who had a great deal to *say*.

*The secret of forming associations is to be able to do it fast enough.* After you have gotten used to practicing association formation you will be able to pick out a new word you hear in a conversation, lock it into place with an association, and never lose the thread of the conversation. To gain facility in this you may practice it while reading or speaking English. If you hear or read the utterance, "And because the storm was threatening to sink the ship the sailors began to *jettison* the cargo," assuming that the meaning of the word *jettison* can be picked up from the context, you may lock its meaning in place with a flash thought by merely thinking of French *jeter* 'to throw.' Later, talk to yourself in inner speech about *jeter-jettison* and you will find weeks or months, perhaps years, later that jettison is a commonly recognizable word, even though you do not go around the house jettisoning your trash in the pit.

When you have reached the point where you can make a flash association of a new word heard in conversation without losing any detail of the conversation, you have arrived.

3. *Words capable of forming weak associations.* A weak association link is one in which the link word does not signal as much phonetic-semantic (sound-meaning) suggestion as would be necessary for a really strong association. You will find that the bulk of the words of any language fall into this group. However, it must not be thought that a perfect association (complete identification) is necessary to suggest the sound and meaning of the native word. After considerable practice you will find that the most minimal association in sound and meaning may be quite sufficient to

bring the word into your thought. The danger of weak associations is that one may cook up a poor association that is actually such a roundabout process that it is worse than no association simply because one is going through too devious a route to arrive at his destination.

Associations should not be with connective words and particles which are of frequent occurrence. In many languages such as Greek and German one must learn the many prefixes or suffixes and save the necessary association formation to identify the *root* of the word complex. In this way one is dealing usually with action and object kinds of words. The use of associations is less efficient with polysyllabic words. However, with some practice an association which calls forth the root or stem of the word is of invaluable aid.

Here are some examples of direct but second rank associations based on Bulu-English. *Nkol* 'hill' is associated with *coal,* as one digs coal out of *hills. Njuk* 'trouble': the *Jews* gave Christ *trouble. Toñ* 'to follow': one should *follow* the *tone* of the African informant. *Liti* 'to show': *litmus* paper *shows* chemical results. *Awu* 'death': he was *wooed* by *death,* or he *died* because he was *wound*ed. *Afup* 'garden': *a food* is produced in the *garden. Joé* 'name': *Joey* Sprague is his *name. Ebuma* 'fruit': *a bloom* becomes a *fruit. Esaé* 'work': *a sigh* comes from some who *work. Mane* 'to finish': I've *mana*ged to *finish. Vom* 'place': *hom*e is the *place. Metyi* 'blood': if I cut *my cheek* there will be *blood. Lik* 'leave behind': what *leak*s out is *left behind. Kon* 'to be sick': if you're too *sick* you lose *con*sciousness. *Bet* 'go up': my *bet goes up* another dollar. *Yam* 'to cook': *yams* are good to *cook.*

One could go on indefinitely making up associations that would be as good as these. The particular association given here is but one out of many. There are others which would serve equally as well. It is entirely subjective and one is free to form the association which strikes his fancy. The only conditions are that the association carries enough sound and meaning similarity to stimulate the Bulu response and is direct enough so that it is easily remembered. The purpose of association links is to reinforce recall and not to substitute for automatization in learning. The sooner one can discard the association link the better. No words locked in place with the help of association links should be allowed to remain in that status. They must be put to work immediately in live conversational situations so that the association link can be pushed out of the way as soon as possible. In the case of dead languages like Greek and Latin, one may continue the links as long as is necessary to gain rapid reading comprehension. Remember that associations will serve their purpose best if we get rid of them as soon as possible through the use of inner speech communication and live situation conversations.

4. *Words incapable of any association link.* Try as you may, calling upon a reserve of several languages, there are some words for which you will find no direct or indirect association. In these cases you must sweat it out. Write them down in familiar utterances, hear them as often as you can, and use them in your inner speech to win them. You may find, in spite of all of this, that they never seem to stay long. Be patient and keep trying. Someday, to your great surprise, some of them will start bobbing up in your thought. Your brain continues to work

for you even after you have given up. The advantage of this classification of words for the purpose of vocabulary building is to give you more time and energy to work on this group. Since you now know the difference between a retainable and nonretainable word, you apply your concentrated effort to the latter group.

### Associations for Distinguishing Minimal Differences

Many words in a language are phonetically different only by one sound, whether that is a regular letter of the alphabet, a tone, a stress, a vowel length, etc. Associations can readily be employed to keep these words straight in your thinking. Take the case of Bulu *nḳú* which with *ú* on high tone means 'signal drum' and *ù* on low tone means 'salt.' The missionary wife who calls to her kitchen boy for *nḳú* 'signal drum' will most likely get a delivery on the salt because the boy knows there are no signal drums in the kitchen supply. This kind of error can be avoided by associating *down tone* with what the salt does — it goes *down* the throat; signal drum vibrations go *up* into the air.

Take the case of Bulu *yem* 'to know' and *yen* 'to see' with which the beginner may have trouble. To avoid confusing these one may do any number of things. If you know something about Old English, you can think of *eyen*, the Old English plural of *eye* which has now become *eyes*. One may associate *yem* 'to know' with *seem*, and *yen* 'to see' with *seen*. *Yen* is a Japanese monetary unit which can be easily seen. The *n* of *yen* may be associated with English *notice* and in this way kept separate from *yem*. Normally it is necessary to have a key for only one of a pair and the other will take care of itself as a remainder. Take the case of *tili* 'to write,' *sili* 'to ask,' and *bili* 'to have.' Here we have three which must be separated, so we will attach a clue to two and leave the third as an independent. For *tili* we will remember the *t* of 'write' and we may say in our inner speech such things as "writili." For *sili* we will associate *s* of 'ask,' "ask-sili." Now we have sufficient association so that *t* of *tili* signals 'write,' *s* of *sili* signals 'ask,' and *bili* 'to have' needs no special clue.

Such words as *oyap* 'far away' and *ayap* 'long' create special problems. Here, again, any good direct clue will serve. *O* of *oyap* can be associated with *over there*. As long as *oyap* is clearly associated, *ayap* should provide no more trouble.

If you confuse *mvu* 'dog' and *mvus* 'behind,' you may end up looking for your "behind" and talking about the good old "dog days" instead of the "days behind." We need an aid to attach to the *s* of *mvus* 'behind.' If you know Spanish, the answer is easy, *atrás* 'behind,' which ends in *s*. If you do not know Spanish, try English second; one who is second is *mvus* 'behind.' Behind times, slow, French *suivre* 'to follow behind,' are other examples. Perhaps you can use the Latin genitive *agminis* 'of the rear line.' Compare it with another African language you may know. Somewhere you will hit upon a good clue. If the *mvu-mvus* kind of problem gives you trouble in your conversation, it is worth a minute of your time to sit down and clear the thing up once and for all. It will save a lot of time and trouble later.

There are real pitfalls contained in the nature of some words. Be careful and do not get trapped. Bulu *fam* 'male' may lead you to associate French *femme* and then via some transvestizing to straighten out the sexes. Remember that the phonetic element in an association is a trigger mechanism which sets you off on the path of the right sound response. However, the meaning aspect of the association triggers the meaning of the foreign word. You have two simultaneous explosions. Make them both count. Avoid the *fam-femme* kind of association in which French *femme* gives you a good push toward the sound of Bulu *fam* but completely confuses you as to the meaning.

### Advanced Stage Associations

Thus far we have dealt with associations in terms of a sound-meaning link from a familiar language to the unfamiliar one. In the second stage (second month) of language learning one should begin to form associations between words within the new language. For example, if one has learned Bulu *nḳú* 'signal drum' and *ḳum* 'wealth,' then later on hears these words fit together into one, he may think of "drum wealth," and a person who has "drum wealth" *nḳuḳum* is a 'chief.' There are similarities in the sounds of hundreds of words in a language, and often it is possible to imagine some associated meaning. If in English you first learned "house" and then later came across the word "mouse," you could easily remember "mouse" on the association of "mouse" is a "midget" animal in a "house." Bulu *ajoé* 'banana' could serve to help you learn *joé* 'nose.' Simply picture a man with a banana for a nose. Of course, unless you practice in inner speech, you will probably really say "banana" instead of "nose," but at least you were close and it is not likely that you will make that mistake twice if you are laughed at!

A further stage of association is when you begin to associate related objects as clusters or complexes of things which just naturally go together. This kind of association is not of the sound-meaning type, but rather the recognition of the interdependence which related cultural items have for each other. In American household vocabulary house cats and alarm clocks become associated, and the pun of "winding up the cat and putting out the alarm clock" reflects the fact that cats and alarm clocks are closely associated in the apartment culture of the U.S. An acquaintance of language as *utterances appropriate to situations* will provide the elements which seem most interrelated in a particular culture and, as language learning develops, these related elements should also be learned as complexes exhibiting their appropriate cultural uses.

You may say by now that the "64-dollar question" has still not been answered. This may well be. However, I am willing to promise you that, if you will discipline yourself to use inner speech and to form good association links, your language learning will increase far more than 64 percent in efficiency. The actual results that can be obtained depend largely upon the *motivation* and *practice* of the language learner, not upon your natural ability to think one way or another.

### Stage III: Consolidation

The third month should be a period in which you make an effort to establish firmly the ground you have covered to this point. Even though you have made considerable use of inner speech communication and association links, you should not plan to turn the world upside down in three months. The third month should be the period of the *rise of confidence* which comes from being able to talk to people about *your* subject, not theirs. It is the period when you take the initiative to force a conversation and make it intelligible and interesting enough so that you can hold on to your listener. In so doing you are ready and open-minded to catch as many new items as you can. Your building system is still the same as in the previous month. but you are now actively taking the lead so that you can convince yourself that what you know can be made intelligible to native listeners. Keep your pencil and pad ready if you are the visual type and pick up new words and expressions. Do not forget that as the talker you have not forgotten to be a good *listener*.

A good exercise to practice at this point is the relating of an episode to your African teacher. Get him to assist you to construct your episode in as idiomatic a fashion as possible. Then, with a few brief notes or key word reminders, practice telling the story to your teacher. Then tell it to yourself in inner speech a few times. Now you are ready. You spy an African loafing in a *chaise longue* and you amble up exchanging the greetings of the day. Then you move the conversation toward the kind of events in your story, and before he knows it you are giving him a blow-by-blow account of your well-rehearsed narrative, which brings him to a sitting position and he is following your every gesture and word. Without doubt, you have convinced one person that you really speak this language.

Now you begin to feel something of confidence and you can hardly wait to start preparing your next episode. After you have done this a few times you will most likely also get a chance to hear some stories in return. Perhaps you are still the timid type who gets all mixed up as soon as your listener sits up and begins to take notice of you. If this is your case, go tell your stories at night in the dying embers of the fire where you will not feel any piercing looks. Better yet, ask around if there are any blind people available. They usually have nothing to do and make excellent people to talk with.

After you have prepared half a dozen narratives about your experiences in some other part of the world, for example among the wild Snacirema tribe (spell it backwards), you will find that you are picking up vocabulary, but also you are getting a more secure feeling for what you had learned in stages I and II. The way to increase your confidence is to speak before people. Tell in your next episode how the Snacirema tribe lives in a city. (Incidentally, if you call them Snacirema instead of Americans, you will be surprised how much more you will learn about them.) The rise of confidence provides you with new and fresh motivation and you will feel a great urge to improve and move ahead. Perhaps at the end of your third month you are ready to speak in church. In the same way in which you have prepared your episodes now prepare your sermon. Do not have it all written out line for line. Do like you did with the stories. Have a small list of ten or twelve words which will give you the signal for the idea you are trying to express. When you have said all that you plan to say, sit down; you are finished. Next time, you can make it longer.

This third month stage of taking the initiative for speaking is aimed primarily at building up your confidence. Some people need this more than others. The one who is already overconfident may find himself inadequate and suffer a defeat. At least he should know where he stands now. There may be the danger of feeling quite satisfied at one's progress at the end of the third month, and consequently at the end of the third year there is very little improvement that the native speaker can see.

### Stage IV: Language in Culture: The Road to Meaning

The three stages so far have been three months given to preparation for the task of speaking in public with a degree of confidence in one's ability to express his thoughts with a minimum of linguistic or emotional disturbance. You will now soon find yourself out in your mission station or post beginning your duties. At this point you will decide the fate of your language learning. Most people will continue to learn and absorb until they feel adequate to handle the mission station linguistic and cultural situations. Here is the temptation of committing a serious error. One is apt to be led to think that the management of a mission hospital, school, station, or church is a true reflection of the raw stuff of which the African language and thought is made. The truth is that these are all white man institutions to which the African himself is adjusting and attempting to learn to think and operate under the guise of the white man's assumptions.

It is because of this that a young missionary in the middle of his first term may be heard to remark, "I have had two language schools and I have not learned a new word since the end of my first six months in the country." This is because the missionary has become quite sufficient linguistically for handling his routine around the hospital, school, shop, or church session. Whether or not the missionary moves ahead now depends on his determination to get into *African situations* which are not often found on mission stations. The man or woman who continues to practice the learning techniques we have discussed and who does so in a great variety of *African situations* will not become stagnated with a " 'nuff to get by" attitude. There is nothing which can so effectively lead one on into the thought patterns of the African's mind and language as a genuine desire to know the people among whom one works. This information is equally valid for the doctor, the teacher, the translator, or the pastor. The first three stages were only to get hold of the bottom rung on the ladder. Whether the missionary will rest contented at this level or will continue to climb will depend upon no one but himself. Remember that one can become exceedingly fluent with little, and the less one knows about the language and its meaning the more one is apt to misjudge African motives and behavior.

Witnessing to the eternal Word of God through the channels of a network enmeshed in a strange language and unfamiliar patterns of thought provides the oldest and still the greatest of all missionary challenges.

*Joseph E. Grimes*

**Reprinted from Vol. 6, No. 6 (1959), pp. 275-276.**

# Ethnographic Questions for Christian Missionaries

A NUMBER of missionaries find that a systematic fact-finding program helps them to be in a position of greater spiritual usefulness. At the same time, the intricate detail of most professional ethnographies gives the worker untrained in anthropology the impression that he cannot hope to undertake a worth-while fact-finding program by himself. This is not necessarily the case.

I have therefore compiled a number of questions to which any missionary should be highly motivated to find answers. Without special help he can follow them out to the place where the intricacies he finds are a source of insight rather than discouragement.[1]

[1] The present list of questions is not designed to be an exhaustive check list, but to help missionaries to get started. Many more comprehensive guides to field work may be found in the following useful books:

Royal Anthropological Institution: *Notes and Queries on Anthropology* (sixth edition). London: Routledge and Kegan Paul, Ltd., 1951.

George P. Murdock and others: *Outline of Cultural Materials* (third edition). New Haven: Human Relations Area Files, Inc., 1950.

John W. M. Whiting and others: *Field Manual for the Cross-Cultural Study of Child Rearing*. New York: Social Science Research Council, 1953.

John Ladd: *The Structure of a Moral Code*. Cambridge, Mass.: Harvard University Press, 1957.

R. Herbert Minnich, Jr.: *A Manual of Social Science Material for Missionaries*. Elkhart, Ind.: Mennonite Board of Missions and Charities, 1958.

None of these questions should — or can — be answered with a pat pronouncement. Each one could well form the core of inquiry for a treatise of monograph length, and the missionary should consider eventual publication of his findings in that form. The main outlines of the answers to all the questions should be well in mind by the end of the first six months' residence on the field, at which time the missionary would do well to talk over what he has done with an anthropologist and receive further suggestions. The questions are not of the variety that can properly be put to an informant directly. The missionary must instead use his own ingenuity to find ways of getting concrete data on what he wants to know.

## The Questions

1. Describe thoroughly the person-to-person links by which news and gossip get around the community. These are the channels the gospel also follows.

2. How are decisions regarding various matters reached by the community as a whole? by groups in the community? by households? How do these decision-making patterns influence people's decision about Jesus Christ?

3. What do people of different statuses want most out of life? How does their action show what they think to be most important? What do they think you feel is important?

4. In the community, which persons control the actions of which other persons? in what ways? on what grounds? What is your place in this system?

5. How does each kind of object produced or imported by the community (goods and services) get to its ultimate user?

6. Who lives where? Give all names, ages, titles, and kinship ties to other people. Use maps.

7. How is each individual trained from birth to become a fully participating member of the community? each recognized group within the community? What do they do about people like you who have not gone through these processes?

8. Give a résumé and evaluation of everything that has ever been written about the language, culture, and general area.

9. How is sexual behavior channeled in marriage? outside of marriage? What is the rationale for each practice?

10. Who controls each piece of land, and how is that control expressed? In what ways is the land utilized?

11. How are differences between persons or groups settled, either in or out of court? Do all differences stay settled?

12. Who are considered deviant or marginal by most people? Why? What is done about them? How do you know your work is not limited to deviants?

13. Describe all practices and idea systems of the religion you are trying to see superseded.

14. What groups of people does marriage bring into relationship? What is the nature of that relationship? Who may and who may not get married? Why? Who actually does marry whom, regardless of the rules?

15. What things and ideas from alien sources are fully accepted? partially accepted? By what process did they get accepted? What makes people accept some things from outside and reject others? What has been accepted from you, and what rejected? Why?

---

**Joseph E. Grimes, of the Wycliffe Bible Translators and Summer Institute of Linguistics, is a Ph.D. candidate in linguistics at Cornell University. At various periods since 1951 he has been living among and working with the Huichol Indians of Mexico. Among various articles on the language and the culture of the Huichol is one which appeared in an earlier issue of PRACTICAL ANTHROPOLOGY: "Individualism and the Huichol Church" (Vol. 1, pp. 127-134).**

*William A. Smalley*

**Reprinted from Vol. 7, No. 4 (1960), pp. 145-152.**

# Making and Keeping Anthropological Field Notes

*The individual who is resident among the people of another culture, even though he is not a professional anthropologist, has marvelous opportunities for observation, for casual or intensive interviewing, and for other ways of gaining extensive information about the people around him and their way of life. He often has a very real advantage over many professional anthropologists in the possibility of such contacts over a period of many years. Only a small percentage, however, of missionaries and other such residents abroad make any kind of systematic record of what they learn. This article discusses briefly the advantages of record-keeping, and makes some practical suggestions.*

THE fundamental reason for making and keeping anthropological field notes is of course the need to remember. The factual details of an interview with an old shaman ("medicine man") when, in an unusually confiding mood, he tells about many of the fundamental ceremonies in his repertoire, and gives an extensive picture of their function, can quickly fade. Some of the value of the interview for an understanding of religious life will fade with it. The opportunity to compare accounts gained in other ways, or to study ceremonies actually observed in the light of the shaman's comments is dissipated. The broad, striking features of the interview may remain, but much of the detail of its content is lost forever.

The need to remember is not always fully apparent to the resident abroad. In his first weeks impressions are startlingly vivid. He learns a great deal that is new and interesting. Much of what he observes, reads, and hears is commonplace in the life around him. He may see no need to make notes on it because he knows he will see and hear many of the same things a thousand times. Note-taking may seem to be an impossibly time-consuming and voluminous task. The habit of observing more or less casually, without keeping a record, is thus quickly established and is usually not broken.

The need for a record becomes more apparent later when certain kinds of problems present themselves. In the missionary situation, for example, there may arise a realization that a certain complex of cultural values and practices needs serious study because they have a bearing on the Christian witness, the development of the church, or some other phase of the welfare of people. In the pages of PRACTICAL ANTHROPOLOGY there have been several reports on such problems.[1]

---

[1] Eunice Pike and Florence Cowan, "Mushroom Ritual versus Christianity," Vol. 6, No. 4 (July-August 1959) pp. 145-150; John C. Messenger, Jr., "The Christian Concept of Forgiveness and Anang Morality," Vol. 6,

The anthropologically curious missionary at this point may begin very serious investigation of the phenomena, in the light of everything he knows about the culture. If anything has been previously written on the culture (or this phase of it) he studies it. He starts questioning informants, and observes the problem area of cultural behavior with renewed attention. If he has been keeping notes he most certainly goes over them for the light they may shed on the problem. And whether or not he has previously kept notes, an adequate record at this point becomes imperative. Note-taking and keeping takes on new focus because it is now problem-oriented. As investigation of the problem continues he makes constant reference to earlier notes, so that an adequate overview of the accumulating information is constantly kept in mind.

Another typical situation in which the need for notes becomes very acute arises when the resident abroad wants to write something or in some way share his knowledge about the culture of his environment. Except for brief and often superficial articles, or ones based on very recent investigations of limited problems, records are indispensable. It is so very important that missionaries with cultural insight share their knowledge with their colleagues through PRACTICAL ANTHROPOLOGY and through a manual on the culture of their neighbors. It is possible, of course, to start making notes at the time when the decision to do such writing is made. It is an enormous help, however, if a systematic record has already been kept over the full period of residence.

For the individual who is not a professional anthropologist the question of time is a major deterrent to keeping records of cultural information. In our discussion a variety of techniques will be suggested and the time factor will be taken into consideration. The student of a culture can tailor his own system to suit his needs and temperament.

## Random vs. Problem-Oriented Records

A basic distinction needs to be made first of all between a system of keeping notes in which the observer keeps record of information on any phase of the culture which comes to his attention, as against one in which he has a specifically defined problem, and where he keeps records only of the information which seems specifically to pertain directly to that problem. If a choice has to be made, the second of the two is the more valuable type of record for many reasons. When an investigator can focus on a limited set of problems he can study them much more exhaustively than he can a whole culture. He is more likely to have time to amass the necessary volume of data. The random record may be too general to lead anywhere in particular.

In a problem-oriented record the investigator tries to keep a record which may help to provide the answers to questions which he has formulated for himself. In Haiti, for example, a missionary might well want to study the cultural phenomena related to the present rapid growth of the evangelical church. He would first of all outline some basic questions to which he needed answers.

---

No. 3 (May-June 1959) pp. 97-103; William D. Reyburn, "Kaka Kinship, Sex, and Adultery," Vol. 5, No. 1 (Jan.-Feb. 1958) pp. 1-21; Walter H. Sangree, "The Structure and Symbol Underlying 'Conversion' in Bantu Tiriki," Vol. 6, No. 3 (May-June 1959) pp. 132-134.

What are present attitudes of various classes of people (including both social and religious groups) toward the Roman Catholic church, "Voodoo," and the various evangelical groups? What is the attitude of the various groups toward individuals who are converted? What needs which people feel are met through conversion? What motivates people to resist conversion? What cultural imbalances are created through conversion? What adjustments are being made to compensate for them? In what ways does conversion provide a greater integration and more valuable life as people feel it? What forms of communication provide an effective witness?

Someone more familiar with the Haitian scene could better define the questions than I, but this will be indicative of the scope of one of the kinds of problems which deserves extensive investigation in every walk of Haitian life. Investigation could lead to very useful knowledge for the missionary who undertook it. This is the value of the problem-oriented study.

Unfortunately, however, the problem-oriented record is never really complete in itself. A problem can take on meaning only in relation to the major part of life. Problem-oriented studies in anthropology must be related to the culture as a whole. This poses the need for a more general record as well. Furthermore, the investigator does not always know what problems are going to interest him particularly in the future, and if a random record is not kept as well, valuable information for future problems may not be forthcoming. A problem-oriented record is not as useful for a general survey of the characteristics of the culture for newcomers, either.

Ideally, the best solution is a non-complicated way of keeping a random record which can be expanded at any point where a particularly interesting or important problem comes to the attention of the investigator. In our Haitian example above, the information on the problem defined would be filed in the religion section of a file. The file would include information on all phases of Haitian life. This particular section, however, would have much fuller notes because it was a particular focus of attention for the investigator. The techniques of note-taking and record-keeping discussed here will be applicable to random records, problem-oriented records, or a combination of both.

## Chronological vs. Topical Filing Systems

The easiest way to *take* notes is in sequence, as the information comes to the investigator. "Diary" or "chronological" notes have the additional advantage of helping to reconstruct the informant situation under which information was gained when discrepancies in information turn up. Earlier investigation, likewise, is more suspect than later, because the investigator has not yet built up the necessary background and may misinterpret what he is getting. For most reference purposes, however, chronological notes are relatively useless. The investigator has to read through pages or even whole notebooks to find a certain piece of information. A topical way of *keeping* notes is therefore essential.

A combination of both systems is perfectly possible, however, with almost no extra effort. The procedure outlined here will combine the two, but individuals can select ideas which seem pertinent to their own needs if this is more than they want.

The key to making both chronological and topical records lies in the use of carbon paper. We recommend that all notes be made in triplicate. The original is for the topical file, one carbon for the chronological file, and another carbon for a second chronological file to be mailed to some other place, preferably out of the country, at weekly intervals, or as a few pages of notes accumulate. If, through some disaster, either or both of the main files are lost, it will be possible to reconstruct them from the third copy.

The notes are dated and the pages numbered in chronological order. New pages are simply added to the chronological file as they are completed. The new pages are also slipped into the proper place in the topical file. This assumes, of course, that there is only one topic on a page. Where more than one topic is included, a cross reference to the page should be made at each relevant place in the file. For each of these cross-references a reference to the chronological file will quickly find the information. If experience shows that material is repeatedly being cross-referenced, additional carbons may be added instead, and the additional copies slipped into the file at the various topics covered.

Essential to a good topical file, and one that will not need constant revision and time-consuming re-sorting, is a comprehensive basic plan. We recommend that for a general culture file the investigator use the *Outline of Culture Materials* prepared for the Human Relations Area Files by George Peter Murdock and others.[2] The *Outline* divides cultural phenomena into some seventy primary categories (with a few additional general categories). Each of these has from six to nine subdivisions, with further subdivisions under each. The topics are also extensively cross-referenced. Not all of the thousands of topics in the *Outline* will be relevant for even the most extensive set of notes for any culture. The primary divisions, most of the first subdivisions, and some of the smallest divisions will be useful for any complete general random file.

For a starter a selection from the primary divisions is enough. File dividers or folders[3] should be prepared for each of them. It is very important that these all have the tab in the same place, preferably at the left. Subheadings can then be inserted later when needed, as a volume of information in any primary section becomes too large for convenience. The subheadings would be entered on tabs in the second position from the left. When further subdivision becomes necessary in some of the sections these tabs would be in the third position, etc. The basic structure of the file is therefore immediately apparent at all times.

In a short time, therefore, the primary divisions of a topical file can be prepared, and the investigator is in business. As he makes notes they are simply slipped behind the proper heading, regardless of chronology or of subdivision. As he needs to make reference to a section, and finds material which is quite heterogeneous, subdivision for that section becomes in order, and a few minutes with the *Outline of Culture Materials* makes it possible to restore order to that section. Two files, one expanding chronologically, and the other topically, are all that an investigator

---

[2] *Behavior Science Outlines,* Vol. 1, Human Relations Area Files, 333 Cedar St., New Haven, Conn. 1950. 162 pages.

[3] Questions of size and format will be discussed below.

needs, and when done in this way are not impossibly time-consuming.

## Note and File Format

A basic decision which has to be made at the beginning of any note-taking is the size of paper on which it is to be done. Several considerations enter into this decision. If, for example, the primary source of information is likely to be informant sessions, where extensive, leisurely notes are possible, standard 8½ x 11 (or the European equivalent) is the most practical. If notes are taken directly on the typewriter, as is ideal in an informant situation, this presents no problem in the use of carbons, and saves inserting sheets as often as would be necessary with a smaller format. Furthermore, when it is not possible to take notes by typewriter, carbons can be inserted between the pages of a spiral notebook of these same dimensions.

The greatest problems with this format lie in filing. Folders are virtually necessary if the sheets are to be filed full size. There is a lot of waste paper on many sheets as the investigator sees a new topic emerging and puts in another sheet to make filing by topic easier. Some investigators who use this size sheet for notes cut them in half for the topical file after the page is finished. In this way the half-sheets can be filed behind file dividers, and there is not as much waste. When a topic changes during note-taking, the typewriter is simply turned up to the bottom half of the page. Alternatively, a 5 x 8 format is the most useful. Its major disadvantage is in the more frequent insertion necessary if a typewriter is used.

No matter what the size paper decided on, it should be kept uniform as much as possible. This means that the investigator gets in the habit of carrying his regulation-size paper with him all the time. For those times when he does not have it, however, and has to make notes on the back of an envelope or some other paper, he may either recopy (with full complement of carbons) or simply staple the odd-size paper to a regulation one, and insert it in the topical file, without benefit of chronological file, except perhaps by cross reference.

Every sheet of notes should contain the date, place, informant, and page number (of chronological file). This can be done quickly and easily, by code. For example, 2-2-60/LP/ST/230, which would mean, February 2, 1960, at Luang Prabang (Laos) with Siang Thii as informant and page 230 of the chronological notes. Investigators differ as to whether they double-space or single-space their typewritten material. A good left-hand margin, however, is very important, as there is often need to write in observations later.[4]

## Information on More than One Culture

Many residents abroad find that they are confronted with more than one culture, or at least with more than one distinct sub-culture. It is not usually necessary to have a separate file for each. Usually the investigator will concentrate primarily on one of these groupings and his file will be based on that culture. However, under each heading there may be tabs of a different color for each different culture or sub-culture. In many cases a notation may read something like this: "Rice harvesting techniques identical

[4] If the original is not typewritten, later comments should be written in ink of a different color from the original.

with Khmu" (in which the Khmu is the culture to which primary attention is being given). On the other hand, in certain respects the cultures will be radically different, and the second culture will require full notes if it is to be recorded.

In most cases the resident abroad will concentrate on the one culture with which he has the most contact, not making any extensive or systematic investigation of the others. As cultural information about them comes to his attention, however, he would do well to record it.

### Pictures and Recordings

Photographs and line drawings have long been essential to an anthropological record. Of these, the line drawing is often more essential than the photograph, even when the investigator is as abominable an artist as this writer. That is particularly true in dealing with the technological aspects of culture.

Notes should be made when a photograph is taken, or when a line drawing is made. The notes, together with the photograph or drawing should be included in the file. This is not possible when the photograph is a color slide, but in that case there should be a cross reference to the slide file.

A newer aid to record-keeping, and one which is proving increasingly more valuable, is the tape recorder. The tape recorder is particularly valuable when it is useful to have the full text of what the informant says or of some conversation, or ceremony, or speech, etc. An important point to remember, however, is that except for music, and for some language-learning purposes, a tape recording without a written transcription is not of any ultimate usefulness.

One way of handling this problem is to take notes on tape-recorded material and to incorporate those notes in the file, with a cross reference to the recording. When this is done, record should be kept of the place on the tape where the various items occur, to facilitate finding them. When secretarial help is available, it is very valuable to have actual transcriptions of much of the tape-recorded material. If no such assistance is available, only the most important items can receive such treatment, of course.

### Using Sources of Information

A word concerning the sources of information which is filed is in order, although reference has already been made to some of them. The reading of published materials on the culture gains considerably in ultimate value if some notation of the material is kept, together with exact page references. In some cases the notation may be very brief if the published material will be readily available again. For example: "Long description of the functioning of the chief's authority in the village" (with full reference to book or article and pages). Magazines or newspapers which would otherwise be thrown away may be clipped and the article stapled to a piece of paper which is standard for the topical file. Or, if this is not convenient, there may be a separate clipping file with cross reference in the topical file.

Reading, and the filing of information gained through reading, can be done even before going to the area under study. Upon arrival, observation becomes possible, even without a knowledge of the language or an interpreter. Observation of interpersonal behavior, of skills and techniques. of reactions to emergencies, of formal and ceremonial situations should all be included in the record. There may be certain occasions in which on-the-spot note-taking is impossible or impolite or otherwise inadvisable. In such cases notes should be written up as soon as possible after the event. Some investigators reserve time each evening for writing up notes on the day's events and observations.

Observation and other sources of information to be mentioned below can be considerably sharpened for the inexperienced investigator by the use of a field manual called *Notes and Queries on Anthropology*.[5] Chapters of this book include such topics as Social Structure, Social Life of the Individual, Political Organization, Economics, Ritual and Belief, etc. In these chapters profitable avenues of investigation are suggested, and important clues to look for are indicated.

Direct interviewing, either with informants regularly used for the purpose, or with friends, or with people encountered casually in the course of everyday life is a very major source of information. Probably in most cases the largest percentage of information filed will be from such sources. Here again note-taking is not always possible or wise outside of the formal informant situation, but notes should be made immediately after the interview, and checked as well as possible. Informants should represent people of various social strata, economic and occupational differences, the various religious groups, etc.

The three preceding sources of information are more or less self-evident, but there remains a fourth. This source, sometimes more difficult, not always possible to employ, is nevertheless the most penetrating and satisfying way of gaining information. It is participation in the life of the people. There is no better way to learn how a house is built than to build a house, and at the same time one learns about the structuring of leadership in work groups, about the techniques of handling tools, about taboos and tacit assumptions that run a wide gamut of life.

Participation in some phases of life is impossible, of course. It may be unacceptable to the people themselves. It may be physically impossible to the individual brought up in another culture. It may be beyond his skill. It may be ethically, or morally, or religiously impossible for him. However, the difficulties of participation are often exaggerated by the fear of trying something new, and participation, even on a limited scale, brings insight which is otherwise very difficult, if not impossible.

For the sensitive foreigner, and especially for the missionary, participation can have another by-product, as can the greater understanding arising from systematic investigation. This by-product is that all-important ingredient in communication: emotional identification. It cannot be emphasized enough that participation is not equivalent to identification.[6] Participation may be dry and mechanical. It may be crudely imitative, insensitive to the way in which it is interpreted by bona-fide members of the culture. As an

---

[5] Written by a committee of the Royal Anthropological Institute of Great Britain and Ireland, and published by Routledge and Kegan Paul, Broadway House, 68 Carter Lane, London.

[6] See William D. Reyburn, "Identification in the Missionary Task," Vol. 7, No. 1 (Jan.-Feb. 1960) pp. 1-15.

activity of a sensitive person, on the other hand, participation may be a road to that kind of rapport and empathy which makes genuine friends out of "informants" or "potential converts" or "church members."

As the habit of note-taking and filing develops, and a routine is established, it does not need to be a burden. On the contrary, it may be a stimulus to more fruitful life, as well as a helpful avenue to insight and understanding.